Hands-On Ethical Hacking and Network Defense

Third Edition

Michael T. Simpson

Nicholas D. Antill

D1334196

CENGAGE
Learning·

Australia • Brazil • Mexico • Singapore • United Kingdom • United States

Hands-On Ethical Hacking and Network Defense, **Third Edition**

Michael T. Simpson and Nicholas D. Antill

GM, Science, Technology, & Math:
Balraj Kalsi

Sr. Product Director, Computing:
Kathleen McMahon

Product Team Manager: Kristin McNary

Associate Product Manager: Amy Savino

Director, Development: Julia Caballero

Content Development Manager: Leigh Hefferon

Managing Content Developer:
Emma Newsom

Senior Content Developer:
Natalie Pashoukos

Product Assistant: Abigail Pufpaff

Marketing Director: Michele McTighe

Marketing Managers: Stephanie Albracht and Jeff Tousignant

Marketing Coordinator: Cassie Cloutier

Executive Director, Production:
Martin Rabinowitz

Production Director: Patty Stephan

Senior Content Project Manager:
Brooke Greenhouse

Art Director: Diana Graham

Cover image(s): iStockPhoto.com/BlackJack3D

For product information and technology assistance, contact us at **Cengage Learning Customer & Sales Support, 1-800-354-9706.**

For permission to use material from this text or product, submit all requests online at **www.cengage.com/permissions**. Further permissions questions can be e-mailed to **permissionrequest@cengage.com**.

Library of Congress Control Number: 2016947570

ISBN: 978-1-285-45467-2

Cengage Learning
20 Channel Center Street
Boston, MA 02210
USA

Cengage Learning is a leading provider of customized learning solutions with employees residing in nearly 40 different countries and sales in more than 125 countries around the world. Find your local representative at **www.cengage.com.**

Cengage Learning products are represented in Canada by Nelson Education, Ltd.

To learn more about Cengage Learning, visit **www.cengage.com**.

Purchase any of our products at your local college store or at our preferred online store **www.cengagebrain.com**.

Notice to the Reader

Publisher does not warrant or guarantee any of the products described herein or perform any independent analysis in connection with any of the product information contained herein. Publisher does not assume, and expressly disclaims, any obligation to obtain and include information other than that provided to it by the manufacturer. The reader is expressly warned to consider and adopt all safety precautions that might be indicated by the activities described herein and to avoid all potential hazards. By following the instructions contained herein, the reader willingly assumes all risks in connection with such instructions. The publisher makes no representations or warranties of any kind, including but not limited to, the warranties of fitness for particular purpose or merchantability, nor are any such representations implied with respect to the material set forth herein, and the publisher takes no responsibility with respect to such material. The publisher shall not be liable for any special, consequential, or exemplary damages resulting, in whole or part, from the readers' use of, or reliance upon, this material.

Printed in the United States of America
Print Number: 06   Print Year: 2019

Brief Contents

Table of Contents

CHAPTER 6
Enumeration. **135**

CHAPTER 7
Programming for Security Professionals. **161**

CHAPTER 13
Network Protection Systems

APPENDIX A
Legal Resources

APPENDIX B
Resources

GLOSSARY

INDEX

Foreword

If there's one thing I have learned from teaching security testing and analysis over the years, it's that testing is the easy part. Almost half the students fail analysis. That means almost half the students won't be able to properly secure anything, maybe ever. Don't worry, though, they will still work in security.

I taught more than a few of the OSSTMM Professional Security Tester and Analyst classes myself and reviewed nearly all the certification exams ever taken, and it proved to me that most people can't analyze properly. Which means they can't make good security decisions consistently.

Most students learn the *skills* part of security testing pretty quickly, and a few of them are natural hackers, automatically showing the right combination of resourcefulness, tenacity, and creativity. However, it's extremely rare to find a natural at security analysis, and although good experience makes a better security analyst, it doesn't define the skill. I suppose it's a lot like lie detection.

People are really bad at lie detection, even those who take those expensive training classes, because we tend to assume we're not being lied to. Even the few of us who work in professional positions that deal with liars all the time (police officers, prison guards, tax collectors, mothers, etc.) rarely get feedback that teaches us when we were right.

This is true in security analysis as well. Most security professionals assume that the security products are doing the right thing; and their vendors and peers, who took the same training classes they did, read the same blogs and magazines, even earned the same certifications, assume the same thing. So there's no good feedback on bad security processes that are assumed to be correct from the start. And there's even less incentive to give bad feedback on a product that doesn't work if you're the one who recommended it be bought.

To better understand what's so hard about security analysis, consider the following:

When is it wrong to patch a vulnerability?

Let's take away legacy systems and production downtime and assume it could be quick and automatic and seamless, like the vendors often say it is. All the literature you know probably says to patch, and that patching is part of your security process. But when is it wrong?

When should a network connected to the Internet not have a firewall?

When is it good for a desktop to not run anti-virus software?

When is it acceptable for a password to be sent over the Internet in plaintext?

When is a self-signed certificate the best transport security on a Web server?

When is obfuscation better than encryption?

When is end-to-end encryption bad for security?

These are things you will be confronted with when working in professional, real-world security. You won't find the correct answers in a checklist or a book. You also won't learn the answers through experience. It comes from your security analysis skills. But don't blame yourself if you can't analyze security. Most security professionals can't.

Society is no more designed to assure that people have good security analysis skills than it is designed to assure that we have good security skills. We know we don't because, otherwise, trust wouldn't be the centerpiece of human relationships and compromise wouldn't be the centerpiece of a community. The odd thing is that it's not human nature to be bad at analysis. We have the capacity. We can learn it. It's just that, as a society, it's not encouraged. So this is something you will have to overcome.

Without the ability to do proper security analysis, you won't be able to discern if a product is right for the given environment. You won't be able to know if the tool is giving you the correct answers or even capable of giving you the answers you actually need. You need security analysis to build a robust and reliable defense.

Of course, it's easy to invoke doom and gloom about the one obscure piece of knowledge dangling out of your reach. But it's not out of your reach. You have to choose not to learn it. You have to choose to ignore it. The problem is that most people think they do security analysis at least better than average and ignore the signs that they might not. When confronted with security decisions, they rely on external analysis from "industry experts" to decide for them. This is what's known as "reading the literature," and it refers to doing your job by examining external assessments in decision making. Don't do that.

If you want to be good at security analysis, and I hope you do, then take every opportunity to pick apart every security product to see what it really does, every vulnerability to see how it really works, every trusted process to see why it's really needed. Do this and it won't take long to figure out how much you don't know, the first step toward making a good security analysis.

Security professionals are dangerous until they reach the point of knowing what they don't know and can't ever know. This is when you can actually admit you don't have the answer. No more guessing or assuming what you think the answer might be.

Those are really powerful words in security: I don't know. Admitting it lets you plan proper defenses and compels you to find new ways to see the unseen. It's a hard thing to admit in the business world because you will be judged for it by your employers and you will be mocked for it by your peers. Some in the security community like to harass anyone who doesn't know something that can't be known, as if we need to be in a constant state of posing. The truth is that they don't know either, because there are things we can't know, like what a vulnerability is worth or whether one vulnerability is worse than another. And the sad truth is, they won't admit they don't know or (even sadder) don't even know they don't know.

As you go on, you will get better at analysis, and truths will begin to appear. You will realize that there are only two ways to steal something. You will learn that there are at least 12 properties that help you discern if something can be trusted. You will find that there are only four ways to test anything. You will know that there are 10 types of protection that combine to defend against every threat. And so much more. Then you will be able to reliably apply these truths to whatever you're looking at, whether it's a room, a network, a car, or a person, and make the right security decisions every time.

Well, almost every time—after all, you're not a robot, and our biology tends to get in the way of thinking straight sometimes. But once you can do security analysis, you'll know exactly why.

Pete Herzog
Managing Director, Institute for Security and Open Methodologies (ISECOM)

Pete is the creator of the Open Source Security Testing Methodology Manual (OSSTMM), a standard for proper and thorough security testing, and the co-founder of the open, nonprofit, security research organization ISECOM (www.isecom.org), a certification authority that specializes in verifying applied knowledge.

Introduction

The need for security professionals who understand how attackers compromise networks is growing each day. You can't read the news without seeing an article on identity theft or credit card numbers being stolen from unprotected databases. Since the first edition of *Hands-On Ethical Hacking and Network Defense* was published, the president of the United States has created an organization with the sole purpose of countering cyber threats and attacks. Both public and private companies rely on skilled professionals to conduct test attacks on their networks as a way to discover vulnerabilities before attackers do. "Ethical hacker" is one term used to describe these professionals; others are "security tester" or "penetration tester."

This book isn't intended to provide comprehensive training in security testing or penetration testing. It does, however, introduce security testing to those who are new to the field. This book is intended for novices who have a thorough grounding in computer and networking basics but want to learn how to protect networks by using an attacker's knowledge to compromise network security. By understanding what tools and methods a hacker uses to break into a network, security testers can protect systems from these attacks.

The purpose of this book is to guide you toward becoming a skilled security tester. This profession requires creativity and critical thinking, which are sometimes difficult skills to learn in an academic environment. However, with an open mind and a willingness to learn, you can think outside the box and learn to ask more questions than this book or your instructor poses. Being able to dig past the surface to solve a problem takes patience and the willingness to admit that sometimes there's no simple answer.

There's more to conducting a security test than running exploits against a system and informing your client of existing vulnerabilities. Isn't it possible that you neglected to test for some areas that might be vulnerable to attacks? Haphazard approaches undermine the security profession and expose companies to theft. The goal of this book is to offer a more structured approach to conducting a security test and introduce novices to professional certifications available in this growing field.

Intended Audience

Although this book can be used by people with a wide range of backgrounds, it's intended for those with a Security+ and Network+ certification or equivalent. A networking background is necessary so that you understand how computers operate in a networked environment and can work with a network administrator when needed. In addition, readers must have knowledge of how to use a computer from the command line and how to use popular operating systems, such as Windows 10, Windows 8, and Kali Linux.

This book can be used at any educational level, from technical high schools and community colleges to graduate students. Current professionals in the public and private sectors can also use this book.

New to This Edition

This book includes a bootable DVD that enables you to use Kali Linux on a classroom or home computer running a Windows OS. Kali, a world-renowned security-testing application and OS, makes hands-on activities easier to perform; therefore, you can spend more time learning how to use security tools than learning how to install and configure Linux. To save time spent downloading and installing software on your system, you can do all activities by using the DVD, which contains all the necessary software tools.

This third edition of the book includes:

- Updated discussions and examples of new hacking tools
- Updated discussion of recent vulnerabilities and exploits
- Smartphone security section and updated discussion of embedded devices
- Updated section regarding Web application hacking, security, and Web-hacking tools

Chapter Descriptions

Here's a summary of the topics covered in each chapter of this book:

- **Chapter 1**, "Ethical Hacking Overview," defines what an ethical hacker can and can't do legally. This chapter also describes the roles of security and penetration testers and reviews certifications that are current at the time of publication.
- **Chapter 2**, "TCP/IP Concepts Review," describes the layers of the TCP/IP protocol stack and important ports and reviews IP addressing along with binary, octal, and hexadecimal numbering systems.
- **Chapter 3**, "Network and Computer Attacks," defines types of malicious software, explains methods for protecting against malware attacks, and discusses types of network attacks and physical security.
- **Chapter 4**, "Footprinting and Social Engineering," explores using Web tools for foot-printing and methods of gathering competitive intelligence. It also describes DNS zone transfers and social engineering methods.
- **Chapter 5**, "Port Scanning," explains the types of port scans and describes how to use port-scanning tools, how to conduct ping sweeps, and how to use shell scripting to automate security tasks.
- **Chapter 6**, "Enumeration," describes steps and tools for enumerating operating systems, such as Windows and UNIX/Linux.
- **Chapter 7**, "Programming for Security Professionals," gives you an overview of programming concepts as they relate to network and computer security.
- **Chapter 8**, "Desktop and Server OS Vulnerabilities," discusses vulnerabilities in Windows and Linux and explains best practices for hardening desktop computers and servers running these operating systems.

- **Chapter 9**, "Embedded Operating Systems: The Hidden Threat," explains what embedded operating systems are and where they're used and describes known vulnerabilities and best practices for protecting embedded operating systems.

- **Chapter 10**, "Hacking Web Servers," explains Web applications and their vulnerabilities and describes the tools used to attack Web servers.

- **Chapter 11**, "Hacking Wireless Networks," gives you an overview of wireless technology and IEEE wireless standards. This chapter also covers wireless authentication, wardriving, and wireless hacking tools and countermeasures.

- **Chapter 12**, "Cryptography," summarizes the history and principles of cryptography, explains encryption algorithms and public key infrastructure components, and offers examples of different attacks on cryptosystems.

- **Chapter 13**, "Network Protection Systems," covers a variety of devices used to protect networks, such as routers, firewalls, and intrusion detection and prevention systems.

- **Appendix A**, "Legal Resources," lists state laws affecting network security and provides applicable excerpts from the Computer Fraud and Abuse Act.

- **Appendix B**, "Resources," lists additional reference books, and lists important URLs referenced throughout the book.

Features

To help you understand computer and network security, this book includes many features designed to enhance your learning experience:

- *Chapter objectives*—Each chapter begins with a detailed list of the concepts to be mastered. This list gives you a quick reference to the chapter's contents and serves as a useful study aid.

- *Figures and tables*—Numerous screenshots show you how to use security tools, including command-line tools, and create programs. In addition, a variety of diagrams aid you in visualizing important concepts. Tables are used throughout the book to present information in an organized, easy-to-grasp manner.

- *Hands-on activities*—One of the best ways to reinforce learning about network security and security testing is to practice using the many tools security testers use. Hands-on activities are interspersed throughout each chapter to give you practice in applying what you have learned.

- *Chapter summary*—Each chapter ends with a summary of the concepts introduced in the chapter. These summaries are a helpful way to review the material covered in each chapter.

- *Key terms*—All terms in the chapter introduced with bold text are gathered together in the key terms list at the end of the chapter. This list encourages a more thorough understanding of the chapter's key concepts and is a useful reference. A full definition of each key term is provided in the Glossary at the end of the book.

- *Review questions*—The end-of-chapter assessment begins with review questions that reinforce the main concepts and techniques covered in each chapter. Answering these questions helps ensure that you have mastered important topics.

- *Case projects*—Each chapter closes with one or more case projects that help you evaluate and apply the material you have learned. To complete these projects, you must draw on real-world common sense as well as your knowledge of the technical topics covered to that point in the book. Your goal for each project is to come up with answers to problems similar to those you'll face as a working security tester. To help you with this goal, many case projects are based on a hypothetical company typical of companies hiring security consultants.

- *DVD*—Many security-testing tools used in this book are included on the Kali Linux DVD.

Text and Graphic Conventions

Additional information and exercises have been added to this book to help you better understand what's being discussed in the chapter. Icons throughout the book alert you to these additional materials:

The Note icon draws your attention to additional helpful material related to the subject being covered. In addition, notes with the title "Security Bytes" offer real-world examples related to security topics in each chapter.

Tips offer extra information on resources and how to solve problems.

Caution icons warn you about potential mistakes or problems and explain how to avoid them.

Each hands-on activity in this book is preceded by the Activity icon.

Case Project icons mark end-of-chapter case projects, which are scenario-based assignments that ask you to apply what you have learned.

MindTap

MindTap for *Hands-On Ethical Hacking and Network Defense* is an online learning solution designed to help students master the skills they need in today's workforce. Research shows employers need critical thinkers, troubleshooters, and creative problem-solvers to stay relevant in our fast-paced, technology-driven world. MindTap helps users achieve this with assignments and activities that provide hands-on practice, real-life relevance, and mastery of difficult concepts. Students are guided through assignments that progress from basic knowledge and understanding to more challenging problems.

All MindTap activities and assignments are tied to learning objectives. The hands-on exercises provide real-life application and practice. Readings and "Whiteboard Shorts" support the lecture, while "In the News" assignments encourage students to stay current. Pre- and post-course assessments allow you to measure how much students have learned using analytics and reporting that makes it easy to see where the class stands in terms of progress, engagement, and completion rates. Use the content and learning path as-is, or pick and choose how the material will wrap around your own content. You control what the students see and when they see it. Learn more at *www.cengage.com /mindtap/.*

Instructor Resources

Free to all instructors who adopt *Hands-On Ethical Hacking and Network Defense*, 3e for their courses is a complete package of instructor resources. These resources are available from the Cengage Learning Web site, *www.cengagebrain.com*, by going to the product page for this book in the online catalog and choosing "Instructor Downloads."

Resources include:

- *Instructor's Manual*—This manual includes course objectives and additional information to help your instruction.

- *Cengage Learning Testing Powered by Cognero*—A flexible, online system that allows you to import, edit, and manipulate content from the text's test bank or elsewhere, including your own favorite test questions; create multiple test versions in an instant; and deliver tests from your LMS, your classroom, or wherever you want.

- *PowerPoint Presentations*—A set of Microsoft PowerPoint slides is included for each chapter. These slides are meant to be used as a teaching aid for classroom presentations, to be made available to students for chapter review, or to be printed for classroom distribution. Instructors are also at liberty to add their own slides.

- *Figure Files*—Figure files allow instructors to create their own presentations using figures taken from the text.

Lab Requirements

The hands-on activities in this book help you apply what you have learned about conducting security or penetration tests. The following are the minimum system requirements for completing all activities:

- Computers that boot to Windows 10, with Windows Firewall and any third-party firewall software disabled
- Access to the Internet, with each computer configured to receive IP configuration information from a router running DHCP
- A DVD-ROM drive that allows using bootable DVDs or a bootable USB drive with Kali Linux installed

Operating Systems and Hardware

The Windows activities in this book were designed for Windows 10. However, you can perform most activity steps with only minor modifications on Windows 8.1 and Windows 7. Computers running Windows 10 should meet the following minimum requirements:

- If you plan to run Kali Linux from a USB flash drive instead of from the book's DVD, a PC with BIOS that supports booting from a USB drive and an 8 GB USB flash drive with a minimum 15 MB/second read and write speed
- Video card with 512 MB video RAM
- 60 GB hard drive
- 1.5 GHz 32-bit or 64-bit processor
- 4 GB system RAM (6 GB or more if running Linux in a virtual environment)
- Wireless card for some optional wireless activities
- Mouse or other pointing device and a keyboard

Security-Testing Tools

This book includes hands-on activities that involve using many security tools on the DVD; these tools can also be downloaded as freeware, shareware, or free demo versions. Because Web site addresses change frequently, use a search engine to find tools if the URL listed in an activity is no longer valid. However, every attempt has been made to include all security tools used in hands-on activities on the DVD. Visits to Web sites are mostly limited to research activities.

In addition, you use Microsoft Office Word (or other word-processing software) and need to have e-mail software installed on your computer.

About the Authors

Michael T. Simpson is president/senior consultant of MTS Consulting, Inc., specializing in network security and network design. Mike's certifications include CEH, CISSP, Security+, OSSTMM Professional Security Tester (OPST), OSSTMM Professional Security Analyst (OPSA),

MCSE, MCDBA, MCSD, MCT, and OCP. He has authored or co-authored eight books and has more than 30 years of industry experience, including 20 years with the Department of Defense (DoD), where he designed and configured computer networks and served as an Oracle database administrator, UNIX administrator, and information systems security officer (ISSO).

Nicholas D. Antill is a seasoned information security professional with over 10 years of specialized cybersecurity experience. Nicholas specializes in penetration testing, proactive security controls, and network defense. He holds many industry certifications, including the OSCP, GWAPT, GPEN, GCIH, CISA, CISSP, and GCFE. Nicholas currently manages the ethical hacking program at a large U.S. financial institution. He started his career at a small grocery chain in Pittsburgh, Pennsylvania, where he developed a fascination with network attack and defense techniques. He worked in support of both the U.S. Department of Justice and the U.S. Department of Defense before returning to the private sector.

Acknowledgments

I would like to express my appreciation to former Managing Editor Will Pitkin, who asked me to do this project over 10 years ago, long before others saw the need for such an endeavor. Today, you can't turn on the television or watch a movie without hearing the term "hacker." I would also like to thank the entire editorial and production staff for their dedication and fortitude during this project, including Senior Content Developer, Natalie Pashoukos. Natalie's ability to manage a project of this magnitude, with many moving parts, and still give autonomy to all participants of the project amazes me. Special thanks to Kent Williams, the developmental editor and my savior when deadlines required a helping hand. Kent's keen eye and ability to find errors that were overlooked by both authors and reviewers, made the final product something we are all proud to be a part of. In addition, thanks to Senior Content Project Manager, Brooke Greenhouse, who oversaw the process of shepherding chapters through production. I also appreciate the careful reading and thoughtful suggestions of Technical Editor, Nicole Spoto, and the validation testing provided by Danielle Shaw. In addition, I would like to thank the peer reviewers who evaluated each chapter and offered helpful suggestions and contributions:

Sam Bowne, PhD & CISSP
Instructor
City College San Francisco
San Francisco, CA

Matthew Chapman, PhD
Assistant Professor of Information Technology
University of Hawaii, West Oahu

Lonnie Decker, PhD
Department Chair, Networking Technology and Information Assurance
Davenport University
Midland, MD

I would also like to express my appreciation to my coauthor, Nicholas Antill, who worked many hours updating and rewriting chapters in response to the almost daily changes in this industry we choose to work in. Without Nicholas, there would not be a third edition of *Hands-On Ethical Hacking and Network Defense*! Thanks also to the security testers and IT colleagues who kept us on track and offered assistance.

Dedication

This book is dedicated to my online piano teacher, Robert Chambers (*anykeymusic.com*), who taught me that our fingers could be used on another kind of keyboard that uses sounds instead of words to convey our thoughts.

Kali Linux

The bootable Linux DVD included with this book is a standard install of Kali Linux 2.0, which will be used for performing Linux security-testing activities.

This book's DVD has been tested and verified to work with all hands-on activities. Because Kali Linux is an open-source product, changes and modifications to the software can occur at any time. You might want to connect to Kali repositories to update the OS when updates are available. However, updating might require doing some troubleshooting if the updates cause applications to not function correctly. If you don't want to spend time troubleshooting application errors, use the DVD as is and create a separate DVD with an ISO image that you can modify and update as needed. You can find a link to download Kali Linux here: *http://cdimage.kali.org/kali-2016.2/kali-linux-2016.2-amd64.iso.*

You can run Kali Linux from the DVD without having to install Linux on your hard drive. However, to improve performance, save time, and be able to save settings between sessions, you might want to install it with one of the following methods:

- Install Kali Linux as a virtual machine with free virtualization software, such as VMware Server or VirtualBox. The advantage of using a virtual machine is that it enables you to run Kali and Windows at the same time.

- Install Kali Linux on a USB flash drive with at least 8 GB storage capacity. With this method, you can move your personalized Linux system and run it on any system. With this method, covered in the next section, you can also save files and reports on this drive.

- Install Linux in a dual-boot arrangement with Windows 10. Dual-boot installations can vary depending on the hardware and require some complex steps if BitLocker or other disk encryption is used. Dual-boot installation isn't explained in this book, but you can find plenty of information online.

The Linux activities have been designed with the assumption that you're booting and running Linux directly from the book's Kali DVD. You need to take this into account and modify the beginning steps of Linux activities if you're running Linux from a virtual machine or a USB flash drive or in a dual-boot arrangement.

Creating a Bootable USB Flash Drive

To install Linux from the DVD on a USB flash drive, you need a drive of at least 8 GB. Note that the speed of some flash drives isn't quite adequate for running a live Linux OS. Performance improvements can be substantial if you use a flash drive with faster read and write speeds. For the best results, a flash drive with a minimum of 15 MB/second read and write speed is recommended. You can check Web sites, such as *http://usb.userbenchmark .com/*, for performance benchmarks to help you choose a suitable drive within your budget.

Once you find the proper thumb drive, you'll find up-to-date USB installation instructions on the Kali Linux Web site (*http://docs.kali.org/downloading/kali-linux-live-usb-install*). There are instructions for those using Windows, Linux, or Mac OS X. These instructions walk you through downloading Kali Linux to booting into Kali Linux for the first time. It's important to make sure your software is up-to-date, so be sure to run the `apt-get update` and `apt-get upgrade` commands, which check the Kali Linux repositories for updates.

Installing New Software

Because Kali is an Ubuntu Linux distribution, thousands of free programs are available that you can download and install with just a few simple commands. These programs, which are specific to an OS version, are stored on Internet archives called repositories. To install new software, you can simply use the command `apt-get install` *packagename* (replacing *packagename* with the name of the software package you want to install). If you don't know the software package name, just use a search engine to look it up!

Community Support for Kali Linux

To find the most recent Kali Linux updates and online forums for help in solving problems, visit *www.kali.org*. This Web site is a good place to start if you want to learn more about Kali Linux.

## chapter 1

Ethical Hacking Overview

After reading this chapter and completing the exercises, you will be able to:

- Describe the role of an ethical hacker
- Describe what you can do legally as an ethical hacker
- Describe what you can't do as an ethical hacker

The term "ethical hacker" might seem like an oxymoron—sort of like an ethical pickpocket or ethical embezzler. In this chapter, you learn that ethical hackers are employed or contracted by a company to do what illegal hackers do: break in. Why? Companies need to know what, if any, parts of their security infrastructure are vulnerable to attack. To protect a company's network, many security professionals recognize that knowing what tools the bad guys use and how they think enables them to better protect (harden) a network's security.

Remember the old adage: You're only as secure as your weakest link. The bad guys spend a lot of time and energy trying to find weak links. This book provides the tools you need to protect a network and shares some approaches an ethical hacker—also called a "security tester" or a "penetration tester"—might use to discover vulnerabilities in a network. It's by no means a definitive book on ethical hacking. Rather, it gives you a good overview of a security tester's role and includes activities to help you develop the skills you need to protect a network from attack. This book helps you understand how to protect a network when you discover the methods the bad guys (hackers) or the good guys (ethical hackers) use to break into a network. It also helps you select the most appropriate tools to make your job easier.

Understanding what laws can affect you when performing your job as a security tester is important, especially if you use the testing methods outlined in this book. Also, understanding the importance of having a contractual agreement with a client before performing any aspects of a security test might help you avoid breaking the law.

Introduction to Ethical Hacking

Companies sometimes hire **ethical hackers** to conduct penetration tests. In a **penetration test**, an ethical hacker attempts to break into a company's network or applications to find weak links. In a **vulnerability assessment**, the tester attempts to enumerate all the vulnerabilities found in an application or on a system. In a **security test**, testers do more than attempt to break in; they also analyze a company's security policy and procedures and report any vulnerabilities to management. Security testing, in other words, takes penetration testing to a higher level. As Peter Herzog states in the *Open Source Security Testing Methodology Manual*, "[Security testing] relies on a combination of creativeness, expansion [of] knowledge bases of best practices, legal issues, and client industry regulations as well as known threats and the breadth of the target organization's security presence (or point of risk)."

These issues are just some of the ones security testers must examine. In doing so, they alert companies to areas that need to be monitored or secured. As a security tester, you can't make a network impenetrable. The only way to do that with certainty is to unplug the network cable. When you discover vulnerabilities ("holes") in a network, you can correct them. This process might entail tasks such as updating an operating system (OS) or installing a vendor's latest security patch.

If your job is a penetration tester, you simply report your findings to the company. Then it's up to the company to make the final decision on how to use the information you have supplied. However, as a security tester, you might also be required to offer solutions for securing or protecting the network. This book is written with the assumption that you're working toward becoming a network security professional in charge of protecting a corporate network, so the emphasis is on using a security tester's skills to secure or protect a network.

In this book, you learn how to find vulnerabilities in a network and correct them. A security tester's job is to document all vulnerabilities and alert management and information technology (IT) staff of areas that need special attention.

The Role of Security and Penetration Testers

A **hacker** accesses a computer system or network without the authorization of the system's owner. By doing so, a hacker is breaking the law and can go to prison. Those who break into systems to steal or destroy data are often referred to as **crackers**; hackers might simply want to prove how vulnerable a system is by accessing the computer or network without destroying any data. For the purpose of this book, no distinction is made between the terms "hackers" and "crackers." The U.S. Department of Justice labels all illegal access to computer or network systems as "hacking," and this book follows that usage.

An ethical hacker is a person who performs most of the same activities a hacker does but with the owner or company's permission. This distinction is important and can mean the difference between being charged with a crime or not being charged. Ethical hackers are usually contracted to perform penetration tests or security tests. Companies realize that intruders might attempt to access their network resources and are willing to pay for someone to discover these vulnerabilities first. Companies would rather pay a "good hacker" to discover problems in their current network configuration than have a "bad hacker" discover these vulnerabilities. Bad hackers spend many hours scanning systems over the Internet, looking for openings or vulnerable systems.

Some hackers are skillful computer experts, but others are younger, inexperienced people who experienced hackers refer to as **script kiddies** or **packet monkeys**. These derogatory terms refer to people who copy code or use tools created by knowledgeable programmers without an understanding of how they work. Many experienced penetration testers can write programs or scripts in Python, Ruby, Perl, or C to carry out attacks. (A script is a set of instructions that runs in sequence to perform tasks on a computer system.) You have a chance to write a script in one of these languages in Chapter 7.

A new term has emerged to define a person who hacks computer systems for political or social reasons: **hacktivist**. For several years, the hacktivist group known as Anonymous has wreaked havoc on federal government computer systems as well as those in the private sector. In 2015, the group threatened to release the names of Ku Klux Klan (KKK) members after hacking the organization's Twitter account. This type of hacking is called "hacktivism."

An Internet search on IT job recruiter sites for "penetration tester" produces hundreds of job announcements, many from Fortune 500 companies looking for experienced applicants. A typical ad might include the following requirements:

- Perform vulnerability, attack, and penetration assessments in Internet, Intranet, and wireless environments.
- Perform discovery and scanning for open ports and services.
- Apply appropriate exploits to gain access and expand access as necessary.
- Participate in activities involving application penetration testing and application source code review.
- Interact with the client as required throughout the engagement.

- Produce reports documenting discoveries during the engagement.
- Debrief with the client at the conclusion of each engagement.
- Participate in research and provide recommendations for continuous improvement.
- Participate in knowledge sharing.
- A good understanding of current country, state, and city cyber laws.

Penetration testers and security testers usually have a laptop computer configured with multiple OSs and hacking tools. The Kali Linux DVD accompanying this book contains the Linux OS and many tools needed to conduct actual network and Web application attacks. Learning how to install an OS isn't covered in this book, but you can find books on this topic easily. The most recent versions of Kali Linux can be found at *kali.org*. The procedure for installing security tools varies, depending on the tool and the OS.

Activity 1-1: Determining the Corporate Need for IT Security Professionals

Time Required: 10 minutes

Objective: Examine the many corporations looking to employ IT security professionals.

Description: Many companies are eager to employ or contract security testers for their corporate networks. In this activity, you search the Internet for job postings, using the keywords "IT security," and read some job descriptions to determine the IT skills (as well as any non-IT skills) most companies want an applicant to possess.

1. Start your Web browser, and go to **http://jobsearch.monster.com**.
2. Click the **Search for Jobs** text box, type **IT Security**, and then click the **Search** button.
3. Scroll to the bottom of the first page, and note the number of positions. Select three to five positions, and read the job description information.
4. When you're finished, exit your Web browser.

Security Bytes

An October 2015 article in *The Washington Post*, "How the government tries to recruit hackers on their own turf," describes the U.S. government's attempts at recruiting hackers from major conferences, such as DEFCON and Black Hat, to help secure the nation's networks. Curiously, the term "ethical" didn't precede the word "hacker." One can only hope the hackers who were hired have ethics as well as hacking skills.

Penetration-Testing Methodologies

Ethical hackers who perform penetration tests use one of these models:

- White box model
- Black box model
- Gray box model

In the **white box model,** the tester is told what network topology and technology the company is using and is given permission to interview IT personnel and company employees. For example, the company might print a network diagram showing all the company's routers, switches, firewalls, and intrusion detection systems (IDSs) or give the tester a floor plan detailing the location of computer systems and the OSs running on these systems (see Figure 1-1).

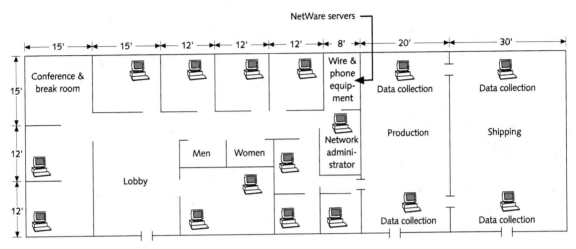

Figure 1-1   A sample floor plan

This background information makes the penetration tester's job a little easier than it is with using the black box model. In the **black box model,** management doesn't divulge to staff that penetration testing is being conducted, nor does it give the tester any diagrams or describe what technologies the company is using. This model puts the burden on the tester to find this information by using techniques you learn throughout this book. This model also helps management see whether the company's security personnel can detect an attack.

The **gray box model** is a hybrid of the white and black box models. In this model, the company gives the tester only partial information. For example, the tester might get information about which OSs are used but not get any network diagrams.

Security Bytes

Hospitals often check the intake procedures medical staff perform by using interns and nurses as "potential patients." In one psychiatric hospital, intake staff was told in advance that some potential patients would be doctors or nurses. Surprisingly, the number of patients admitted that month was unusually low, even though none of the patients were interns or nurses. In the same vein, if a company knows that it's being monitored to assess the security of its systems, employees might behave more vigilantly and adhere to existing procedures. Many companies don't want this false sense of security; they want to see how personnel operate without forewarning that someone might attempt to attack their network.

Certification Programs for Network Security Personnel

As most IT professionals are aware, professional certification is available in just about every area of network security. The following sections cover several applicable certifications. Whether you're a security professional, computer programmer, database administrator, or wide area network (WAN) specialist, professional organizations offer enough certifications and exams to keep you busy for the rest of your career. The following sections cover the most popular IT security certifications and describe some exam requirements briefly. You should have already earned, at minimum, CompTIA Security+ certification or have equivalent knowledge, which assumes networking competence at the CompTIA Network+ level of knowledge, a prerequisite for the Security+ certification. For more details, visit the CompTIA Web site (*www.comptia.org*).

Offensive Security Certified Professional The Offensive Security Certified Professional (OSCP; *https://www.offensive-security.com*) is an advanced certification that requires students to demonstrate hands-on abilities to earn their certificates. It covers network and application exploits and gives students experience in developing rudimentary buffer overflows, writing scripts to collect and manipulate data, and trying exploits on vulnerable systems.

Certified Ethical Hacker The International Council of Electronic Commerce Consultants (EC-Council) has developed a certification designation called **Certified Ethical Hacker (CEH)**. Currently, the multiple-choice CEH exam is based on 22 domains (subject areas) the tester must be familiar with. Knowledge requirements change periodically, so if you're interested in taking this exam, visit EC-Council's Web site (*www.eccouncil.org*) for the most up-to-date information. The 22 domains tested for the CEH exam are as follows:

- Ethics and legal issues
- Footprinting
- Scanning
- Enumeration
- System hacking
- Trojans and backdoors
- Sniffers
- Denial of service
- Social engineering
- Session hijacking
- Hacking Web servers
- Web application vulnerabilities
- Web-based password-cracking techniques
- Structured Query Language (SQL) injection
- Hacking wireless networks
- Viruses and worms
- Physical security

- Hacking Linux
- IDSs, firewalls, and honeypots
- Buffer overflows
- Cryptography
- Penetration-testing methodologies

As you can see, you must be familiar with a vast amount of information to pass this exam. Although you do need a general knowledge of these 22 domains for the exam, in the workplace, you'll most likely be placed on a team that conducts penetration tests. This team, called a **red team** in the industry, is composed of people with varied skills who perform the tests. For example, a red team might include a programming expert who can perform SQL injections or other programming vulnerability testing. (You learn more about SQL injections and programming fundamentals in Chapter 10.) The team might also include a network expert who's familiar with port vulnerabilities and IDS, router, or firewall vulnerabilities. It's unlikely that one person will perform all tests. However, passing the exam requires general knowledge of all the domains listed. Reading this book and working through the activities and case projects will help you gain this knowledge.

Open Source Security Testing Methodology Manual Professional Security Tester

The OSSTMM Professional Security Tester (OPST) certification is designated by the **Institute for Security and Open Methodologies (ISECOM)**, a nonprofit organization that provides security training and certification programs for security professionals. The OPST certification uses the **Open Source Security Testing Methodology Manual (OSSTMM)**, written by Peter Herzog, as its standardized methodology. You'll use many of its methodologies throughout this book. Because the manual is updated periodically, you should check the ISECOM site (*www.isecom.org*) regularly to download the most current version.

The exam covers some of the following topics:

- *Professional*—Rules of engagement (defining your conduct as a security tester)
- *Enumeration*—Internet packet types, denial-of-service testing
- *Assessments*—Network surveying, controls, competitive intelligence scouting
- *Application*—Password cracking, containment measures
- *Verification*—Problem solving, security testing

The exam requires testers to not only answer multiple-choice questions but also conduct security testing on an attack network successfully. This practical-application portion of the exam ensures that testers can apply their knowledge to a real-world setting. For more information on this certification, visit *www.isecom.org*.

Certified Information Systems Security Professional

The Certified Information Systems Security Professional (CISSP) certification for security professionals is issued by the International Information Systems Security Certification Consortium (ISC²). Even though the CISSP certification isn't geared toward the technical IT professional, it has become one of the standards for many security professionals. The exam doesn't require testers to have technical knowledge in IT; it tests security-related managerial skills. CISSPs are usually more concerned with policies and procedures than the actual tools for conducting security tests or penetration tests, so they don't need the skills of a technical IT professional. ISC^2 requires exam takers to have 5 years of experience before taking the 5-hour exam, so don't rush into it until you've been in the industry a while. The exam covers questions from the following 10 domains:

- Security and Risk Management
- Asset Security (Protecting Security of Assets)
- Security Engineering (Engineering and Management of Security)
- Communication and Network Security (Designing and Protecting Network Security)
- Identity and Access Management (Controlling Access and Managing Identity)
- Security Assessment and Testing (Designing, Performing, and Analyzing Security Testing)
- Security Operations (Foundational Concepts, Investigations, Incident Management, and Disaster Recovery)
- Software Development Security (Understanding, Applying, and Enforcing Software Security)

For more information on this certification, visit *www.isc2.org*.

SANS Institute   The **SysAdmin, Audit, Network, Security (SANS) Institute** offers training and IT security certifications through **Global Information Assurance Certification (GIAC)**. Two related certifications in ethical hacking are the GIAC Certified Penetration Tester (GPEN) and the GIAC Certified Web Application Tester (GWAPT). In addition to its well-respected certification, SANS offers its training courses through an accredited university, SANS Technology Institute. Alongside its training and degree programs, SANS disseminates research documents on computer and network security worldwide at no cost. One of its most popular documents is the Top 25 Software Errors list, which describes the most common network exploits and suggests ways of correcting vulnerabilities. This list offers a wealth of information for penetration testers or security professionals, and you examine it in Activity 1-2. For more information on security certification exams, visit *www.sans.org* or *www.giac.org*.

Which Certification Is Best?   Deciding which certification exam to take can be difficult. Both penetration testers and security testers need technical skills to perform their duties effectively. They must also have a good understanding of networks and the role of management in an organization, skills in writing and verbal communication, and a desire to continue learning. Any certification, if it encourages you to read and study more, is worth its weight in gold. The argument that a certification is just a piece of paper can be countered by saying "So is a hundred dollar bill, but it's nice to have in your wallet!" The danger of certification exams is that some participants simply memorize terminology and don't have a good grasp of the subject matter or complex concepts, much like students who have managed to pass a final exam by cramming but then forget most of the information after taking the test. Use the time you spend studying for a certification exam wisely, discovering areas in which you might need improvement instead of memorizing answers to questions.

By learning the material in this book, you can acquire the skills you need to become a competent IT security professional and pass exams covering ethical hacking, penetration-testing methods, and network topologies and technologies. Regardless of the exam you take, however, the most critical point to remember is that there are laws governing what you can or can't do as an ethical hacker, a security tester, or a penetration tester. Following the laws and behaving ethically are more important than passing an exam.

Again, visit Web sites for the organizations conducting certification testing because exam requirements change as rapidly as technology does. For example, several years ago, the CISSP exam had no questions on wireless networking because the technology wasn't widely available, but now the exam covers wireless technology.

Activity 1-2: Examining the Top 25 Most Dangerous Software Flaws

Time Required: 15 minutes

Objective: Examine the SANS list of the most common network exploits.

Description: As fast as IT security professionals attempt to correct network vulnerabilities, someone creates new exploits, and network security professionals must keep up to date on these exploits. In this activity, you examine some current exploits used to attack networks. Don't worry—you won't have to memorize your findings. This activity simply gives you an introduction to the world of network security.

Be aware that Web sites change often. You might have to dig around to find the information you're looking for. Think of it as practice for being a skilled security tester.

1. Start your Web browser, and go to **www.sans.org**.

2. Under Resources, click the **Top 25 Programming Errors** link. (Because Web sites change as rapidly as the price of gas, you might have to search to find this link.)

3. Read the contents of the Top 25 list. (This document changes often to reflect the many new exploits created daily.) The list is organized into three categories: Insecure Interaction Between Components, Risky Resource Management, and Porous Defenses.

4. Investigate the first few flaws by clicking the **CWE-#** link. For each flaw, note the consequences and its prevalence.

5. When you're finished, exit your Web browser.

What You Can Do Legally

Because laws involving computer technology change as rapidly as technology itself, you must keep abreast of what's happening in your area of the world. What's legal in Des Moines might not be legal in Indianapolis, for example. Finding out what's legal in your state or country can be just as difficult as performing penetration tests, however. Many state officials aren't aware of the legalities surrounding computer technology. This confusion also makes it difficult to prosecute wrongdoers in computer crimes. The average citizen on a jury doesn't want to send a person to jail for doing something the state prosecutor hasn't clearly defined as illegal.

As a security tester, you must be aware of what you're allowed to do and what you should not or cannot do. For example, some security testers know how to pick a deadbolt lock, so a locked door wouldn't deter them from getting physical access to a server. However, testers must be knowledgeable about the laws for possessing lockpicks before venturing out to a corporate site with tools in hand. In fact, laws vary from state to state and country to country. In some states, the mere possession of lockpicking tools constitutes a crime, whereas other states allow possession as long as a crime hasn't been committed. In one state, you might be charged with a misdemeanor for possessing these tools; in another state, you might be charged with a felony.

The Open Organisation of Lockpickers (TOOOL) is worth taking a look at if you are considering this skill in your arsenal. Their Website, *http://toool.us/laws.html*, makes it easy for you to do a quick look at the laws in each state before your pack your suitcase with your lockpicking tools!

Laws of the Land

As with lockpicking tools, having some hacking tools on your computer might be illegal. You should contact local law enforcement agencies and ask about the laws for your state or country before installing hacking tools on your computer. You can see how complex this issue gets as you travel from state to state or country to country. New York City might have one law, and a quick drive over the George Washington Bridge brings you to the laws of New Jersey. Table A-1, in Appendix A, compares Vermont's computer crime statutes to New York's to demonstrate the variety of verbiage the legal community uses.

Laws are written to protect society, but often the written words are open to interpretation, which is why courts and judges are necessary. In Hawaii, for example, the state must prove that the person charged with committing a crime on a computer had the "intent to commit a crime." So just scanning a network isn't a crime in Hawaii. Also, the state has the even more difficult task of having to prove that the computer used in committing a crime had been used by only one person—the one alleged to have committed the crime. If the person charged with the crime claims that more than one person had access to the computer used to gather evidence of wrongdoing, the state can't use that computer as evidence.

What do these laws have to do with a network security professional using penetration-testing tools? Laws for having hacking tools that allow you to view a company's network infrastructure aren't as clearly defined as laws for possession of lockpicking tools because laws haven't been able to keep up with the speed of technological advances. In some states, running a program that gives an attacker an overview and a detailed description of a company's network infrastructure isn't seen as a threat.

As another example of how laws can vary, is taking photos of a bank's exterior and interior legal? Security personnel at a bank in Hawaii say you would be asked to stop taking photos and leave the premises. An FBI spokesperson put it in simple terms: You can be asked to stop taking photos if you're on private property. Taking photos across the street from the bank with a zoom lens is legal, but if you use the photos to commit a crime in the future, an attorney would tell you the charges against you might be more serious. Because of the fear of terrorism, in certain parts of the United States and many parts of Europe, taking photos of bridges, train stations, and other public areas is illegal.

The point of mentioning all these laws and regulations is to make sure you're aware of the dangers of being a security tester or a student learning hacking techniques. Table 1-1 lists just a small fraction of the cases prosecuted in the past few years; in these cases,

State and year	Description
Massachusetts, 2013	Aaron Swartz was charged with 13 felony counts under the Computer Fraud and Abuse Act after connecting to MIT's computer networks and downloading 2.7 million articles from JSTOR, a digital library of academic journals. *Note:* The movie *Internet's Own Boy*, the story of Aaron Swartz, is available free at *https://www.youtube.com/watch?v=vXr-2hwTk58*.
Massachusetts, 2014	Cameron Lacroix, 25, of New Bedford, Massachusetts, was sentenced to 4 years in prison and 3 years of supervised release for computer hacking and credit card theft. Lacroix, a community college student, hacked into law enforcement agencies' servers that contained sensitive information, such as arrest warrants, police reports, and sex offender information. He also accessed the Massachusetts chief of police's e-mail account and hacked into his college's server to change his grades and those of two other students.
Georgia, 2014	Sergei Nicolaevich Tsurikov, 30, of Tallinn, Estonia, was sentenced to 11 years in prison for conspiracy to commit wire fraud and computer intrusion. U.S. Attorney Sally Quillian Yates said the hack was one of the most sophisticated and organized computer fraud attacks ever conducted. It involved more than 44 counterfeit payroll debit cards and the withdrawal of more than $9 million.
Delaware, 2014	Nathan Leroux, 20, of Bowie, Maryland; Sanadodeh Nesheiwat, 28, of Washington, New Jersey; David Pokora, 22, of Mississauga, Ontario, Canada; and Austin Alcala, 18, of McCordsville, Indiana, were indicted for stealing gaming technology and Apache helicopter training software. The four hackers used SQL injection (covered in Chapter 10) and stolen usernames and passwords to hack into Microsoft Corporation, Epic Games Inc., Valve Corporation, Zombie Studios, and the U.S. Army. After they had access to computer systems, they stole unreleased software, trade secrets, source programming code, and other proprietary information. The cyber theft included the popular Xbox game *Call of Duty: Modern Warfare 3*.
Texas, 2014	Fidel Salinas, 27, of Donna, Texas, an alleged member of the hacktivist group Anonymous, faces up to 10 years in federal prison for allegedly cyberstalking a female victim, attempting to gain unauthorized access to her Web site, and attempting to open user accounts in her name without her permission. The indictment also claims that Salinas made more than 14,000 hacking attempts on the administration page of the Hidalgo County Web site's server, causing a denial of service (discussed in Chapter 3) and incurring a cost of more than $10,000 to respond to the attack.
New York, 2014	Lauri Love, 30, of Suffolk, England, was charged with hacking into the Federal Reserve. He allegedly used SQL injection to exploit a vulnerability in the Federal Reserve's servers; stole confidential information, such as names, phone numbers, and e-mail addresses; and posted the information to a Web site he had already hacked. He's believed to have hacked into thousands of networks, including those of the U.S. Army and NASA. If convicted, he faces up to 10 years in a federal prison.
Wisconsin, 2014	James L Santelle, 24, of Postville, Iowa, was sentenced to 24 months' probation and ordered to pay $110,932.71 in restitution for participating in a distributed denial-of-service attack against the Angel Soft (bathroom tissue) Web site. The company claimed it lost several hundred thousand dollars over a 3-day period as a result.

Table 1-1   An overview of recent hacking cases

many people have been sentenced to prison for "hacking," the term used by the Department of Justice. Most attacks involved more than just scanning a business, but this information shows that the government is getting more serious about punishment for cybercrimes. Some of the most infamous cases are hacks carried out by college students, such as the eBay hack of 1999. As you read the information in this table, note that some hackers used software to crack passwords of logon accounts. This act, performed by many security professionals when given permission to do so by a network's owner, is a federal offense when done without permission and can add substantial prison time to a hacker's sentence.

Security Bytes

A September 2013 Forbes.com article, 6 *High-Paying Jobs of the Future*, listed ethical hacker second in jobs for the future, with median salary of $92,200 per year. However, Thomas Frey, author of *Communicating with the Future*, had an interesting comment in his analysis: "[W]e need to officially distinguish between what is and isn't ethical."

Is Port Scanning Legal?

Some states consider port scanning (covered in Chapter 5) as noninvasive or nondestructive in nature and deem it legal. This isn't always the case, however, so you must be prudent before you start using penetration-testing tools. In some cases, a company has filed criminal charges against hackers for scanning its system, but judges ruled that no damage was done to the network, so the charges were dismissed. It's just a matter of time before a business will claim that its network is also private property, and it should have the right to say that scanning is not allowed.

Because the federal government currently doesn't see these infringements as a violation of the U.S. Constitution, each state is allowed to address these issues separately. However, a company could bring up similar charges against you if you decide to practice using the tools you learn in this book. Even if you're found innocent in your state, the legal costs could be damaging to your business or personal finances. Therefore, researching your state laws before using what you learn in this book is essential, even if you're using the tools for the benefit of others, not criminal activity. As of this writing, you can check *www.ncsl.org/research/telecommunications-and-information-technology /computer-hacking-and-unauthorized-access-laws.aspx* for each state's laws on unauthorized access and hacking. (If this URL doesn't work, go to the home page at *www.ncsl .org* and do a search.) Spending time at this site is certainly preferable to spending time in court or prison.

When traveling outside the United States, be aware of the cyber laws of the country you're visiting. For example, driving a car equipped with an antenna designed to identify wireless access points is a crime in Germany.

You should also read your ISP contract, specifically the section usually called "Acceptable Use Policy." Most people just glance over and accept the terms of their contract. Figure 1-2 is an excerpt from an actual ISP contract. Notice that section (c) might create some problems

---

Acceptable Use Policy

(a)   PacInfo Net makes no restriction on usage provided that such usage is legal under the laws and regulations of the State of Hawaii and the United States of America and does not adversely affect PacInfo Net customers. Customer is responsible for obtaining and adhering to the Acceptable Use Policies of any network accessed through PacInfo Net services.

(b)   PacInfo Net reserves the right without notice to disconnect an account that is the source of spamming, abusive, or malicious activities. There will be no refund when an account is terminated for these causes. Moreover, there will be a billing rate of $125 per hour charged to such accounts to cover staff time spent repairing subsequent damage.

(c)   Customers are forbidden from using techniques designed to cause damage to or deny access by legitimate users of computers or network components connected to the Internet. PacInfo Net reserves the right to disconnect a customer site that is the source of such activities without notice.

Figure 1-2   An example of an acceptable use policy

if you run scanning software that slows down network access or prevents users from accessing network components.

Another ISP responded to an e-mail about the use of scanning software with the following message:

> Any use of the Service that disturbs the normal use of the system by HOL or by other HOL customers or consumes excessive amounts of memory or CPU cycles for long periods of time may result in termination pursuant to Section 1 of this Agreement. Users are strictly prohibited from any activity that compromises the security of HOL's facilities. Users may not run IRC "bots" or any other scripts or programs not provided by HOL.

> Regards,

> Customer Support
> Hawaii Online

The statement prohibiting the use of Internet Relay Chat (IRC) bots or any other scripts or programs not provided by the ISP might be the most important for penetration testers. An IRC "bot" is a program that sends automatic responses to users, giving the appearance of a person being on the other side of the connection. For example, a bot can be created that welcomes new users joining a chat session, even though a person isn't actually present to welcome them. Even if you have no intentions of creating a bot, the "any other scripts or programs" clause should still raise an eyebrow.

Table A-2 in Appendix A shows which legal statutes to look at before you begin your journey. The statutes listed in the table might have changed since the writing of this book, so keeping up with your state laws before trying penetration-testing tools is important. In Activity 1-3, you research the laws of your state or country, using Table A-2 as a guide.

Activity 1-3: Identifying Computer Statutes in Your State or Country

Time Required: 30 minutes

Objective: Learn what laws might prohibit you from conducting a network penetration test in your state or country.

Description: For this activity, you use Internet search engines to gather information on computer crime in your state or country (or a location selected by your instructor). You have been hired by ExecuTech, a security consulting company, to gather information on any new statutes or laws that might have an impact on the security testers they employ. Write a one-page memo to Bob Lynch, director of security and operations, listing any applicable statutes or laws and offering recommendations to management. For example, you might note in your memo that conducting a denial-of-service attack on a company's network is illegal because the state's penal code prohibits this type of attack unless authorized by the owner.

Federal Laws

You should also be aware of applicable federal laws when conducting your first security test (see Table 1-2). Federal computer crime laws are getting more specific about cybercrimes and intellectual property issues. In fact, the government now has a new branch of computer crime called "computer hacking and intellectual property (CHIP)."

Federal law	Description
The Computer Fraud and Abuse Act. Title 18, Crimes and Criminal Procedure. Part I: Crimes, Chapter 47, Fraud and False Statements, Sec. 1030: Fraud and related activity in connection with computers	This law makes it a federal crime to access classified information or financial information without authorization.
Electronic Communication Privacy Act. Title 18, Crimes and Criminal Procedure. Part I: Crimes, Chapter 119, Wire and Electronic Communications Interception and Interception of Oral Communications, Sec. 2510: Definitions and Sec. 2511: Interception and disclosure of wire, oral, or electronic communications prohibited	These laws make it illegal to intercept any communication, regardless of how it was transmitted.
U.S. PATRIOT Act, Sec. 217. Interception of Computer Trespasser Communications	This act largely sought to amend previous privacy and surveillance laws and fund government surveillance programs. Among many other things, it created new ways for the government to monitor individuals and allowed victims of cybercrimes to monitor the activity of trespassers on their systems.
Homeland Security Act of 2002, H.R. 5710, Sec. 225: Cyber Security Enhancement Act of 2002	This amendment to the Homeland Security Act of 2002 specifies sentencing guidelines for certain types of computer crimes.
The Computer Fraud and Abuse Act. Title 18, Crimes and Criminal Procedure, Sec. 1029: Fraud and related activity in connection with access devices	This law makes it a federal offense to manufacture, program, use, or possess any device or software that can be used for unauthorized use of telecommunications services.

Table 1-2   Federal computer crime laws

Federal law	Description
Stored Wire and Electronic Communications and Transactional Records Act. Title 18, Crimes and Criminal Procedure. Part I: Crimes, Chapter 121, Stored Wire and Electronic Communications and Transactional Records Act, Sec. 2701: Unlawful access to stored communications	This law defines unauthorized access to computers that store classified information.
(a) Offense. Except as provided in subsection of this section whoever (1) intentionally accesses without authorization a facility through which an electronic communication service is provided; or (2) intentionally exceeds an authorization to access that facility; Sec. 2702: Disclosure of contents	

Table 1-2 Federal computer crime laws (*continued*)

Security Bytes

Even though you might think you're following the requirements set forth by the client who hired you to perform a security test, don't assume that management will be happy with your results. One tester was reprimanded by a manager who was upset that security testing revealed all the logon names and passwords. The manager believed that the tester shouldn't know this information and considered stopping the security testing.

Activity 1-4: Examining Federal Computer Crime Laws

Time Required: 15 minutes

Objective: Increase your understanding of U.S. federal laws related to computer crime.

Description: For this activity, use Internet search engines to gather information on U.S. Code, Title 18, Sec. 1030, which covers fraud and related activity in connection with computers. Write a summary explaining how this law can affect ethical hackers and security testers.

What You Cannot Do Legally

After reviewing the state and federal laws on computer crime, you can see that accessing a computer without permission, destroying data, and copying information without the owner's permission are illegal. It doesn't take a law degree to understand that certain actions are illegal, such as installing viruses on a network that deny users access to network resources. As a security tester, you must be careful that your actions don't prevent the client's employees from doing their jobs. If you run a program that uses network resources to the extent that a user is denied access to them, you have violated federal law. For example, denial-of-service (DoS) attacks, covered in Chapter 3, should not be initiated on your client's networks.

Get It in Writing

As discussed, you can cause a DoS attack inadvertently by running certain hacking programs on a client's network. This possibility is what makes your job difficult, especially if you're conducting security tests as an independent contractor hired by a company instead of being an employee of a large security company that has a legal team to draw up a contract with the client. Employees of a security company are protected under the company's contract with the client.

For the purposes of this discussion, assume you're an independent contractor who needs a little guidance in creating a written contract. Some contractors don't believe in written contracts, thinking they undermine their relationships with clients. The old handshake and verbal agreement work for many consultants, but consulting an attorney is always wise. Some think it's a matter of trust, and others argue that a written contract is just good business. Consultants who haven't received payment from the client usually vote yes on the contract question. Similarly, users often aren't convinced of the importance of backing up important documents until their computers crash. Don't be like them and wait until you're in court to wish you had something in writing.

If you want additional information, you can consult books on working as an independent contractor, such as *Getting Started as an Independent Computer Consultant* (Mitch Paioff and Melanie Mulhall, 2008, ISBN 978-0-98192-970-5) and *The Consulting Bible: Everything You Need to Know to Create and Expand a Seven-Figure Consulting Practice* (Alan Weiss, 2011, ISBN 978-0-470-92808-0). The Internet can also be a helpful resource for finding free contract templates that can be modified to fit your business situation. The modifications you make might create more problems than having no contract at all, however, so having an attorney read your contract before it's signed is a good investment of your time and money.

Are you concerned? Good. Most books or courses on ethical hacking gloss over this topic, yet it's the most important part of the profession. If your client gives you a contract drawn up by the company's legal department, consulting a lawyer can save you time and money. Attempting to understand a contract written by attorneys representing the company's best interests warrants an attorney on your side looking out for your best interests. The complexity of law is too much for most laypeople to understand. Keeping up with computer technology is difficult enough. Both fields are changing constantly, but law is even more complex, as it changes from state to state.

Figure B-1 in Appendix B shows an example of a contract you might want to use, with modifications, after joining the Independent Computer Consultants Association (ICCA) Visit *www.icca.com* for information on how you can become a member. Read through the legal language in this figure, and then do Activity 1-5.

Activity 1-5: Understanding a Consulting Contract

Time Required: 30 minutes

Objective: Increase your understanding of a consulting contract.

Description: For this activity, review the sample contract shown in Appendix B. This contract can't be used unless you're a member of the ICCA, but it's an excellent example of how a contract might be worded. After reading the contract, write a one-page summary discussing the areas you would modify or add to. Include any sections important for a penetration tester that are missing.

Security Bytes

Because the job of an ethical hacker is fairly new, the laws are changing constantly. Even though a company has hired you to test its network for vulnerabilities, be careful that you aren't breaking any laws in your state or country. If you're worried that one of your tests might slow down the network because of excessive bandwidth use, this concern should signal a red flag. The company might consider suing you for lost time or monies caused by this delay.

Ethical Hacking in a Nutshell

After reading all the dos and don'ts, you might have decided to go into a different profession. Before switching careers, however, take a look at the skills a security tester needs to help determine whether you have what it takes to do this job:

- *Knowledge of network and computer technology*—As a security tester, you must have a good understanding of networking concepts. You should spend time learning and reviewing TCP/IP and routing concepts and be able to read network diagrams. If you don't have experience working with networks, it's important that you start now. Being a security tester is impossible without a high level of expertise in this area. You should also have a good understanding of computer technologies and OSs. Read as much as you can on OSs in use today, paying particular attention to Linux systems and Windows OSs because most security testing is done on these popular systems.

- *Ability to communicate with management and IT personnel*—Security testers need to be good listeners and must be able to communicate verbally and in writing with management and IT personnel. Explaining your findings to CEOs might be difficult, especially if they don't have a technical background. Your reports should be clear and succinct and offer constructive feedback and recommendations.

- *An understanding of the laws that apply to your location*—As a security tester, you must be aware of what you can and can't do legally. Gathering this information can be difficult when working with global companies, as laws can vary widely in other countries.

- *Ability to apply the necessary tools to perform your tasks*—Security testers must have a good understanding of tools for conducting security tests. More important, you must be able to think outside the box by discovering, creating, or modifying tools when current tools don't meet your needs.

Security Bytes

If being liked by others is important to you, you might want to consider a different profession than security testing. If you're good at your job, many IT employees resent your discovering vulnerabilities in their systems. In fact, it's one of the only professions in which the better you do your job, the more enemies you make!

Chapter Summary

- Many companies hire ethical hackers to perform penetration tests. The purpose of a penetration test is to discover vulnerabilities in a network. A security test is typically done by a team of people with varied skills, sometimes referred to as a "red team," and goes further to recommend solutions for addressing vulnerabilities.

- Penetration tests are usually conducted by using one of three models: white box model, black box model, and gray box model. The model the tester uses is based on the amount of information the client is willing to supply. In some tests, the client doesn't want the tester to have access to any of the company's information. In other words, the client is saying "Find out what you can about my company without my help."

- Security testers can earn certifications from multiple sources. The most popular certifications are CEH, CISSP, and OCSP. Each certification requires taking an exam and covers different areas the tester must master. Because test requirements change periodically, visit the certification company's Web site to verify exam requirements.

- As a security tester or penetration tester, you must be aware of what you're allowed or not allowed to do by law. Contacting your local law enforcement agency is a good place to start before beginning any security testing.

- Your ISP might have an acceptable use policy in the contract you signed. It could limit your ability to use many of the tools available to security testers. Running scripts or programs not authorized by the ISP can result in termination of services.

- State and federal laws pertaining to computer crime should be understood before conducting a security test. Federal laws are applicable for all states, whereas state laws can vary. Being aware of the laws that apply is imperative.

- Get it in writing. As an independent contractor, having the client sign a written contract allowing you to conduct penetration testing before you begin is critical. You should also have an attorney read the contract, especially if you or the company representative made any modifications.

- You need to understand the tools available to conduct security tests. Learning how to use them should be a focused and methodical process.

Key Terms

black box model
Certified Ethical Hacker (CEH)
Certified Information Systems Security Professional (CISSP)
crackers
ethical hackers
Global Information Assurance Certification (GIAC)
gray box model
hacker

hacktivist
Institute for Security and Open Methodologies (ISECOM)
Offensive Security Certified Professional (OCSP)
Open Source Security Testing Methodology Manual (OSSTMM)
OSSTMM Professional Security Tester (OPST)

packet monkeys
penetration test
red team
script kiddies
security test
SysAdmin, Audit, Network, Security (SANS) Institute
vulnerability assessment
white box model

Review Questions

1. The U.S. Department of Justice defines a hacker as which of the following?

   a. A person who accesses a computer or network without the owner's permission

   b. A penetration tester

   c. A person who uses phone services without payment

   d. A person who accesses a computer or network system with the owner's permission

2. A penetration tester is which of the following?

   a. A person who breaks into a computer or network without permission from the owner

   b. A person who uses telephone services without payment

   c. A security professional who's hired to break into a network to discover vulnerabilities

   d. A hacker who breaks into a system without permission but doesn't delete or destroy files

3. Some experienced hackers refer to inexperienced hackers who copy or use prewritten scripts or programs as which of the following? (Choose all that apply.)

   a. Script monkeys

   b. Packet kiddies

   c. Packet monkeys

   d. Script kiddies

4. What three models do penetration or security testers use to conduct tests?

5. A team composed of people with varied skills who attempt to penetrate a network is called which of the following?

   a. Green team

   b. Blue team

   c. Black team

   d. Red team

6. How can you find out which computer crime laws are applicable in your state?

   a. Contact your local law enforcement agencies.

   b. Contact your ISP provider.

   c. Contact your local computer store vendor.

   d. Call 911.

7. What portion of your ISP contract might affect your ability to conduct a penetration test over the Internet?

   a. Scanning policy

   b. Port access policy

   c. Acceptable use policy

   d. Warranty policy

8. If you run a program in New York City that uses network resources to the extent that a user is denied access to them, what type of law have you violated?

   a. City

   b. State

   c. Local

   d. Federal

9. Which federal law prohibits unauthorized access of classified information?

   a. Computer Fraud and Abuse Act, Title 18

   b. Electronic Communication Privacy Act

   c. Stored Wire and Electronic Communications and Transactional Records Act

   d. Fifth Amendment

10. Which federal law prohibits intercepting any communication, regardless of how it was transmitted?

    a. Computer Fraud and Abuse Act, Title 18

    b. Electronic Communication Privacy Act

    c. Stored Wire and Electronic Communications and Transactional Records Act

    d. Fourth Amendment

11. Which federal law amended Chapter 119 of Title 18, U.S. Code?

    a. Computer Fraud and Abuse Act, Title 18

    b. Electronic Communication Privacy Act

    c. Stored Wire and Electronic Communications and Transactional Records Act

    d. U.S. PATRIOT Act, Sec. 217: Interception of Computer Trespasser Communications

12. To determine whether scanning is illegal in your area, you should do which of the following?

    a. Refer to U.S. code.

    b. Refer to the U.S. PATRIOT Act.

    c. Refer to state laws.

    d. Contact your ISP.

13. What organization offers the CEH certification exam?

    a. ISC^2

    b. EC-Council

    c. SANS Institute

    d. GIAC

14. What organization designates a person as a CISSP?

    a. ISC^2

    b. EC-Council

    c. SANS Institute

    d. GIAC

15. What is an OSCP?

    a. Open Security Consultant Professional

    b. Offensive Security Certified Professional

    c. Official Security Computer Programmer

    d. OSSTMM Security Certified Professional

16. As a security tester, what should you do before installing hacking software on your computer?

    a. Check with local law enforcement agencies.

    b. Contact your hardware vendor.

    c. Contact the software vendor.

    d. Contact your ISP.

17. Before using hacking software over the Internet, you should contact which of the following? (Choose all that apply.)

    a. Your ISP

    b. Your vendor

    c. Local law enforcement authorities to check for compliance

    d. The FBI

18. Which organization issues the Top 25 list of software errors?

    a. SANS Institute

    b. ISECOM

    c. EC-Council

    d. OPST

19. A written contract isn't necessary when a friend recommends a client. True or False?

20. A security tester should have which of the following attributes? (Choose all that apply.)

    a. Good listening skills

    b. Knowledge of networking and computer technology

    c. Good verbal and written communication skills

    d. An interest in securing networks and computer systems

Case Projects

Case Project 1-1: Determining Legal Requirements for Penetration Testing

Alexander Rocco Corporation, a large real estate management company in Maui, Hawaii, has contracted your computer consulting company to perform a penetration test on its computer network. The company owns property that houses a five-star hotel, golf courses, tennis courts, and restaurants. Claudia Mae, the vice president, is your only contact at the company. To avoid undermining the tests you're conducting, you won't be introduced to any IT staff or employees. Claudia wants to determine what you can find out about the company's network infrastructure, network topology, and any discovered vulnerabilities, without any assistance from her or company personnel.

Based on this information, write a report outlining the steps you should take before beginning penetration tests of the Alexander Rocco Corporation. Research the laws applying to the state where the company is located, and be sure to reference any federal laws that might apply to what you have been asked to do.

Case Project 1-2: Researching Hacktivists at Work

In 2015, Anonymous hacked the official Twitter account of the KKK (Ku Klux Klan), an extremist, secret society formed after the Civil War to advocate for white supremacy. KKK members wear white robes and hoods to hide their identities. The hacktivists stated that because the KKK had previously threatened to harm a group of protesters, they would retaliate by releasing the names of prominent people who were KKK members.

Research hacktivism, and write a one-page paper that answers the following questions:

- Is hacktivism an effective political tool?
- Did any of the hacktivists you researched go too far?
- Can hacktivism ever be justified?

## chapter 2

TCP/IP Concepts Review

After reading this chapter and completing the exercises, you will be able to:

- Explain the TCP/IP protocol stack
- Explain the basic concepts of IP addressing
- Explain the binary, octal, and hexadecimal numbering systems

Almost everything you do as a network security analyst or security tester depends on your understanding of networking concepts and knowledge of Transmission Control Protocol/ Internet Protocol (TCP/IP). It's assumed you already understand networking concepts and TCP/IP and are CompTIA Network+ certified or have equivalent knowledge. This chapter, however, serves as a review of how these topics relate to IT security and security testers. In the activities and case projects, you apply your knowledge of TCP/IP and networking concepts to security-testing techniques.

Most of the tools both hackers and security testers use run over IP, which is a standard networking protocol. However, IP version 4 (IPv4), still the most widely used version, was developed without security functions in mind, so professionals need the knowledge and skills to tighten up security holes resulting from the use of IP.

In this chapter, you examine the TCP/IP protocol stack and IP addressing and review the binary, octal, and hexadecimal numbering systems and the ports associated with services that run over TCP/IP.

Overview of TCP/IP

For computers to communicate with one another over the Internet or across an office, they must speak the same language. This language is referred to as a **protocol**, and the most widely used is **Transmission Control Protocol/Internet Protocol (TCP/IP)**. No matter what medium connects workstations on a network—copper wires, fiber-optic cables, or a wireless setup— the same protocol must be running on all computers if communication is going to function correctly.

You've probably already studied TCP/IP, but a little review is helpful to make sure you have a thorough understanding. TCP/IP is more than simply two protocols (TCP and IP). It's usually referred to as the TCP/IP stack, which contains four distinct layers (see Figure 2-1). The Network layer is concerned with physically moving bits across a medium (whether it's copper wire, fiber-optic cables, or wireless), and the Internet layer is responsible for routing packets by using IP addresses. The Transport layer is concerned with controlling the flow of data, sequencing packets for reassembly, and encapsulating the segment with a TCP or User Datagram Protocol (UDP) header. The Application layer is where applications and protocols, such as HTTP and Telnet, operate.

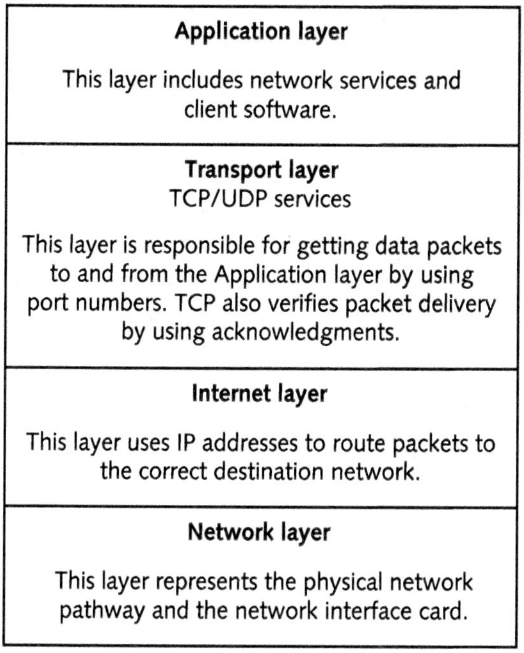

Figure 2-1 The TCP/IP protocol stack

This chapter discusses only the Application, Transport, and Internet layers, covered in the following sections, because security testing doesn't usually involve getting down to the Network layer's hardware level. However, there are computer attacks that use physical hardware, such as a keylogger (covered in Chapter 3).

The Application Layer

The Application-layer protocols are the front end to the lower-layer protocols in the TCP/IP stack. In other words, this layer is what you can see and touch. Table 2-1 lists some of the

Application	Description
Hypertext Transfer Protocol (HTTP)	The primary protocol used to communicate over the Web (see RFC 2616 at *www.ietf.org* for details)
File Transfer Protocol (FTP)	Allows different OSs to transfer files between one another
Simple Mail Transfer Protocol (SMTP)	The main protocol for transmitting e-mail messages across the Internet
Simple Network Management Protocol (SNMP)	Primarily used to monitor devices on a network, such as monitoring a router's state remotely
Secure Shell (SSH)	Enables users to securely log on to a remote server and issue commands interactively
Internet Relay Chat (IRC)	Enables multiple users to communicate over the Internet in discussion forums
Telnet	Enables users to insecurely log on to a remote server and issue commands interactively

Table 2-1 Application-layer programs

main applications and protocols running at this layer. These applications and protocols are discussed again in the "TCP Ports" section.

The Transport Layer

The Transport layer is where data is encapsulated into segments. A segment can use TCP or UDP as its method for connecting to and forwarding data to a destination host (or node). TCP is a **connection-oriented protocol**, meaning the sender doesn't send any data to the destination node until the destination node acknowledges that it's listening to the sender. In other words, a connection is established before data is sent. For example, if Computer A wants to send data to Computer B, it sends Computer B a SYN packet first. A **SYN** packet is a query to the receiver, much like asking "Hello, Computer B. Are you there?" Computer B sends back an acknowledgment called a **SYN-ACK** packet, which is like replying "Yes, I'm here. Go ahead and send." Finally, Computer A sends an **ACK** packet to Computer B in response to the SYN-ACK. This process, called a **three-way handshake**, involves the following steps:

1. Host A sends a TCP packet with the SYN flag set (*i.e.,* a SYN packet) to Host B.

2. After receiving the packet, Host B sends Host A its own SYN packet with an ACK flag (a SYN-ACK packet) set.

3. In response to the SYN-ACK packet from Host B, Host A sends Host B a TCP packet with the ACK flag set (an ACK packet).

TCP Segment Headers   As a security professional, you should know the critical components of a TCP header: TCP flags, the initial sequence number (covered later in "Initial Sequence Number"), and source and destination port numbers (covered later in "TCP Ports"). Figure 2-2 shows a diagram of the TCP header.

16-bit	32-bit
Source Port	Destination Port
Sequence Number	
Acknowledgement Number (ACK)	
Offset Reserved U A P R S F	Window
Checksum	Urgent Pointer
Options and Padding	

Figure 2-2   TCP header diagram

Hackers leverage knowledge of these TCP header components. You need to understand these components before learning how they can be abused. Then, and only then, can you check whether your network has vulnerabilities in these areas. Remember, to protect a network, you need to know the basic methods of hacking into networks. You examine more details on TCP headers in Activity 2-1.

Description: As an IT security professional, you should be aware of the ports used in a network infrastructure. A good way to test whether a service is running on a server is to telnet to the port using that service. For example, the SMTP service uses port 25. In this activity, you telnet to your classroom's mail server from your Windows computer. If your classroom doesn't have a mail server configured, connect to your ISP's mail server and send an e-mail from your e-mail account.

Security Bytes

If you can't connect to a mail server with the commands in Activities 2-2 and 2-3, you should still read through the steps and examine the figures to give you an idea of what a successful telnet connection looks like.

1. Telnet is disabled by default in Windows Vista and later, so if you're running one of these OSs, you'll need to enable it. Open Control Panel and click **Programs and Features**. On the left, click **Turn Windows features on or off**. In the Windows Features dialog box, scroll down and click the **Telnet Client** check box (see Figure 2-4). You can select other services you want to enable at this time, too. When you're finished, click **OK**, then close the Windows Features window and Control Panel.

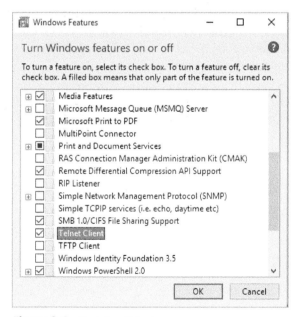

Figure 2-4   Enabling Telnet

Source: Microsoft

2. To open a command prompt window in Windows 10, right-click the **Start button,** and choose Command Prompt.

3. Type **telnet *RemoteMailServer* 25** (substituting your own server name for *RemoteMailServer*) and press **Enter**. You must enter the port number of the service you're attempting to connect to. In this case, you use port 25 for SMTP.

4. After getting the prompt shown in Figure 2-5, type **helo** *LocalDomainName* and press **Enter**. The mail server accepts almost anything you enter after the **helo** command as valid, but you should use your actual domain name.

```
220 Lab-Server-EH Microsoft ESMTP MAIL Service, Version: 8.5.9600.16384 ready at
    Sun, 15 Nov 2015 21:25:16 -0800
HELO Lab-Server-EH
250 Lab-Server-EH Hello [192.168.185.155]
mail from: non-entity@nowhere.com
250 2.1.0 non-entity@nowhere.com....Sender OK
rcpt to: administrator@Lab-Server-EH
250 2.1.5 administrator@Lab-Server-EH
data
354 Start mail input; end with <CRLF>.<CRLF>
This is a test message!
.
250 2.6.0 <LAB-SERVER-EHMvObjH00000002@Lab-Server-EH> Queued mail for delivery
quit
221 2.0.0 Lab-Server-EH Service closing transmission channel

Connection to host lost.

C:\Users\Administrator>
```

Figure 2-5   Using Telnet to send e-mail

Source: Microsoft

5. You can now enter your e-mail address, which is displayed in the recipient's From field. You can enter a bogus address, as shown in Figure 2-4, which is how someone can spoof an e-mail, but you should enter your correct e-mail address for this activity. Type **mail from:** *YourMailAccount* and press **Enter**.

6. You should get a "250 OK" message. You can then enter the recipient's e-mail address. (You can also send a message to yourself.) Type **rcpt to:** *RecipientMailAccount* and press **Enter**. You can enter a bogus address here, too, but the e-mail isn't actually sent unless the *RecipientMailAccount* is valid.

7. After getting a "Recipient OK" message, you're ready to start creating your message. Type **data** and press **Enter**. Type your message, press **Enter**, and then type . (a single period) and press **Enter** to end your message. You should get a message saying that your e-mail was queued.

If you make a typo, you have to re-enter your commands. Pressing Backspace or using the arrow keys doesn't work.

8. To end the Telnet session, type **quit** and press **Enter**. You will see the "Connection to host lost" message shown previously in Figure 2-4. You can leave the command prompt window open for the next activity.

Activity 2-3: Connecting to Port 110 (POP3)

Time Required: 30 minutes

Objective: Use the **telnet** command to access port 110 on your mail server, log on, and retrieve an e-mail message that has been sent to your e-mail account.

Description: The POP3 service uses port 110. In this activity, you telnet to your classroom's mail server from your Windows computer. If your classroom doesn't have a mail server configured, connect to your ISP's mail server and retrieve an e-mail message that has been sent to your mailbox.

1. Open a command prompt window, if necessary.

2. Type **telnet** *RemoteMailServer* 110 (substituting your server name for *Remote-MailServer*) and press **Enter**.

3. After getting the +OK message (see Figure 2-6), you must enter the user command for logging on to your account. Type **user** *YourMailAccount* and press **Enter**.

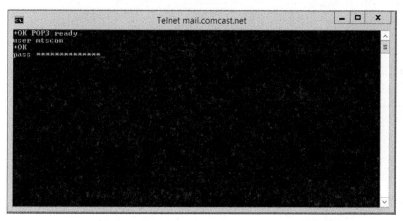

Figure 2-6 Logging on to an e-mail server

Source: Microsoft

4. Next, you're prompted to enter your password. Type **pass** *YourPassword* and press **Enter**.

5. After being authenticated by the mail server, you get a message similar to Figure 2-7 showing the number of messages in your mailbox. To list all the messages, type **list** and press **Enter**.

Figure 2-7 Viewing e-mail messages in a mailbox

Source: Microsoft

6. To retrieve a specific message, you use the `retr` command followed by the message number. For example, to retrieve message number 1, type **retr 1** and press **Enter** (see Figure 2-8).

Figure 2-8 Retrieving an e-mail message

Source: Microsoft

7. Type **quit** and press **Enter**. This command deletes any messages marked for deletion, logs you off the mail server, and ends the Telnet session.

8. To view open ports on your Windows computer, you can use the `netstat` command. Figure 2-9 shows the result of running `netstat` while multiple ports are open. Open another command prompt window, type **netstat,** and press **Enter**.

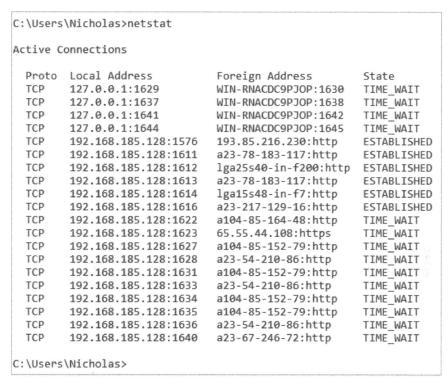

```
C:\Users\Nicholas>netstat

Active Connections

  Proto  Local Address            Foreign Address          State
  TCP    127.0.0.1:1629           WIN-RNACDC9PJOP:1630      TIME_WAIT
  TCP    127.0.0.1:1637           WIN-RNACDC9PJOP:1638      TIME_WAIT
  TCP    127.0.0.1:1641           WIN-RNACDC9PJOP:1642      TIME_WAIT
  TCP    127.0.0.1:1644           WIN-RNACDC9PJOP:1645      TIME_WAIT
  TCP    192.168.185.128:1576     193.85.216.230:http       ESTABLISHED
  TCP    192.168.185.128:1611     a23-78-183-117:http       ESTABLISHED
  TCP    192.168.185.128:1612     lga25s40-in-f200:http     ESTABLISHED
  TCP    192.168.185.128:1613     a23-78-183-117:http       ESTABLISHED
  TCP    192.168.185.128:1614     lga15s48-in-f7:http       ESTABLISHED
  TCP    192.168.185.128:1616     a23-217-129-16:http       ESTABLISHED
  TCP    192.168.185.128:1622     a104-85-164-48:http       TIME_WAIT
  TCP    192.168.185.128:1623     65.55.44.108:https        TIME_WAIT
  TCP    192.168.185.128:1627     a104-85-152-79:http       TIME_WAIT
  TCP    192.168.185.128:1628     a23-54-210-86:http        TIME_WAIT
  TCP    192.168.185.128:1631     a104-85-152-79:http       TIME_WAIT
  TCP    192.168.185.128:1633     a23-54-210-86:http        TIME_WAIT
  TCP    192.168.185.128:1634     a104-85-152-79:http       TIME_WAIT
  TCP    192.168.185.128:1635     a104-85-152-79:http       TIME_WAIT
  TCP    192.168.185.128:1636     a23-54-210-86:http        TIME_WAIT
  TCP    192.168.185.128:1640     a23-67-246-72:http        TIME_WAIT

C:\Users\Nicholas>
```

Figure 2-9   Using the `netstat` command to view open ports

Source: Microsoft

9. If the results show no active ports open, try typing **netstat -a** and pressing Enter. This command lists all connections and listening ports on your system (see Figure 2-10). Notice the many TCP and UDP ports listed.

```
Microsoft Windows [Version 10.0.10586]
(c) 2015 Microsoft Corporation. All rights reserved.

C:\Users\Nicholas>netstat -a

Active Connections

   Proto  Local Address          Foreign Address         State
   TCP    0.0.0.0:135            WIN-RNACDC9PJOP:0        LISTENING
   TCP    0.0.0.0:445            WIN-RNACDC9PJOP:0        LISTENING
   TCP    0.0.0.0:1536           WIN-RNACDC9PJOP:0        LISTENING
   TCP    0.0.0.0:1537           WIN-RNACDC9PJOP:0        LISTENING
   TCP    0.0.0.0:1538           WIN-RNACDC9PJOP:0        LISTENING
   TCP    0.0.0.0:1539           WIN-RNACDC9PJOP:0        LISTENING
   TCP    0.0.0.0:1541           WIN-RNACDC9PJOP:0        LISTENING
   TCP    0.0.0.0:1566           WIN-RNACDC9PJOP:0        LISTENING
   TCP    0.0.0.0:7680           WIN-RNACDC9PJOP:0        LISTENING
   TCP    192.168.185.128:139    WIN-RNACDC9PJOP:0        LISTENING
   TCP    192.168.185.128:1576   193.85.216.230:http     ESTABLISHED
   TCP    192.168.185.128:1596   a23-217-129-19:http     TIME_WAIT
   TCP    192.168.185.128:1597   a104-68-142-251:http    TIME_WAIT
   TCP    192.168.185.128:1598   a23-217-129-11:http     TIME_WAIT
   TCP    192.168.185.128:1600   a-0001:https            TIME_WAIT
   TCP    192.168.185.128:1604   a-0001:https            TIME_WAIT
   TCP    192.168.185.128:1606   a-0001:https            TIME_WAIT
   TCP    192.168.185.128:1608   207.46.7.252:http       TIME_WAIT
   TCP    192.168.185.128:1611   a23-78-183-117:http     ESTABLISHED
   TCP    192.168.185.128:1612   lga25s40-in-f8:http     ESTABLISHED
   TCP    192.168.185.128:1613   a23-78-183-117:http     ESTABLISHED
   TCP    192.168.185.128:1614   lga15s48-in-f7:http     ESTABLISHED
   TCP    192.168.185.128:1615   a23-67-246-179:http     TIME_WAIT
   TCP    192.168.185.128:1616   a23-217-129-16:http     ESTABLISHED
   TCP    192.168.185.128:1620   a23-67-246-97:http      TIME_WAIT
   TCP    192.168.185.128:1621   a104-85-164-64:http     TIME_WAIT
   TCP    192.168.185.128:1622   a104-85-164-48:http     ESTABLISHED
   TCP    [::]:135               WIN-RNACDC9PJOP:0        LISTENING
   TCP    [::]:445               WIN-RNACDC9PJOP:0        LISTENING
   TCP    [::]:1536              WIN-RNACDC9PJOP:0        LISTENING
   TCP    [::]:1537              WIN-RNACDC9PJOP:0        LISTENING
   TCP    [::]:1538              WIN-RNACDC9PJOP:0        LISTENING
   TCP    [::]:1539              WIN-RNACDC9PJOP:0        LISTENING
   TCP    [::]:1541              WIN-RNACDC9PJOP:0        LISTENING
   TCP    [::]:1566              WIN-RNACDC9PJOP:0        LISTENING
   TCP    [::]:7680              WIN-RNACDC9PJOP:0        LISTENING
```

Figure 2-10   Using `netstat` with the -a option

Source: Microsoft

10. Minimize the command prompt window, and start a Web browser.

11. Connect to **google.com**. Maximize the command prompt window, type **netstat** again, and press **Enter**. Notice the new entry indicating that port 443 (HTTPS) is now being connected to.

12. Close the command prompt window and any other open windows.

User Datagram Protocol   User Datagram Protocol (UDP) is a fast but unreliable delivery protocol that also operates on the Transport layer. Imagine trying to compete in the mail courier business and touting that your service is fast but unreliable. It would probably be difficult to sell. However, UDP is a widely used protocol on the Internet because of its speed. It doesn't need to verify whether the receiver is listening or ready to accept the packets. The sender doesn't care—it just sends, even if the receiver isn't ready to accept the packet. See why it's faster? Some applications that use UDP have built-in utilities to warn recipients of undeliverable messages, but UDP doesn't. In other words, it depends on the higher layers of the TCP/IP stack to handle these problems. Think of UDP as someone announcing over a loudspeaker that school will be closed that afternoon. Some lucky students will hear the message, and some won't. This type of delivery protocol is referred to as **connectionless**.

The Internet Layer

The Internet layer of the TCP/IP stack is responsible for routing a packet to a destination address. Routing is done by using a logical address, called an IP address. Like UDP, IP addressing packet delivery is connectionless. IP addressing is covered in more detail later in "IP Addressing," but first take a look at another protocol operating at the Internet layer.

Internet Control Message Protocol Internet Control Message Protocol (ICMP) is used to send messages related to network operations. For example, if a packet can't reach its destination, you might see the "Destination Unreachable" error.

ICMP makes it possible for network professionals to troubleshoot network connectivity problems (with the `ping` command) and track the route a packet traverses from a source IP address to a destination IP address (with the `traceroute` command). Security professionals can use ICMP type codes (see Table 2-2) to block ICMP packets from entering or leaving a network. For example, a router can be configured to not allow an ICMP packet with the type code 8 to enter a network. Try pinging *www.microsoft.com* and see what happens. Microsoft doesn't allow its IP address to be pinged, which is the type code 8 (Echo).

ICMP type code	Description
0	Echo Reply
3	Destination Unreachable
4	Source Quench
5	Redirect
6	Alternate Host Address
8	Echo
9	Router Advertisement
10	Router Solicitation
11	Time Exceeded
12	Parameter Problem
13	Timestamp
14	Timestamp Reply
15	Information Request
16	Information Reply

Table 2-2   ICMP type codes (*continues*)

ICMP type code	Description
17	Address Mask Request
18	Address Mask Reply
19	Reserved (for Security)
20–29	Reserved (for Robustness Experiment)
30	Traceroute
31	Datagram Conversion Error
32	Mobile Host Redirect
33	IPv6 Where-Are-You
34	IPv6 I-Am-Here
35	Mobile Registration Request
36	Mobile Registration Reply
37	Domain Name Request
38	Domain Name Reply
39	Skip
40	Photuris
41–255	Reserved

Table 2-2   ICMP type codes (*continued*)

For a more detailed description of ICMP, see RFC 792.

IP Addressing

An IPv4 address consists of 4 bytes divided into two components: a network address and a host address. Based on the starting decimal number of the first byte, you can classify IP addresses as Class A, Class B, or Class C, as shown in Table 2-3.

Address class	Range	Address bytes	Number of networks	Host bytes	Number of hosts
Class A	1–126	1	126	3	16,777,214
Class B	128–191	2	16,128	2	65,534
Class C	192–223	3	2,097,152	1	254

Table 2-3   TCP/IP address classes

Security Bytes

The 127 address missing from Table 2-3 is used for loopback and testing. It's not a valid IP address that can be assigned to a network device. Class D and Class E addresses are reserved for multicast and experimental addressing and aren't covered in this chapter.

From Table 2-3, you can determine, for example, that a user with the IP address 193.1.2.3 has a Class C address, and a user with the IP address 9.1.2.3 has a Class A address. An IP address is composed of 4 bytes (an octet). A byte is equal to 8 bits, which also equals an octet, so you sometimes see an IP address defined as four octets instead of 4 bytes. The following list describes each address class:

- *Class A*—The first byte of a Class A address is reserved for the network address, making the last 3 bytes available to assign to host computers. Because a Class A address has a three-octet host address, Class A networks can support more than 16 million hosts. (For more information on determining how many hosts a network can support, see "Reviewing the Binary Numbering System" later in this chapter.) The number of Class A addresses is limited, so these addresses are reserved for large corporations and governments. Class A addresses have the format *network.node.node.node*.

- *Class B*—These addresses are divided evenly between a two-octet network address and a two-octet host address, allowing more than 65,000 hosts per Class B network address. Large organizations and ISPs are often assigned Class B addresses, which have the format *network.network.node.node*.

- *Class C*—These addresses have a three-octet network address and a one-octet host address, resulting in more than 2 million Class C addresses. Each address supports up to 254 hosts. These addresses, usually available for small businesses and home use, have the format *network.network.network.node*.

Subnetting allows a network administrator to divide these networks into smaller segments. The use of subnets is important for both performance and security purposes. In addition to a unique network address, each network must be assigned a subnet mask, which helps distinguish the network address bits from the host address bits.

Consider the following example

The IP address 128.214.018.016 represented in binary is:

```
10000000.11010110.00010010.00010000
```

If we define a subnet mask of 255.255.255.0, it's expressed in binary as:

```
11111111.11111111.11111111.00000000
```

The subnet part of the IP address is:

```
10000000.11010110.00010010
```

The host address is:

```
00010000
```

You can determine which subnet the IP address belongs in by performing a bitwise AND operation on the IP address and the subnet mask. This calculation is vertically for each column. With the AND operation, if both bits are 1, the resulting value is 1. Otherwise, the resulting value is 0.

```
10000000.11010110.00010010.00010000 AND
11111111.11111111.11111111.00000000 =
10000000.11010110.00010010.00000000
```

This calculation results in the subnet of 128.215.018.0, meaning that our original IP address 128.214.018.016, with a subnet mask of 255.255.255.0, belongs in the subnet 128.214.018.0.

An understanding of these concepts is important for a security professional, but many free subnetting calculators exist on the Internet.

CIDR Notation

IPv4 allows for roughly 4.3 billion unique IP addresses. That sounds like a lot of addresses. However, with a growing number of Internet-connected devices, almost all of the world's IPv4 addresses are in use. The long-term solution is IPv6 addressing, which is discussed in a few paragraphs. The short-term fix was CIDR (Classless Inter-Domain Routing), which was developed in 1993 and helped prolong the life of IPv4 by allowing for more efficient IP-assignment space.

Here is an example of a subnet in CIDR notation: 192.168.1.0/24. In CIDR, the number following the "/" is the prefix. A subnet using a CIDR prefix of 24 is analogous to a Class C subnet. 192.168.0.0/16 and 192.0.0.0/8 are CIDR notations for Class B and Class A networks, respectively. CIDR optimizes the way IP space was assigned, or allocated, by allowing engineers more options to right-size assignments. By assigning a /23 containing 512 addresses to an organization that requires 400 IP addresses, CIDR conserves over 65,000 addresses (almost an entire Class B) that would have been required under a classful assignment. A list of important CIDR prefixes is found in Table 2-4. A full listing of CIDR address options can be found through an Internet search.

CIDR prefix	# Class C equivalent	Number of usable hosts
/27	1/8th of a Class C	30 hosts
/26	1/4th of a Class C	62 hosts
/25	1/2 of a Class C	126 hosts
/24	1 Class C	254 hosts
/23	2 Class C	510 hosts
/22	4 Class C	1022 hosts
/21	8 Class C	2046 hosts
/20	16 Class C	4094 hosts
/19	32 Class C	8190 hosts
/18	64 Class C	16,382 hosts
/17	128 Class C	32,766 hosts
/16	1 Class B	65,534 hosts
/15	2 Class B	131,070 hosts

Table 2-4   CIDR addressing

CIDR prefix	# Class C equivalent	Number of usable hosts
/14	4 Class B	262,142 hosts
/13	8 Class B	524,286 hosts
/12	16 Class B	1,048,574 hosts
/11	32 Class B	2,097,150 hosts
/10	64 Class B	4,194,302 hosts
/9	128 Class B	8,388,606 hosts
/8	1 Class A	16,777,214 hosts

Table 2-4   CIDR addressing (*continued*)

Planning IP Address Assignments

When IP addresses are assigned, companies need to assign a unique network address to each network segment that's separated by a router. For example, a company has been issued two IP addresses: 193.145.85.0 and 193.145.86.0 (or 193.145.85.0/24 and 193.154.86.0/24 in CIDR notation). Looking at the first byte of each address, the company determines that both are Class C addresses. With a default subnet mask of 255.255.255.0, 254 host addresses can be assigned to each segment. You use the formula $2x - 2$ for this calculation, with x representing the number of unmasked bits. For this example, x equals 8 because there are 8 bits in the fourth octet:

$$2^8 - 2 = 254$$

You must subtract 2 in the formula because the network portion and host portion of an IP address can't contain all 1s or all 0s. Remember, you can't assign a network user the IP address 192.168.8.0 if you used the 255.255.255.0 mask. Also, you can't give a user an address of 192.168.8.255 because it would produce all 1s in the host portion of an IP address; this address is reserved as a broadcast address to all nodes on the segment 192.168.8.0.

To access entities and services on other networks, each computer must also have the IP address of its gateway. Before sending a packet to another computer, the TCP/IP Internet layer uses the sending computer's subnet mask to determine the destination computer's network address. If this address is different from the sending computer's network address, the sending computer relays the packet to the IP address specified in the gateway parameter. The gateway computer then forwards the packet to its next destination. In this way, the packet eventually reaches the destination computer.

For example, if a Linux server has the IP address 192.168.8.2 and the subnet mask 255.255.255.0, and a user has a computer with the IP address 192.168.9.200 and the subnet mask 255.255.255.0, the company must configure a default gateway address. The default gateway sends the message to a router, which routes it to the different network segment. If the default gateway isn't configured on the user's computer, and this user attempts to use the `Ping` command to contact the server, he or she gets the "Destination Unreachable" message (see Table 2-2). The user's computer can't connect to the other host—a Linux server located on a different network segment—because there's no router to help it. The router's job is to take packets destined for a computer on a different network segment from the sending computer and send them on their way.

As a security professional, you must understand these basic network concepts before attempting to conduct a penetration test on a network, especially one that's been subnetted. In a subnetted network, it might be easy to mistake a broadcast address as a valid host address, a major blunder that could cause a denial-of-service attack after thousands of packets are sent to all hosts on a network instead of to the one host you were trying to reach. Just be sure to verify the IP address you're sending packets to before pressing Enter!

IPv6 Addressing

As a security professional, you should spend some time reviewing the IP addressing system Internet Protocol version 6 (IPv6). As mentioned, IPv4 wasn't designed with security in mind, and many current network vulnerabilities are caused by this oversight. This section gives you some basics of IPv6, but reading RFC 2460 (*www.ietf.org/rfc/rfc2460.txt*) is recommended for more details.

IPv6 was developed to increase the IP address space and provide additional security. Instead of the 4 bytes used in IPv4, IPv6 uses 16 bytes, or a 128-bit address, so 2^{128} addresses are available—about 2000 IP addresses for every square foot on the planet. You might think this many IP addresses aren't necessary, but they'll be needed. As you learn in Chapter 9, many new products, such as toasters, microwaves, refrigerators, and TVs, will be accessible via the Internet and need IP addresses.

Here's an example of an IPv6 number: 1111:0cb7:75a2:0110:1234:3a2e:1113:7777. If it looks odd to you, the review of hexadecimal numbers later in the chapter might refresh your memory. The colons separate each group of four hexadecimal numbers. However, the good news is that being a good security tester doesn't require being an expert at translating or memorizing these long numbers.

As a security tester, you should be aware that all newer OSs are configured to enable IPv6, but some router-filtering devices, firewalls, and intrusion detection systems (IDSs) are not. This makes it possible for hackers to bypass these security systems using IPv6. You can find numerous articles online that discuss the weaknesses with IPv4, IPv6, and the protocols that support them. Bad guys spend hours reading these types of articles. Security testers should, too!

Overview of Numbering Systems

As a security professional, your knowledge of numbering systems will also come into play. The following sections offer a quick review of the binary, octal, and hexadecimal numbering systems.

Reviewing the Binary Numbering System

You learned base-10 math in elementary school, although you might not have realized it at the time. When you see the number 3742, for example, you recognize it as "three thousand seven hundred and forty-two." By placing each number in a column, as shown in the following lines, you can see that each number has a different value and magnitude. This numbering system uses 10 as its base and goes from right to left, multiplying the base number in each column by an exponent, starting from zero. Valid numbers in base 10 are 0 through 9. That is, each column can contain any number from 0 to 9.

```
1000   100    10    1
10³    10²    10¹   10⁰
3      7      4     2
```

As you can see, you get 3742 by multiplying 2 by 1, 4 by 10, 7 by 100, and 3 by 1000, and then adding all these values. The binary numbering system, on the other hand, uses 2 as its base. Each binary digit (bit) is represented by a 1 or 0. Bits are usually grouped by eight because a byte contains 8 bits. Computer engineers chose this numbering system because logic chips make binary decisions based on true or false, on or off, and so forth. With 8 bits, a programmer can represent 256 different colors for a video card, for example. (Two to the power of eight, or 2^8, equals 256.) Therefore, black can be represented by 00000000, white by 11111111, and so on.

Another example of using binary numbering can be seen in file permissions for users: r (read), w (write), and x (execute). A 1 represents having the permission, and a 0 removes the permission. Therefore, 111 (rwx) means all permissions apply, and 101 (r-x) means the user can read and execute the file but not write to it. (The - symbol indicates that the permission isn't granted.) Those familiar with UNIX will recognize this numbering system. UNIX allows using the decimal equivalent of binary numbers, so for the binary 111, you enter the decimal number 7. For the binary 101, you enter the decimal number 5. Confused? You'll be a binary expert in a few minutes, so hang in there.

To simplify the concept of binary numbers, think of a room with two light switches, and consider how many different combinations of positions you could use for the switches. For example, both switches could be off, Switch 1 could be off and Switch 2 could be on, and so forth. Here's a binary representation of these switch positions:

```
0   0   (off, off)
0   1   (off, on)
1   0   (on, off)
1   1   (on, on)
```

The two switches have four possible occurrences, or 2^x power; x represents the number of switches (bits) available. For the light switches, x equals 2.

Examples of Determining Binary Values Now that you've been introduced to the basic concepts, you can see how bits are used to notate binary numbers. First, however, you must learn and memorize the columns for binary numbers, just as you did for base 10 numbering:

```
128   64   32   16   8   4   2   1
```

From right to left, these numbers represent increasing powers of two. Using the preceding columns, try to determine the value of the binary number 01000001:

```
128   64    32    16    8    4    2    1
2⁷    2⁶    2⁵    2⁴    2³   2²   2¹   2⁰
0     1     0     0     0    0    0    1
```

The byte in the preceding example represents the decimal number 65. You calculate this value by adding each column containing a 1 (64 + 1). Now try another example with the binary number 11000001:

128	64	32	16	8	4	2	1
2^7	2^6	2^5	2^4	2^3	2^2	2^1	2^0
1	1	0	0	0	0	0	1

To convert the binary number to decimal (base 10), add the columns containing 1s:

$$128 + 64 + 1 = 193$$

Adding the values in these columns can be tedious, but in the following section, you learn some tricks of the trade to help you translate binary to decimal quickly. However, make sure to memorize each binary column before working through the remaining examples in this chapter.

Understanding Nibbles Psychologists have found that people have difficulty memorizing numbers of seven digits or more. This difficulty is why phone numbers have only seven digits and a dash follows the first three numbers; the dash gives your brain a chance to pause before moving on to the next four numbers.

Likewise, binary numbers are easier to read when there's a separation between them. For example, 1111 1010 is easier to read than 11111010. If you need to convert a binary number written as 11111010, you should visualize it as 1111 1010. In other words, you break the byte into two nibbles (sometimes spelled "nybbles"). A nibble is half a byte, or 4 bits. The 4 bits on the left are called the high-order nibble, and the 4 bits on the right are the low-order nibble.

The following examples show how to convert a low-order nibble to a decimal number. Note the pattern at work in the binary numbers as you go through the examples:

0000 = 0

0001 = 1

0010 = 2

0011 = 3

0100 = 4

0101 = 5

0110 = 6

0111 = 7

1000 = 8

1001 = 9

1010 = 10

1011 = 11

1100 = 12

2

1101 = 13

1110 = 14

1111 = 15

The largest decimal number you can represent with 4 low-order bits is 15. You should memorize these numbers if you can, especially the ones that have convenient memory aids. For example, 1010 is equal to the decimal number 10. Just remember the phrase "It's 10, silly, 10!" 1011 is just as easy: "Not 10, but 11." You can make up your own tricks, but you can always simply add the columns if you forget.

You can also practice converting decimal numbers into binary numbers by using license plate numbers as you drive to work. For example, if a license plate number ends with 742, you should visualize 0111, 0100, 0010. (You can eliminate the leading zeros after a few days of practice.) When you get comfortable with the low-order nibble and can identify a sequence of 4 bits quickly, you can move to the high-order side.

For example, what does the binary number 1010 1010 equal in decimal? On the low-order side, you can quickly convert 1010 to the decimal number 10. The high-order side is also 10, but it's 10 times 16, or 160. Now, we add the low-order side of 10 to our high-order side of 160 to get our answer, 170. You can always add the columns if you're confused:

128 + 32 = 160

Any value in the high-order nibble is multiplied by the number 16. For example, the binary number 0010 0000 is equal to 32. You can multiply the nibble value of 2 by 16, but in this case it's easier to recognize the 1 in the 32 column, which makes the answer 32.

You should memorize the following high-order nibble values, which will help you with subnetting. As you should recall from subnetting basics, 128, 192, 224, and so on are used as subnet masks.

1000 = 128

1100 = 192

1110 = 224

1111 = 240

If you recognize 1111 0000 as 240, the binary number 1111 1000 should be easy to calculate as 248. By the same token, the binary number 1111 1111 is equal to the decimal 255, or 240 + 15, the largest number you can represent with 8 bits.

To help you convert numbers correctly, note that all odd numbers have the low-order bit turned on. For example, 1001 can't be an even number, such as 10 or 8, because the low-order bit is turned on. You can also guess that the number is larger than 8 because the 8 column bit is turned on. Similarly, you can identify 0101 as converting to a decimal number lower than 8 because the 8 column isn't turned on and identify it as an odd number because the low-order bit is on.

There are other easy ways to memorize and break down binary numbers. For example, 1010 is 10, and 0101 converts to half of 10: 5. The two numbers are mirror images of each other in binary, and one **TIP** number is half of the other in decimal. In the same way, 1110 equals 14 and 0111 is 7. In the high-order nibble, 1110 equals 224, and 0111 in the high-order nibble equals 112 (half of 224). This trick helps you convert binary numbers quickly. For example, the binary number 0101 1010 equals 90. In this number, the high-order nibble converts to 80 because 1010 equals 160. The low-order nibble converts to 10, and quick addition gives you the final answer of 90.

Reviewing the Octal Numbering System

An octal number is a base-8 number, so it's written by using these eight values: 0, 1, 2, 3, 4, 5, 6, and 7. Because you're a binary expert now, it's easy to see how binary converts to octal. An octal digit can be represented with only 3 bits because the largest digit in octal is 7. The number 7 is written as 00000111, or 111 if you drop the leading zeros. The binary equivalent of the octal number 5 is then 101.

To see how this concept relates to network security, take a look at UNIX permissions again. Octal numbering is used to express the following permissions on a directory or file: owner permissions, group permissions, and other permissions. Setting the permission (rwxrwxrwx) for a directory means that the owner of the directory, members of a group, and everyone else (other) have read, write, and execute permissions for this directory.

Because each category has three unique permissions, and because each permission can be expressed as true or false (on or off), 3 bits are used. You don't need all 8 bits because 3 bits (rwx) are enough. Recall from binary numbering that 0 is counted as a number, so with 3 bits, there are eight possible occurrences: 000, 001, 010, 011, 100, 101, 110, and 111. Using octal numbering, 001 indicates that the execute (x) permission is granted, 010 indicates that the write (w) permission is granted but not read and execute, and so on. The octal number 7 indicates all 1s (111), or 1 + 2 + 4. So, in UNIX and Linux systems, 777 (in binary, 111 111 111) indicates that the owner, group, and other have all permissions (rwx) to a file or directory.

Reviewing the Hexadecimal Numbering System

A hex number is written with two characters, each representing a nibble. Hexadecimal is a base-16 numbering system, so its valid numbers range from 0 to 15. Like base 2 (binary), hex uses exponents that begin with 0 and increase from right to left:

```
4096   256   16    1

16³    16²   16¹   16⁰

A      0     C     1
```

Fortunately, in hex you have to memorize only the final two columns: 1 and 16. As you can see from the preceding example, the value contains alphabetic characters—valid hex numbers range from 0 to 15, and hex solves the problem of expressing two-digit numbers in a single slot by using letters. For example, A represents the number 10, B stands for 11, C is 12, D is 13, E is 14, and F is 15.

Hex numbers are sometimes expressed with "0×" in front of them. For example, 0×10 equals decimal number 16. As with decimal and binary numbers, you multiply the value in each column by the value of the column to determine hex numbers. In the previous example, you simply multiply 1 by 16 to get 16. To convert a hex number to binary, you write each nibble from left to right. For example, 0×10 is 0001 0000 in binary and 0×24 is 0010 0100. As a security professional, sometimes you need to review output from software that displays values in hexadecimal numbers. For example, the Tcpdump tool, covered in Chapter 5, uses hexadecimal numbers in much of its output, especially if the systems being analyzed use IPv6. As explained, all IPv6 addresses are in hexadecimal notation.

Security Bytes

Could knowing hexadecimal save your life if you were trapped on Mars? *Spoiler alert*: It worked for Matt Damon's character, astronaut **NOTE** Mark Watney, in the 2015 movie *The Martian*. Watney needed a way to communicate with NASA that made use of cards positioned around a circle and a camera that rotated 360 degrees. However, the 26-character alphabet created problems with the camera angles. He needed a smaller alphabet. Fortunately, hexadecimal has only 16 characters. Writing the hexadecimal characters he got from an ASCII table, which contains 255 characters, he could communicate with NASA. For example, the letter A in ASCII is equivalent to 41 in hex. Many free ASCII-to-hex converters are available online. You can use them to enter a two-digit hex number and get the ASCII letter equivalent. (There's one at *www .rapidtables.com/convert/number/ascii-to-hex.htm*. Try writing the word HELP! in hex. Don't forget the exclamation point.)

Reviewing the Base-64 Numbering System

Base-64 has a number of uses both legitimate and not. A common use for base-64 is for the encoding and transportation of binary files sent through e-mail. All you need to know right now is that there are a number of ways in which attackers can use base-64 to obfuscate their actions.

Base-64 character mappings are shown in Table 2-5.

Character or symbol	Representation in base-64
Uppercase A to Z	0–25
Lowercase a to z	26–51
Numerals 0 to 9	52–61
+ and / symbols	62, 63

Table 2-5 Base-64 character mappings

To represent 0 to 63 characters, you need only 6 bits, or 2^6. So, the binary representation of the letter A is 000000, B is 000001, C is 000010, and so on. Z is represented as 011001. Just remember that the high-order bit is the 32 column, not the 128 column, as with 8 bits. The lowest number you can represent with 6 bits is 000000 (0), and the highest number is 111111 (63). To convert a base-64 number to its decimal equivalent, simply break the sequence into groups of four characters and represent each character by using 6 bits (24 bits = 6 × 4).

As an example, here is how to convert the base-64 string SGFwcHkgQmlydGhkYXk= into its decimal equivalent. In this example, the first four characters—S, G, F, and w—are written as three 8-bit numbers (24 bits = 3 × 8).

1. Convert the decimal value of each letter to binary:

   S = 18 decimal, binary 010010

   G = 6 decimal, binary 000110

   F = 5 decimal, binary 000101

   w = 48 decimal, binary 110000

2. Rewrite the four binary groups into three groups of 8 bits. For example, starting with the lower-order bit of the binary equivalent of "w," writing from right to left produces [01]110000. The bracketed binary numbers represent the first two lower-order bits from the F binary equivalent, 1 and 0:

   01001000 01100001 01110000

3. Convert the binary into its decimal equivalent:

   01001000 = 72 ASCII   H

   01100001 = 97 ASCII   a

   01110000 = 112 ASCII   p

Repeat Steps 1 to 3 for the next four base-64 numbers, cHkg, until each letter's base-64 number is converted. (One or two equal signs are used when 3 bytes [24 bits] aren't needed to represent the integer.) What does the base-64 string convert to? Your answer should be "Happy Birthday."

Base-64 decoders are available for free online. As a security professional, you don't need to know how to convert base-64 code manually, but it's important to see how numbering systems are used in practical applications, not just academic exercises.

Activity 2-4: Working with Binary and Octal Numbering

Time Required: 30 minutes

Objective: Apply your skills in binary and octal numbering to configuring *nix directory and file permissions.

Description: As a security professional, you need to understand different numbering systems. For example, if you work with routers, you might have to create access control lists (ACLs) that filter inbound and outbound network traffic, and most ACLs require understanding binary numbering. Similarly, if you're hardening a Linux system, your understanding of binary helps you create the correct umask and permissions. UNIX uses base-8 (octal) numbering for creating directory and file permissions. You don't need to do this activity on a computer; you can simply use a pencil and paper.

1. Write the octal equivalents for the following binary numbers: 100, 111, 101, 011, and 010.

2. Write how to express *nix owner permissions of r-x in binary. (Remember that the - symbol means the permission isn't granted.) What's the octal representation of the binary number you calculated? (The range of numbers expressed in octal is 0 to 7. Because *nix has three sets of permissions, three sets of 3 binary bits logically represent all possible permissions.)

3. In binary and octal numbering, how do you express granting read, write, and execute permission to the owner of a file and no permissions to anyone else?

4. In binary and octal numbering, how do you express granting read, write, and execute permission to the owner of a file, read and write permission to group, and read permission to other?

5. In UNIX, a file can be created by using a umask, which enables you to modify the default permissions for a file or directory. For example, a directory has the default permission of octal 777. If a UNIX administrator creates a directory with a umask of octal 020, what effect does this setting have on the directory? *Hint*: To calculate the solution, you can subtract the octal umask value from the octal default permissions.

6. The default permission for a file on a UNIX system is octal 666. If a file is created with a umask of octal 022, what are the effective permissions? Calculate your results.

Chapter Summary

- TCP/IP is the most widely used protocol for communication over the Internet. The TCP/IP stack consists of four layers that perform different functions: Network, Application, Transport, and Internet.

- The Application-layer protocols are the front end to the lower-layer protocols. Examples of protocols operating at this layer are HTTP, SMTP, Telnet, and SNMP.

- The Transport layer is responsible for encapsulating data into segments and uses UDP or TCP headers for connections and for forwarding data. TCP is a connection-oriented protocol. UDP is a connectionless protocol.

- The critical components of TCP segment headers are TCP flags, the ISN, and source and destination port numbers.

- TCP ports identify the services running on a system. Port numbers from 1 to 1023 are considered well-known ports. A total of 65,535 port numbers are available.

- The Internet layer is responsible for routing a packet to a destination address. IP addresses as well as ICMP messages are used in this layer. IP, like UDP, is a connectionless protocol. ICMP is used to send messages related to network operations. A type code identifies the ICMP message type and can be used to filter out network traffic.

- IP addresses consist of 4 bytes, also called "octets," which are divided into two components: a network address and a host address. Three classes of addresses are used on the Internet: A, B, and C.

- IPv6 addresses consist of 16 bytes and are written in hexadecimal notation.

- The binary numbering system is used mainly because logic chips make binary decisions based on true or false, on or off. Binary numbers are represented by 0 or 1.

- The octal numbering system (base 8) uses numbers from 0 to 7. Only 3 bits of the binary numbering system are used because the highest number in base 8 is the number 7, which can be written with 3 binary bits: 111.

- Hexadecimal is a base-16 numbering system that uses numbers from 0 to 15. After 9, the numbers 10, 11, 12, 13, 14, and 15 are represented as A, B, C, D, E, and F.

- Base64 is a numbering system that uses numbers from 0 to 63. Numbers 0–61 are represented with alpha-numeric characters; 62 and 63 are symbols.

Key Terms

ACK	Internet Control Message Protocol (ICMP)	SYN-ACK
connection-oriented protocol		TCP flag
connectionless	network session hijacking	three-way handshake
initial sequence number (ISN)	port	Transmission Control Protocol/Internet Protocol (TCP/IP)
Internet Assigned Numbers Authority (IANA)	protocol	User Datagram Protocol (UDP)
	SYN	

Review Questions

1. The `netstat` command indicates that POP3 is in use on a remote server. Which port is the remote server most likely using?

   a. Port 25

   b. Port 110

   c. Port 143

   d. Port 80

2. On a Windows computer, what command can you enter to show all open ports being used?

   a. `netstat`

   b. `ipconfig`

   c. `ifconfig`

   d. `nbtstat`

3. Which protocol uses UDP?

   a. FTP

   b. Netstat

   c. Telnet

   d. TFTP

4. Which protocol offers guaranteed delivery and is connection oriented?

    a. UDP

    b. IP

    c. TCP

    d. TFTP

5. TCP communication can be likened to which of the following?

    a. Announcement over a loudspeaker

    b. Bullhorn at a sporting event

    c. Driving on a highway

    d. Phone conversation

6. Which of the following protocols is connectionless? (Choose all that apply.)

    a. UDP

    b. IP

    c. TCP

    d. SPX

7. Which command verifies the existence of a node on a network?

    a. `ping`

    b. `ipconfig`

    c. `netstat`

    d. `nbtstat`

8. FTP offers more security than TFTP. True or False?

9. List the three components of the TCP/IP three-way handshake.

10. What protocol is used for reporting or informational purposes?

    a. IGMP

    b. TCP

    c. ICMP

    d. IP

11. List the six flags of a TCP packet.

12. A UDP packet is usually smaller than a TCP packet. True or False?

13. What port, other than port 110, is used to retrieve e-mail?

    a. Port 25

    b. Port 143

    c. Port 80

    d. Port 135

14. What port does DNS use?

    a. Port 80

    b. Port 69

    c. Port 25

    d. Port 53

15. What command is used to log on to a remote server, computer, or router?

    a. `ping`

    b. `traceroute`

    c. `telnet`

    d. `netstat`

16. Which of the following is *not* a valid octal number?

    a. 5555

    b. 4567

    c. 3482

    d. 7770

17. The ISN is set at which step of the TCP three-way handshake?

    a. 1, 2, 3

    b. 1, 3

    c. 1

    d. 1 and 2

18. A `ping` command initially uses which ICMP type code?

    a. Type 0

    b. Type 8

    c. Type 14

    d. Type 13

19. "Destination Unreachable" is designated by which ICMP type code?

    a. Type 0

    b. Type 14

    c. Type 3

    d. Type 8

20. What's the hexadecimal equivalent of the binary number 1111 1111?

    a. FF

    b. 255

    c. EE

    d. DD

Case Projects

CASE PROJECTS

Case Project 2-1: Determining the Services Running on a Network

Alexander Rocco Corporation has multiple OSs running in its many branch offices. Before conducting a penetration test to determine the network's vulnerabilities, you must analyze the services currently running on the network. Bob Kaikea, a member of your security team who's experienced in programming and database design but weak in networking concepts, wants to be briefed on network topology issues at Alexander Rocco Corporation.

Write a memo to Bob summarizing port numbers and services that run on most networks. The memo should discuss the concepts of well-known ports and give a brief description of the most commonly used ports: 20, 21, 23, 25, 53, and 110.

Case Project 2-2: Investigating Possible E-mail Fraud

A vice president at Alexander Rocco Corporation says he received a hostile e-mail message from an employee in the Maui office. Human Resources has informed him that the message's contents are grounds for termination, but the vice president wonders whether the employee actually sent the message. When confronted, the employee claims he didn't send the message and doesn't understand why the message shows his return address.

Write a memo to the vice president, outlining the steps an employee might have taken to create an e-mail message and make it appear to come from another employee's account. Be sure to include some SMTP commands the culprit might have used.

## chapter 3

Network and Computer Attacks

After reading this chapter and completing the exercises, you will be able to:

- Describe the different types of malicious software and what damage they can do
- Describe methods of protecting against malware attacks
- Describe the types of network attacks
- Identify physical security attacks and vulnerabilities

As an IT security professional, you need to be aware of the ways an intruder can attack your network. Attacks include unauthorized attempts to access network resources or systems, attempts to destroy or corrupt information, and attempts to prevent authorized users from accessing resources. You must have a good understanding of both network security and computer security. Network security involves protecting the network infrastructure as well as stand-alone systems. Therefore, computer security is necessary to protect computers and laptops that aren't part of a network infrastructure but still contain important or confidential information. Protective measures include examining physical security (right down to checking door locks) and assessing the risks associated with a lack of physical security.

This chapter gives you a strong foundation on what attackers are doing. Just as law enforcement personnel must be aware of the methods criminals use, you must know what computer attackers are up to. How can a denial-of-service attack be used to shut down a company? How can worms and viruses be introduced into a company's corporate database? How can a laptop or desktop computer be removed from your office with little risk of the intruder being caught or stopped? In this chapter, you get an overview of attack methods and protective measures. To understand the importance of physical security, you also learn that a skilled attacker can pick a lock in seconds.

Malicious Software (Malware)

Typically, network attacks are initiated to steal data that can be used or sold for financial gain or to carry out a sociopolitical agenda. **Malware** is malicious software, such as a virus, worm, or Trojan program, introduced into a network to help an attacker accomplish these goals. The lines between these categories of malware are blurring, with advanced malware now having rich target-dependent functionality that covers multiple categories. You will see malware in this chapter's tables that spans multiple categories. Previously, the main goal of malware was to destroy or corrupt data or to shut down a network or computer system. Today, more often than not, the goal is to make money. Scores of cybercrime organizations have warehouses full of programmers who do nothing but write malware with signatures unknown to antivirus programs. Malware was once targeted specifically at Windows, Linux, and other traditional operations systems. Now, it is written to target tablets, smartphones, and other Internet-connected devices. The following sections cover different types of malware that attackers use.

Security Bytes

Security professionals know that the Russian Business Network (RBN, also known by many other names) is one of the most well-structured cybercrime organizations in existence. The RBN's specialties are creating malware; hosting child pornography, spam, and phishing Web sites; and committing identity theft. RBN has employed experienced and dangerous computer programmers and hackers. When you learn how to use a security tool, remember that the bad guys are learning how to use it, too. Don't give up, however! The good guys need good hackers who can give the bad guys a run for their money.

Viruses

A **virus** is a program that attaches itself to a file or another program, often sent via e-mail. The key word is "attaches." A virus doesn't stand on its own, so it can't replicate itself or operate without the presence of a host. A virus attaches itself to a host file or program (such as Microsoft Word), just as the flu attaches itself to a host organism, and then performs whatever the creator designed it to do.

Figure 3-1 shows an example of a phishing message that has multiple links to Web sites containing malicious code. The phishing e-mail sender uses social engineering to lure a user into following a malicious link. When the malicious link is followed, the user's browser visits a site containing a virus that automatically downloads and executes.

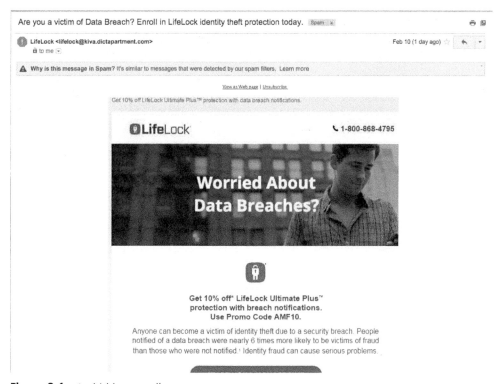

Figure 3-1   A phishing e-mail message

Ransomware, a type of virus that locks a target system until a ransom is paid, is a growing trend in viruses. Over the years, ransomware creators have become more sophisticated. Now, it is common to find a ransomware virus that captures credentials to cloud storage and prevents a user from accessing those accounts in addition to files on his or her local desktop.

The bad news about viruses is that there's no foolproof method of preventing them from attaching themselves to computers, no matter how skilled you are as a security professional. Many antivirus software packages are available, but none can guarantee protection because new viruses are created constantly. Antivirus software compares signatures (hashes or code patterns) and common malicious programmatic behaviors (heuristic analysis) of known viruses against every file on a computer; if there's a match, the software warns you that the program or file is infected. These signatures are kept in a **virus signature file** that the antivirus software maintains. If the virus isn't known, however, the antivirus software doesn't detect a match. Therefore, updating virus signature files regularly is crucial. Many antivirus software packages offer automatic updates. For example, with Symantec Endpoint Protection (SEP), administrators can configure a server that handles pushing antivirus updates to client computers in an organization.

Table 3-1 shows some common viruses that have plagued computer systems. As of this writing, thousands of viruses and variants are being created each day. Listing all known viruses would take up this entire book.

Virus	Description
CryptoLocker	As of January 2016, this "ransomware" virus is estimated to have infected over 250,000 computers. This malware locks the user's files in an encrypted container and requires the victim to pay ransom for their decryption. Like most malware, it is delivered through an e-mail that is designed to trick the user in to clicking on a malicious link or attachment. Once a machine is infected, the victim has a set amount of time to pay the ransom if they want to retrieve their files. Payment is currently only accepted via BitCoin and averages about $300 USD per victim.
MalumPOS	A recent trend in malware has been to target devices responsible for processing payments, referred to as POS (Point of Sale) systems. The MalumPOS virus was used in mid 2015 to attack POS devices at hotel chains. This virus was programmed to find, intercept, copy, and exfiltrate payment card information (e.g., credit/debit card numbers and other information stored on the magnetic track of a credit card).
Carbanak	This virus is spread via phishing e-mails that almost always target financial institutions. These phishing e-mails contain a word document and a malicious .cpl file (keep this in mind for the upcoming base-64 decoding exercise). Once initial access is gained, the malware runs a number of checks to ensure it's able to gain the proper privileges to further its attack. Once proper privileges are gained or verified, a backdoor is opened to a few remote servers under the control of an unknown (to this point) malicious actor. This malware has been used to facilitate fraudulent transactions in financial institutions' funds transfer systems and ATM machines.
Gumblar	First detected in March 2009, this malware spread by mass-hacking hundreds of thousands of Web sites, which then exploited visiting browsers via Adobe PDF and Flash vulnerabilities. The malware steals FTP credentials that are used to further compromise Web sites that the victim maintains. It also hijacks Google searches and blocks access to antivirus update sites to prevent removal. Recent variations install a backdoor that attempts to connect to a botnet.
Gpcode	This "ransomware" virus detected in 2008 isn't widespread but is unique because it uses practically unbreakable 1024-bit asymmetric key encryption to hide a user's documents on the computer and hold them for ransom until the victim pays to get the encryption key.

Table 3-1   Common computer viruses

It seems that many people have nothing but time on their hands to create these destructive programs. The following warning was returned to a user with a file called Price.cpl attached to the e-mail. The e-mail provider rejected sending the e-mail because the attachment was recognized as a potential virus.

Trojan Programs

The most insidious attacks against networks and computers worldwide take place via **Trojan programs**. Trojans disguise themselves as useful programs and can install a backdoor or root-kit on a computer. **Backdoors or rootkits** are programs that give attackers a means of regaining access to the attacked computer later. A rootkit is created after an attack and usually hides itself in the OS tools, so it's almost impossible to detect. Back Orifice is a good example of a popular Trojan over the past decade. It allows attackers to take full control of the attacked computer, similar to the way Windows XP Remote Desktop functions, except that Back Orifice works without the user's knowledge. The program has been around since 1999, but it's now marketed as an administrative tool rather than a hacking tool. Table 3-3 lists some ports that Trojan programs use.

Trojan program	TCP ports used
W32.Korgo.A	13, 2041, and 3067
Backdoor.Rtkit.B	445
Backdoor.Systsec, Backdoor.Zincite.A	1034
W32.Beagle.Y@mm	1234
W32.Mytob.MX@mm	7000
Agobot, Backdoor.Hacarmy.C, Linux.Backdoor.Kaitenh, Backdoor.Clt, Backdoor.IRC.Flood.E, Backdoor.Spigot.C, Backdoor.IrcContact, Backdoor.DarkFtp, Backdoor.Slackbot.B	6667
Backdoor.Danton	6969
Backdoor.Nemog.C	4661, 4242, 8080, 4646, 6565, and 3306

Table 3-3   Trojan programs and ports

The programmer who wrote Backdoor.Slackbot.B, for example, can control a computer by using Internet Relay Chat (IRC), which is on port 6667. A good software or hardware firewall would most likely identify traffic that's using unfamiliar ports, but Trojan programs that use common ports, such as TCP port 80 (HTTP) or UDP port 53 (DNS), are more difficult to detect. Also, many home users and small businesses don't manage which ports are open or closed on their firewalls.

Security Bytes

Many software firewall products for home users do a good job of recognizing port-scanning programs or detecting connection attempts from a computer via a questionable port, such as port 6667. However, many of these firewalls prompt users to allow or disallow this traffic. The problem is that users who aren't aware of these Trojan programs simply click Allow when warned about suspicious activity on a port. Also, many Trojan programs use standard ports to conduct their exploits, which makes it difficult for average users to distinguish between suspicious activity and normal Internet traffic. You should educate network users about these basic concepts if there's no corporate firewall or a corporate policy establishing rules and restrictions.

Spyware

If you do a search on the keyword "spyware," you'll be bombarded with hundreds of links. Some simply tout spyware removal, but some install spyware on a computer when the user clicks the Yes button in a dialog box asking whether the computer should be checked for spyware (see Figure 3-2). When you click the Yes button, the spyware installation begins.

Figure 3-2   A spyware initiation program

A **spyware** program sends information from the infected computer to the person who initiated the spyware program on your computer. This information could be confidential financial data, passwords, PINs—just about any data stored on your computer. You need to make sure users understand that this information collection is possible, and spyware programs can register each keystroke entered. It's that simple. This type of technology not only exists but is prevalent. It can be used to record and send everything a user enters to an unknown person located halfway around the world. Tell users they shouldn't assume that physical security measures, such as locked doors, are enough to keep all intruders out.

Activity 3-4: Identifying Spyware

Time Required: 30 minutes

Objective: Examine prevalent spyware programs.

Description: Network security professionals know that spyware is one of the worst types of malicious attacks on corporate networks. Spyware can be installed on any computer through various means; the most common approach is installing spyware automatically after a user clicks a hyperlink or runs a program without verifying its authenticity. You should be aware of any new spyware programs as well as software that can remove spyware from a computer.

1. Start your Web browser, if necessary, and go to **www.google.com**. Type **spyware** in the text box, and click **Google Search**.

2. List some of your search results.

3. Write a description of spyware based on one of the sites you listed in Step 2.

4. In your Web browser, go to **www.spywareguide.com**. On the home page, click the **SpywareGuide Product Database** link.

5. Click one of the links you found in Step 4, and write a brief description of the spyware. (*Note*: The list is in alphabetical order; you can scroll through it with the arrow keys.)

6. Leave your Web browser open for the next activity.

Adware

The difference between spyware and **adware** is a fine line. Both programs can be installed without users being aware of their presence. Adware, however, sometimes displays a banner that notifies users of its presence. Adware's main purpose is to determine a user's purchasing habits so that Web browsers can display advertisements tailored to this user. The biggest problem with adware is that it slows down the computer it's running on.

Security Bytes

Network security begins with each user understanding how vulnerable a computer is to attack. However, being aware of malware's presence, just as you're aware of unscrupulous telemarketers who call you during dinnertime, can better equip you to make valid decisions. If someone offers to sell you property in Tahiti for $99.95 over the phone and asks for your credit card number, you'd refuse. Computer users should be just as skeptical when prompted to click an OK button or install a free computer game.

Protecting Against Malware Attacks

Protecting an organization from malware attacks is difficult because new viruses, worms, and Trojan programs appear daily. Fortunately, antivirus programs can detect many malware programs. For example, Figure 3-3 shows McAfee antivirus software detecting a potentially unwanted program. Educating users about these types of attacks and other attacks, covered later in this section, is also important. After all, users can't be patched. Antivirus programs

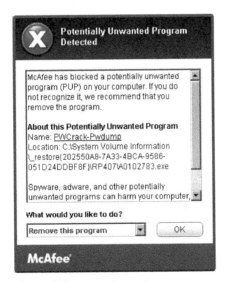

Figure 3-3   Detecting a virus

Source: McAfee

can mitigate some risks associated with malware, but users who aren't trained thoroughly can open holes into a network that no technology can protect against.

Educating Your Users

No matter how hard you try to protect a network from malware being introduced, it's nearly impossible to prevent infection. It is, however, possible to minimize the damage and the frequency with which computers become infected.

An important non-technical consideration is conducting structured training of all employees and management. In fact, many U.S. government agencies make security awareness programs mandatory, and many private-sector companies are following their example. A simple but effective method of educating users is e-mailing monthly security updates to all employees to inform them of the most recent viruses, spyware, and adware detected on the Internet. In addition to structured training, some organizations are now actively phishing their own employees and sending them to training content if they accidentally clicked on something they should not have.

To help prevent malicious code from being introduced into corporate networks, many organizations are looking to application **whitelisting** as a last line of defense. Application whitelisting comes in a few different forms, but ultimately it allows only approved programs to run on a computer. For example, programs such as Word.exe, Excel.exe, and Safari.exe would be whitelisted. All programs not on the whitelist would be prevented from executing on the user's computer, including that malicious program attached to a phishing e-mail a user clicks on.

Another recommendation you should make to a client is to update virus signature files as soon as they're available from the vendor. Most antivirus software does this updating automatically or prompts the user to do so. An organization cannot depend on employee vigilance to protect its systems, so centralizing all antivirus updates from a corporate server is prudent.

To counter the introduction of spyware and adware into a corporate network, you should invest in an antivirus product. While many antivirus packages don't fully address the problem of spyware and adware, it is an important first step. As of this writing, two popular spyware and adware removal programs are SpyBot Search and Destroy and Malwarebytes Anti-Malware (MBAM). Many other Web sites offer these programs, but remember to use caution when downloading any programs from unknown Web sites.

You can also help protect a network by installing a firewall (covered in more detail in Chapter 13). Many of the top antivirus vendors also offer software firewalls for home and small-business users who don't have a hardware firewall or an intrusion detection system (IDS) installed. Companies using firewalls can follow the vendor's configuration instructions. For example, the W32/Sobig.F worm uses UDP port 8998 to contact the attacker's server. By blocking all outbound traffic on this port, you can prevent this attack from occurring. Also, many services are started by default on a computer, and they don't need to be. For example, the average home user or small-business owner doesn't typically use Telnet. This service shouldn't be active on most computers because it's vulnerable to many outside attacks.

Avoiding Fear Tactics   You'd be surprised how many users don't know that clicking an icon in an e-mail message can activate a virus or Trojan program or allow another person to access their computers from a remote location. Consequently, some security professionals use fear tactics to scare users into complying with security measures. Their approach is to tell users that if they don't take a particular action, their computer systems will be attacked by every malcontent who has access to the Internet. This method is sometimes used to generate business for security testers and, in this context, is not only unethical, but also against the OSSTMM's Rules of Engagement. The rule states: "The use of fear, uncertainty, and doubt may not be used in the sales or marketing presentations, websites, supporting materials, reports, or discussion of security testing for the purpose of selling or providing security tests. This includes but is not limited to crime facts, criminal or hacker profiling, and statistics."

Your approach to users or potential customers should promote awareness rather than instill fear. You should point out to users how important it is not to install programs—especially those not approved by the company—on their desktops because of the possibility of introducing malware. Users should be aware of potential threats, not terrified by them.

In addition, when training users, be sure to build on the knowledge they already have. For example, some users are familiar with Windows Remote Assistance or other remote control programs, such as TeamViewer and VNC. Users' experience with these programs makes the job of explaining how an intruder can take control of their computers easier because they already know the technology is available.

Intruder Attacks on Networks and Computers

An **attack** is defined as any attempt by an unauthorized person to access, damage, or use network resources or computer systems. Typically, an attack happens when a weakness or **vulnerability** is exploited. An **exploit** is a specially crafted string of data intended to take advantage of a vulnerability. **Network security** is concerned with the security of computers or devices that are part of a network infrastructure. **Computer security** is defined as securing a stand-alone computer that's not part of a network infrastructure. The FBI, CIA, and Interpol warn that computer crime is the fastest growing type of crime worldwide. After all, attacking a corporate network from the comfort of home is much easier than breaking into a business at 3:00 a.m. Speaking on the subject of the difficulty of prosecuting computer criminals, FBI agent Arnold Aanui, Jr., from the Honolulu FBI Cybercrime Division, stated in an interview: "Even if the FBI tracks down the computer used in a crime, if more than one person has access to that computer, the FBI can't arrest the alleged perpetrator because any one of the users might have committed the crime." Unless the laws change so that the punishment for committing these crimes becomes more of a deterrent, security professionals will be busy for many years.

Security Bytes

In an affluent neighborhood in Hawaii, the FBI stormed into a quiet residential home with warrants in hand, prepared to arrest the occupant and confiscate his desktop computer, which was alleged to contain records of drug transactions and other incriminating evidence. While FBI personnel were cautiously entering the front of the house, they heard a gunshot from a rear bedroom. When they entered the room, they saw a man seated on the bed and a 12-gauge shotgun leaned against a closed door. He had just emptied a round into the computer, destroying the hard drives so thoroughly that the data couldn't be recovered. The FBI agents could have tried sending the disks to a lab that specialized in data recovery from hard disks but decided not to because they believed they had enough evidence from other sources.

Denial-of-Service Attacks

As the name implies, a **denial-of-service (DoS) attack** prevents legitimate users from accessing network resources. In a DoS attack, attackers aren't attempting to access the information on a remote computer. However, they might be using the attack to cripple the network.

As a security tester, you don't usually install a virus or worm on a customer's computer as part of your testing. Similarly, you should know how a DoS attack can take place and attempt to protect a company from it, but conducting the attack yourself isn't wise. Doing so would be like a safety consultant blowing up a refinery after being hired to look for safety hazards. You simply need to explain how the attack could be carried out.

An old but useful example of a DoS attack is the **Ping of Death attack**. This attack causes the victim computer to freeze and malfunction. It is not as common as it was during the late 1990s. The attacker simply creates an ICMP packet (discussed in Chapter 2) that's larger than the maximum-allowed 65,535 bytes. The large packet is fragmented into smaller packets and reassembled at its destination. The user's system at the destination point can't handle the reassembled oversized packet, thereby causing the system to crash or freeze. This is also an example of a buffer overflow attack, which is discussed later in this chapter.

Distributed Denial-of-Service Attacks

A **distributed denial-of-service (DDoS) attack** is launched against a host from multiple servers or workstations. In a DDoS attack, a network could be flooded with billions of packets; typically, each participant in the attack sends only a few of the total number of packets. If one server bombards an attacked server with hundreds or even thousands of packets, available network bandwidth could drop to the point that legitimate users notice a performance degradation. Now imagine 1000 servers or even 10,000 distributed servers involved, with each server sending several thousand IP packets to the attacked server. There you have it: a DDoS attack.

Keep in mind that participants in the attack often aren't aware their computers are taking part in the attack. They, too, have been attacked by the culprit. In fact, in one DDoS attack, a company was flooded with IP packets from thousands of Internet routers and Web servers belonging to Yahoo.com.

A Dark DDoS attack is a smokescreen to distract network defenders while another stealthier and likely more damaging attack is occurring. By focusing network defenders on a sustained "noisy" DDoS attack, the attacker can carry out a fraudulent transaction or exfiltration of data that might have been caught if the defenders had not focused on the DDoS.

Security Bytes

Security professionals will be studying one of the world's most widespread DDoS attacks for years. Estonia, in Northern Europe, fell victim to a DDoS attack in 2007 that shut down government Web sites, banks, and other financial institutions. The malicious traffic came from all over the world, including the United States and Canada. DDoS attacks are difficult to stop because owners of the compromised computers, referred to as **zombies**, are unaware that their systems are sending malicious packets to a victim thousands of miles away. These compromised computers are usually part of a **botnet** (a network of "robot" computers) following instructions from a central location or system. For more information, do a search on "Estonia DDoS."

Buffer Overflow Attacks

A number of buffer overflow attacks on many different OSs have taken place over the years. In a **buffer overflow attack**, an attacker finds a vulnerability in poorly written code that doesn't check for a defined amount of memory space use. If a program defines a variable size of 64 bytes (the total amount of memory the variable is supposed to use), and the program writes data over the 64-byte mark without triggering an error or preventing this occurrence, you have a buffer overflow. For example, the QEMU virtualization software reserved a buffer of 512 bytes to receive data from a virtual floppy disk, but a researcher found a way to send more than 512 bytes and take control of the VM host from inside a virtual machine. Basically, the attacker writes code that overflows the buffer, which is possible because the program accepts unvalidated user input. The trick is to not fill the overflowed memory with meaningless data, but to fill it with executable program code. That way, the OS runs the code, and the attacker's program does something harmful. Usually, the code elevates the attacker's permissions to an administrator's level or creates a service that allows an attacker to remotely access the target system. Table 3-4 describes some current buffer overflow vulnerabilities.

Buffer overflow	Description
GHOST	This vulnerability made headlines across the globe when it was discovered by security researchers at Qualys. Under the right conditions, GHOST could be exploited to gain administrative access to a remote system with no credentials. The vulnerability resulted from a weakness with the "glibc" library, central component of Linux operating systems. For more details, visit *https://community.qualys.com/blogs/laws-of-vulnerabilities/2015/01/27/the-ghost-vulnerability*.
Cisco ASA Internet Key Exchange	Cisco Security Advisory for CVE-2016-1287 (*https://tools.cisco.com/security/center/content/CiscoSecurityAdvisory/cisco-sa-20160210-asa-ike*) discusses this serious buffer overflow vulnerability in Cisco's ASA product line. Attackers could send a specially crafted packet to the affected device, which would allow them to gain full administrative privileges. This attack could be carried out from anywhere on the Internet if ASAs are in use on a company's perimeter.
StageFright Android Overflow Vulnerability	Buffer overflows not only affect traditional operating systems but mobile devices as well. This vulnerability, CVE-2015-1538, was found in Android's media playback libraries. Researchers found that a special MMS (Multimedia Messaging Service) message sent to a target Android device could cause an overflow, which allows for remote code execution without any user interaction.
Windows Server Service	Microsoft Security Bulletin MS08-067 (*www.microsoft.com/technet/security/Bulletin/MS08-067.mspx*) discusses this buffer overflow vulnerability, which makes it possible for attackers to run arbitrary code placed in memory. This vulnerability allowed the infamous Conficker worm to spread.

Table 3-4   Buffer overflow vulnerabilities

In defense of programmers, most are not adequately trained to write programs with computer security in mind. In the past, programs were written for ease of use and to create efficient executable code that ran quickly and used as few computer resources as possible. Today, the trend is to make sure programmers are aware of how their code might be vulnerable to attack, but checking for security vulnerabilities as a standard practice still isn't widespread. Most universities do not offer courses on writing programs with security in mind.

Independent and sponsored initiatives, such as Open Web Application Security Project (OWASP) and Building Security In Maturity Model (BSIMM), are encouraging secure development and helping organizations build better software. At Microsoft, programmers are now rewarded for writing code that doesn't show up later as a vulnerability in the system. In Activity 3-5, you take a look at some software with vulnerabilities caused by overlooking the security factor in the program design.

Activity 3-5: Researching Software Vulnerabilities

Time Required: 30 minutes

Objective: Examine some vulnerabilities released by the U.S. Computer Emergency Readiness Team (US-CERT).

Description: As a security professional conducting a security test on a customer's network, you need to investigate any vulnerabilities that might be exploited. After discovering vulnerabilities that might affect a client's network, you must create documentation of your findings and make recommendations to correct the problem. In this activity, you examine vulnerabilities reported by US-CERT and learn what solutions or recommendations you might give to customers.

1. Start your Web browser, if necessary, and go to **www.us-cert.gov/ncas**.

2. Click the "Bulletins" link, then click the most recent bulletin.

3. Investigate the first few vulnerabilities. Pick one and use the links under the "Source and Patch Info" column to answer the following questions: What recommendations would you give to someone whose system had been exploited because of this vulnerability? Can anything be done to prevent exploitation of this vulnerability?

4. Exit your Web browser.

Activity 3-5 gives you insight into software vulnerabilities used to exploit an OS or software running on an OS. Usually, a buffer overflow's main purpose is to insert code into the overwritten area of memory that elevates the attacker's permissions or give an attack remote access to a machine.

Eavesdropping

An attacker can listen in on unencrypted network communications in order to intercept confidential information or gather credentials that can be used to extend the attack. Eavesdropping can be accomplished with sniffing tools designed to capture copies of packets being sent across a network (e.g., tcpdump and wireshark). Later, these captured packets, typically stored in a .pcap file, can be reconstructed and scoured for data and credentials. Useful tools for viewing .pcap files include RSA's NetWitness Investigator and CapAnalysis. To defend against the threat of eavesdropping, network equipment and applications should be forced to communicate only over encrypted protocols and utilize valid, trusted certificates.

Man-in-the-Middle

One step beyond eavesdropping is a man-in-the-middle attack. Attackers can inject themselves between two parties or systems communicating with one another in order to manipulate messages being passed back and forth. Man-in-the-middle attacks are covered in more depth in Chapter 12.

Network Session Hijacking

Network session hijacking enables an attacker to join a TCP session and make both parties think he or she is the other party. This attack, discussed briefly in Chapter 2 in relation to initial sequence numbers (ISNs), is a complex attack that's beyond the scope of this book.

Addressing Physical Security

Protecting a network from attacks is not always a software issue. You should have some basic skills in protecting a network from physical attacks as well. No matter how effective your firewall is, you must secure servers and computers from an attack from within the organization. In fact, there's a higher chance that an attacker who breaks into the network is from inside the company rather than outside.

Security Bytes

On a military base in Hawaii, a pickup truck parked in front of an office building, and the driver entered the building and walked into an empty office. He disconnected a computer from the network, carried it out of the office, placed it in the truck's flatbed, and drove off, never to be seen again. When upper management questioned the staff, employees said they remembered seeing someone walking out of the building with the computer but assumed he was a help desk employee. Physical security is only as strong as the weakest link. All employees need to be aware of what's happening in their work environment. For example, if they notice a stranger sitting in front of a computer downloading files, they should contact security and then confront the person. Employees should be vigilant and not depend on security personnel alone to pay attention.

Keyloggers

Keyloggers are hardware devices or software that can be used to capture keystrokes on a computer. If you are conducting a security test on a system and need to obtain passwords, keyloggers can be a helpful tool. Of course, you should have written permission from the client before using software or hardware keyloggers. Software keyloggers behave like viruses or Trojan programs. A hardware keylogger is a small device—often smaller than an inch long. It can usually be installed in less than 30 seconds. It's a simple matter of unplugging the keyboard, plugging the keylogging device into a USB port, and then plugging the keyboard into the keylogging device's USB port.

Some common hardware keyloggers are Key Grabber and KeyGhost. Key Grabber automatically goes in to record mode, once installed. In order to enter playback mode, a key combination can be entered to enable a hidden flash drive. In this flash drive, the attacker will find LOG.TXT, which contains a log regarding every keystroke entered since the device was installed. In Figure 3-4, the Key Grabber keylogger program has captured John's e-mail credentials and a private message; John is informing Bob that he is going to quit his job.

```
LOG - Notepad
File Edit Format View Help
mail.google.com [Ent]
jsmith123@gmail.com[Tab]p@ssw0rd123[Ent]
bob.smith@gmail.com [Tab] Bob, This is private, so don't tell anyone else! [Ent]
I'm QUITTING! [Ent]
[Ent]
-John
```

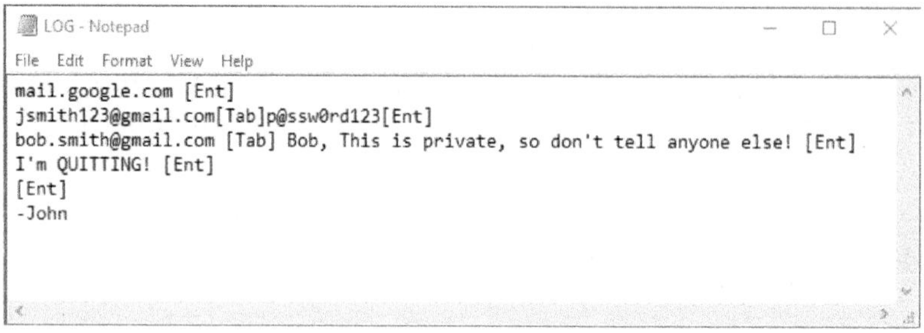

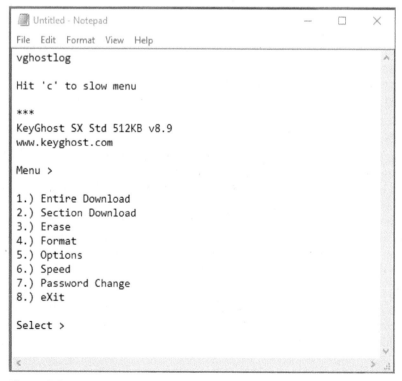

Figure 3-4 An e-mail message captured by Key Grabber

Source: Key Grabber

Figure 3-5 shows the menu in KeyGhost. Key Grabber and KeyGhost were created for companies or even parents who want to monitor computers. You can acquire a plastic shrink-fit covering that can be melted with a lighted match onto the keyboard connection so that the user can't unplug (or notice) the unit before conducting questionable activity on the computer.

```
Untitled - Notepad
File Edit Format View Help
vghostlog

Hit 'c' to slow menu

***
KeyGhost SX Std 512KB v8.9
www.keyghost.com

Menu >

1.) Entire Download
2.) Section Download
3.) Erase
4.) Format
5.) Options
6.) Speed
7.) Password Change
8.) eXit

Select >
```

Figure 3-5 The KeyGhost menu

Source: KeyGhost

Unfortunately, attackers can also use keylogger devices. An unscrupulous employee can connect a keylogger to a manager's computer and retrieve confidential information later. Installing this device does require access to the computer, which might pose a problem if the manager's office is locked. However, as mentioned, keyloggers are also available as software (spyware) that's loaded on a computer, and retrieved information can be e-mailed or transferred to a remote location.

When doing random visual tests of computers in your organization, keep an eye out for any suspicious hardware attached to the keyboard cable that wasn't installed by security personnel. This check is a simple way to monitor for keyloggers (or even computer systems) that the company didn't install.

Behind Locked Doors

As a security professional, you should be aware of the types of locks used to secure a company's assets. If an intruder gets physical access to a server, whether it's running Linux, Windows, or another OS, it doesn't matter how good your firewall or IDS is. Encryption or public key infrastructure (PKI) enforcements don't help in this situation, either. If intruders can sit in front of your server, they can hack it. Simply put, *lock up your server*.

In the same way that terrorists can learn how to create a bomb by doing Internet research, attackers can find countless articles about lock picking. One Web site, "Lockpicking–by Deviant Ollam" (*http://deviating.net/lockpicking/*), discusses the vulnerabilities of a variety of locks and has videos to show lockpicking techniques. In just a few days of practice, the average person can learn how to pick a typical American home lock in less than 5 minutes. Those who have more time on their hands, such as hackers, can learn to pick a deadbolt lock in under 30 seconds. If you're responsible for protecting a network infrastructure that has night-shift workers, don't assume that locked doors or cabinets can keep out unscrupulous employees with time on their hands. Typically, fewer employees are around during nonstandard business hours, which makes it easier for them to get into areas to which they might not normally have access. Your server room should have the best lock your company can afford. Take the time to look into locks that organizations such as the Department of Defense use, where protecting resources might be a life-or-death situation. Spending $5000 to $10,000 on a lock isn't unheard of in these organizations.

Rotary locks that require pushing in a sequence of numbered bars are more difficult to crack than deadbolt locks. However, neither lock type keeps a record of who has entered the locked room, so some businesses require using card access for better security. With this method, a card is scanned, and access is given to the cardholder while documenting the time of entry. This method also makes it possible for one card to allow access to several doors without having to issue multiple keys or having users memorize different combinations.

Security Bytes

Some legitimate sites offer tools and manuals on lock picking for police or security professionals. You might have to fill out some forms, but it could be worth your while if you plan to become a security professional. For example, if you're conducting a security test on an organization that has a locked server room and you want to gain access, knowing how to pick a lock could be beneficial. Remember, however, that you must get written permission from management before conducting this level of testing.

 Most police officers take a class to learn the basics of lock picking. When ordering lockpicking tools, be aware that many states or countries consider the mere possession of these tools a crime, as mentioned in Chapter 1. Remember that possession of certain hacking tools is also illegal.

Chapter Summary

- Security professionals must be aware of attacks that can take place on both network infrastructures and stand-alone computers.

- Network and computer attacks can be perpetrated by insiders as well as outside attackers.

- Malicious software (malware), such as viruses, worms, and Trojan programs, can attack a network or computer. A virus attaches itself to a host. A worm can replicate and propagate itself without attaching itself to a host. A Trojan program disguises itself as a useful program or application and can install a backdoor or rootkit on a computer.

- Users can install spyware programs inadvertently, thinking they're installing software to protect their computers. Spyware can record information from a user's computer and send it to the attacker.

- Security professionals can minimize the damage and likelihood of an infection by following best practices and implementing technical and non-technical measures.

- Adware programs can also be installed without users' knowledge. They're used to discern users' buying patterns for the purpose of sending Web advertisements tailored to their buying habits but can slow down a computer system.

- A denial-of-service (DoS) attack prevents authorized users from accessing network resources. The attack is usually accomplished through excessive use of bandwidth, memory, and CPU cycles.

- A distributed denial-of-service (DDoS) is an attack on a host from multiple servers or computers.

- The main purpose of buffer overflows is to insert executable code into an area of memory that elevates the attacker's permissions to the level of an administrator or allows an attacker remote access to the target system.

- In a Ping of Death attack, the attacker crafts an ICMP packet to be larger than the maximum 65,535 bytes, which causes the recipient system to crash or freeze. Most systems today aren't affected by this exploit.

- In session hijacking, the attacker joins a TCP session and makes both parties think he or she is the other party.

- Keyloggers make it possible to monitor what's being entered on a computer system. They can be installed on a keyboard connector easily and use a word processing program to store information. Security personnel should conduct random checks of computer hardware to detect these devices.

- Physical security is everyone's responsibility. All desktop systems and servers must be secured.

3

Key Terms

adware	keyloggers	Trojan program
attack	macro virus	virus
backdoor	malware	virus signature file
botnet	network security	vulnerability
buffer overflow attack	Ping of Death attack	whitelisting
computer security	ransomware	worm
denial-of-service (DoS) attack	rootkit	zombies
distributed denial-of-service (DDoS) attack	shell	
exploit	spyware	

Review Questions

1. What is the main purpose of malware?

   a. Financial gain or destruction

   b. Learning passwords

   c. Discovering open ports

   d. Identifying an operating system

2. A computer _____ relies on a host to propagate throughout a network.

   a. worm

   b. virus

   c. program

   d. sniffer

3. An exploit that attacks computer systems by inserting executable code in areas of memory because of poorly written code is called which of the following?

   a. Buffer overflow

   b. Trojan program

   c. Virus

   d. Worm

4. Which of the following exploits might hide its destructive payload in a legitimate application or game?

   a. Trojan program

   b. Macro virus

   c. Worm

   d. Buffer overflow

5. Antivirus software should be updated annually. True or False?

6. Which of the following doesn't attach itself to a host but can replicate itself?

   a. Worm

   b. Virus

   c. Trojan program

   d. Buffer overflow

7. Which of the following is an example of a macro programming language?

   a. C++

   b. Shell

   c. Basic

   d. Visual Basic for Applications

8. One purpose of adware is to determine users' purchasing habits. True or False?

9. List three types of malware.

10. A software or hardware component that records each keystroke a user enters is called which of the following?

    a. Key sniffer

    b. Keylogger

    c. Trojan program

    d. Buffer overflow

11. List three worms or viruses that use e-mail as a form of attack.

12. The Ping of Death is an exploit that sends multiple ICMP packets to a host faster than the host can handle. True or False?

13. What type of network attack relies on multiple servers participating in an attack on one host system?

    a. Trojan attack

    b. Buffer overflow

    c. Denial-of-service attack

    d. Distributed denial-of-service attack

14. What exploit is used to elevate an attacker's permissions by inserting executable code in the computer's memory?

   a. Trojan program

   b. Buffer overflow

   c. Ping of Death

   d. Buffer variance

15. What component can be used to reduce the risk of a Trojan program or rootkit sending information from an attacked computer to a remote host?

   a. Base-64 decoder

   b. Keylogger

   c. Telnet

   d. Firewall

16. To reduce the risk of a virus attack on a network, you should do which of the following?

   a. Use antivirus software.

   b. Educate users about opening attachments from suspicious e-mail.

   c. Keep virus signature files current.

   d. All of the above

17. The base-64 numbering system uses _____ bits to represent a character.

   a. 4

   b. 6

   c. 7

   d. 8

18. An exploit that leaves an attacker with another way to compromise a network later is called which of the following? (Choose all that apply.)

   a. Rootkit

   b. Worm

   c. Backroot

   d. Backdoor

19. Which of the following is a good place to begin your search for vulnerabilities in Microsoft products?

   a. Hacking Web sites

   b. Microsoft Security Bulletins

   c. Newsgroup references to vulnerabilities

   d. User manuals

20. An exploit discovered for one OS might also be effective on another OS. True or False?

Case Projects

Case Project 3-1: Determining Vulnerabilities for a Database Server

You have interviewed Ms. Erin Roye, an IT staff member, after conducting your initial security testing of the Alexander Rocco Corporation. She informs you that the company is running an older version of Oracle's database, Oracle 10g, for its personnel database. You decide to research whether Oracle 10g has any known vulnerabilities that you can include in your report to Ms. Roye. You don't know whether Ms. Roye has installed any patches or software fixes; you simply want to create a report with general information.

Based on this information, write a memo to Ms. Roye describing any CVEs (common vulnerabilities and exposures) or CAN (candidate) documents you found related to Oracle 10g. (*Hint*: A search of the CVE Web site sponsored by US-CERT, *https://cve.mitre.org/,* can save you a lot of time.) If you do find vulnerabilities, your memo should include recommendations and be written in a way that doesn't generate fear or uncertainty but encourages prudent decision-making.

Case Project 3-2: Investigating Possible Vulnerabilities of Microsoft IIS 6.0

Carrell Jackson, the Web developer for Alexander Rocco Corporation, has informed you that Microsoft IIS 6.0 is used for the company's Web site. He's proud of the direction the Web site is taking and says it has more than 1000 hits per week. Customers can reserve hotel rooms, schedule tee times for golf courses, and make reservations at any of the facility's many restaurants. Customers can enter their credit card information and receive confirmations via e-mail.

Based on this information, write a memo to Mr. Jackson listing any technical cybersecurity alerts or known vulnerabilities of IIS 6.0. If you find vulnerabilities, your memo should include recommendations and be written in a way that doesn't generate fear or uncertainty but encourages prudent decision-making.

## chapter 4

Footprinting and Social Engineering

After reading this chapter and completing the exercises, you will be able to:

- Use Web tools for footprinting
- Conduct competitive intelligence
- Describe DNS zone transfers
- Identify the types of social engineering

In this chapter, you learn how to use tools readily available on the Internet to find out how a company's network is designed. You also learn the skills needed to conduct competitive intelligence and how to use these skills for information gathering. Before you conduct a security test on a network, you need to perform most, if not all, of the footprinting tasks covered in this chapter.

This chapter also explains the tactics of attackers who use social engineering to get information from a company's key employees. In addition, you examine some of the less glamorous methods attackers use—such as looking through garbage cans, wastepaper baskets, and dumpsters for old computer manuals, discarded disks, and other materials—to find information that can enable them to break into a network.

Using Web Tools for Footprinting

In movies, before a thief robs a bank or steals jewelry, he "cases the joint" by taking pictures and getting floor plans. Movie thieves are usually lucky enough to get schematics of alarm systems and air-conditioning/ventilation systems, too. At least, that's how Hollywood portrays thieves. Any FBI agent would tell you that most real-life thieves aren't that lucky. However, the smart ones who don't get caught are meticulous and cautious. Many attackers do case the joint to look over the location, find weaknesses in the security system, and determine what types of locks and alarm systems are being used. They try to gather as much information as possible before committing a crime.

As a security tester, you, too, must find out as much as you can about the organization that hired you to test its network security. That way, you can advise management of any problem areas. In computer jargon, the process of finding information on a company's network is called **footprinting**. You might also hear the term "reconnaissance" used, and you should be familiar with both terms.

An important concept is that footprinting is passive, or nonintrusive; in other words, you aren't accessing information illegally or gathering unauthorized information with false credentials. With passive reconnaissance, you are not even engaging with the remote systems, but rather attempting to glean information about your target from other sources. Passive activities are likely to go unnoticed. Active footprinting, on the other hand, means you are actually prodding the target network in ways that might seem suspicious to network defenders. This includes things like port scans, DNS zone transfers, and interacting with a target's Web server. With active footprinting techniques, you are likely to be logged. The security tester (or attacker) tries to discover as much as possible about the organization and its network using both passive and active techniques. Table 4-1 lists some of the many tools available for footprinting; many are available in the latest version of Kali Linux.

 Many command-line utilities included for Linux systems aren't part of a Windows environment. For example, the `dig`, `netcat`, and `wget` commands don't work from a Windows 10 command prompt, but **NOTE** you can usually download Windows versions from the Web sites listed in Table 4-1. Security testers should spend time learning to use these command-line tools on a Linux system.

Tool	Function
Google (*www.google.com*)	Uncover files, systems, sites, and other information about a target using advanced operators and specially crafted queries. Some of these queries can be found at the Google Hacking Database (GHDB) (*https://www.exploit-db.com/google-hacking-database/*).
Maltego (*https://www.paterva.com*)	Discover relevant files, e-mail addresses, and other important information with this powerful graphic user interface (GUI) tool.
Recon-ng (*https://bitbucket.org/LaNMaSteR53/recon-ng*)	Automate footprinting with this powerful, advanced framework utilizing search engines, social media, and many other sources.
Netcraft Site Report (*http://toolbar.netcraft.com/site_report*)	Uncover the underlying technologies that a Web site operates on.
WayBackMachine (*https://archive.org/web/*)	Search through previous versions of the Web site to uncover historical information about a target.
Google Groups (*http://groups.google.com*)	Search for e-mail addresses in technical or nontechnical newsgroup postings.
Zed Attack Proxy (*https://www.owasp.org/index.php/OWASP_Zed_Attack_Proxy_Project*)	This is a useful Web site analysis tool. Can spider/crawl remote Web sites and even produce a list of vulnerabilities that might be present on a remote Web site.
Whois (*www.arin.net* or *www.whois.net*)	Gather IP and domain information.
Domain Dossier (*http://centralops.net/co/domaindossier.aspx*)	This Web tool is useful in gathering IP and domain information (whois, DNS, traceroute).
Web Data Extractor (*www.rafasoft.com*)	Extract contact data, such as e-mail, phone, and fax information, from a selected target.
FOCA (*www.elevenpaths.com/labstools/foca/index.html*)	Extract metadata from documents on Web sites to reveal the document creator's network logon and e-mail address, information on IP addresses of internal devices, and more.
Namedroppers (*www.namedroppers.com*)	Run a domain name search; more than 30 million domain names updated daily.
White Pages (*www.whitepages.com*)	Conduct reverse phone number lookups and retrieve address information.
Metis (*www.severus.org/sacha/metis*)	Gather competitive intelligence from Web sites.
`dig` (command available on all *nix systems; can be downloaded from *http://www.isc.org/downloads/bind/* for Windows platforms)	Perform DNS zone transfers; replaces the `nslookup` command.
`netcat` (command available on all *nix systems; can be downloaded from *https://nmap.org/ncat/* for Windows platforms)	Read and write data to ports over a network.
`wget` (command available on all *nix systems; can be downloaded from *http://gnuwin32.sourceforge.net/packages/wget.htm* for Windows platforms)	Retrieve HTTP, HTTPS, and FTP files over the Internet.

Table 4-1   **Summary of Reconnaissance tools**

In this chapter, you use the Domain Dossier utility to get information about a company's Web presence and see how DNS zone transfers can be used to determine computers' IP address ranges and hostnames.

Security Bytes

Each year, Department of Defense (DoD) employees are required to complete security awareness training that emphasizes the dangers of terrorists and spies being able to collect unclassified information. This information can be found in newspapers, Web sites, and TV and radio news programs, but information can also be gathered from Facebook, LinkedIn, and Twitter pages. By putting small pieces of information together, terrorists can get a fairly detailed picture of the DoD's activities. The DoD wants its employees to realize that discussing seemingly inconsequential information might be more dangerous than imagined. This information, when combined with information from other sources, can be damaging to national security.

For example, a sailor meets a friend in a restaurant and mentions that he'll be gone for 6 months. At the same restaurant, a civilian working for the DoD mentions over lunch with a friend that she has to work a lot of overtime ordering more supplies. As you can see, terrorists could easily pick up both pieces of information by listening in on conversations. This example might sound far-fetched, but it's a major method of gathering intelligence. The point is that you, too, need to pay attention to all information that's available, whether it's on a Web site, in e-mail headers, or in an employee's statement in an interview. Unfortunately, attackers check Web pages and newsgroups, examine IP addresses of companies, and look for postings from IT personnel asking questions about OSs or firewall configurations. Remember that after gathering a piece of information, you shouldn't stop there. Continue to dig to see what else potential attackers could discover.

Conducting Competitive Intelligence

If you want to open a piano studio to compete against another studio that has been in your neighborhood for many years, getting as much information as possible about your competitor is wise. How could you know the studio was successful without being privy to its bank statements? First, many businesses fail after the first year, so the studio being around for years is a testament to the owner doing something right. Second, you can simply park your car across the street from the studio and count the students entering to get a good idea of the number of clients. You can easily find out the cost of lessons by calling the studio or looking for ads in newspapers, flyers, telephone books, billboards, and so on. Numerous resources are available to help you discover as much as is legally possible about your competition. Business people have been doing this for years. Now this information gathering, called **competitive intelligence,** is done on an even higher level through technology. As a security professional, you should be able to explain to your clients the methods competitors use to gather information. To limit the amount of information a company makes public, you need a good understanding of what a competitor would do to discover confidential information.

Security Bytes

Just because you're able to find information about a company and its employees doesn't mean you should divulge it. For example, you discover that an employee is visiting a dating service Web site or questionable newsgroups. As long as this activity doesn't jeopardize the company in any way, as a security tester, you're not obligated to inform the company. Depending on the laws of your country or state, privacy issues might affect your decision on how to handle this situation. Security professionals and company officials can be sued for releasing confidential information of this nature.

Analyzing a Company's Web Site

Attacks often begin by gathering information from a company's Web site, because Web pages are an easy way for attackers to discover critical information about an organization. Many tools are available for this type of information gathering. One example, Zed Attack Proxy (ZAP), is a powerful tool for Linux, MacOSX, and Windows that can be downloaded free (*https://github.com/zaproxy*). The screenshots in this section are intended to show one of the many tools that can be used to gather information about a company's Web site and discover any existing vulnerabilities. The specific tool used isn't important. What's important is that you understand the process a security tester uses when beginning a security test.

ZAP requires having Java installed (downloaded from *https://www.java.com*). Figure 4-1 shows the main window of ZAP.

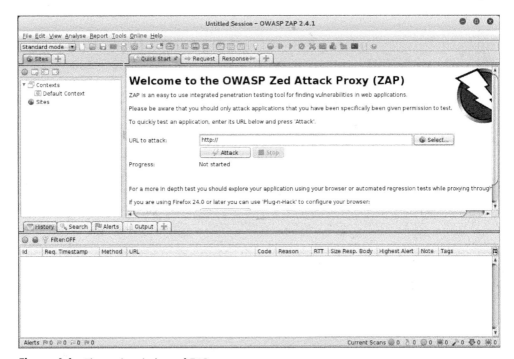

Figure 4-1   The main window of ZAP

Source: Apache 2 License

ZAP has a feature called "Plug-n-Hack" that automatically edits the configuration of a Web browser to direct traffic through ZAP proxy. This allows the ZAP tool to intercept and manipulate traffic sent between your Web browser and the target Web server. To use the Plug-n-Hack feature, you would click the Plug-n-Hack button in the ZAP welcome screen or browse to the URL listed using Firefox. Figure 4-2 shows the welcome message created by the ZAP proxy.

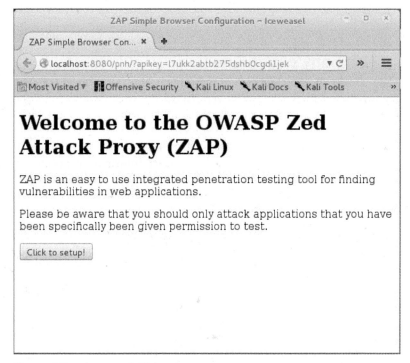

Figure 4-2   Plug-n-Hack Welcome Message

Source: Apache 2 License

Once the browser is configured, the attacker can browse to the target site. After this, the target site should appear in the ZAP tool interface. In the ZAP interface, the site can be right-clicked and selected for spidering. **Spidering** (or **crawling**) is an automated way to discover pages of a Web site by following links. Within a matter of seconds, the filenames of Web pages on the "spidered" site are displayed under the Spider tab (see Figure 4-3).

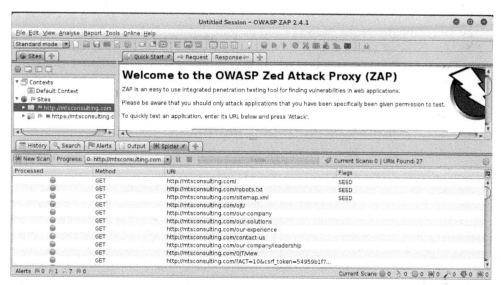

Figure 4-3   Displaying filenames of Web pages on a site

Source: Apache 2 License

After the site has been spidered, we can actively scan the site using the ZAP "Active Scan" feature. This sends the Web server a series of requests designed to identify vulnerabilities. Once complete, vulnerabilities will display under the Alerts tab in the bottom frame of the ZAP interface. This information is also exportable into an HTML report format. Figure 4-4 shows an example HTML report, with a summary of findings on the top and medium-risk vulnerability details on the bottom.

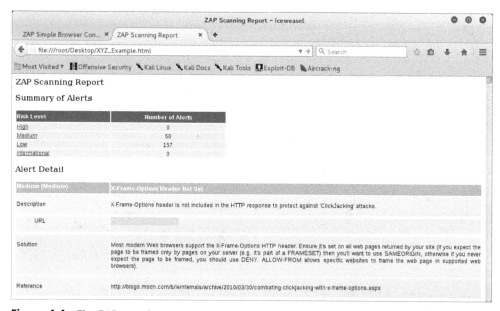

Figure 4-4   The ZAP scanning report

Source: Apache 2 License

As you can see, the scan feature allows testing areas of the site that might have problems. Any vulnerabilities in the Web site are indicated in the Risk Level column as either High, Medium, Low, or Informational. In this example, the risk level is flagged as Medium. Gathering competitive intelligence through scans of this type is time consuming, and the more you find out, the deeper you want to dig. Setting a reasonable time frame for this phase of your investigation is important, or you might spend too much time on this activity. On the other hand, you don't want to rush your information gathering, because much of what you learn can be used for further testing and investigation. The following section covers additional tools you can use for gathering information.

Using Other Footprinting Tools

The Whois utility is a commonly used Web tool for gathering IP address and domain information. With just a company's Web address, you can discover a tremendous amount of information. Unfortunately, attackers can also make use of this information. Often companies don't realize they're publishing information on the Web that computer criminals can use. The Whois utility gives you information on a company's IP addresses and any other domains the company might be part of. In Activity 4-1, you practice using the Domain Dossier Whois function.

Activity 4-1: Using Footprinting Tools

Time Required: 30 minutes

Objective: Learn how to use footprinting tools, such as the Domain Dossier Whois function.

Description: Security testers need to know how to use tools for gathering information about networks. With the Whois function, you can discover which network configuration factors might be used in attacking a network.

1. Start your Web browser, and go to **http://centralops.net/co/domaindossier.aspx**.

2. Type **mit.edu** in the domain or IP address text box, check the **"domain whois record"** check box, then click the **go** button. Scroll down to view the information displayed (see Figure 4-5).

Figure 4-5   Viewing information with the Domain Dossier Whois function

3. Note the IP addresses and name servers listed. Chapter 5 covers port scanning and explains how these IP addresses can be used to gather more information about name servers.

4. Try entering several other organizations' domain names in the domain or IP address text box and repeat Steps 2 and 3. Note that some organizations are more discreet about what is listed in their output screens. For example, when describing an administrative contact, giving just a job title is better than listing an actual name, as you'll soon discover.

5. Leave your Web browser open for the next activity.

Using E-mail Addresses

After seeing the information you can gather with the commands covered in this chapter, you might wonder what else you can do. Knowing a user's e-mail address can help you dig even further. Based on an e-mail account listed in DNS output, you might discover that the company's e-mail address format is first-name initial followed by last name and the *@companyname.com* sequence. You can guess other employees' e-mail accounts by getting a company phone directory or searching the Internet for any *@companyname.com* references. *Groups.google.com* is the perfect tool for this job. In Activity 4-2, you use it to find company e-mail addresses.

Activity 4-2: Identifying Company E-mail Accounts

Time Required: 30 minutes

Objective: Determine e-mail addresses for company employees.

Description: Knowing the e-mail addresses of employees can help you discover security vulnerabilities and gather competitive intelligence data. For example, you might discover that an employee has joined a newsgroup using his or her company e-mail account and shared proprietary information about the company. IT employees, when posting technical questions to a newsgroup, might reveal detailed information about the company's firewall or IDS, or a marketing director might mention a new ad campaign strategy the company is considering.

1. Start your Web browser, if necessary, and go to **http://groups.google.com**.

2. On the search page, type **@microsoft.com** and press **Enter**. This method is a fast and easy way to find e-mail accounts of people posting questions to the Microsoft domain.

3. Scroll down the list of items and try to find postings from employees who work at different companies. (*Hint*: Choose entries containing "Re:" in the listing. They're usually responses to questions sent by employees.) The list will vary, but it should give you an idea of the danger in using a company's e-mail address when posting questions to forums or newsgroups.

Remember that messages posted to newsgroups aren't private and that people can look them up for many years. You can test this by entering any e-mail address you've used in the past 10 years to post newsgroup messages. You might be surprised to find your messages **TIP** are still available for anyone to see. As a security tester, you should recommend that employees use a Web-based e-mail account (such as Outlook or Gmail) rather than company e-mail accounts for posting messages to newsgroups.

4. In a new query, type **@cisco.com** and press **Enter**. Now you can find out who's posting questions to the security company Cisco. Most likely, the postings are from users of Cisco's products. Can you see how an attacker could use this information?

5. Scroll through the list and look for questions from employees of the security company and customers wanting advice. Could attackers use this information for malicious purposes?

6. Did you find any information that could be useful to a security tester? How old are many of the returned links?

7. To view more recent postings, modify your query to include "2015" and "2016." (Include the quotation marks around search terms to make sure you don't get phone numbers or addresses containing these numbers in your search results.)

The name used in the activity was obtained from the Whois utility. However, if you know a user's e-mail address, you can enter it in the *groups.google.com* search page. In Case Project 4-1, you get a chance to search on a specific e-mail address. If you were conducting a security test in the real world, you would search for e-mail accounts of IT staff and other key personnel.

Using HTTP Basics

As you learned in Chapter 3, HTTP operates on port 80. A security tester can pull information from a Web server by using HTTP commands. You've probably seen HTTP client error codes before, such as 404 Not Found. A basic understanding of HTTP can be beneficial to security testers, and you don't have to learn too many codes to get data from a Web server. If you know the return codes a Web server generates, you can determine what OS is used on the computer where you're conducting a security test. Table 4-2 lists common HTTP client errors, and Table 4-3 lists HTTP server errors that might occur.

Error	Description
400 Bad Request	Request not understood by server
401 Unauthorized	Request requires authentication
402 Payment Required	Reserved for future use
403 Forbidden	Server understands the request but refuses to comply
404 Not Found	Unable to match request
405 Method Not Allowed (*Note:* Methods are covered later in this chapter.)	Request not allowed for the resource
406 Not Acceptable	Resource doesn't accept the request
407 Proxy Authentication Required	Client must authenticate with proxy
408 Request Timeout	Request not made by client in allotted time
409 Conflict	Request couldn't be completed because of an inconsistency
410 Gone	Resource is no longer available
411 Length Required	Content length not defined
412 Precondition Failed	Request header fields evaluated as false
413 Request Entity Too Large	Request is larger than server is able to process
414 Request-URI (uniform resource identifier) Too Long	Request-URI is longer than the server is willing to accept

Table 4-2 HTTP client errors

Error	Description
500 Internal Server Error	Request couldn't be fulfilled by the server
501 Not Implemented	Server doesn't support the request
502 Bad Gateway	Server received invalid response from the upstream server
503 Service Unavailable	Server is unavailable because of maintenance or overload
504 Gateway Timeout	Server didn't receive a timely response
505 HTTP Version Not Supported	HTTP version not supported by the server

Table 4-3   HTTP server errors

In addition, you need to understand some of the available HTTP methods, shown in Table 4-4. You don't have to be fluent in using HTTP methods, but you need to be well versed enough to use the most basic HTTP method: GET / HTTP/1.1.

Method	Description
GET	Retrieves data by URI
HEAD	Same as the GET method, but retrieves only the header information of an HTML document, not the document body
OPTIONS	Requests information on available options
TRACE	Starts a remote Application-layer loopback of the request message
CONNECT	Used with a proxy that can dynamically switch to a tunnel connection, such as Secure Sockets Layer (SSL)
DELETE	Requests that the origin server delete the identified resource
PUT	Requests that the entity be stored under the Request-URI
POST	Allows data to be posted (i.e., sent to a Web server)

Table 4-4   HTTP methods

For a more detailed definition of HTTP methods, see RFC 2616.

If you know HTTP methods, you can send a request to a Web server and, from the generated output, determine what OS the Web server is using. You can also find other information that could be used in an attack, such as known vulnerabilities of operating systems and other software, as you learned in Chapter 3. After you determine which OS version a company is running, you can search for any exploits that might be used against that network's systems.

Activity 4-3: Using HTTP Methods

Time Required: 30 minutes

Objective: Determine Web server information by using HTTP methods.

Description: Armed with the information gathered from a company Web server by using basic HTTP methods, a security tester can discover system vulnerabilities and use this information for further testing. For example, querying a Web server might reveal that the server is running the Linux OS and using Apache software. In this activity, you use the `nc` (netcat) command to connect to port 80 and then use HTTP methods.

4

If you can't get results in this activity by using pitt.edu, the Web site has probably changed its security and won't allow using the HEAD or OPTIONS methods. If so, try using isecom.org instead of mit.edu.

1. Boot your computer into Linux with the Kali 2.0 DVD. Then open a command shell by clicking the **Terminal** icon on the panel taskbar. At the command prompt, type **nc pitt.edu 80** and press **Enter**. (Port 80 is the HTTP port.)

2. On the next line, type **OPTIONS / HTTP/1.1** and press **Enter**. (Note the spaces around the slash character between the words OPTIONS and HTTP.)

3. On the next line, type **HOST:127.0.0.1** and press **Enter** twice. After several seconds, you see the screen shown in Figure 4-6.

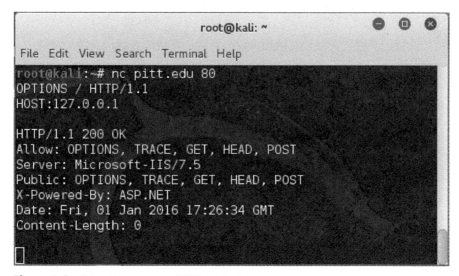

Figure 4-6 Using the OPTIONS HTTP method

4. What information generated from the nc command might be useful to a security tester? What other options are available when accessing this Web server? (*Note*: Use Figure 4-6 to answer the question if the command doesn't work at this time.)

5. Type **nc pitt.edu 80** and press **Enter**.

6. On the next line, type **HEAD / HTTP/1.0** and press **Enter** twice to retrieve header information. Your screen should look similar to Figure 4-7. Note the additional information the HEAD method produced, such as indicating that the connection has been closed and specifying the content length (0 bytes).

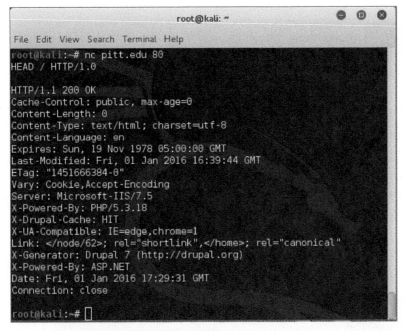

```
root@kali: ~                                        ⊖  ▢  ✕

 File  Edit  View  Search  Terminal  Help
root@kali:~# nc pitt.edu 80
HEAD / HTTP/1.0

HTTP/1.1 200 OK
Cache-Control: public, max-age=0
Content-Length: 0
Content-Type: text/html; charset=utf-8
Content-Language: en
Expires: Sun, 19 Nov 1978 05:00:00 GMT
Last-Modified: Fri, 01 Jan 2016 16:39:44 GMT
ETag: "1451666384-0"
Vary: Cookie,Accept-Encoding
Server: Microsoft-IIS/7.5
X-Powered-By: PHP/5.3.18
X-Drupal-Cache: HIT
X-UA-Compatible: IE=edge,chrome=1
Link: </node/62>; rel="shortlink",</home>; rel="canonical"
X-Generator: Drupal 7 (http://drupal.org)
X-Powered-By: ASP.NET
Date: Fri, 01 Jan 2016 17:29:31 GMT
Connection: close

root@kali:~# ▯
```

Figure 4-7   Using the HEAD HTTP method

7. Close the Terminal shell and log off Linux for the next activity.

To see additional parameters that can be used with the nc command, you can type nc -h at the command prompt (see Figure 4-8).

```
                              root@kali: ~                    ●  ◎  ⊗

 File  Edit  View  Search  Terminal  Help
root@kali:~# nc -h
[v1.10-41]
connect to somewhere:   nc [-options] hostname port[s] [ports] ...
listen for inbound:     nc -l -p port [-options] [hostname] [port]
options:
        -c shell commands    as `-e'; use /bin/sh to exec [dangerous!!]
        -e filename          program to exec after connect [dangerous!!]
        -b                   allow broadcasts
        -g gateway           source-routing hop point[s], up to 8
        -G num               source-routing pointer: 4, 8, 12, ...
        -h                   this cruft
        -i secs              delay interval for lines sent, ports scanned
        -k                   set keepalive option on socket
        -l                   listen mode, for inbound connects
        -n                   numeric-only IP addresses, no DNS
        -o file              hex dump of traffic
        -p port              local port number
        -r                   randomize local and remote ports
        -q secs              quit after EOF on stdin and delay of secs
        -s addr              local source address
        -T tos               set Type Of Service
        -t                   answer TELNET negotiation
        -u                   UDP mode
        -v                   verbose [use twice to be more verbose]
        -w secs              timeout for connects and final net reads
        -C                   Send CRLF as line-ending
        -z                   zero-I/O mode [used for scanning]
port numbers can be individual or ranges: lo-hi [inclusive];
hyphens in port names must be backslash escaped (e.g. 'ftp\-data').
root@kali:~# █
```

Figure 4-8   `netcat` parameters

Other Methods of Gathering Information

So far, you have learned several methods for gathering information from company Web sites and e-mail addresses. With just a URL, you can determine which Web server and OS a company is using and learn the names of IT personnel, for example. You need to be aware of other methods attackers use to gather information about a company. Some of these methods, such as using cookies and Web bugs, are unscrupulous.

Detecting Cookies and Web Bugs   A cookie is a text file generated by a Web server and stored on a user's browser. The information in this file is sent back to the Web server when the user returns to the Web site. For example, a returning customer can be shown a customized Web page when he or she revisits an online store's Web site. Some cookies can cause security issues because unscrupulous people might store personal information in cookies that can be used to attack a computer or server.

A **Web bug** is a 1-pixel × 1-pixel image file referenced in an <IMG> tag, and it usually works with a cookie. Its purpose is similar to that of spyware and adware: to get information about the person visiting the Web site, such as an IP address, when the Web bug was viewed, and the type of browser used to view the page. All this information can be useful to hackers. Web bugs are not from the same Web site as the Web page creator. They come from third-party companies specializing in data collection. Because Web bugs are just another image file, usually a GIF, they can't be blocked by a browser or rejected by a user. Also, Web bugs usually match the color of the Web page's background, which renders them invisible. If you don't have a tool for detecting Web bugs, usually the only way to find them is examining the Web page's source code to find a file in an < IMG > tag loading from a different Web server than other image files on the page. Security professionals need to be aware of cookies and Web bugs to keep these information-gathering tools off company computers.

Activity 4-4: Discovering Cookies in Web Pages

Time Required: 30 minutes

Objective: Determine whether cookies are present in Web pages.

Description: Many companies include cookies in their Web pages to gather information about visitors to their Web sites. This information might be used for competitive intelligence or, for example, to determine visitors' buying habits. Security testers should know how to verify whether a Web page contains cookies.

1. Boot your computer into Windows, and start the Mozilla Firefox Web browser. If you have been using this browser in Windows, cookies are probably loaded on your computer already, so you need to clear them and then visit a new site.

2. To clear any cookies from your computer, click on the menu button on the top right of the Firefox window. Then choose **Options** from the menu. In the Options dialog box, click the **Privacy** icon and click on the **clear your recent history** linked text.

3. In the **Clear All Recent History** dialog box (if necessary, click the Details arrow), unselect everything but Cookies and click **Clear Now**. Click **Cancel** and open a new tab, leaving the options tab open in the background.

4. Go to **www.amazon.com**. Return to the Options tab and click **remove individual cookies**. Examine the new cookies that have been created by clicking on each folder. Do any of the cookies have personal information stored?

5. If time permits, visit some sites that require signing in with an account logon and password. See whether these sites create any cookies with personal information.

6. Click the **Close** button twice to return to the Amazon Web page, and leave your Web browser open for the next activity.

Activity 4-5: Examining Web Bugs and Privacy

Time Required: 30 minutes

Objective: Gain an understanding of data collection with Web bugs.

Description: Web bugs are considered more invasive than cookies. As a security professional, you should understand how companies use them to gather information on users who visit Web sites.

1. Start your Web browser in Windows, if necessary, and go to **www.knowprivacy.org**.

2. Click the **Web Bugs** tab on the home page, and read all sections.

3. Which Web sites have the most Web bugs? (List the top five.)

4. The article explains that Google creates incentives for site operators to share data by offering premium services only to Web sites willing to share data they gather from Web bugs. Break up into teams of three or four students, and be prepared to argue for Google or the Know Privacy organization.

5. After reading the article, exit your Web browser.

Using Domain Name System Zone Transfers

Another way to gather information when footprinting a network is through Domain Name System (DNS). As you know from learning basic networking concepts, DNS is the network component responsible for resolving hostnames to IP addresses and vice versa. People would much rather memorize a URL than an IP address. Unfortunately, using URLs comes at a high price. DNS is a major area of potential vulnerability for network attacks.

Without going into too much detail, DNS uses name servers to resolve names. After you determine what name server a company is using, you can attempt to transfer all the records for which the DNS server is responsible. This process, called a **zone transfer**, can be done with the `dig` command. (For those familiar with the `nslookup` command, `dig` is now the recommended command.) To determine a company's primary DNS server, you can look for a DNS server containing a Start of Authority (SOA) record. An SOA record shows for which zones or IP addresses the DNS server is responsible. After you determine the primary DNS server, you can perform another zone transfer to see all host computers on the company network. In other words, the zone transfer gives you an organization's network diagram. You can use this information to attack other servers or computers that are part of the network infrastructure.

Activity 4-6: Identifying IP Addresses by Using Zone Transfers (Optional)

Time Required: 30 minutes

Objective: Perform a zone transfer on a DNS server.

Description: When footprinting a network, finding the IP addresses and hostnames of all servers, computers, and other nodes connected to the network is important. With commands such as `dig`, you can perform zone transfers of DNS records. You can then use this information to create network diagrams and establish a good picture of how the network is organized. For example, you can see how many hosts are on the network and how many subnets have been created.

In this example, mit.edu is used to demonstrate conducting a zone transfer so that you can see what kind of information can be gathered from a zone transfer. At the time of this writing, the zone transfer with mit.edu worked. However, many universities are tightening security and no longer allow zone transfers, but you should still know the steps for performing one.

1. Boot your computer into Linux with the Kali Linux DVD and open a Terminal shell. At the command prompt, type **dig NS zonetransfer.me** and press **Enter**. You should see a screen similar to Figure 4-9. Two name servers, indicated by "NS," are listed: nsztm1.digi.ninja, and nsztm2.digi.ninja. (This information might change by the time you read this book. If so, ask your instructor for guidelines.) You can see the information that was available to a hacker when the zone transfers are performed. These commands shouldn't work if a DNS administrator has configured DNS correctly. As you'll learn, however, sometimes administrators don't do what they should, which leaves systems vulnerable to attacks.

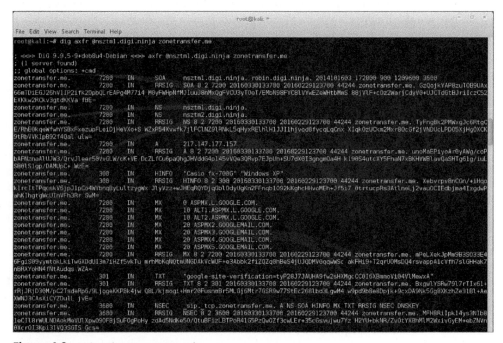

Figure 4-9   Using the `dig` command

Source: © 2016 Internet Systems Consortium

2. To perform a zone transfer on the nsztm1.digi.ninja DNS server, type **dig axfr @nsztm1.digi.ninja zonetransfer.me** and press **Enter**. nsztm1.digi.ninja is the server on which you're attempting the zone transfer, and the second zonetransfer.me statement is the domain where the server is located.

3. After a short wait, your screen should fill with a few records.

4. Do the transfer again, but this time use the |less parameter by typing **dig axfr @nsztml.digi.ninja zonetransfer.me |less** and pressing **Enter**.

5. Press **Enter** or the **spacebar** to view additional records, and then press q to quit. Close the Terminal shell, and log off Linux.

TIP As a security tester, you should always be aware that an attack might be successful one day and unsuccessful another day. So, if an attack works, copy all files and data obtained in the hack to a hard disk or thumb drive as quickly as possible. In the example here, the security tester would have already obtained the information she needed and saved it to her company's server. It would not matter if DNS were properly reconfigured correctly after the zone transfer took place. Game over!

The tools you've just learned about aren't the only way to get information. Sometimes information about a company is gathered by using nontechnical skills. In fact, the best hackers aren't necessarily the most technically adept people. Instead, they possess a more insidious—and often underestimated—skill called social engineering, discussed in the following section.

Introduction to Social Engineering

The art of social engineering has been around much longer than computers. **Social engineering** means using knowledge of human nature to get information from people. In computer attacks, the information is usually a password to a network or other information an attacker could use to compromise a network. A salesperson, for example, can get personal information about customers, such as income, hobbies, social life, drinking habits, music preferences, and the like, just by asking the customer the right questions. A salesperson uses charm and sometimes guile to relax customers and even attempts to bond with customers by pretending to be empathetic with them. After leaving the store, customers might regret some of the information they gave freely, but if the salesperson was personable, they might not think twice about it. Social engineers might also use persuasion tactics, intimidation, coercion, extortion, and even blackmail to gather the information they need. They are probably the biggest security threat to networks and the most difficult to protect against.

You have probably heard the saying "Why try to crack a password when you can simply ask for it?" Many attackers do just that: They ask for it. Unfortunately, many users give attackers everything they need to break into a network. Anyone who has worked at a help desk or in network support knows this to be true. Even if a company policy states that passwords must not be given to anyone, users often think this policy doesn't apply to IT personnel. How many times have users said their passwords out loud when an IT technician is seated in front of their computers? IT personnel don't want to know a user's password. They especially don't want a user to say it aloud or on the telephone or type it in e-mails. Yet users often don't consider their company passwords private, so they don't guard passwords as they might PINs for their ATM cards. They might not think that what they have on their company's computers is important or would be of interest to an attacker. Social engineers know how to put these types of users at ease. The following is an example of a typical social-engineering tactic.

First, the social engineer poses as "Mike," a name he found after performing a zone transfer and examining the company's DNS server. Mike might not be the current IT point of contact (POC), but it doesn't matter. Depending on the company's size, users often don't know everyone on the IT staff. The social engineer then places a call for Sue, an employee name he found from the zone transfer information and several company Web pages that showed the format of e-mail addresses. To get the phone number, he simply calls the company's main switchboard and asks for Sue. Then he says he wants to leave a message for Sue and asks to be directed to her voice-mail. "Sue's in the office now," replies the friendly receptionist. "Would you like me to connect you to her?" The social engineer says, "Darn, my other line is ringing. I misplaced her extension. Can you please give it to me, and I'll call her back in a few minutes? I really have to get that call."

In this exchange, his tactic is to create a sense of urgency yet remain cordial. It usually works because most receptionists don't see a problem with connecting a caller to an employee or giving an employee's direct number or extension. After all, the caller knows Sue's name and seems to know her. "Extension 4100," the receptionist says. "Thanks! Gotta go," the social engineer replies.

After 30 minutes or so, the social engineer calls the company again. "Hello. Extension 4101, please," he asks. The receptionist connects him, and a man answers "Bob Smith, Accounting." "Sorry, Bob. Mike here. I was calling Sue, but I guess I got your extension by mistake. Sue was having a problem connecting to the Internet, so we're checking IP address information. We just fixed her system. Are you also having a problem?" Bob says, "It looks like only the accounting department is having a problem with the VLAN config." Mike then asks, "Still running Windows XP, or are you all using Windows 10 now?" Bob answers no but tells Mike which operating system he's using. Bob probably feels as though he knows Mike, even though he doesn't.

Another way to find out how the IT staff operates is for Mike to pose as Bob and call with a question or problem he's having. Mike would then learn how the help desk person handles the call. Does the help desk issue a help ticket? Does Bob have to give any information to the caller other than his name and phone number? Many help desk offices require assigning a unique number to the help call until the problem is solved.

The social engineer used Sue's name to give his call more credibility. Also, because he had gathered information about the operating system through other means, he took advantage of that knowledge, as shown by his Windows version question. Mike might try to go for the kill now, or he might decide to attempt the final attack with Sue. If he calls her, he can talk about Bob as though they're old friends. What he wants is Bob or Sue's password. He might try the following ploy: "Bob, there's a good chance we'll have to shut down accounting's network connectivity for an hour or so. I could reduce this time for your system to five minutes if I could work on the problem from here. Only problem is I need your password. I already have your logon account as bsmith@gmail-info.com. Is that correct?" Chances are good that Bob will give his password to Mike over the telephone.

Not all social engineering takes place on the telephone, but it's probably the most common method because it's anonymous and allows a social engineer to carry out multiple attacks in the same organization. This method can be more difficult if one or two employees hear different stories from the same person. However, a well-dressed person carrying a clipboard can also be successful in gathering information from employees. This approach requires more courage because the social engineer has to face the people from whom he's attempting to gather information.

Social engineers study human behavior. They can recognize personality traits, such as shyness or insecurity, and understand how to read body language: slouched shoulders, avoidance of eye contact, nervous fidgeting, and so on. If the ploy is conducted over the telephone, the person's tone of voice can give the social engineer clues. Many profess to practice on people they date or try to get useless information from unsuspecting victims just to hone their skills. Like a tiger seeking out the weakest gazelle in the herd, social engineers can identify the most vulnerable person in an organization. They know who to approach and who to avoid.

Security Bytes

A security professional's most difficult job is preventing social engineers from getting crucial information from company employees. No matter how thorough a security policy is or how much money is spent on firewalls and intrusion detection systems (IDSs), employees are still the weakest link in an organization. Attackers know this fact and use it. Employees must be trained and tested periodically on security practices. Just as fire drills help prepare people to evacuate during a fire, random security drills can improve a company's security practices. For example, randomly selecting and testing employees each month to see whether they give their passwords to someone inside or outside the organization is a good way to find out whether your security memos are being read and followed.

Social engineers use many different techniques in their attempts to gain information from unsuspecting people:

- *Urgency*—"I need the information now or the world will come to an end!" For example, a social engineer might tell a user he needs the information quickly or the network will be down for a long time, thus creating a false sense of urgency.

- *Quid pro quo*—"I can make your life better if you give me the information I need." The social engineer might promise the user faster Internet access, for example, if he or she helps by supplying information.

- *Status quo*—"Everyone else is doing it, so you should, too." By using the names of other employees, a social engineer can easily convince others to reveal their passwords.

- *Kindness*—This tactic is probably the most dangerous weapon social engineers wield. People want to help those who are kind to them. The saying "It's easier to catch flies with honey than with vinegar" also applies to social engineering.

- *Position*—Convincing an employee that you're in a position of authority in the company can be a powerful means of gaining information. This is especially true in the military, where rank has its privileges. Social engineers can claim that a high-ranking officer is asking for the information, so it's imperative to give it as quickly as possible.

Security Bytes

As a security tester, you should never use social-engineering tactics unless the person who hired you gives you permission in writing. You should also confirm on which employees you're allowed to perform social-engineering tests and document the tests you conduct. Your documentation should include the responses you received, and all test results should, of course, be confidential. Figures 4-10 and 4-11 show social-engineering templates included in the OSSTMM. You can print them from your copy of the OSSTMM on the book's DVD.

OSSTMM Social Engineering Template

Company	
Company Name	
Company Address	
Company Telephone	
Company Fax	
Company Web Page	
Products and Services	
Primary Contacts	
Departments and Responsibilities	
Company Facilities Location	
Company History	
Partners	
Resellers	
Company Regulations	
Company Info Security Policy	
Company Traditions	
Company Job Postings	
Temporary Employment Availability	
Typical IT Threats	
People	
Employee Information	
Employee Names and Positions	
Employee Place in Hierarchy	
Employee Personal Pages	
Employee Best Contact Methods	
Employee Hobbies	
Employee Internet Traces (SENET, Forums)	
Employee Opinions Expressed	
Employee Friends and Relatives	
Employee History (Including Work History)	
Employee Character Traits	
Employee Values and Priorities	
Employee Social Habits	
Employee Speech and Speaking Patterns	
Employee Gestures and Manners	

Figure 4-10   The OSSTMM social-engineering template

OSSTMM Social Engineering Telephone Attack Template

Attack Scenario	
Telephone #	
Person	
Description	
Results	

Figure 4-11   The OSSTMM telephone attack template

Training users not to give outsiders any information about OSs is important. Employees should also be taught to confirm that the person asking questions is indeed the person he or she claims to be. Employees shouldn't be embarrassed to ask the person for a company phone number to call back instead of trusting the person on the other end of the phone line. Simply making employees aware that most hacking is done through social engineering, not programming skills, can make them more aware of how attackers operate.

The Art of Shoulder Surfing

Another method social engineers use to gain access to information is **shoulder surfing**. A shoulder surfer is skilled at reading what users enter on their keyboards, especially logon names and passwords. This skill certainly takes practice, but with enough time, it can be mastered easily. Shoulder surfers also use this skill to read PINs entered at ATMs or to detect long-distance authorization codes that callers dial. ATM theft is much easier than computer shoulder surfing because a keypad has fewer characters to memorize than a computer keyboard. If the person throws away the receipt in a trash can near the ATM, the shoulder surfer can match the PIN with an account number and then create a fake ATM card. Often shoulder surfers use binoculars or high-powered telescopes to observe PINs being entered, making it difficult to protect against this attack.

Security Bytes

A common tactic of shoulder surfers is using smartphone cameras to take photos of unaware shoppers' credit cards in supermarkets and stores. With this technique, they can get the credit card number and expiration date. Combining this technique with observing the shopper entering his or her PIN increases the risk of identity theft.

Many keyboard users don't follow the traditional fingering technique taught in typing classes. Instead, they hunt and peck with two or three fingers. However, shoulder surfers train themselves to memorize key positions on a standard keyboard. Armed with this knowledge, they can determine which keys are pressed by noticing the location on the keyboard, not which finger the typist is using.

Shoulder surfers also know the popular letter substitutions most people use when creating passwords: $ for s, @ for a, 1 for i, 0 for o, and so forth. Many users think p@$$w0rd is difficult to guess, but it's not for a skilled shoulder surfer. In addition, many users are required to use passwords containing special characters, and often they type these passwords more slowly to make sure they enter the correct characters. Slower typing makes a shoulder surfer's job easier.

Security Bytes

With so many people taking their mobile devices to airports, commercial airlines warn customers to be aware of shoulder surfers. In the tight confines of an airplane, someone could easily observe the keys pressed and read the data on a screen. Products that prevent off-axis viewing of screens, such as screen overlays or a security lens, are recommended for travelers. Many employees conduct business on airplanes, and shoulder surfers can use the information they gather to compromise computer systems at the company.

To help prevent shoulder-surfing attacks, you must educate users to not type logon names and passwords when someone is standing directly behind them—or even standing nearby. You should also caution users about typing passwords when someone nearby is talking on a cell phone because of the wide availability of camera phones. To further reduce the risk of shoulder surfing, make sure all computer monitors face away from the door or the cubicle entryway. Warn your users to change their passwords immediately if they suspect someone might have observed them entering their passwords.

Security Bytes

When you're entering a long-distance access code at a pay phone, a shoulder surfer holding a calculator while pretending to talk on the phone next to you can simply enter each number you press into his or her calculator. With this method, he or she doesn't have to memorize a long sequence of numbers. The calculator entry contains the access code for placing a long-distance call charged to your phone card.

The Art of Dumpster Diving

Another method social engineers use to gain access to information is **dumpster diving**. Although it's certainly not a glamorous form of gathering information, you'd be surprised at what you can find by examining someone's trash. For example, discarded computer manuals can indicate what OS is being used. If the discarded manual is for Windows Server 2012, there's a good chance the new system is a more recent Windows OS, such as Windows Server 2016. Sometimes network administrators write notes in manuals or even jot down passwords, and social engineers can make use of this information.

Company phone directories are another source of information. A dumpster diver who finds a directory listing company employees can use this information to pose as an employee for the purpose of gathering information. Company calendars with meeting schedules, employee vacation schedules, and so on can be used to gain access to offices that won't be occupied for a specified time period. Trash can be worth its weight in gold for the dumpster diver who knows what to do with it. Here are some other items that can be useful to dumpster divers:

- Financial reports
- Interoffice memos
- Discarded computer programs
- Company organizational charts showing managers' names
- Resumes of employees
- Company policies or systems and procedures manuals
- Professional journals or magazines
- Utility bills
- Solicitation notices from outside vendors
- Regional manager reports
- Quality assurance reports
- Risk management reports
- Minutes of meetings
- Federal, state, or city reports
- Employee charge card receipts

Dumpster diving can produce a tremendous amount of information, so educating your users on the importance of proper trash disposal is critical. Disks or hard drives containing company information should be formatted with "disk-cleaning" software that writes binary 0s on all portions of the disks. This formatting should be done at least seven times to ensure that all previous data is unreadable. Old computer manuals should be discarded offsite so that dumpster divers can't associate the manuals with the company. Before disposal, all these items should be placed in a locked room with adequate physical, administrative, and technical safeguards. All documents should be shredded, even if the information seems innocuous. Social engineers know how to pull together information from many different sources. Putting a puzzle together from many small pieces makes it possible for attackers to break into a network.

The Art of Piggybacking

Sometimes security testers need to enter part of a building that's restricted to authorized personnel. In this case, a tester or an attacker uses a technique called **piggybacking**. Piggybacking is trailing closely behind an employee who has access to an area without the person realizing you didn't use a PIN or a security badge to enter the area. Those skilled in piggybacking watch authorized personnel enter secure areas and wait for the opportune time to join them quickly at the security entrance. They count on human nature and the desire of others to be polite and hold open a secured door. This ploy usually works, especially if the piggybacker has both hands full and seems to be struggling to remove an access card from a purse or pants pocket. Some piggybackers wear a fake badge around their necks or pretend to scan a security card across a card reader. If they're detected, they might say their card has been giving them problems and use their social-engineering skills to convince the security guard to let them through.

A good preventive measure against piggybacking is using turnstiles at areas where piggybacking can occur. However, the best preventive measure is to train personnel to notify security when they notice a stranger in a restricted area. Employees must feel a vested interest in area security and should not rely on security personnel. Employees should be taught not to hold secured doors open for anyone, even people they know. Educate your users to get in the habit of making sure all employees use their access cards to gain entry into a restricted area and to report any suspicious or unknown people to security.

Security Bytes

A well-dressed security tester walked into a hospital with a laptop and sat down in the waiting area next to the nurses' station. He **NOTE** was able to access passwords and logon information on his laptop and collected data for more than a week without being questioned by security or hospital personnel. In fact, the security tester felt as though he was invisible. Doctors, nurses, administrators, and other hospital personnel never questioned the presence of the stranger in their midst, even though he had covered most of the waiting room table with legal pads and his laptop. After the security test was completed, it was determined that everyone thought the stranger was working for someone else in the area. No one felt responsible for finding out who the stranger was and why he was there.

Activity 4-7: Learning Piggybacking Skills

Time Required: 30 minutes

Objective: Learn how piggybacking can be used to gain access to restricted areas.

Description: In this activity, you learn the piggybacking skills used to gain access to areas restricted to authorized personnel. Assume you're conducting a security test and need access to a company's server room. To enter the room, you must scan an access card over a card reader, and then push open a door within several seconds, during which time a bell rings softly. If the door isn't opened in the allotted time, the card must be swiped again. Form teams of two and demonstrate to the class how you would use piggybacking to get into the classroom if it was secured. One student should pretend to be an authorized user while the other student uses piggybacking techniques to gain entry. Have a class discussion about these attempts, and note which one was the most successful.

Phishing

Almost everyone with an e-mail address has received a **phishing** e-mail at some point. "Update your account details" is a typical subject line. The message is usually framed as an urgent request to visit a Web site to make sure you're not locked out of an account, such as your online banking service. The Web site is a fake, but if you're tricked into giving out your personal account data, the money you lose is real. Figure 4-12 shows an actual phishing e-mail purportedly from PayPal. One clue that the e-mail isn't legitimate is that the recipient is addressed by the generic "Dear Customer" instead of his or her name.

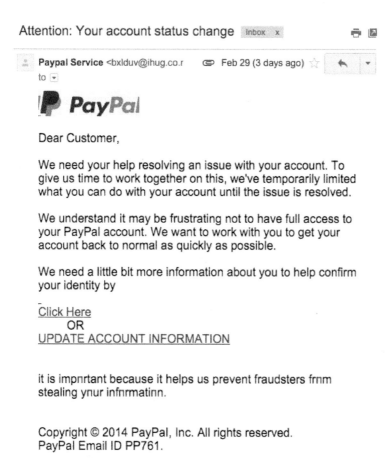

4

Figure 4-12   A phishing e-mail

What's potentially more dangerous to companies is **spear phishing,** another attack carried out by e-mail that combines social engineering with exploiting vulnerabilities. Attackers have used spear phishing to steal millions of dollars. Unlike phishing, this attack is directed at specific people in an organization and uses social engineering based on previous reconnaissance data to hook victims. A spear phishing e-mail might appear to come from a sender the recipient knows and mention topics of mutual interest. The goal is to entice victims into opening an attachment or clicking a link; this action installs the "spear phished" malware, which can have devastating effects on an organization's network. Some security consulting companies incorporate spear phishing attacks as part of their testing, using tools that can inject shell code into Adobe PDF files. One example of these tools is Metasploit (included on the Kali Linux DVD and discussed in Chapter 7). These tools make the technical engineering of a spear phishing attack so easy a caveman could do it. E-mail authentication technologies—such as Sender Policy Framework, DomainKeys Identified Mail, S/MIME, and PGP—as well as security awareness training for users and constant vigilance help reduce the threat of phishing and spear phishing.

Chapter Summary

- Footprinting is the process of gathering network information with Web tools and utilities. Web tools for gathering information about a network infrastructure include Whois, Namedroppers, and Google.

- Corporate information can be gathered by using competitive intelligence gained through observation and Web tools.

- IP addresses and domain names can be found by using tools such as Domain Dossier and the `dig` command.

- Security testers must be aware of how cookies and Web bugs can be used to retrieve information and access data without a user's knowledge.

- Zone transfers can be used to get information about a network's topology and view all the network's host computers and domains.

- Social engineering is the ability to use an understanding of human nature to get information from unsuspecting people.

- Social engineers use many methods to convince users to give them information, such as creating a false sense of urgency, pretending to have a position of authority, being kind and friendly, offering something in return for complying with the request, or giving the impression that everyone else has complied with the request.

- Educating company personnel about social-engineering attacks is important, but random testing can also be done to ensure that employees are following company policies.

- Attackers use techniques such as shoulder surfing, dumpster diving, piggybacking, and phishing to gather confidential information.

Key Terms

competitive intelligence	phishing	spidering (or crawling)
cookie	piggybacking	spear phishing
dumpster diving	shoulder surfing	Web bug
footprinting	social engineering	zone transfer

Review Questions

1. Which of the following is a fast and easy way to gather information about a company? (Choose all that apply.)

   a. Conduct port scanning.

   b. Perform a zone transfer of the company's DNS server.

   c. View the company's Web site.

   d. Look for company ads in phone directories.

2. To find information about the key IT personnel responsible for a company's domain, you might use which of the following tools? (Choose all that apply.)

   a. Whois

   b. Whatis

   c. Domain Dossier

   d. Nbtstat

3. _____ is one of the components most vulnerable to network attacks.

   a. TCP/IP

   b. WINS

   c. DHCP

   d. DNS

4. Which of the following contains host records for a domain?

   a. DNS

   b. WINS

   c. Linux server

   d. UNIX Web clients

5. Which of the following is a good Web site for gathering information on a domain?

   a. *www.google.com*

   b. *www.namedroppers.com*

   c. *http://centralops.net/co/*

   d. *www.arin.net*

   e. All of the above

6. A cookie can store information about a Web site's visitors. True or False?

7. Which of the following enables you to view all host computers on a network?

   a. SOA

   b. `ipconfig`

   c. Zone transfers

   d. `HTTP HEAD` method

8. What's one way to gather information about a domain?

   a. View the header of an e-mail you send to an e-mail account that doesn't exist.

   b. Use the `ipconfig` command.

   c. Use the `ifconfig` command.

   d. Connect via Telnet to TCP port 53.

9. Which of the following is one method of gathering information about the operating systems a company is using?

   a. Search the Web for e-mail addresses of IT employees.

   b. Connect via Telnet to the company's Web server.

   c. Ping the URL and analyze ICMP messages.

   d. Use the `ipconfig /os` command.

10. To determine a company's primary DNS server, you can look for a DNS server containing which of the following?

    a. Cname record

    b. Host record

    c. PTR record

    d. SOA record

11. When conducting competitive intelligence, which of the following is a good way to determine the size of a company's IT support staff?

    a. Review job postings on Web sites such as *www.monster.com* or *www.dice.com*.

    b. Use the `nslookup` command.

    c. Perform a zone transfer of the company's DNS server.

    d. Use the `host -t` command.

12. If you're trying to find newsgroup postings by IT employees of a certain company, which of the following Web sites should you visit?

    a. *http://groups.google.com*

    b. *www.google.com*

    c. *www.samspade.com*

    d. *www.arin.org*

13. Which of the following tools can assist you in finding general information about an organization and its employees? (Choose all that apply.)

    a. *www.google.com*

    b. *http://groups.google.com*

    c. `netcat`

    d. `nmap`

14. What's the first method a security tester should attempt to find a password for a computer on the network?

    a. Use a scanning tool.

    b. Install a sniffer on the network.

    c. Ask the user.

    d. Install a password-cracking program.

15. Many social engineers begin gathering the information they need by using which of the following?

    a. The Internet

    b. The telephone

    c. A company Intranet

    d. E-mail

16. Discovering a user's password by observing the keys he or she presses is called which of the following?

    a. Password hashing

    b. Password crunching

    c. Piggybacking

    d. Shoulder surfing

17. Shoulder surfers can use their skills to find which of the following pieces of information? (Choose all that apply.)

    a. Passwords

    b. ATM PINs

    c. Long-distance access codes

    d. Open port numbers

18. Entering a company's restricted area by following closely behind an authorized person is referred to as which of the following?

    a. Shoulder surfing

    b. Piggybacking

    c. False entering

    d. Social engineering

19. What social-engineering technique involves telling an employee that you're calling from the CEO's office and need certain information ASAP? (Choose all that apply.)

    a. Urgency

    b. Status quo

    c. Position of authority

    d. Quid pro quo

20. Before conducting a security test by using social-engineering tactics, what should you do?

    a. Set up an appointment.

    b. Document all findings.

    c. Get written permission from the person who hired you to conduct the security test.

    d. Get written permission from the department head.

4

Case Projects

Case Project 4-1: Using an E-mail Address to Determine a Network's Operating System

Alexander Rocco Corporation has multiple OSs running in its many offices. Before conducting a security test to determine the vulnerabilities you need to correct, you want to determine whether any OSs are running that you're not aware of. Christy Fitzgerald, the network administrator/security officer, is resistant to giving you information after he learns you're there to discover network security vulnerabilities. He sees you as a threat to his position. After several hours of interviews, you can ascertain only that Mike's personal e-mail address is *vetman2601@gmail.com*, and an old RHEL server is running on one of the company's systems. Based on this information, answer the following questions:

1. What tools might you use after learning Mike's e-mail address?

2. What can you determine by entering Mike's e-mail address into Google? What about just the handle "vetman2601"?

3. Could the information you learned from Google be used to conduct vulnerability testing?

Write a memo to the IT manager, Bob Jones, about the potential issues with running a old RHEL 5.8 server, and mention the importance of patch hygiene. Make sure your memo explains how you gathered this information and offers constructive feedback. Your memo shouldn't point a finger at any company employees; it should discuss problems on a general level.

Case Project 4-2: Using Dumpster-Diving Skills

You have observed that Alexander Rocco Corporation uses Alika's Cleaning Company for its janitorial services. The company's floors are vacuumed and mopped each night, and the trash is collected in large bins placed outside for pickup on Tuesdays and Fridays. You decide to visit the dumpster Thursday evening after the cleaning crew leaves. Wearing surgical gloves and carrying a large plastic sheet, you place as much of the trash on the sheet as possible. Sorting through the material, you find the following items: a company phone directory; a Windows NT training kit; 23 outdated Oracle magazines; notes that appear to be programs written in HTML, containing links to a SQL Server database; 15 company memos from key employees; food wrappers; an empty bottle of expensive vodka; torn copies of several resumes; an unopened box of new business cards; and an old pair of women's running shoes.

Based on this information, write a two-page report explaining the relevance these items have. What recommendations, if any, might you give to Alexander Rocco management?

## chapter 5

Port Scanning

After reading this chapter and completing the exercises, you will be able to:

- Describe port scanning and types of port scans
- Describe port-scanning tools
- Explain what ping sweeps are used for
- Explain how shell scripting is used to automate security tasks

Port scanning, also referred to as service scanning, is the process of examining a range of IP addresses to determine what services are running on a network. As you learned in Chapter 2, open ports on a computer can identify the services running on it. For example, HTTP uses port 80 to connect to a Web service. Instead of pinging each IP address in a range of addresses and waiting for an ICMP Echo Reply (type 0) to see whether a computer can be reached, you can use scanning tools to simplify this procedure. After all, pinging several thousand IP addresses manually is time consuming.

Port-scanning tools can be complex, so you need to devote time to learning their strengths and weaknesses and understanding how and when you should use these tools. In this chapter, you look at port-scanning tools that enable you to identify services running on a network and use this knowledge to conduct a security test. In addition, you see how to use shell scripting to automate ping sweeps and other security-testing tasks.

Introduction to Port Scanning

In Chapter 4, you performed a zone transfer with the `dig` command to determine a network's IP addresses. Suppose the zone transfer indicates that a company is using a subnetted Class C address with 126 available host IP addresses. How do you verify whether all these addresses are being used by computers that are up and running? You use a port scanner to ping the range of IP addresses you discovered.

A more important question a security tester should ask is "What services are running on the computers that were identified?" **Port scanning** is a method of finding out which services a host computer offers. For example, if a server is hosting a Web site, is it likely that the server has port 80 open? Are any of the services vulnerable to attacks or exploits? Are any services not being filtered by a firewall, thus making it possible to load a Trojan program that can send information from the attacked computer? Which computer is most vulnerable to an attack? You already know how to search for known vulnerabilities by using the Common Vulnerabilities and Exposures (*www.cve.mitre.org*) and US-CERT (*www.us-cert.gov*) Web sites. There are also port-scanning tools that identify vulnerabilities—for example, Angry IP Scanner (*angryip.org*), a free port scanner with a GUI interface (see Figure 5-1). Using this tool, an attacker can quickly identify an open port and then launch an exploit to attack the system.

## chapter 6

Enumeration

After reading this chapter and completing the exercises, you will be able to:

- Describe the enumeration step of security testing
- Enumerate Windows OS targets and services
- Enumerate *nix OS targets and services

Enumeration takes port scanning to the next level. Now that you know how to discover live systems on a network, the next steps are finding what resources are shared on the systems, discovering logon accounts and passwords, and gaining access to network resources. Enumeration involves connecting to a remote system, not just identifying that a system is present on a network. Hackers aren't satisfied with knowing that computer systems are running on a network; their goals are to find live systems and gain access to them. For security testers, enumeration is a more intrusive part of testing, and not having permission from the network's owner for this step could result in being charged with a criminal offense. Make sure to have a Rules of Engagement (ROE) in place to clearly define what actions you will be taking, and make sure to get written permission. In this step, you attempt to retrieve information and gain access to servers by using company employees' logon accounts. Knowledge of operating systems and how they store information can be helpful in enumeration. Not knowing how shares or file permissions are handled in Windows and Linux can make accessing information and finding possible vulnerabilities more difficult. In this chapter, you learn some basics of various OSs and the tools for enumerating them. Some of these tools have been covered previously and some are new, but they make enumeration as easy as entering a single command or clicking a button.

Introduction to Enumeration

In previous chapters, you have seen how to perform a zone transfer, use the `dig` command, and discover what computers are live on a network. The next step in security testing is **enumeration**, the process of extracting the following information from a network:

- Resources or shares on the network
- Network topology and architecture
- Usernames or groups assigned on the network
- Information about users and recent logon times

To determine what resources or shares are on a network, security testers must use port scanning and footprinting first to determine what OS is used. If a network is running a Windows OS, for example, testers can use specific tools to view shares and possibly access resources. As mentioned, enumeration is more intrusive because you're not just identifying a resource; you're attempting to access it. It goes beyond passive scanning of a network to find open ports. For example, sometimes this process entails guessing passwords after determining a username. In Activity 6-1, you use NBTscan ("NBT" means NetBIOS over TCP/IP), a tool for enumerating Windows OSs that's part of the Kali Linux suite of security tools.

 In some of this chapter's activities, you work with a partner so that one partner boots into Windows and the other boots into Linux with the Kali Linux DVD. The reason for doing this is to have some **NOTE** Windows computers running in the classroom so that the enumeration tools you're working with can find systems to enumerate. NetBIOS doesn't run on Linux by default.

Activity 6-1: Using the NBTscan Tool

Time Required: 5 minutes

Objective: Learn how to use the NBTscan tool.

Description: In this activity, you work with a partner and use the NBTscan tool to find systems running NetBIOS.

1. Discuss with your partner and decide which one will boot into Windows and which one will boot into Linux with the Kali Linux DVD.

2. Open a Terminal shell, type **nbtscan -h | less,** and press **Enter** to view the help page. Using this information, enter the NBTscan command to scan a range of IP addresses on your network and see whether any computers are identified. Can you identify your partner's Windows computer in the output? Figure 6-1 shows an example of output from the NBTscan command. Note the computers with NetBIOS names. The command also reveals the computers' MAC addresses.

```
                                    root@kali: ~                          ⊖  ◻  ⊗
File  Edit  View  Search  Terminal  Help
root@kali:~# sudo nbtscan 192.168.185.0/24 -r
Doing NBT name scan for addresses from 192.168.185.0/24

IP address          NetBIOS Name      Server    User            MAC address
------------------------------------------------------------------------------
192.168.185.0    Sendto failed: Permission denied
192.168.185.129  WIN-1PT0UL5NKFB  <server>  <unknown>      00:0c:29:97:cc:a7
192.168.185.155  EHSRV            <server>  <unknown>      00:0c:29:8f:d0:f6
192.168.185.183  <unknown>                  <unknown>
192.168.185.255  Sendto failed: Permission denied
root@kali:~#
```

Figure 6-1   NBTscan finds computers running NetBIOS

3. Shutdown Kali Linux and boot into Windows. Your partner should boot into Linux with the Kali Linux DVD and do Steps 1 and 2.

4. If necessary, shutdown Linux and boot into Windows for the next activity.

Enumerating Windows Operating Systems

To understand how an attacker might gain access to resources or shares on a Windows network, in this section you take a brief look at Windows OSs. Chapter 8 delves into more detail on Microsoft attacks; this chapter focuses on the Windows OS as it relates to enumeration. By default, very little information can be enumerated from Window's systems after Windows 7. Table 6-1 describes Windows OSs from Windows 95 to Windows 10.

Windows OS version	Description
Windows 95	The first Microsoft GUI product that didn't rely on DOS, Windows 95 was the beginning of plug and play and the ActiveX standard used in all Windows versions today. A major enhancement was the Registry, a database storing information about the system's hardware and software. Previously, this information was stored in files. Windows 95 ran on stand-alone and networked computers and used the FAT16 file system. Version OSR2 added support for FAT32.
Windows 98 and Me	More stable than their predecessors, with an improved file system (FAT32), new hardware support, and better backup and recovery tools. The enumeration process for Windows Me is the same as for Windows 98.
Windows NT 3.51 Server/Workstation	Created with security and enhancement of network functionality in mind. Emphasized domains instead of workgroups and used the client/server model instead of peer-to-peer networks; the server was responsible for authenticating users and giving them access to network resources. The client/server model also allowed having many computers in a domain instead of the limited number of computers in a workgroup. NTFS replaced FAT16 and FAT32 because of the difficulty in incorporating security in these file systems. NTFS included file-level security features not possible in FAT.
Windows NT 4.0 Server/Workstation	These upgrades to Windows NT 3.51 had improved GUIs and performance.
Windows 2000 Server/Professional	In this upgrade to NT, Microsoft included Active Directory (AD) for object storage. AD was more scalable than other available solutions for managing large networks. It used Lightweight Directory Access Protocol (LDAP), which is still in use today. Also, this update included the first version of Microsoft Management Console (MMC) and Encrypted File System (EFS). Enumeration of these OSs includes enumerating Active Directory.
Windows XP Professional	Included Windows 2000 features, such as standards-based security, improved manageability, and the MMC. In addition, Windows XP had an improved user interface and better plug-and-play support. Security improvements in the kernel data structures made them read only to prevent rogue applications from affecting the OS core, and Windows File Protection was added to prevent overwriting core system files. With Service Pack 2 (SP2), security was improved further with features such as Data Execution Prevention (DEP) and a firewall that's enabled by default. DEP fixed a security exposure caused by vulnerable running services that hackers often use for buffer overflow attacks, and the firewall made it more difficult for hackers to exploit Windows service vulnerabilities and enumerate shares and services. In fact, enumeration of Windows XP SP2 and later systems can be difficult without modifying the configuration. Disabling the Windows Firewall is common in corporate networks, but this practice gives hackers additional attack surface. In these environments, the enumeration processes used for earlier Windows versions still work much the same way in Windows XP Professional.
Windows Server 2003	Windows Server 2003 included improvements over Windows 2000 in some security areas, such as Internet Information Services (IIS), and came in four editions. Generally, all editions included Remote Desktop, load balancing, VPN support, management services (such as Windows Management Instrumentation [WMI]), and .NET application services. The higher-end editions offered better support for PKI, certificate services, and Active Directory as well as enhancements to reliability, scalability, manageability, and security. Again, even with improvements in security and stability, enumeration techniques described for other Windows versions are effective with Windows Server 2003.

Table 6-1   Windows OS descriptions

Windows OS version	Description
Windows Vista	Vista comes in several editions and is the first Windows version to introduce User Account Control (UAC) and built-in full drive encryption, called BitLocker (available in Vista Enterprise and Ultimate editions). UAC allows running Vista in nonprivileged mode to prevent unwanted code or user actions from damaging or controlling the computer (maliciously or inadvertently). However, UAC has been widely criticized because of its intrusive security prompts that force many users to disable it. In Windows 7, you can configure the frequency of these prompts. Also introduced in this release was Address Space Layout Randomization (ASLR), which makes exploitation of overflow-type vulnerabilities much more difficult. By default, Vista in a stand-alone environment can be difficult to enumerate without modifying its configuration.
Windows Server 2008	Features security options similar to Vista, including BitLocker drive encryption and UAC. Vista and Windows Server 2008 support Network Access Protection (NAP), which reduces the possibility of rogue systems being able to access network resources. Features, services, and roles in Windows Server 2008 can be fine-tuned to meet specific needs. A command-line version that requires fewer resources, called Server Core, is available for certain server roles. This version is designed to reduce maintenance, use of resources, and the "attack surface." Hyper-V, a full-featured virtualization product, is included with Windows Server 2008 and allows installing guest OSs, such as Linux and other Windows versions.
Windows 7	Builds on the security advances made in Vista with the introduction of AppLocker, which allows for control over application execution. The inclusion of the Action Center in Windows 7 allows users to view potential configuration in one simple interface. Other improvements include refinements to the UAC feature and Windows Defender, which protects the system from known spyware.
Windows 8.1	Boasting "ground breaking malware resistance," Windows 8.1 comes with features that make user-level infection much less dangerous by limiting the privileges of basic users. In addition, Windows 8.1 includes a number of heap integrity checks designed to make exploitation more difficult. Windows Defender was upgraded to a full anti-malware product. SmartScreen extended to the OS to alert when an application is launched on a PC. For the first time, SecureBoot prevents execution of non-trusted boot content, preventing rootkits/bootkits.
Windows Server 2012	With this edition, Microsoft introduced Authentication Silos to prevent pass-the-hash attacks, a major weakness in all earlier versions of Windows servers. It also includes enhanced support for Domain Name System Security Extensions (DNSSEC), which relies on digital signatures to prove zone ownership.
Windows 10	Designed for use on tablets and traditional PCs, Windows 10 can be found in more places than ever. Numerous security enhancements were brought to Windows 10. One of the more progressive enhancements is that it only allows trusted apps by default through Device Guard. It also added Credential Guard, which uses virtualization to protect access tokens from theft by attackers.
Windows Server 2016	(Please note that the features discussed here are based on a Beta version.) Windows Server 2016 features a number of security upgrades. The most important, Windows Containers, allows for application isolation to protect applications from one another. Windows Defender (malware protection) is now enabled by default. In this version, the option for telnet server is eliminated completely (telnet client is still available). A feature named Just Enough Administration (JEA) allows for more granular access control settings on tasks.

Table 6-1 **Windows OS descriptions (*continued*)**

6

 Many of the enumeration techniques that work with older Windows OSs still work with the newer versions.

NetBIOS Basics

Before learning how to enumerate Microsoft systems, you need to review the basics of how **Network Basic Input/Output System (NetBIOS)** works. NetBIOS is a Windows programming interface that allows computers to communicate across a local area network (LAN). Most Windows OSs use NetBIOS to share files and printers. NetBIOS listens on UDP ports 137 (NetBIOS Name service) and 138 (NetBIOS Datagram service) and TCP port 139 (NetBIOS Session service). File and printer sharing in Windows also requires an upper-level service called Server Message Block (SMB), which runs on top of NetBIOS. In Windows 2000 and later, SMB listens on TCP port 445 and doesn't need to use NetBIOS over TCP/IP unless support for older Windows versions is required.

The computer names you assign to Windows systems are called NetBIOS names and have a limit of 16 characters; the last character is reserved for a hexadecimal number (00 to FF) that identifies the service running on the computer. Therefore, you can use only 15 characters for a computer name, and NetBIOS adds the last character automatically to identify the service that has registered with the OS. For example, if a computer is running the Server service, the OS stores this information in a NetBIOS table.

A NetBIOS name must be unique on a network. Table 6-2 lists the NetBIOS suffixes that correspond to the services, or resource types, running on a computer. You don't need to memorize all these suffixes, but note that some identify the computer or server being enumerated as

NetBIOS name	Suffix	Description
<computer name>	00	The Workstation service registered the computer name (also called the NetBIOS name).
<computer name>	20	Registered by the Server service. A computer must have this service running to share printers or files.
<computer name>	22	Registered by the Microsoft Exchange Interchange service.
<computer name>	23	Registered by the Microsoft Exchange Store service. A store is where mailboxes and public folders are stored.
<computer name>	24	Registered by the Microsoft Exchange Directory service.
<computer name>	87	Signifies that Microsoft Exchange Message Transfer Agent (MTA) is running on this computer.
<domain name>	00	Indicates that Domain Name System (DNS) is running.
<domain name>	1C	Identifies the computer as a domain controller.
<iNet~Services>	1C	Indicates that IIS is running.
<IS~computer name>	00	Also indicates that IIS is running.

Table 6-2   Important NetBIOS names and suffixes

a stand-alone computer or domain controller. Hackers often exert more effort to attack computers identified as domain controllers because these systems store more information, including logon names for user accounts and network resources. A more comprehensive list of NetBIOS suffixes can be found in this book's appendices.

NetBIOS Null Sessions

Historically, one of the biggest vulnerabilities of NetBIOS systems is a **null session,** which is an unauthenticated connection to a Windows computer that uses no logon and password values. Many of the enumeration tools covered in this chapter establish a null session to gather information such as logon accounts, group membership, and file shares from an attacked computer. This vulnerability has been around for more than a decade and is still present in Windows XP. Null sessions have been disabled by default in Windows Server 2003, although administrators can enable them if they're needed for some reason. In Windows Vista and Server 2008, null sessions aren't available and can't be enabled, even by administrators.

NetBIOS Enumeration Tools

The Nbtstat command is a powerful enumeration tool included with Windows. To display the NetBIOS table, you issue the nbtstat -a *IPaddress* command. (If you want to run Nbtstat locally, the command is nbtstat -s.) Figure 6-2 shows the entry WDSGDC101 <20>. The 20 represents the Server service running on the WDSGDC101 computer. The NetBIOS table also shows that DC1 is a domain controller, as indicated by the 1C suffix.

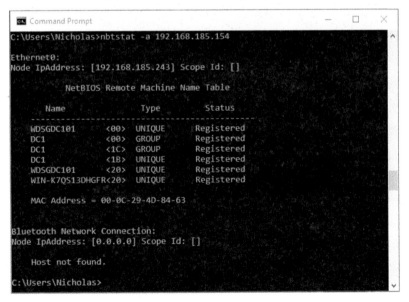

Figure 6-2 Using the Nbtstat command

Another built-in Windows tool is the `net view` command, which gives you a quick way to see whether there are any shared resources on a computer or server. To see the syntax for this command, type `net view ?`. Using the `net view` command, an attacker can view remote shares, as shown in Figure 6-3.

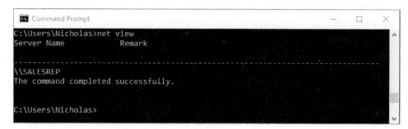

Figure 6-3   Using the `Net view` command

You can also use the IP address of computers you discovered with port-scanning tools. For example, Figure 6-4 shows the command used on a remote Windows 10 computer. A share name called EMPPASSWORDS is displayed. The next command an attacker could use against this computer is `\\SALESREP\emppasswords` to explore the share drive and look for passwords.

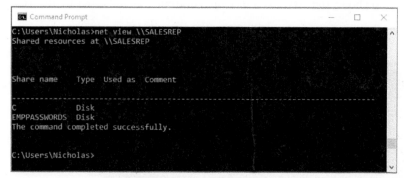

Figure 6-4   Using the `Net view` command with a hostname

Although you can download or buy enumeration tools, you should learn how to take advantage of the tools available in Windows. A simple command-line utility can give you the name of a logged-on user, and a guess of that user's password can give you access to the system quickly. Many password-cracking programs can determine a password in a matter of seconds. The Department of Defense uses one called L0phtcrack. (You can download a free trial version at *www.l0phtcrack.com/download.html.*) However, security testers can often guess passwords without needing a special program because some users are careless when creating passwords. For example, many users, despite guidelines in company security policies, use simple passwords, such as "password" or "p@$$w0rd."

Activity 6-2: Using Built-in Windows NetBIOS Tools

Time Required: 30 minutes

Objective: Learn to use the Windows `Nbtstat`, `Net view`, and `Net use` commands.

Description: In this activity, you work with a partner to examine the Windows tools for viewing NetBIOS services and shares. After using the `Nbtstat` command to discover a network computer or server that's sharing a resource, you use the `Net view` and `Net use` commands to enumerate these shared resources and possibly access them from your computer.

1. Start your computer and log on to Windows, if necessary.

2. Right-click **Start** and go to the **File Explorer.** Choose **This PC** from the list on the left, double-click **Local Disk (C:),** and then click the **Home** tab on the top; point to **New Folder.** Type *YourFirstName* for the folder name and press **Enter.**

3. Right-click the folder you just created and point to **Share with** and click on **Specific people.** In the Properties dialog box, type **Everyone,** click **Add** check box, and then click **Share.**

4. Open a command prompt window, and then type **ipconfig** and press **Enter.** Write down your IP address and tell it to your partner.

5. Next, type **net view ***Partner'sIPaddress* and press **Enter.** What does the command produce as output?

6. You use the `Net use` command to connect to a computer containing shared folders or files. To see the information this command returns, type **net use ?** and press **Enter.** Your screen should look like Figure 6-5.

```
C:\Users\Nicholas>net use ?
The syntax of this command is:

NET USE
[devicename | *] [\\computername\sharename[\volume] [password | *]]
        [/USER:[domainname\]username]
        [/USER:[dotted domain name\]username]
        [/USER:[username@dotted domain name]
        [/SMARTCARD]
        [/SAVECRED]
        [[/DELETE] | [/PERSISTENT:{YES | NO}]]

NET USE {devicename | *} [password | *] /HOME

NET USE [/PERSISTENT:{YES | NO}]

C:\Users\Nicholas>
```

Figure 6-5 Viewing help for the **Net use** command

7. Next, type **net use ***Partner'sIPaddress\Partner'sSharedFolder* and press **Enter.** What are the results of this command?

8. At the command prompt, type **nbtstat -a** *Partner'sIPaddress* and press **Enter**. What are the results of this command?

9. Close all open windows, and decide which partner will boot with Kali Linux for the next activity.

Additional Enumeration Tools

As you have seen, several built-in Windows tools can assist you in enumerating NetBIOS systems. In the following activity, you examine some additional tools for this task.

Activity 6-3: Using Windows Enumeration Tools

Time Required: 30 minutes

Objective: Learn to use Windows network mapping and enumeration tools.

Description: In this activity, you explore and test some Windows enumeration tools included with Kali Linux. As in Activity 6-1, one partner keeps his or her computer booted into Windows, and the other boots with Kali Linux.

1. Boot your computer into Linux with the Kali Linux DVD.

2. Open a **Terminal** window and type **enum4linux –h** to view the usage details for enum4linux. Now, use the tool to enumerate your partner's Windows shares: Type **enum4linux -S** *Partner'sIPaddress*. The results should be similar to what is shown in Figure 6-6. If enum4linux fails to enumerate shares, it might be that Windows 10 now disables guest access to list shares remotely by default. If you have an older version of Windows, you will probably see results. If Activity 6-2 worked, your partner's computer was probably added to the "HomeGroup." You should do a quick Internet search to understand more about Windows "HomeGroup." We can see that modern versions of Windows hardly give us any information back! This tool is much more effective against older versions of Windows.

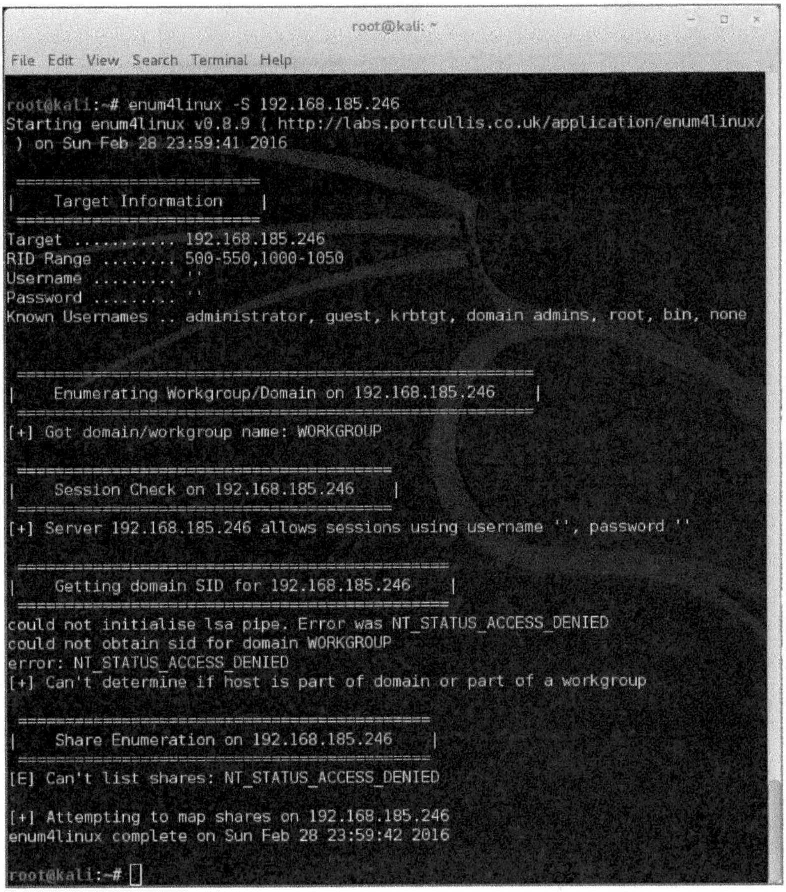

Figure 6-6   enum4linux's results

3. Click the **Applications** button and **Information Gathering** to see other available tools (see Figure 6-7).

Figure 6-7   Kali information-gathering tools

4. Spend a few minutes exploring the functions of some of these tools. Don't hesitate to experiment or search the Internet for more information. Besides enum4linux and NMap, are any other tools suited for enumerating Windows systems?

5. Switch computers with your partner, and the one who ran Windows previously should perform this activity. When you're finished, make sure both computers are booted into Linux with the Kali Linux DVD for the next activity.

DumpSec DumpSec is a popular enumeration tool for Windows NT, 2000, and XP systems. It is produced by Foundstone, Inc. and can be downloaded from *www.system tools.com*. The information you can gather with this tool is astonishing. For example, after connecting to a Windows server, you can download—or, as it's called in DumpSec, "dump"—the following information:

- Permissions for shares
- Permissions for printers
- Permissions for the Registry

- Users in column or table format
- Policies (such as local, domain, and group policies)
- Rights
- Services

Hyena Hyena, available at *www.systemtools.com*, is an excellent GUI tool for managing and securing Windows OSs. The interface is easy to use and gives security professionals a wealth of information.

With just a click, you can look at the shares and user logon names for Windows servers and domain controllers. If any domains or workgroups are on the network, this tool displays them, too. Hyena can also display a graphical representation of the following areas:

- Microsoft Terminal Services
- Microsoft Windows Network
- Web Client Network
- Find User/Groups

Nessus and OpenVAS (aka Greenbone Security Assistant) Chapter 5 introduced the OpenVAS, or Greenbone Security Assistant (GSA), tool. GSA operates in client/server mode and is the open-source descendant of Nessus, a popular tool for identifying vulnerabilities. Both OpenVAS and Nessus are discussed in this section. Nessus and OpenVAS are both compatible with and easy to install on Kali Linux. You can download the latest Nessus version for Windows, Linux, Mac OS X, and FreeBSD at *www.tenable.com* free for personal, noncommercial use. OpenVAS installation instructions for Kali Linux can be found at *https://www.kali.org/penetration-testing/openvas-vulnerability-scanning/*. Although Nessus is discussed often in this book, you can use Nessus or OpenVAS interchangeably for most purposes when enumerating systems. For example, Figure 6-8 shows OpenVAS reporting a list of software and versions from a remote windows host.

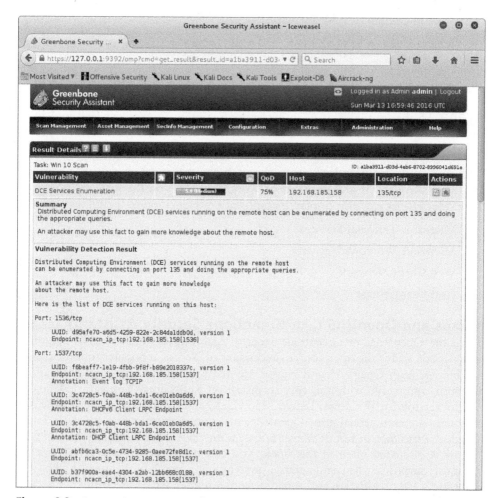

Figure 6-8   OpenVAS enumerates software and versions on a remote host

Even though you aren't using Nessus in activities, seeing examples of how the tool is used is important because it's used in almost every company—both public and private sectors—conducting security testing. The latest version of Nessus Server and Client can run on Windows, Mac OS X, FreeBSD, and most Linux distributions. Nessus is easy to install and takes just minutes to configure. This tool can come in handy when you need to enumerate different OSs on a large network.

Nessus is now only available via a Web interface via port 8834. Browsing to the Nessus Web interface and authenticating brings up the Scans page shown in Figure 6-9. On this screen, you create, edit, and delete scans. If you click the New Scan button, you can select a scan template that is suitable for your goals.

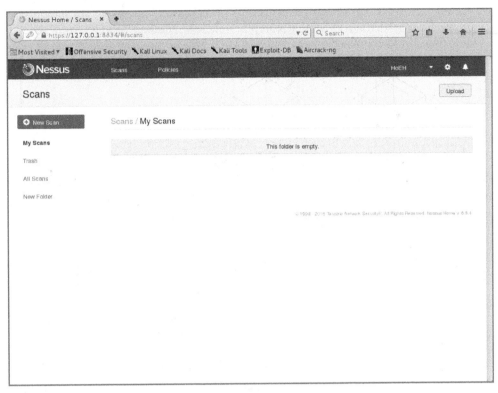

Figure 6-9   The Nessus Scans page

In Figure 6-10, the previously saved session HoEH_Lab.nessus is selected.

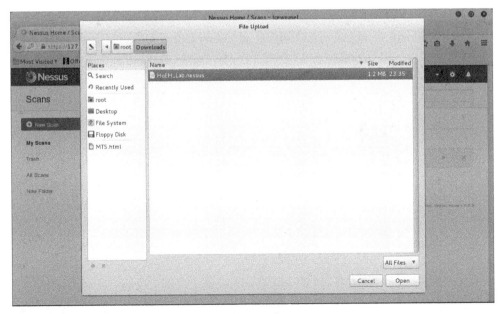

Figure 6-10   Opening a previously saved Nessus session

The next several figures show Nessus in action. Figure 6-11 shows six NetBIOS names that Nessus has gathered, indicating computer names, running services, and so forth. Nessus identifies the computer name as WIN-1PT0UL5NKFB and the workgroup or domain name as WORKGROUP. This information could be useful for later attacks.

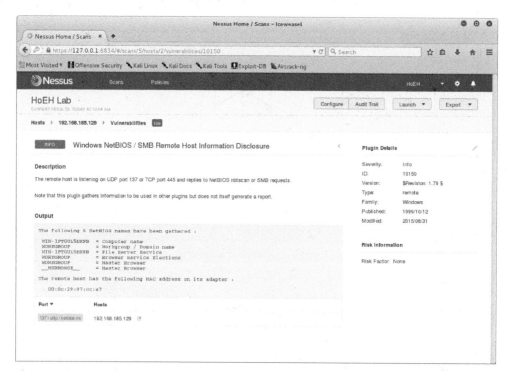

Figure 6-11   Nessus enumerates a NetBIOS system

The Windows computer that Nessus is enumerating indicates a security problem: The EMPPASSWORDS share can be accessed (see Figure 6-12). Hackers can see that this share contains a file called passwords.txt, meaning it probably contains employee passwords—useful information for launching an attack.

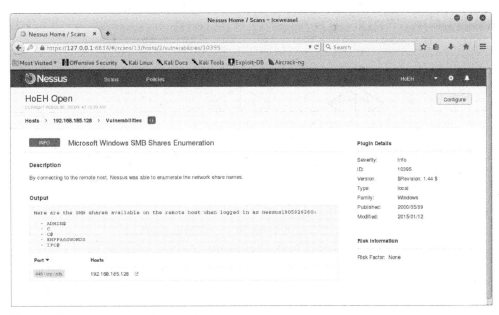

Figure 6-12   Enumerating shares in Nessus

Nessus is also helpful in identifying the OS and service pack running on a computer. Figure 6-13 shows that the system with the IP address 192.168.185.128 is running Windows 10 installed. Nessus does more than just enumerate Windows OSs, as you see in the following section.

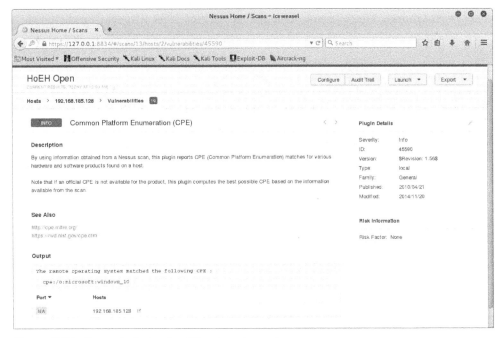

Figure 6-13   Nessus indicates the OS and service pack

Enumerating *nix Operating System

Of the OSs covered in this chapter, UNIX is the oldest. Most computer vendors have developed their own flavors of this popular OS, but because of copyright restrictions (only AT&T can use the name UNIX), they can't use "UNIX" in their product names. Other variations of UNIX include the following:

- Solaris (Sun Microsystems) and OpenSolaris
- HP-UX (Hewlett-Packard)
- Mac OS X and OpenDarwin, based on FreeBSD
- AIX (IBM)
- BSD UNIX (University of California at Berkley)
- FreeBSD (BSD-based UNIX, developed by contributors)
- OpenBSD (BSD-based UNIX, developed by contributors)
- NetBSD (BSD-based UNIX, developed by contributors)
- Linux, including the following distributions:
    - Ubuntu (Debian based, sponsored by Canonical)
    - Kali Linux (Debian based)
    - Red Hat Enterprise Linux (released commercially by Red Hat)
    - Fedora Linux (developed by contributors and sponsored by Red Hat)
    - Debian Linux (developed by contributors)
    - SUSE Linux (Micro Focus) and OpenSUSE
    - Mandriva Linux (distant commercial fork of 1990 Red Hat)
    - Slackware (oldest surviving Linux distribution)

As you can see, many organizations have a UNIX version. Linux, created by Linus Torvalds, is just that: a variation of UNIX originally designed for inexpensive Intel PCs. With all the UNIX variations available, it's no wonder that many computer professionals are using this OS. Recent versions of Linux are easier to install and configure and include GUIs and Web browsers that make the software less complicated to use. With Grand Unified Bootloader (GRUB), you can have your desktop computer or laptop start in both Windows and Linux. Even novice computer users can install the latest version easily. Most Linux distributions have Live CD/DVD or flash versions that you can try without installing them on your hard drive.

*nix Enumeration

An old but still popular network management service for network administrators is **Simple Network Management Protocol (SNMP)**, which enables remote administration. The SNMP service can run on both Windows and *nix, but for this section we will focus on *nix. SNMP is useful for administrators who want to see system statistics, version numbers, and other detailed host information remotely. For this reason, it is also useful for hackers. By default, the SNMP service uses "public" as a credential for read-only access and "private" for read-write access. SNMPWalk is a tool useful in enumerating hosts running SNMP with the default configuration (see Figure 6-14). If attackers know the processor architecture (typically 32-bit or 64-bit) and the detailed version number of the remote operating system, they will have an easier time finding exploits that will be successful. The SNMP daemon (snmpd) listens on UDP port 161.

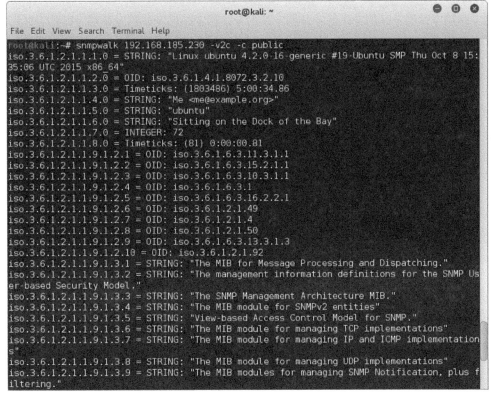

Figure 6-14 Using the SNMPWalk command

Nessus is also helpful in *nix enumeration. Figure 6-15 shows what Nessus found when scanning a Ubuntu 15.10 system.

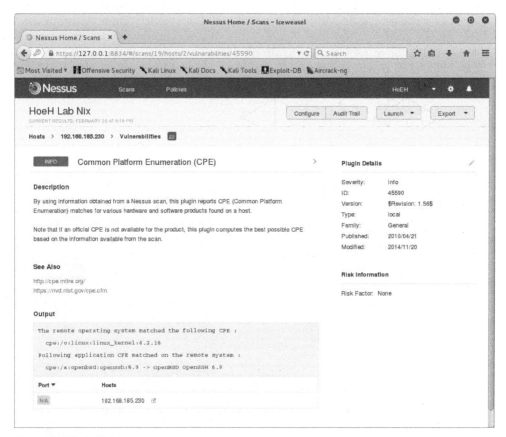

Figure 6-15 Nessus enumerates a Linux system

If you don't have access to Nessus, NMap script scanning can also help an attacker gain information about remote *nix hosts. Figure 6-16 shows what NMap found when scanning a Ubuntu 15.10 system.

```
                            root@kali: ~                    ⊖  ▣  ✕
 File  Edit  View  Search  Terminal  Help
|_   256 fd:5e:87:5b:e0:33:59:c9:75:ea:37:5a:2c:20:66:66 (ECDSA)
MAC Address: 00:0C:29:EB:39:38 (VMware)

Nmap done: 1 IP address (1 host up) scanned in 1.38 seconds
root@kali:~# nmap 192.168.185.230 -sC -sV

Starting Nmap 7.01 ( https://nmap.org ) at 2016-02-29 00:44 EST
Nmap scan report for 192.168.185.230
Host is up (0.00039s latency).
Not shown: 999 closed ports
PORT   STATE SERVICE VERSION
22/tcp open  ssh     OpenSSH 6.9p1 Ubuntu 2ubuntu0.1 (Ubuntu Linux; protocol 2.0
)
| ssh-hostkey:
|   1024 92:d8:90:6b:2d:c7:7a:d1:8d:e6:49:4c:e8:b0:0c:04 (DSA)
|   2048 3b:1f:d2:bf:98:2c:e4:3f:14:35:fe:14:3b:53:3f:c3 (RSA)
|_  256 fd:5e:87:5b:e0:33:59:c9:75:ea:37:5a:2c:20:66:66 (ECDSA)
MAC Address: 00:0C:29:EB:39:38 (VMware)
Service Info: OS: Linux; CPE: cpe:/o:linux:linux_kernel

Service detection performed. Please report any incorrect results at https://nmap
.org/submit/ .
Nmap done: 1 IP address (1 host up) scanned in 1.68 seconds
root@kali:~# █
```

Figure 6-16   NMap script scan enumerates a Linux system

An older but sometimes useful enumeration tool for both security testers and hackers is the Finger utility, which enables you to find out who's logged in to a *nix system with one simple command. Finger is both a client and a server. The Finger daemon (fingerd) listens on TCP port 79.

Activity 6-4: Enumerating *nix Web Servers with NMap

Time Required: 30 minutes

Objective: Learn to use the NMap tool on local and remote *nix systems.

Description: In this activity, you use the NMap command to enumerate your computer and see how this powerful command can gather information from a remote system. You'll also learn how to start and stop services on your local machine.

1. If necessary, boot your computer into Linux with the Kali Linux DVD.

2. For this exercise, we will be enabling a few services that could put your machine at risk if you don't take the proper precautions! Before continuing, you need to change your password by using the command **passwd root**.

3. Most Linux services are started from a series of scripts stored in the directory /etc/init.d/. We can view the contents of this folder with the following command: **ls /etc/init.d/**.

4. Start the ssh and samba services on your local host with the following commands: **/etc/init.d/ssh start** and **/etc/init.d/samba start**.

5. Use Nmap to run a scripted scan of the localhost (127.0.0.1). What results were returned? What version of SSH is your computer running? What version of Samba?

6. Are there any vulnerabilities associated with these versions of SSH or Samba?

7. Use the following commands to stop the services you enabled: **/etc/init.d/sshd stop** and **/etc/init.d/samba stop**. Shut down your Kali Linux computer.

Chapter Summary

- Enumeration is the process of extracting usernames, passwords, and shared resources from a system.

- Enumeration can give an attacker insight into sensitive areas of a network, systems running old software, or even simple misconfigurations that the attacker can take advantage of.

- Enumerating Windows targets can be done with built-in Windows tools, such as the Nbtstat, Net view, and Net use commands, or with a variety of other utilities. Also, other utilities such as enum4linux can enumerate Windows from various versions of *nix. Newer versions of Windows are much more difficult to enumerate because of advances in Windows security over time.

- Enumeration of *nix systems can be done with tools used for enumerating other OSs, such as Nessus and its open-source descendant, OpenVAS.

- SNMP can be used to enumerate both *nix and Windows hosts that are running the SNMP service/daemon with the default configuration.

Key Terms

enum4linux

enumeration

Network Basic Input/Output System (NetBIOS)

null session

Simple Network Management Protocol (SNMP)

Review Questions

1. Which of the following testing processes is the most intrusive?

   a. Port scanning

   b. Enumeration

   c. Null scanning

   d. Numeration

2. Security testers conduct enumeration for which of the following reasons? (Choose all that apply.)

   a. Gaining access to shares and network resources

   b. Obtaining user logon names and group memberships

   c. Discovering services running on computers and servers

   d. Discovering open ports on computers and servers

3. Which of the following tools can be used to enumerate Windows systems? (Choose all that apply.)

   a. OpenVAS or Nessus

   b. Reddit

   c. DumpIt

   d. Hyena

4. Enumeration of Windows systems can be more difficult if port _____ is filtered.

   a. 110/UDP

   b. 443/UDP

   c. 80/TCP

   d. 139/TCP

5. A null session is enabled by default in all the following Windows versions except:

   a. Windows 95

   b. Windows Server 2008

   c. Windows 98

   d. Windows 2000

6. The Net view command can be used to see whether there are any shared resources on a server. True or False?

7. To identify the NetBIOS names of systems on the 193.145.85.0 network, which of the following commands do you use?

   a. nbtscan 193.145.85.0/24

   b. nbtscan 193.145.85.0-255

   c. nbtstat 193.145.85.0/24

   d. netstat 193.145.85.0/24

8. Which of the following is a Windows command-line utility for seeing NetBIOS shares on a network?

   a. Net use

   b. Net user

   c. Net view

   d. Nbtuser

9. The Nbtstat command is used to enumerate *nix systems. True or False?

10. A NetBIOS name can contain a maximum of _____ characters.

   a. 10

   b. 11

   c. 15

   d. 16

11. Which of the following commands connects to a computer containing shared files and folders?

   a. Net view

   b. Net use

   c. Netstat

   d. Nbtstat

12. Which port numbers indicate NetBIOS is in use on a remote target?

   a. 135 to 137

   b. 389 to 1023

   c. 135 to 139

   d. 110 and 115

13. Which of the following is the vulnerability scanner from which OpenVAS was developed?

   a. OpenVAS Pro

   b. Nessus

   c. ISS Scanner

   d. SuperScan

14. Most NetBIOS enumeration tools connect to the target system by using which of the following?

   a. ICMP packets

   b. Default logons and blank passwords

   c. Null sessions

   d. Admin accounts

15. What is the best method of preventing NetBIOS attacks?

   a. Filtering certain ports at the firewall

   b. Telling users to create difficult-to-guess passwords

   c. Pausing the Workstation service

   d. Stopping the Workstation service

16. Which of the following is a commonly used UNIX enumeration tool?

   a. Netcat

   b. Nbtstat

   c. Netstat

   d. SNMPWalk

17. Which of the following commands should you use to determine whether there are any shared resources on a Windows computer with the IP address 193.145.85.202?

   a. `netstat -c 193.145.85.202`

   b. `nbtscan -a 193.145.85.202`

   c. `nbtstat -a 193.145.85.202`

   d. `nbtstat -a \\193.145.85.202`

18. The Windows Net use command is a quick way to discover any shared resources on a computer or server. True or False?

6

Case Projects

CASE PROJECTS

Case Project 6-1: Enumerating Systems on the Alexander Rocco Network

After conducting enumeration of the Alexander Rocco network, you discover several Windows computers with shared folders for the Help Desk Department. You're concerned when you access one of the shared folders containing information for help desk personnel and find an Excel spreadsheet listing e-mail addresses and passwords for all employees. Help desk employees use this shared folder to access the Excel spreadsheet if users call saying they have forgotten their passwords and need this information even when they're away from their offices.

Based on this information, write a one-page memo to the IT manager, Donald Lee, describing the steps you would take after this discovery. The memo should also mention any information you find in the OSSTMM that relates to your discovery and offer recommendations.

Case Project 6-2: Researching enum4Linux on the Internet

You are given permission to use your credentials to run some basic security checks on the Alexander Rocco domain. You don't have access to Nessus or OpenVAS, so you have to use other tools to enumerate the domain. After some research, you come across the enum4linux tool. To make sure your boss is okay with this tool, you need to tell him why you want to use enum4linux and what it's capable of.

Write a one-page memo on the enum4linux tool in which you describe the goal of your enumeration and the checks available in enum4linux. Your memo should persuade your boss into letting you use the tool for enumeration purposes.

## chapter 7

Programming for Security Professionals

After reading this chapter and completing the exercises, you will be able to:

- Explain basic programming concepts
- Write a simple C program
- Explain how Web pages are created with HTML
- Describe and create basic Perl programs
- Explain basic object-oriented programming concepts

As a security professional, you need to know how both hackers and security testers use computer programming. This chapter describes the basic skills of programming. You won't be an expert programmer after this chapter, but you'll have a clearer idea of how programs are written. Removing the mystique eliminates the fear many networking professionals experience when hearing the word "programming." Having a basic understanding of programming can also help you in developing custom security tools or modifying existing tools when you're conducting security tests. In fact, most security tester positions require being able to create customized security tools. Just as a good carpenter knows how to modify a tool to fit a special job, security testers should know how to modify computer tools created for one purpose so that they can be used for other functions.

This chapter gives you a general overview of C, HTML, and Perl. Becoming a programmer takes a lot of time and practice, but this chapter gives you an opportunity to examine some programs and practice writing a couple yourself.

Introduction to Computer Programming

Just as book editors must understand the rules and syntax of the English language, computer programmers must understand the rules of programming languages and deal with syntax errors. A command's syntax must be exact, right down to the placement of semicolons and parentheses. One minor mistake and the program won't run correctly, or even worse, it produces unpredictable results. Being a programmer takes a keen eye and patience; keep in mind that errors aren't unusual the first time you try to create a program.

Unfortunately, most colleges don't teach programming with security in mind. Many current attacks on operating systems and applications are possible because of poor programming practices. Mary Ann Davidson, Oracle's chief security officer (CSO), speaks all over the world on this topic. She argues that software developers focus on "cool technology" and the latest programming languages. "They don't think like attackers," she stated to an audience filled with more than 1000 information assurance professionals. "Nor is there a requirement for software developers to demonstrate proficiency in safe, secure programming as a condition of matriculation," she added.

Details on this issue are beyond the scope of this book, but if you decide to pursue programming or software engineering as a major, urge the college you're attending to cover this important topic. Oracle's CSO offered some suggestions to change the higher education system. She believes security should be part of every computer science class, "not just in a single class that students file and forget," and computer science textbooks should be written to emphasize secure programming more. Grades should be based in part on the "hackability" of code students submit for assignments, and students should be required to use automated tools to find vulnerabilities in their coding. Security must be integrated into any software engineering project from its inception, not after the fact.

This chapter's intention is to whet your appetite and give you an overview of programming. To begin, take a look at some programming fundamentals in the following section.

Programming Fundamentals

Manuals filled with a programming language's syntax and commands can take up a lot of space on your shelves, but you can learn some basics in any programming language without consulting manuals. In fact, you can begin writing programs with just a little knowledge of some programming fundamentals, which you can remember with the acronym BLT (as in bacon, lettuce, and tomato): branching, looping, and testing.

Branching, Looping, and Testing (BLT) Most programming languages have a way
to branch, loop, and test. For example, a function in a C program can branch to another **function** in the program, perform a task there, and then return to its starting point. A function is a mini program within the main program that carries out a task. For example, you can write a function that adds two numbers and then returns the answer to the function that called it. **Branching** takes you from one area of a program (a function) to another area. **Looping** is the act of performing a task over and over. The loop usually completes after **testing** is conducted on a variable and returns a value of true or false. Although you don't need to worry about the syntax for now, examine the following program to see where it uses branching, looping, and testing:

```c
#include <stdio.h>
main()
{
    int a = 1; // Variable initialized as integer, value 1
    if (a > 2) ; //Testing whether "a" is greater than 2
      printf("a is greater than 2");
    else
      GetOut(); // Branching: calling a different function
GetOut() // Do something interesting here
  {
      for(int a=1; a<11; a++) // Loop to display 10 times
      {
      printf("I'm in the GetOut() function");
      }
  }
}
```

There you have it: the BLT of computer programming. Of course, there's a lot more to learn in programming, but by knowing how to do these three actions, you can examine a program and understand its functionality.

A program contains different functions, or modules, that perform specific tasks. Say you're writing a program for making a BLT sandwich. The first step is to list the tasks in this process. In computer lingo, you're writing an **algorithm** (a recipe) to make a BLT sandwich. You keep an algorithm as simple as possible, but creating an algorithm is one of the most important programming skills to master.

Skipping a step in an algorithm can cause problems. For example, not rinsing the lettuce might result in a **bug** in your sandwich. Similarly, not reviewing your program's code carefully might result in having a bug in your program—an error that causes unpredictable results. Bugs are worse than syntax errors because a program can run successfully with a bug, but the output might be incorrect or inconsistent. Performing tasks in the incorrect order might also create havoc. For example, putting mayonnaise on the bread before toasting it can result in soggy toast. The following list is an example of an algorithm for making a BLT sandwich:

- Purchase the ingredients.
- Gather all the utensils needed for making the sandwich.
- Clean the tomatoes and lettuce.
- Slice the tomatoes and separate the lettuce leaves.
- Fry the bacon.
- Drain the bacon.
- Toast the bread.
- Put mayonnaise on the toast.
- Put the fried bacon, sliced tomato, and lettuce leaves on the toast.
- Join the two slices of toasted bread.

A programmer would then convert this algorithm into **pseudocode**. Pseudocode isn't a programming language; it's an English-like language you can use to help create the structure of your program. The following example is the pseudocode that addresses purchasing all the ingredients needed for a BLT sandwich before you write the programming code:

```
PurchaseIngredients Function
    Call GetCar Function
    Call DriveToStore Function
    Purchase Bacon, Bread, Tomatoes, Lettuce, and Mayonnaise at store
End PurchaseIngredients Function
```

After writing pseudocode, you can then begin writing your program in the language of your choosing. Are outlining an algorithm and writing pseudocode necessary for every computer program you write? No. If the program you're writing has very few lines of code, you can skip these steps, but for beginning programmers, these two steps are helpful.

Documentation When writing any program, documenting your work is essential. To do this, you add comments to the code that explain what you're doing. Documentation not only makes your program easier for someone else to modify; it also helps you remember what you were thinking when you wrote the program. The phrase "No comment" might be appropriate for politicians or Wall Street investors with inside trading information, but not for programmers.

Although documentation is important, many programmers find it time consuming and tedious. Often they think their code is self-explanatory and easy enough for anyone to maintain and modify, so documenting their work isn't necessary. You'll soon discover, however, that without good documentation, you won't understand the lines of code you wrote three weeks ago, let alone expect a stranger to figure out your train of thought. For example, the following comments can help the next programmer understand why a new function was added to an existing program:

```
/* The following function was added to the program June 15, 2016
per a request from the Marketing Department.
It appears that reports generated by the sales() function were
not giving the marketing folks information about sales in Asia.
This new function now uses data from text files from the offices
*/ in Tokyo and Hong Kong. - Bob C. Twins
```

Software engineering companies don't retain programmers who don't document their work because they know that 80% of the cost of software projects is maintenance. They also know that an average of 10 bugs for every 1000 lines of code is the industry standard. For example, Windows 10 is estimated to contain over 50 million lines of code, but Microsoft software engineers, partly because of strict documentation rules and Secure Software Development Lifecycle Practices, are able to limit bugs to fewer than the average. In general, Microsoft is below the industry standard on the average number of bugs. With bugs being so prevalent in many programs, however, it's easy to see how attackers can discover vulnerabilities in software. Programmers can easily overlook problems in thousands of lines of code that might create a security hole attackers can exploit.

Activity 7-1: Writing Your First Algorithm

Time Required: 10 minutes

Objective: Learn to write an algorithm.

Description: Programmers must be able to think logically and approach problem solving in logical steps or tasks. Missing a step can have disastrous effects, so you should train yourself to think in a structured, logical way. A good way to test whether you can follow a step-by-step approach is by doing exercises that encourage you to think in this manner. For this activity, list at least 10 steps for making scrambled eggs. When writing the steps, make sure you don't take anything for granted. Assume someone with no knowledge of cooking—or even of eggs—will try to follow your algorithm.

Learning the C Language

Many programming languages are available to security testers. You'll begin your journey with an introduction to one of the most popular programming languages: C, developed by Dennis Ritchie at Bell Laboratories in 1972. The C language is both powerful and concise. In fact, UNIX, which was first written in **assembly language**, was soon rewritten in C. Not many programmers want to write programs in binary (machine code) or machine language, so assembly language was developed. It uses a combination of hexadecimal numbers and expressions, such as mov, add, and sub, so writing programs in this language is easier than in machine language.

This chapter gives you a basic overview of the C language. At many colleges, an entire course is devoted to learning this language; others skip C and teach C++, an enhancement of the C language. Many security professionals and hackers still use C because of its power and cross-platform usability.

A **compiler** is a program that converts a text-based program, called source code, into executable or binary code. Table 7-1 lists some available C compilers. Most C compilers can also create executable programs in C++. The Intel and Microsoft compilers must be purchased, but many other compilers are free and can be found with an Internet search.

Compiler	Description
Intel compilers for Windows and Linux	Intel's C++ compiler for developing applications for Windows servers, desktops, and handheld PDAs. The Intel Linux C++ compiler claims to optimize the speed of accessing information from a MySQL database, an open-source database program used by many corporations and e-commerce companies.
Microsoft Visual C++ Compiler	This compiler is widely used by programmers developing C and C++ applications for Windows platforms.
GNU C and C++ compilers (GCC)	These free compilers can be downloaded for Windows and *nix platforms. Most *nix systems include the GNU GCC compiler.

Table 7-1 C language compilers

What's dangerous about C is that a beginner can make some big blunders. For example, a programmer can accidentally write to areas of memory that could cause the program to crash, or worse, give an attacker the ability to take control of the remote system. Usually, what's written is executable code that might give an attacker a backdoor into the system, escalate an attacker's privileges to that of an administrator, or simply crash the program. This type of attack is usually possible because the programmer didn't check users' input. For example, if users can enter 300 characters when prompted to enter their last names, an attacker can probably enter executable code at this point of the program. When you see the term "buffer overflow vulnerability," think "poor programming practices." Keep in mind that although C is easy to learn and use, errors in using it can result in system damage.

Anatomy of a C Program

Many veteran programmers can't think of the C language without remembering the "Hello, world!" program, the first program a C student learns:

```
/* The famous "Hello, world!" C program */

#include <stdio.h> /* Load the standard IO library. The library contains
functions your C program might need to call to perform various tasks. */

main()
{
    printf("Hello, world!\n\n");
}
```

That's it. You can write these lines of code in almost any text editor, such as Notepad if you're using Windows or the vim editor if you're using Linux. The following sections explain each line of code in this program.

Many C programs use the /* and */ symbols to comment large portions of text instead of using the // symbols for one-line comments. For example, you can type the /* symbols, add as many lines of comment text as needed, and then type the closing */ symbols. Forgetting to add the */ at the end of comment text can cause errors when compiling the program, so be careful.

The #include statement is used to load libraries that hold the commands and functions used in your program. In the Hello, world! example, the #include <stdio.h> statement loads the stdio.h library, which contains many C functions.

The parentheses in C mean you're dealing with a function. C programs must contain a main() function, but you can also add your own functions to a C program. Note that after the main() function, an open brace (the { symbol) is on a line by itself. Braces show where a block of code begins and ends. In the Hello, world! program, the closing brace indicates the end of the program. Forgetting to add a closing brace is a common mistake.

Inside the main() function, the program calls another function: printf(). When a function calls another function, it uses parameters, also known as arguments. Parameters are placed between opening and closing parentheses. In this example, the parameters "Hello, world! \n\n" are passed to the printf() function. The printf() function then displays (prints) the words "Hello, world!" onscreen, and the \n\n characters add two new lines after the Hello, world! display. Table 7-2 lists some special characters that can be used with the printf() function.

Character	Description
\n	New line
\t	Tab

Table 7-2   Special characters for use with the printf() function

Declaring Variables

A variable represents a numeric or string value. For example, you can solve $x + y = z$ if you know two of the variable values. In programming, you can declare variables at the beginning of a program so that calculations can be carried out without user intervention. A variable might be defined as a character or characters, such as letters of the alphabet, or it can be assigned a numeric value, as in the expression $int\ x = 1$. Table 7-3 shows some variable types used in C.

Variable type	Description
Int	Use this variable type for an integer (positive or negative number).
Float	This variable type is for a real number that includes a decimal point, such as 1.299999.
Double	Use this variable type for a double-precision floating-point number.
Char	This variable type holds the value of a single letter.
String	This variable type holds the value of multiple characters or words.
Const	A constant variable is created to hold a value that doesn't change for the duration of your program. For example, you can create a constant variable called TAX and give it a specific value: const TAX =.085. If this variable is used in areas of the program that calculate total costs after adding an 8.5% tax, it's easier to change the constant value to a different number if the tax rate changes, instead of changing every occurrence of 8.5% to 8.6%.

Table 7-3   Variable types in C

If the `printf()` function contains values other than a quoted sentence, such as numbers, you need to use **conversion specifiers**. A conversion specifier tells the compiler how to convert the value in a function. For example, `printf("Your name is %s!", name);` displays the following if you have assigned the value Sue to the `string` variable called `name`:

Your name is Sue!

Table 7-4 lists conversion specifiers for the `printf()` function.

Specifier	Type
%c	Character
%d	Decimal number
%f	Floating decimal or double number
%s	Character string

Table 7-4   Conversion specifiers in C

In addition to conversion specifiers, programmers use operators to compare values, perform mathematical calculations, and the like. Most likely, programs you write will require calculating values based on mathematical operations, such as addition or subtraction. Table 7-5 describes mathematical operators used in C.

Operator	Description
+ (unary)	Doesn't change the value of the number. Unary operators use a single argument; binary operators use two arguments. Example: +(2).
– (unary)	Returns the negative value of a single number.
++ (unary)	Increments the unary value by 1. For example, if a is equal to 5, ++a changes the value to 6.
–– (unary)	Decrements the unary value by 1. For example, if a is equal to 5, ––a changes the value to 4.
+ (binary)	Addition. For example, a + b.
– (binary)	Subtraction. For example, a – b.
* (binary)	Multiplication. For example, a * b.
/ (binary)	Division. For example, a / b.
% (binary)	Modulus. For example, 10 % 3 is equal to 1 because 10 divided by 3 leaves a remainder of 1.

Table 7-5   **Mathematical operators in C**

You might also need to test whether a condition is true or false when writing a C program. To do that, you need to understand how to use relational and logical operators, described in Table 7-6.

Operator	Description
==	Used to compare the equality of two variables. In a == b, for example, the condition is true if variable a is equal to variable b.
!=	Not equal; the exclamation mark negates the equal sign. For example, the statement if a != b is read as "if a is not equal to b."
>	Greater than.
<	Less than.
>=	Greater than or equal to.
>=	Less than or equal to.
&&	The AND operator; evaluates as true if both sides of the operator are true. For example, if ((a > 5) && (b > 5)) printf ("Hello, world!"); prints only if both a and b are greater than 5.
||	The OR operator; evaluates as true if either side of the operator is true.
!	The NOT operator; the statement ! (a == b), for example, evaluates as true if a isn't equal to b.

Table 7-6   **Relational and logical operators in C**

Using compound assignment operators as a sort of shorthand method, you can perform more complex operations with fewer lines of code. For example, TotalSalary +-5 is a shorter way of writing TotalSalary = TotalSalary + 5. Similarly, TotalSalary -= 5 means the TotalSalary variable now contains the value TotalSalary – 5.

Many beginning C programmers make the mistake of using a single equal sign (=) instead of the double equal sign (==) when attempting to test the value of a variable. A single equal sign (the assignment **TIP** operator) is used to assign a value to a variable. For example, a = 5 assigns the value 5 to the variable a. To test the value of variable a, you can use the statement if (a == 5). If you mistakenly write the statement as if (a = 5), the value 5 is assigned to the variable a, and then the statement is evaluated as true. This happens because any value not equal to zero is evaluated as true, and a zero value is evaluated as false.

Although this chapter covers only the most basic elements of a program, with what you have learned so far, you can write a C program that displays something onscreen. Security testers should gain additional programming skills so that they can develop tools for performing specific tasks, as you see in "Understanding Perl" later in this chapter.

Branching, Looping, and Testing in C Branching in C is as easy as placing a function in your program followed by a semicolon. The following C code does nothing, but it shows you how to begin writing a program that can be developed later. For example, in the following code, the prompt(); statement (indicated by the semicolon at the end) at the beginning branches to go to the prompt() function:

```
main()
{
    prompt();        //Call function to prompt user with a question
    display();       //Call function to display graphics onscreen
    calculate();     //Call function to do complicated math
    cleanup();       //Call function to make all variables equal to
                     //zero

    prompt()
    {
    [code for prompt() function goes here]

    }
    display()
    {
    [code for display() function goes here]

    }
    [and so forth]

}
```

When the program runs, it branches to the prompt() function and then continues branching to the functions listed subsequently. By creating a program in this fashion, you can develop each function or module one at a time. You can also delegate writing other functions to people with more experience in certain areas. For example, you can have a math wizard write the calculate() function if math isn't your forte.

C has several methods for looping. The **while loop** is one way of having your program repeat an action a certain number of times. It checks whether a condition is true, and then continues looping until the condition becomes false. Take a look at the following example (with the important code bolded) and see whether you can understand what the program is doing:

```
main()

{

    int counter = 1;      //Initialize (assign a value to)
                          //the counter variable

    while (counter <= 10) //Do what's inside the braces until false

    {
        printf("Counter is equal to %d\n", counter);
        ++counter; //Increment counter by 1;
    }

}
```

Figure 7-1 shows the output of this program. In this example, when the counter variable is greater than 10, the while loop stops processing, which causes printf() to display 10 lines of output before stopping.

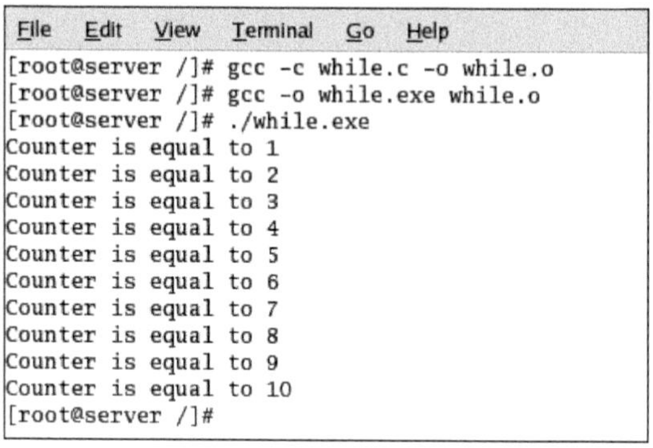

Figure 7-1 A while loop in action

The **do loop** performs an action first and then tests to see whether the action should continue to occur. In the following example, the do loop performs the print() function first, and then checks whether a condition is true:

```
main()

{

    int counter = 1;                  //Initialize counter variable
    do

    {
        printf("Counter is equal to %d\n", counter);
        ++counter;                    //Increment counter by 1
```

```
   } while (counter <= 10);        //Do what's inside the braces
                                   until false


}
```

Which is better to use: the `while` loop or the do loop? It depends. The `while` loop might never execute if a condition isn't met. A do loop always executes at least once.

The last loop type in C is the **for loop**, one of C's most interesting pieces of code. In the following `for` loop, the first part initializes the `counter` variable to 1, and then the second part tests a condition. It continues looping as long as the `counter` variable's value is equal to or less than 10. The last part of the `for` loop increments the `counter` variable by 1. Figure 7-2 shows an example of a `for` loop.

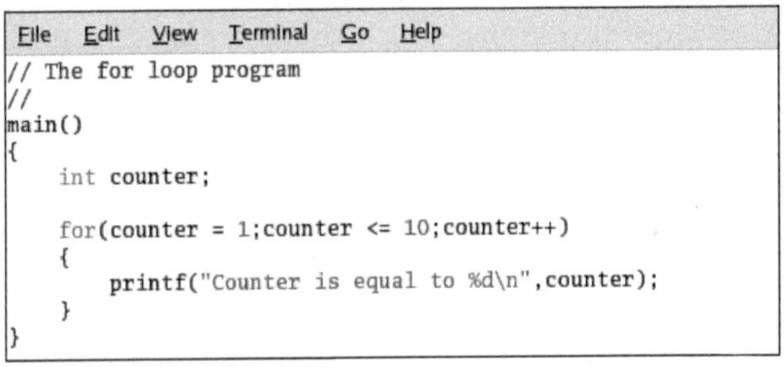

```
File  Edit  View  Terminal  Go  Help
// The for loop program
//
main()
{
    int counter;

    for(counter = 1;counter <= 10;counter++)
    {
        printf("Counter is equal to %d\n",counter);
    }
}
```

Figure 7-2 A for loop

```
for (int counter = 1;counter <= 10;counter++);
```

You might see some C programs with a `for` loop containing nothing but semicolons, as in this example:

```
for (;;)
{
    printf("Wow!");
}
```

This code is a powerful, yet dangerous, implementation of the `for` loop. The `for(;;)` tells the compiler to keep doing what's in the brackets over and over and over. You can create an endless loop with this statement if you don't have a way to exit the block of code that's running. Usually, a programmer has a statement inside the block that performs a test on a variable, and then exits the block when a certain condition is met.

Activity 7-2: Learning to Use the GNU GCC Compiler

Time Required: 30 minutes

Objective: Learn how to use the GNU GCC compiler included with most *nix operating systems.

Description: In the past, programmers had to read through their code line by line before submitting the job to the mainframe CPU. The job included all the commands the CPU would execute. If a program was full of errors, the mainframe operator notified the programmer, who had to go through the code again and fix the errors. With today's compilers, you can write a program, compile it, and test it yourself. If the compiler finds errors, it usually indicates what they are so that you can correct the code and compile the program again. In this activity, you create a C program that contains errors and try to compile the program. After seeing the errors generated, you correct the program and then recompile it until you get it right.

1. Boot your computer into Linux with the Kali Linux DVD.

2. At the shell prompt, type **vim syntax.c** and press **Enter** to use the vim editor.

3. To enter insert mode, type **i**.

4. Type the following code, pressing **Enter** after each line:

```
#include <stdio.h>

main()
{
    int age
    printf("Enter your age: ");
    scanf("%d", &age);
    if (age > 0)
    {
        printf("You are %d years old\n", age);
    }
}
```

5. Exit and save the file by pressing **Esc** and then pressing **:** (a colon). At the : prompt, type **wq** and press **Enter**.

6. To compile the program, type **gcc -o syntax syntax.c** and press **Enter**. The -o switch tells the compiler to create an output file called syntax. The compiler returns an error (or several errors) similar to the one in Figure 7-3. The error varies depending on the compiler version you use. In any event, you should be warned that there was a syntax error before printf() because there was no semicolon after the int age statement.

```
[root@server root]# gcc -c syntax.c -o syntax.o
syntax.c: In function `main':
syntax.c:4: syntax error before "printf"
[root@server root]#
```

Figure 7-3 Example of a syntax error message

If there are no errors in the source code you created, you get a shell prompt.

Sometimes you can correct an error easily by looking at the line number of the first error detected.

7. To correct the missing semicolon error, you can use the vim editor again. Type **vim syntax.c** and press **Enter**. Type **a** to enter Append mode. Add a semicolon to the end of the line containing the variable declaration int age.

8. Save and exit the program.

9. Compile the program again by typing **gcc -o syntax syntax.c** and pressing **Enter**. (You can also use the up arrow key to return to previous commands.)

10. If you entered everything correctly, you should be at the shell prompt. To run the program, type **./syntax** and press **Enter**.

11. Log off the Kali Linux session for the next activity.

Security Bytes

There are two schools of thought on how to handle syntax errors. Many programmers believe the compiler should check for errors in their code and spend little time reading and stepping through their programs, looking for syntax or logic errors. They just compile it and see what errors pop up. Others refuse to compile the program until they have examined the code thoroughly and are confident it's accurate and syntactically correct. For beginning programmers, examining the code carefully before compiling helps make you a better programmer. You'll increase your skills and develop the keen eye needed to spot a missing brace or semicolon.

Understanding HTML Basics

HTML is a markup language used mainly for indicating the formatting and layout of Web pages, so HTML files don't contain the kind of programming code you see in a C program. As a security professional, you should understand basic HTML syntax because it's still the basis of Web development. No matter what language is used to create Web pages, HTML statements are used, so knowing HTML is the foundation for learning other Web languages.

Security professionals often need to examine Web pages and recognize when something looks suspicious. You should understand what HTML's limitations are, be able to read an HTML file, and have a basic understanding of what's happening. This section isn't going to make you a Web developer, but it does introduce some HTML basics so that you have a foundation for exploring and learning other programming and scripting languages.

 Today, many Web sites use Extensible Markup Language (XML). Although this language isn't covered in this book, it's a good one to study if you want to specialize in Web security. Learning additional Web-development languages, such as Extensible HTML (XHTML; see *www.w3c.org* for more information), Perl, JavaScript, PHP, and Python can also enhance your skills as a security professional.

Creating a Web Page with HTML

You can create an HTML Web page in Notepad and then view it in a Web browser. Because HTML is a markup language, not a programming language, it doesn't use branching, looping, or testing. The following is a simple example of HTML code:

```
<!--This is how you add a comment to an HTML Web page-->
<HTML>
<HEAD>
<TITLE>Hello, world--again</TITLE>
</HEAD>
<BODY>
This is where you put page text, such as marketing copy for an e-commerce
business.
</BODY>
</HTML>
```

The < and > symbols denote HTML tags, which act on the data they enclose. Notice that each tag has a matching closing tag that includes a forward slash (/). For example, the <HTML> tag has the closing tag </HTML>, as do the <HEAD>, <TITLE>, and <BODY> tags. Most HTML Web pages contain these four tags. Table 7-7 describes some common formatting tags used in an HTML Web page.

Opening tag	Closing tag	Description
<H1>, <H2>, <H3>, <H4>, <H5>, and <H6>	</H1>, </H2>, </H3>, </H4>, </H5>, and </H6>	Formats text as different heading levels. Level 1 is the largest font size, and level 6 is the smallest.
<P>	</P>	Used to mark the beginning and end of a paragraph.
<B>	</B>	Formats enclosed text in bold.
<I>	</I>	Formats enclosed text in italics.

Table 7-7 HTML formatting tags

There are more tags for formatting tables and lists, but this table gives you a general overview of HTML tags. You can find many references to learn more about creating HTML Web pages (refer to Appendix B). In Activity 7-3, you get a chance to practice creating a Web page, using Notepad as the editor.

7

Activity 7-3: Creating an HTML Web Page

Time Required: 30 minutes

Objective: Create an HTML Web page.

Description: As a security tester, you might be required to view Web pages to check for possible Web security issues. A basic knowledge of HTML can help you with this task. In this activity, you create a simple HTML Web page and then view it in your Web browser.

1. Start your computer in Windows. If in Windows 10, right-click the **Windows Logo**, select **Run**, type **notepad MyWeb.html**, and press **Enter**. If you're prompted to create a new file, click **Yes**.

2. In the new Notepad document, type the following lines, pressing **Enter** after each line:

   ```
   <!-- This HTML Web page has many tags -->
   <HTML>
   <HEAD>
   <TITLE>HTML for Security Testers</TITLE>
   </HEAD>
   ```

3. Type the next two lines, pressing **Enter** *twice* after each line:

   ```
   <BODY>
   <H2>Security Tester Web Site</H2>
   ```

4. Type **<P><B>There are many good Web sites to visit for security testers. For vulnerabilities click</B>** and press **Enter**.

5. Type **<A HREF="HTTP://www.cve.mitre.org"><FONT COLOR="red">here!</FONT></A>** and press **Enter**.

6. Type **</P>** and press **Enter**.

7. Type **</BODY>** and press **Enter**. On the last line, type **</HTML>** to end your code.

8. Verify that you have typed everything correctly. Your file should look similar to Figure 7-4. When you're done, save the file.

Figure 7-4 HTML source code

9. To test whether you have created the Web page correctly, start your File Explorer and navigate to the default location—typically, C:\Users*YourUserName*\Documents). Right-click the **MyWeb.html** file you created, and from the Open with menu, select **Internet Explorer**. If you entered the information correctly, your Web page should look like the one shown in Figure 7-5.

Figure 7-5 An HTML Web page

10. Click the **here!** hyperlink you created to check whether you're sent to the correct Web site. If not, make corrections to your HTML code.

11. When you're finished, exit your Web browser, but leave Windows running for the next activity.

Understanding Perl

Many scripts and programs for security professionals are written in Practical Extraction and Report Language (Perl), a powerful scripting language. Perl and Python are two very popular languages for security professionals; this book will cover the basics of Perl. In this section, you see why this language is so popular, examine the syntax of the language, and practice writing Perl scripts. You also create a utility for examining the configuration of a Windows computer.

Background on Perl

Perl, developed by Larry Wall in 1987, can run on almost any platform, and *nix-based OSs invariably have Perl installed already. The Perl syntax is similar to C, so C programmers have few difficulties learning Perl. Table 7-8 is a brief timeline of this language. For more details, visit *http://history.perl.org/PerlTimeline.html*.

Perl version	Date	Description
Version 1.0000	December 1987	Wall describes his scripting language as being optimized for scanning text files and extracting information from those files.
Version 2.0000	June 1988	New features added, such as recursive subroutine calls, local variables allowed in blocks and subroutines, a sort operator, and much more.
Version 3.0000	October 1989	Modified to handle binary data and pass arguments to subroutines by reference (previously by value only) and offers debugger enhancements and new functions.
Version 4.0000	March 1991	Modified to include an artistic license and GPL (GNU Public License). Wall receives the *Dr. Dobbs Journal* Excellence in Programming Award in his final 4.036 version released in 1993.
Version 5.0000	October 1994	Complete rewrite of Perl with more extensive documentation, additional functions, and the introduction of object-oriented programming for Perl. The most current version as of this writing is 5.22.1.
Version 6.0000	Not released	Wall wants this version to be a rewrite of version 5.0 but wants the Perl community to participate in the rewriting. Perl 6 will also include Parrot (a language-independent interpreter) as part of its design.

Table 7-8   Perl timeline

Hackers use Perl to create automated exploits and malicious bots, but system administrators and security professionals use it to perform repetitive tasks and conduct security monitoring. Before examining the Perl syntax, in Activity 7-4 you write your first Perl script. As with any programming language, the best way to learn Perl is by using it.

Activity 7-4: Writing a Perl Script Using GVim

Time Required: 60 minutes

Objective: Write a Perl script using GVim.

Description: Security professionals and hackers alike use the Perl scripting language. Many hacking programs are written in Perl, so any skills you develop in this language will help you in your career. In this activity, write a basic Perl script. In the other activities, vim was used. For this activity, we will use the graphical version of vim, called GVim. The usage is very similar, but you can click to navigate instead of relying on the keyboard commands.

1. Boot your computer into Linux with the Kali Linux DVD.

2. Open a terminal window, then change the directory to the desktop using the **cd ~/Desktop** command.

3. Type **gvim first.pl** and press **Enter**.

4. Select the **Syntax** tab on the top of the GVim window and select **Automatic**. This enables syntax highlighting for your Perl project.

5. On the first line, type **# This is my first Perl script program** and press **Enter**.

6. Next, type **# I should always have documentation in my scripts!** and press **Enter** twice.

7. Add another comment to describe what the code in instruction 6 does: **#This code displays "Hello security testers" to the screen**. Press **Enter** twice.

8. Next, type **print "Hello security testers!\n\n";** and press **Enter**.

9. Your script should look similar to Figure 7-6. Be careful not to miss a semicolon or quotation mark. Remember that programming requires a keen eye.

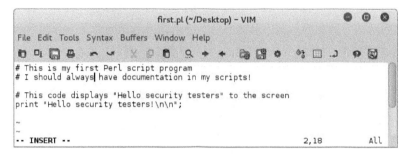

Figure 7-6 Creating the first.pl Perl script

10. Save the file

11. At the command prompt, type **perl first.pl** and press **Enter**.

12. If you didn't make any errors, your screen should look like Figure 7-7. If you did get errors, read through your code and compare it with the lines of code in this activity's steps. Correct any errors and save the file again.

Figure 7-7 Running the first.pl Perl script

13. Close the command prompt window, and leave Windows running for the next activity.

Understanding the Basics of Perl

Knowing how to get help quickly in any programming language is useful. The `perl -h` command gives you a list of parameters used with the `perl` command (see Figure 7-8).

Figure 7-8 Using the perl -h command

If you want to know what the print command does, you can use perldoc -f print, which produces the output shown in Figure 7-9. Before you can use the perldoc command in Kali, you'll have to use the apt-get install perl-doc command to install this feature.

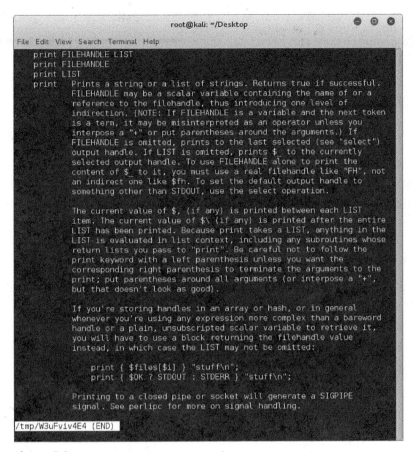

Figure 7-9 Using the `perldoc` command

As you can see, this command gives you a detailed description of the Perl `print` command, which is almost identical to the C `print` command. Perl also has the `printf` command for formatting complex variables. Table 7-9 shows how to use this command to format specific data. Note the similarities to C.

Formatting character	Description	Input	Output
`%c`	Character	`printf '%c', "d"`	d
`%s`	String	`printf '%s', "This is fun!"`	This is fun!
`%d`	Signed integer in decimal	`printf '%+d %d', 1, 1`	+1 1
`%u`	Unsigned integer in decimal	`printf '%u', 2`	2
`%o`	Unsigned integer in octal	`printf '%o', 8`	10
`%x`	Unsigned integer in hexadecimal	`printf '%x', 10`	a

Table 7-9 Using `printf` to format output (*continues*)

Formatting character	Description	Input	Output
%e	Floating-point number in scientific notation	printf '%e', 10;	1.000000e+001 (depending on the OS)
%f	Floating-point number in fixed decimal notation	printf '%f', 1;	1.000000

Table 7-9   Using printf to format output (*continued*)

Understanding the BLT of Perl

As you learned previously, all programming languages must have a way to branch, loop, and test. The following sections use code examples to show you how Perl handles these BLT functions. As you examine these examples, keep the following syntax rules in mind:

- The sub keyword is used in front of function names.
- Variables begin with the $ symbol.
- Comment lines begin with the # symbol.
- The & symbol indicates a function.

Except for these minor differences, Perl's syntax is much like the C syntax. This similarity is one of the reasons many security professionals with C programming experience choose Perl as a scripting language.

Branching in Perl   In a Perl program, to go from one function to another, you simply call the function by entering its name in your source code. In the following example, the &name_best_guitarist line branches the program to the sub name_best_guitarist function:

```
# Perl program illustrating the branching function
# Documentation is important
# Initialize variables
$first_name = "Jimi";
$last_name = "Hendrix";
&name_best_guitarist;
sub name_best_guitarist
{
    printf "%s %s %s", $first_name, $last_name, "was the best!";
}
```

Looping in Perl   Suppose you want to send an important message to everyone in your class by using the Net send command. Because you're sending the same message to multiple users, it's a repetitive task that requires looping. In Activity 7-5, you write a Perl script to do just that: Send a message to everyone in the class. As you learned in C, you have several choices for performing a loop. In this section, you learn about two of Perl's looping mechanisms: the for loop and the while loop.

The Perl for loop is identical to the C for loop:

```
for (variable assignment; test condition; increment variable)
{
    a task to do over and over
}
```

Substituting the variable $a, you have the following code:

```
for ($a = 1; $a <= 10; $a++)
{
    print "Hello, security testers!\n"
}
```

This loop prints the phrase 10 times. Next, try getting the same output by using the while loop, which has the following syntax:

```
while (test condition)
{
    a task to do over and over
}
```

The following code produces the same output as the for loop:

```
$a = 1;
while ($a <= 10)
{
    print "Hello, security testers!\n";
    $a++
}
```

Security Bytes

Chris Nandor, known for developing the Mac Classic version of Perl 5.8.0, became one of the first hackers to use a Perl script in an online election. Apparently, his Perl script added more than 40,000 votes for several Red Sox players during an online election in 1999 for the All-Stars game. Similarly, in 1993, an online election involving the Denver Broncos traced more than 70,000 votes coming from one IP address. The power of the loop!

Testing Conditions in Perl Most programs must be able to test the value of a variable or condition. The two looping examples shown previously use the less than or equal operator (<=). Other operators used for testing in Perl are similar to C operators. Table 7-10 lists the operators you can use in Perl.

Operator	Function	Example
+	Addition	$total = $sal + $commission
−	Subtraction	$profit = $gross_sales − $cost_of_goods
*	Multiplication	$total = $cost * $quantity
/	Division	$GPA = $total_points / $number_of_classes
%	Modulus	$a % 10 = 1
**	Exponent	$total = $a**10
Assignments		
=	Assignment	$Last_name = "Rivera"
+=	Add, then assignment	$a+=10; shorthand for $a=$a+10
−=	Subtract, then assignment	$a−=10; shorthand for $a=$a−10
*=	Multiply, then assignment	$a*=10; shorthand for $a=$a*10
/=	Divide, then assignment	$a/=10; shorthand for $a=$a/10
%=	Modulus, then assignment	$a%=10; shorthand for $a=$a%10
**=	Exponent and assignment	$a**=2; shorthand for $a=$a**2
++	Increment	$a++; increment $a by 1
−−	Decrement	$a−−; decrement $a by 1
Comparisons		
==	Equal to	$a==1; compare value of $a with 1
!=	Not equal to	$a!=1; $a is not equal to 1
>	Greater than	$a>10
<	Less than	$a<10
>=	Greater than or equal to	$a>=10
<=	Less than or equal to	$a<=10

Table 7-10   Perl operators

Often you combine these operators with Perl conditionals, such as the following:

- `if`—Checks whether a condition is true. Example:

```
if ($age < 12) {
    print "You must be a know-it-all!";
}
```

- `else`—Used when there's only one option to carry out if the condition is not true. Example:

```
if ($age) > 12 {
    print "You must be a know-it-all!";
        }
    else
```

```
   {
      print "Sorry, but I don't know why the sky is blue.";
   }
```

- elsif—Used when there are several conditionals to test. Example:

```
if (($age > 12) && ($age < 20))
   {
      print "You must be a know-it-all!";
   }
elsif ($age > 39)
   {
      print "You must lie about your age!";
   }
else
   {
      print "To be young...";
   }
```

- unless—Executes unless the condition is true. Example:

```
unless ($age == 100)
   {
      print "Still enough time to get a bachelor's degree.";
   }
```

The message is displayed until the $age variable is equal to 100. With some practice and lots of patience, these examples can give you a start at creating functional Perl scripts.

Activity 7-5: Writing a Perl Script That Uses Ping and Notify-Send

Time Required: 30 minutes

Objective: Write a Perl script that uses branching, looping, and testing components.

Description: Security professionals often need to automate or create tools to help them conduct security tests. In this activity, you write a Perl script that uses the notify-send command and a for loop to select IP numbers from the classroom range your instructor has provided. You can use the following reference for the Perl ping command: *http://perldoc.perl.org/Net/Ping.html*.

1. Write down the IP address range used in the class network.

2. Open a terminal window and type **apt-get install libnotify-bin**. This will install the notification service we will use in this activity.

3. Change the directory to the desktop with **cd ~/Desktop**. Now, type **gvim ping.pl** and press **Enter**.

4. Type **# ping.pl** on the first line and press **Enter**.

5. Type **# Program to ping workstations in the classroom** and press **Enter**.

6. Type **# If the ping is successful, a message is sent to the screen** and press **Enter**.

7. Type **# Program assumes a Class C address (w.x.y.z) where w.x.y is the network portion of the IP address** and press **Enter**.

8. Type **# The "z" octet will be incremented from 1 to 254 with a for loop unless otherwise directed by the instructor** and press **Enter** three times.

9. Type **use Net::Ping; # Loads the Net library** and press **Enter** once.

10. Type **$p = Net::Ping->new(); # Creates a new ping object with default settings** and press **Enter** twice.

11. The next line initializes the variable you're using to hold your network ID. Type **$class_IP = "192.168.185"; # Network ID–** (change to reflect your topology) and press **Enter** twice.

12. The next lines of code are the `for` loop, which increments the last octet of the network IP address to all available IP addresses in your class. Type **for ($z=1; $z<255; $z++) {** and press **Enter** once.

13. Type the following lines (adding two spaces at the beginning of lines to indent them, as shown in Figure 7-10) and press **Enter** after each line:

    $wkstation = "$class_IP.$z"; # Creates the host to be scanned for this iteration of the for loop

    print "Looking for live systems to attack, Trying $wkstation \n"; #Displays status message

    system("notify-send '$wkstation is ready to attack!'") if $p->ping($wkstation); # Sends message if ping is successful

    }

14. Type **}** and press **Enter** to end your program, which should look similar to Figure 7-10.

```
ping.pl (~/Desktop) – VIM

File  Edit  Tools  Syntax  Buffers  Window  Help

# Program to ping workstations in the classroom
# If the ping is successful, a message is sent to the screen
# Program accumes a Class C address (w.x.y.z) where w.x.y is the network portion of the address
# The "z" octet will be incremented from 1-254 with a for loop unless other instructed by the in
structor

use diagnostics;

use Net::Ping; # Loads the Net library

$p = Net::Ping->new(); #Creates a new ping object with default settings

$class_IP = "192.168.185"; #Network ID

for ($z=1;$z<255;$z++) {
  $wkstation = "$class_IP.$z"; #creates the host to be scanned for this iteration of the for loo
p
  print "Looking for live systems to attack, Trying $wkstation \n"; #Displays status message
  system("notify-send '$wkstation is ready to attack!'") if $p->ping($wkstation); #Sends message
  if ping is successful
  }
~
                                                                          1,1           All
```

Figure 7-10   Creating the ping.pl Perl script

15. To improve this program's documentation, add comment lines to your code stating the author and date written and explaining any complex algorithms.

16. Go through each line of code and make sure the syntax is correct. Note that the `$class_IP` variable holds the network portion of your class's IP address range. After verifying the syntax and contents of the Perl script, save it and return to the terminal window.

17. Run your script by typing **perl ping.pl** and pressing **Enter**. If you have no errors, your program should begin pinging IP addresses, as shown in Figure 7-11. If a live address is found, you'll see a notification at the bottom of the screen.

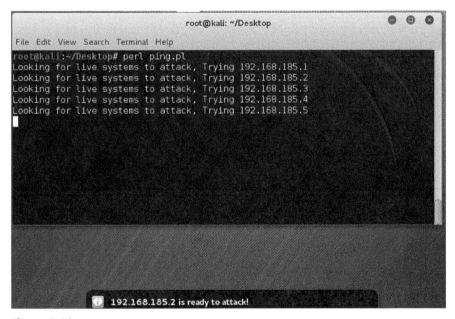

Figure 7-11   Running ping.pl on a live network

18. To terminate the Perl script, press **Ctrl+C**. Leave the command prompt window open for the next activity.

Understanding Object-Oriented Programming Concepts

Just when you think you're comfortable with a technology concept, something new comes along. Although the concept of object-oriented programming isn't new to experienced programmers, it might not be familiar to those just learning how to write their first Perl script, for example. Perl 5.0 uses object-oriented programming concepts, and Perl 6.0 will be based solely on this model, so this section covers some basic object-oriented concepts as a foundation for writing another Perl script. This section is by no means a complete discussion of a complex concept. Learning object-oriented programming takes time and practice, and this section merely introduces you to the fundamental concepts.

Components of Object-Oriented Programming

The version of Perl you installed has additional functions that can make program calls to the Windows application programming interface (Win API). Programmers should know what functions are available in different OSs so that they can write programs that interact with these functions. For example, a C programmer knows that the Win API has the `NodeName()` function, which returns the NetBIOS computer name. To use this function, the programmer references it with `Win32::NodeName()`. The `::` separates the name of the **class**, `Win32`, from the member function, `NodeName()`. In object-oriented programming, classes are structures that hold pieces of data and functions. The following code example shows the `Employee` class in C++. Classes can be written in many object-oriented languages (e.g., Java, Object COBOL, and Perl). What's important is recognizing what a class looks like:

```
// This is a class called Employee created in C++
class Employee
{
    public:
        char firstname[25];
        char lastname[25];
        char PlaceOfBirth[30];
        [code continues]

};
void GetEmp()
{
    // Perform tasks to get employee info
    [program code goes here]

}
```

Win32 API is now officially known as Win API to reflect its support in the latest 64-bit systems. However, for the purposes of this section, Win32 API is used interchangeably with Win API.

The structure created in this code can contain employee information as well as a function that performs a lookup. A function contained in a class is called a member function. As mentioned, to access a member function, you use the class name followed by two colons and the member function's name:

```
Employee::GetEmp()
```

The `Win32` class contains many functions you can call from your Perl script. Table 7-11 describes some commonly used Win32 API functions.

Function	Description
GetLastError()	Returns the last error generated when a call was made to the Win32 API.
OLELastError()	Returns the last error generated by the object linking and embedding (OLE) API.
BuildNumber()	Returns the Perl build number.
LoginName()	Returns the username of the person running Perl.
NodeName()	Returns the NetBIOS computer name.
DomainName()	Returns the name of the domain the computer is a member of.
FsType()	Returns the name of the file system, such as NTFS or FAT.
GetCwd()	Returns the current active drive.
SetCwd(newdir)	Enables you to change to the drive designated by the newdir variable.
GetOSName()	Returns the OS name.
FormatMessage(error)	Converts the error message number into a descriptive string.
Spawn(command, args, $pid)	Starts a new process, using arguments supplied by the programmer and the process ID ($pid).
LookupAccountSID(sys, sid, $acct, $domain, $type)	Returns the account name, domain name, and security ID (SID) type.
InitiateSystemShutdown(machine, message, timeout, forceclose, reboot)	Shuts down a specified computer or server.
AbortSystemShutdown(machine)	Aborts the shutdown if it was done in error.
GetTickCount()	Returns the Win32 tick count (time elapsed since the system first started).
ExpandEnvironmentalStrings (envstring)	Returns the environmental variable strings specified in the envstring variable.
GetShortPathName(longpathname)	Returns the 8.3 version of the long pathname. In DOS and older Windows programs, filenames could be only eight characters, with a three-character extension.
GetNextAvailableDrive()	Returns the next available drive letter.
RegisterServer(libraryname)	Loads the DLL specified by libraryname and calls the DLLRegisterServer() function.
UnregisterServer(libraryname)	Loads the DLL specified by libraryname and calls the DLLUnregisterServer() function.
Sleep(time)	Pauses the number of milliseconds specified by the time variable.

Table 7-11   Win32 API functions

Attackers and security professionals can use these functions to discover information about a remote computer. Although these functions aren't difficult to understand, becoming proficient at using them in a program takes time and discipline. For security professionals who need to know what attackers can do, gaining this skill is worth the time and effort.

In Activity 7-6, you create a Perl script that uses some of the Win32 API functions listed in Table 7-11. This script gives you the following information about the Windows computer you have been using for this book's activities:

- Logon name of the user
- Computer name
- File system
- Current directory
- OS name

Activity 7-6: Creating a Perl Script That Uses the Win32 API

Time Required: 30 minutes

Objective: Install Perl on Windows and learn how to access the Win32 API from a Perl script.

Description: In this activity, you'll install ActivePerl 5.X and write a basic Perl script, using the formatting functions you have already learned and the Win32 API functions in Table 7-11. If possible, work in groups of three to four students. You can use the following reference to learn more about the Win32 API: *http://search.cpan.org/~jdb/Win32-0.52/Win32.pm*.

1. Start your Web browser and go to **http://activestate.com/activeperl**.

2. On the ActivePerl page, click the **Download ActivePerl** link. Now, click the **Download ActivePerl 5.X...** button. *(Note: Websites may change over time so you might have to search around the page to find the download link.)*

3. After the file has been downloaded, locate and run the install. If necessary, respond to any security prompts.

4. In the welcome window of the ActivePerl Setup Wizard, click **Next**.

5. Read the license agreement, verify that the **I accept the terms in the License Agreement** option button is selected, and then click **Next**.

6. By default, the wizard will install all components on your hard drive, as shown in Figure 7-12. (Note that the screens you see might differ slightly, depending on the version you downloaded.) If you want to see the total disk space required, click the **Disk Usage** button, then click **OK**. Click **Next** to accept the features.

Figure 7-12   Installing ActivePerl features

7. In the Choose Setup Options window (see Figure 7-13), accept the default selections, then click **Next**.

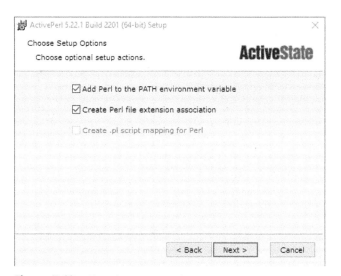

Figure 7-13   Choosing setup options

8. In the Ready to Install window, click **Install**. Click **Yes** on the UAC prompt, if necessary. After several minutes, the program is installed.

9. In the last window, click **Finish**. Read the release notes, which are displayed in your Web browser automatically.

10. To begin writing your Perl script, open a command prompt window and switch to the **C:\Perl** directory. Type **notepad Win32.pl** and press **Enter**. Click **Yes** when prompted to create a new file.

11. In the new Notepad document, type **# Win32.pl** on the first line and press **Enter**.

12. Use what you've learned in this chapter to write comments for documenting the program. Be sure to enter the author name, date, and a brief description of what the program does, such as the functions it accesses from the Win32 API.

13. After your lines of documentation, press **Enter** several times to create blank lines for separating your comments from the program code. Then type **use win32;** and press **Enter**. (*Note*: Don't forget the semicolon.)

14. You need five pieces of information (noted in the bulleted list before this activity) from the Win32 API. Attempt to write the code for getting this information, and then save the program. If you need assistance, use the following steps.

15. Type **$login = Win32::LoginName();** and press **Enter**. This line populates the `$login` variable with the information gathered from `LoginName()`.

16. Next, type the following lines to populate the other variables needed to complete the task, pressing **Enter** after each line:

```
$NetBIOS = Win32::NodeName();
$filesystem = Win32::FsType();
$Directory = Win32::GetCwd();
$os_name = Win32::GetOSName();
```

17. The following variables need to be displayed onscreen. Type the lines of code as shown, pressing **Enter** after each line. When you're done, your window should look similar to Figure 7-14.

```
print "$login\n";
print "$NetBIOS\n";
print "$filesystem\n";
print "$Directory\n";
print "$os_name\n";
```

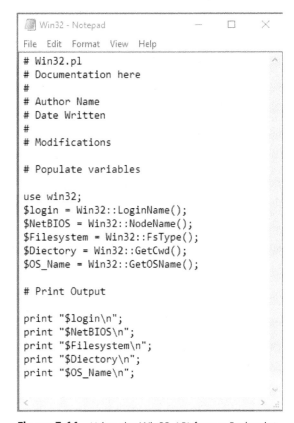

Figure 7-14 Using the Win32 API from a Perl script

18. After typing all the code, save the program, run it, and debug any errors. Figure 7-15 shows the output. What's wrong with this report?

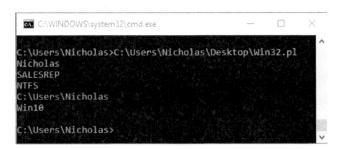

Figure 7-15 Running the win32.pl Perl script

19. Spend time improving the report's formatting so that anyone reading the output could understand its meaning.

20. Are there any improvements your group thinks should be made to the script? Explain. What other information might be beneficial for a security professional to get from this report?

21. Select a spokesperson from your group to do a 3- to 5-minute presentation on the final script, and state why your program is the most marketable. After all the presentations, have the class choose a winner.

22. Close all open windows.

An Overview of Ruby

Another object-oriented language many security testers use is Ruby, which is similar to Perl. Security testers also use Metasploit (*www.metasploit.com*), a Ruby-based program included on this book's DVD, to check for vulnerabilities on computer systems. Metasploit contains hundreds of exploits that can be launched on a victim's computer or network, which makes it a useful tool for hackers. Security testers using Metasploit should understand the basics of Ruby and be able to modify Ruby code to suit different environments and targets. For example, security testers might need to modify code for a reverse shell module in Ruby so that it's compatible with the target system where they're conducting vulnerability tests (see Figure 7-16). A reverse shell is a backdoor initiated from inside the target's network that makes it possible to take control of the target even when it's behind a firewall. Google "Reverse Shell" to learn more about it.

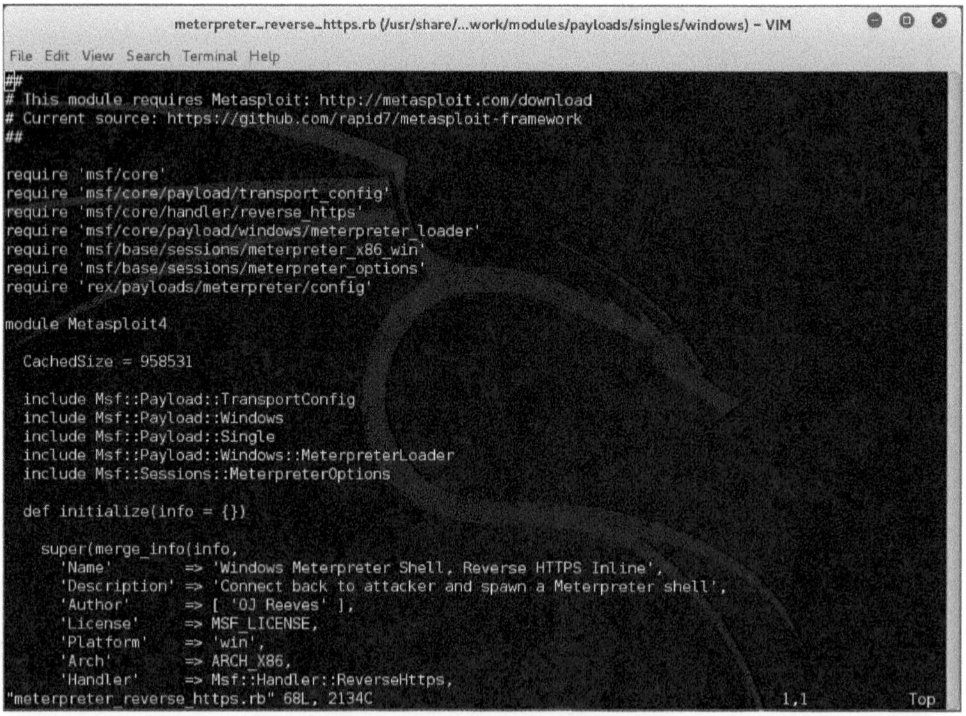

Figure 7-16   Modifying reverse shell payload code in Ruby

Figure 7-17 shows some of the many exploits written in Ruby. Note the .rb extension, for Ruby, in program names. In Figure 7-18, the security tester has opened the module for the MS15-020 vulnerability exploit in vim for editing. As you can see, the Ruby syntax is similar to that of object-oriented programming, and the module includes detailed descriptions of the Ruby code.

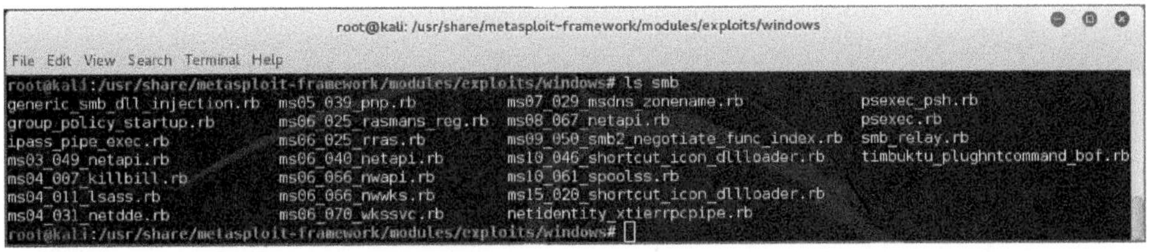

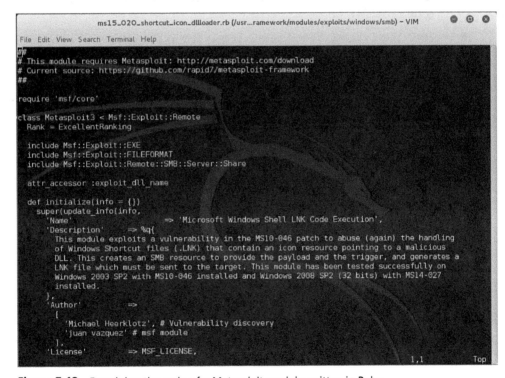

Figure 7-17   Metasploit modules in Ruby

Figure 7-18   Examining the code of a Metasploit module written in Ruby

Chapter Summary

- Writing an algorithm and using pseudocode are good habits to adopt when writing programs.

- Clear documentation of program code is essential.

- C is one of the most popular programming languages for security professionals and hackers alike.

- Learning the BLT of any programming language can help you master the fundamentals of programming. Branching, looping, and testing are the most important aspects of programming.

- Many C compilers are available. GNU GCC is an open-source C compiler included with most Linux implementations.

- HTML is the primary language used to create Web pages. Security professionals need to recognize when something looks suspicious in a Web page, so they should be able to read an HTML file.

- Security professionals should have a basic knowledge of Perl and C because many security tools are written in these languages. Security professionals who understand these programming languages can modify security tools and create their own customized tools.

- With object-oriented programming, programmers can create classes, which are structures containing both data and functions. Functions in these classes are programs that perform specific tasks.

- WinAPI (formerly called Win32 API) is an interface to the Windows OS that programmers can use to access information about a computer running Windows, such as the computer name, OS name, and so forth.

- Ruby is a flexible, object-oriented programming language similar to Perl. Security testers and attackers use Metasploit, containing exploit modules written in Ruby, to check for vulnerabilities or to attack systems.

Key Terms

algorithm	compiler	looping
assembly language	conversion specifier	pseudocode
branching	do loop	testing
bug	for loop	while loop
class	function	

Review Questions

1. A C program must contain which of the following?

   a. Name of the computer programmer

   b. A main() function

   c. The #include <std.h> header file

   d. A description of the algorithm used

2. An algorithm is defined as which of the following?

   a. A list of possible solutions for solving a problem

   b. A method for automating a manual process

   c. A program written in a high-level language

   d. A set of instructions for solving a specific problem

3. A missing parenthesis or brace might cause a C compiler to return which of the following?

   a. System fault

   b. Interpreter error

   c. Syntax error

   d. Machine-language fault

4. List three logical operators used in C programming.

5. Most programming languages enable programmers to perform which of the following actions? (Choose all that apply.)

   a. Branching

   b. Testing

   c. Faulting

   d. Looping

6. Before writing a program, many programmers outline it first by using which of the following?

   a. Pseudocode

   b. Machine code

   c. Assembly code

   d. Assembler code

7. Which of the following C statements has the highest risk of creating an infinite loop?

   a. while (a > 10)

   b. while (a < 10)

   c. for (a = 1; a < 100; ++a)

   d. for (;;)

8. To add comments to a Perl script, you use which of the following symbols?

   a. `//`

   b. `/*`

   c. `#`

   d. `<!--`

9. Documentation of a program should include which of the following? (Choose all that apply.)

   a. Author

   b. Date written

   c. Explanation of complex algorithms

   d. Modifications to the code

10. Name two looping mechanisms used in Perl.

11. In C, which looping function performs an action first and then tests to see whether the action should continue to occur?

    a. `for loop`

    b. `while loop`

    c. `do loop`

    d. `unless loop`

12. What is the result of running the following C program?

```
main()
{
  int a = 2; if (a = 1)
    printf("I made a mistake!");
  else
    printf("I did it correctly!");
}
```

    a. "Syntax error: illegal use of ;" is displayed.

    b. "I made a mistake!" is displayed.

    c. "Syntax error: variable not declared" is displayed.

    d. "I did it correctly!" is displayed.

13. Using the following Perl code, how many times will "This is easy..." be displayed onscreen?

```
for ($count=1; $count <= 5; $count++)
{
  print "This is easy...";
}
```

    a. 6

    b. 4

    c. None (syntax error)

    d. 5

Many of the explanations on the CVE Web site are complex and might be difficult to understand. What's important, however, is that you're able to research a vulnerability that's relevant to the security test you're conducting. For example, if the system you're testing uses the Remote Desktop Connection Client noted in CVE-2013-1296, you might need to do research on what Remote Desktop Connection is and whether the version the company is running is vulnerable. You might also have to visit the Microsoft Web site to see whether any patches or security updates are available for this vulnerability. For example, searching on "CVE-2013-1296" on Google reveals a number of results. If you follow the link to technet.microsoft.com for MS 13-029, you'll be taken to "Microsoft Security Bulletin MS13-029—Critical: Vulnerability in Remote Desktop Client Could Allow Remote Code Execution (2828223)."

As a security tester, you must be able and willing to go beyond the basics to perform your job effectively. A security tester is an investigator who doesn't stop at one piece of information. You are the Monk of the IT world, always saying "You'll thank me later...."

Security testers can use information from the CVE site to test a Windows computer and make sure it's been patched with updates from Microsoft that address these known vulnerabilities. Hackers visit Web sites that offer exploit programs to run against these vulnerabilities, but exploits should only be used in specific cases, as a security tester and with prior approval. In other words, you don't want to blow up a refinery to demonstrate the company's security flaws; you want to inform the company when its systems are vulnerable to attack. Many of these known vulnerabilities are found on ports that port-scanning tools can easily detect as being open. For example, SMB (tcp/139 or tcp/445), SMTP (tcp/25), HTTPS (tcp/443), and RPC (tcp/135) might be vulnerable to attack.

Tools like Nessus and OpenVAS will help to automate some of the process of identifying vulnerabilities for you, but make sure you understand the results that the tool provides by doing further research. When you're conducting research, don't skim the CVE and CAN information. Remember, attention to detail is what separates skillful security testers from the mediocre. As Pete Herzog states in the OSSTMM: "Do sweat the small stuff, because it's all small stuff."

Windows File Systems

The purpose of any file system, regardless of the OS, is to store and manage information. The file system organizes information that users create as well as the OS files needed to boot the system, so the file system is the most vital part of any OS. In some cases, this critical component of the OS can be a vulnerability.

File Allocation Table File Allocation Table (FAT), the original Microsoft file system, is supported by nearly all desktop and server OSs from 1981 to now. Because of its broad support, FAT12 is also the standard file system for most removable media other than CDs and DVDs. Later versions, such as FAT16, FAT32, and Extended FAT (exFAT, developed for Windows Embedded CE), provide for larger file and disk sizes. For example, FAT32 allows a single file to be up to 4 GB and a disk volume to be up to 8 terabytes (TB). The most serious shortcoming of FAT is that it doesn't support file-level access control lists (ACLs), which are necessary for setting permissions on files. For this reason, using FAT in a multiuser environment results in a critical vulnerability. Microsoft addressed this problem and other shortcomings of FAT when it introduced its first OS for enterprises, Windows NT.

NTFS New Technology File System (NTFS) was first released as a high-end file system in Windows NT 3.1, and in Windows NT 3.51, it added support for larger files and disk volumes as well as ACL file security. Subsequent Windows versions have included upgrades for compression, disk quotas, journaling, file-level encryption, transactional NTFS, symbolic links, and self-healing. NTFS is used today for Windows 10 systems. Even with strong security features, however, NTFS has some inherent vulnerabilities; some may refer to these vulnerabilities as features. For example, one little-known NTFS feature is alternate data streams (ADSs), written for compatibility with Apple Hierarchical File System (HFS). An ADS can "stream" (hide) information behind existing files without affecting their function, size, or other information, which makes it possible for system intruders to hide exploitation tools and other malicious files. Several methods can be used to detect ADSs. In Windows Vista and later, a switch has been added to the Dir command: Enter dir /r from the directory you want to analyze to display any ADSs. For previous Windows versions, you need to download a tool such as Streams.exe from *https://technet.microsoft.com/en-us/sysinternals/bb897440.aspx*. Whatever method you use, you need to determine whether any ADS you detect is supposed to be there. A better and more efficient method of detecting malicious changes to the file system is using host-based file-integrity monitoring tools, such as Tripwire (*www.tripwire.com*) or Log-Rhythm (*www.logrhythm.com*). A *nix-based version of Tripwire is also available.

Remote Procedure Call

Remote Procedure Call (RPC) is an interprocess communication mechanism that allows a program running on one host to run code on a remote host. The Conficker worm took advantage of a vulnerability in RPC to run arbitrary code on susceptible hosts. Microsoft Security Bulletin MS08-067, posted October 23, 2008, advised users of this critical vulnerability that allowed attackers to run their own code and offered a patch to correct the problem. Even though the vulnerability was published in advisories and a patch was available weeks before the Conficker worm hit on November 21, 2008, millions of computers were affected. Stuxnet, which surfaced in 2010, used the same flaw that Conficker used to spread its infection three years prior!

Microsoft Baseline Security Analyzer (MBSA, discussed in more detail later in "Tools for Identifying Vulnerabilities in Windows") is an excellent tool for determining whether a system is vulnerable due to an RPC-related issue and for many other configuration and patching items as well. MSBA can quickly identify missing patches and misconfigurations. In Activity 8-1, you download and install MBSA on your Windows computer.

Activity 8-1: Downloading and Installing MBSA

Time Required: 30 minutes

Objective: Download and install Microsoft Baseline Security Analyzer.

Description: In this activity, you download and install MBSA, a helpful tool for discovering vulnerabilities in Windows systems.

1. In Windows, start your Web browser and go to **https://www.microsoft.com/en-us/download/details.aspx?id=7558.**

2. Click the **Download** link, and then check the box corresponding to your version of Windows (32 bit or 64 bit)—usually, MBSASetup-x86-EN.msi or MBSASetup-x64-EN.msi.

3. After the download is finished, browse to the location of the saved file and double-click the setup executable file. If you see a warning message, click **Run** or **OK** to continue. The MBSA Setup Wizard starts.

4. After closing all running Windows applications, click **Next**.

5. Click the **I accept the license agreement** option button, and then click **Next**.

6. Follow the prompts, accepting the default settings unless your instructor advises you otherwise.

7. When the installation is finished, start MBSA by clicking **Start** and clicking **Microsoft Baseline Security Analyzer** under recently added or by double-clicking the desktop icon, if available.

8. Take some time to explore the interface and familiarize yourself with the program. Leave MBSA running for the next activity.

NetBIOS

As you learned in Chapter 6, NetBIOS is software loaded into memory that enables a program to interact with a network resource or device. Network resources are identified with 16-byte NetBIOS names. NetBIOS isn't a protocol; it's just the interface to a network protocol that enables a program to access a network resource. It usually works with **NetBIOS Extended User Interface (NetBEUI)**, a fast, efficient protocol that requires little configuration and allows transmitting NetBIOS packets over TCP/IP and various network topologies, such as token ring and Ethernet. NetBIOS over TCP/IP is called NBT in Windows 2000 Server; in Windows Server 2003, it's called NetBT. (NetBIOS isn't available in Windows Vista, Server 2008, and later versions of Windows.)

Systems running newer Windows OSs can share files and resources without using NetBIOS; however, NetBIOS is still used for backward compatibility, which is important when corporate budgets don't allow upgrading every computer on the network. In addition, customer expectations must be met. Customers expect, for example, that a document created in Word 97 can still be read in Word 2003. In fact, they demand it. Therefore, software developers face the challenge of improving OS security yet still ensuring compatibility with less secure predecessors. As long as newer Windows OSs have to work with older NetBIOS-based systems, security will always be a challenge.

Server Message Block

In Windows, **Server Message Block (SMB)** is used to share files and usually runs on top of NetBIOS, NetBEUI, or TCP/IP. Several hacking tools that target SMB can still cause damage to Windows networks. Two well-known SMB hacking tools are L0phtcrack's SMB Packet Capture utility and SMBRelay, which intercept SMB traffic and collect usernames and password hashes.

Interestingly, it took Microsoft seven years to patch the vulnerability these hacking tools exploited. Many security researchers point to this situation as another example of the problem caused by ensuring backward compatibility. By continuing to use a protocol with a known vulnerability (which can also be described as a design flaw), Microsoft exposes its products to attack and exploitation.

Microsoft introduced SMB2 in Windows Vista, and this version has several new features and is faster and more efficient. In addition, in Windows 7, Microsoft avoided reusing code from Windows XP in the OS but still allowed backward capability by including an option for a virtualized Windows XP environment, called Windows XP Mode.

Common Internet File System

Common Internet File System (CIFS) is a standardized protocol that replaced SMB in Windows 2000 Server and later, but to allow backward compatibility, the original SMB is still used. CIFS is a remote file system protocol that enables computers to share network resources over the Internet. In other words, files, folders, printers, and other resources can be made available to users throughout a network. For sharing to occur, there must be an infrastructure that allows placing these resources on the network and a method to control access to resources. CIFS relies on other protocols to handle service announcements notifying users what resources are available on the network and to handle authentication and authorization for accessing these resources. CIFS is also available for many *nix systems.

The Network Neighborhood or My Network Places services use broadcast protocols to announce resources available on a network. Essentially, a computer calls over the network connection "Here I am! My NetBIOS name is Salesmgr, and I have lots of files and folders to share with anyone out there." To share files and folders, CIFS relies on SMB, but it offers many enhancements, including the following:

- Locking features that enable multiple users to access and update a file simultaneously without conflicts
- Caching and read-ahead/write-behind capability
- Support for fault tolerance
- Capability to run more efficiently over slow dial-up lines
- Support for anonymous and authenticated access to files to improve security

To prevent unauthorized access to these files, CIFS relies on SMB's security model. An administrator can select two methods for server security:

- *Share-level security*—A folder on a disk is made available to users for sharing. A password can be configured for the share but isn't required.
- *User-level security*—The resource is made available to network users; however, a username and password are required to access the resource. The SMB server maintains an encrypted version of users' passwords to enhance security.

Windows 2000 Server and later listen on most of the same ports as Windows NT, which means many old attacks might still work on newer OSs. For example, by recognizing which ports are open on a Windows Server 2003 or 2008 system, a security tester can find vulnerabilities that allow introducing a Trojan or other remote control program for capturing authorized users' passwords and logon names. Most attackers look for servers designated as

domain controllers (servers that handle authentication). Windows Server 2003 and 2008 domain controllers are used to authenticate user accounts, so they contain much of the information attackers want to access. By default, Windows Server 2003 and 2008 domain controllers using CIFS listen on the following ports:

- DNS (port 53)
- HTTP (port 80)
- Kerberos (port 88)
- RPC (port 135)
- NetBIOS Name Service (port 137)
- NetBIOS Datagram Service (port 139)
- LDAP (port 389)
- HTTPS (port 443)
- SMB/CIFS (port 445)
- LDAP over SSL (port 636)
- Active Directory global catalog (port 3268)

In Windows Server 2003 and 2008, a domain controller uses a global catalog (GC) server to locate resources in a domain containing thousands or even millions of objects. For example, if a user wants to locate a printer with the word "color" in its description, he or she can use a GC server, which contains attributes such as the resource's name and location and points the user to the network resource.

Null Sessions

As you learned in Chapter 6, a null session is an anonymous connection established without credentials, such as a username and password. Also called an anonymous logon, a null session can be used to display information about users, groups, shares, and password policies. Null sessions are necessary only if networks need to support older Windows versions. Nonetheless, many organizations still have null sessions enabled, even though all their old Windows systems have been removed from the network. You can use the Nbtstat, Net view, Netstat, Ping, Pathping, and Telnet commands to enumerate NetBIOS vulnerabilities.

Web Services

Older versions of Web services and IIS would enable numerous features by default, leaving systems with a large attack surface. Microsoft developed the IIS Lockdown Wizard specifically for locking down IIS versions 4.0 and 5.0. You can download it from *http://support .microsoft.com/kb/325864*. As a security tester, however, you should encourage clients to upgrade any OS and any software that's no longer supported instead of using security workarounds, such as the IIS Lockdown Wizard.

IIS 5.0 is installed by default in Windows 2000 Server, and many administrators aren't aware of it until a problem occurs. On networks still using Windows 2000 Server, don't assume there's no Web server on your network just because you didn't specifically install one.

Although IIS 6.0 (Windows Server 2003) through IIS 10.0 (Windows Server 2016) are installed in a "secure by default" mode, previous versions left crucial holes that made it possible for attackers to sneak into a network. Regardless of the IIS version a system runs, keeping systems patched is important, and system administrators should still be aware of what patches are installed and which services are running on their Web servers. Configuring only necessary services and applications is a wise move.

MS SQL Server

Older versions of Microsoft SQL Server have many potential vulnerabilities that can't be covered in detail in this book. The most common critical SQL vulnerability is the null SA password. All versions before SQL Server 2005 have a vulnerability that could allow remote users to gain System Administrator (SA) access through the SA account on the server. During SQL Server 6.5 and 7 installations, the user is prompted—but not required—to set a password on this account. SQL Server 2000 uses Windows Integrated authentication by default, but the user can also select mixed-mode authentication. In this authentication mode, an SA account with a blank password is created, and this account can't be disabled. If attackers find this account, they have administrative access to not only the database, but also potentially the database server.

Buffer Overflows

As you learned in Chapter 3, a buffer overflow occurs when data is written to a buffer (temporary memory space) and, because of insufficient bounds checking, corrupts data in memory next to the allocated buffer. Normally, this problem occurs when dangerous functions use input that has not been properly validated. Because of design flaws, several functions don't verify that the numbers or strings they accept fit in the buffer supplied to hold them. If this lack of verification is exploited, it can allow attackers to run shell code. Both C and C++ lack built-in protection against overwriting data in memory, so applications written in these languages are vulnerable to buffer overflow attacks. Because these programming languages are widely used, buffer overflow vulnerabilities are prevalent in many applications and OSs. Buffer overflow attacks don't require an authenticated user and can be carried out remotely. Fortunately, modern frameworks (e.g., ReactJS and AngularJS) include sanitizing routines and other security features to help developers code more securely. However, it's still up to the developer to use these features to create secure code.

 Several Microsoft buffer overflow exploit plug-ins are available free for download and are included with Metasploit on this book's DVD. If you have access to these exploit tools, you can be sure that attackers will, too.

Passwords and Authentication

You've already learned that the weakest security link in any network is authorized users. Unfortunately, this link is the most difficult to secure, as it relies on people who might not realize that their actions could expose their organization to a major security breach, resulting in damaged systems, stolen or destroyed information, malware infection, and so forth. There might also be legal issues to deal with after an attack, and a company can lose customers' confidence as a result.

Companies should take steps to address this vulnerability. A comprehensive password policy is critical, as a username and password are often all that stands between an attacker and access. A password policy should include the following:

- Change passwords regularly on system-level accounts quarterly.
- Require users to change their passwords quarterly.
- Require a minimum password length of at least eight characters (and 15 characters for administrative accounts).
- Require complex passwords; in other words, passwords must include letters, numbers, symbols, punctuation characters, and preferably both uppercase and lowercase letters.
- Passwords can't be common words, words found in the dictionary (in any language), or slang, jargon, or dialect.
- Passwords must not be identified with a particular user, such as birthdays, names, or company-related words.
- Never write a password down or store it online or in a file on the user's computer.
- Don't hint at or reveal a password to anyone over the phone, in e-mail, or in person.
- Use caution when logging on to make sure no one sees you entering your password.
- Limit reuse of old passwords.

In addition to these guidelines, administrators can configure domain controllers to enforce password age, length, and complexity. On Windows 2000 Server and Windows Server 2003 domain controllers, some aspects of a password policy can be enforced, such as the following:

- *Account lockout threshold*—Set the number of failed attempts before the account is disabled temporarily.
- *Account lockout duration*—Set the period of time the user account is locked out after a specified number of failed logon attempts.

On Windows Server 2008, Windows Server 2012, and Windows Server 2016 domain controllers, multiple password policies can be enforced. For example, one password policy might require a complex password of 15 or more characters for administrator accounts, and another password policy might require only 8 characters for user accounts with no administrative privileges. Despite the best efforts to promote security by enforcing password policies, it's still entirely possible that a password can be cracked. The latest tools that incorporate rainbow tables can crack complex passwords surprisingly fast. You explore password cracking in more detail in Chapter 12.

Tools for Identifying Vulnerabilities in Windows

Many tools are available for discovering Windows vulnerabilities. Using more than one tool for analysis is advisable, so learning a variety of methods and tools is beneficial to your career. Familiarity with several tools also helps you pinpoint problems more accurately. Some tools might report deceptive results, and if these results aren't verified with another method, you might not have an accurate assessment to report. Popular OS vulnerability scanners include Tripwire IP360, Tenable Nessus, QualysGuard, and Open-VAS, which you were introduced to in previous chapters. All these products scan both Linux and Windows OSs. In addition, several tools are specifically for Windows, and you learned about some in Chapter 6. In this following section, you explore a Windows tool for assessing Windows systems.

Built-in Windows Tools

This section focuses on MBSA, which you installed in Activity 8-1. Although security problems exist in all computer systems, many attacks can be avoided with careful system analysis and maintenance, which can include anything from establishing an efficient, regular update scheme to reviewing log files for signs of unusual activity. When Microsoft learns of problems or vulnerabilities in its software, it publishes patches, security updates, service packs, and hotfixes to address them as soon as possible. Microsoft has also addressed the problem of finding configuration errors, missing patches, and so on, and MBSA is an excellent, free resource for this task (see Figure 8-1). This tool is capable of checking for patches, security updates, configuration errors, blank or weak passwords, and more.

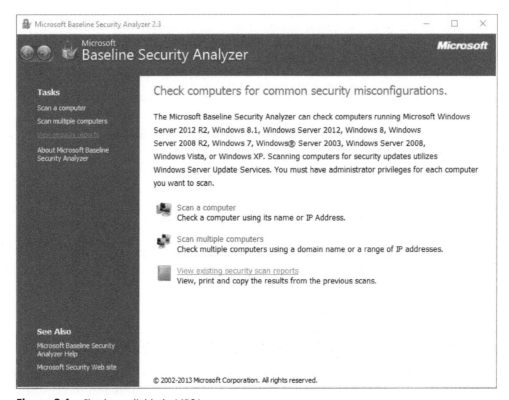

Figure 8-1   Checks available in MBSA

Source: © 2016 Microsoft

Table 8-2 summarizes MBSA's scanning capabilities. Note that these scans aren't performed, even in full-scan mode, if the associated product isn't installed on the system you're scanning. More information and complete instructions are available in the MBSA Help interface or the Microsoft Security Tools Web site (*https://technet.microsoft.com /en-us/security/cc297183.aspx*).

Type of check	Checks for:
Security update checks	Missing Windows, IIS, and SQL Server security updates Missing Exchange Server security updates Missing IE security updates Missing Windows Media Player and Office security updates Missing Microsoft Virtual Machine (VM) and Microsoft Data Access Components (MDAC) security updates Missing MSXML and Content Management Server security updates
Windows checks	Account password expiration and whether blank or simple passwords are used for local user accounts File system type on hard drives Whether the Auto Logon feature is enabled Whether the Guest account is enabled and the number of local Administrator accounts RestrictAnonymous Registry key setting List shares on the computer and any unnecessary services running Windows version and whether Windows auditing is enabled Firewall status and Automatic Updates status
IIS checks	Whether the IIS Lockdown tool is running Whether IIS sample applications and the IIS Admin virtual folder are installed Whether IIS parent paths are enabled Whether MSADC and Scripts virtual directories are installed Whether IIS logging is enabled Whether IIS is running on a domain controller
SQL checks	Whether the Administrators group belongs in the Sysadmin role and whether the CmdExec role is restricted to Sysadmin only Whether SQL Server is running on a domain controller Whether the SA account password is exposed and the Guest account has database access Access permissions to SQL Server installation folders Whether the Everyone group has access to SQL Server Registry keys Whether SQL Server service accounts are members of the local Administrators group Whether SQL Server accounts have blank or simple passwords SQL Server authentication mode type and number of Sysadmin role members
Desktop application checks	IE security zone settings for each local user Whether IE Enhanced Security Configuration is enabled for Administrator accounts Whether IE Enhanced Security Configuration is enabled for non-Administrator accounts Microsoft Office security zone settings for each local user

Table 8-2   Checks performed by MBSA in full-scan mode

Using MBSA Any computer meeting the system requirements shown in Table 8-3 can scan another computer or be scanned locally or remotely by MBSA. MBSA has its origins in the HFNetChk scanner created by Mark Shavlik, a Windows NT developer. Microsoft collaborated with Shavlik to develop and refine MBSA. The latest MBSA version uses the dynamic features of Windows Update.

Action	Requirements
To scan the local computer	Any Windows operating system, XP or later XML parser (the most recent version of the MSXML parser is recommended) World Wide Web service to perform local IIS administrative vulnerability checks Workstation and Server services enabled
A computer running the tool that's scanning remote machines	Any Windows operating system, XP or later XML parser (the most recent version of the MSXML parser is recommended) IIS Common Files (Note: IIS 6.0/7.0 Common Files are required for scanning an IIS 6.0/7.0 server remotely.) Workstation service and Client for Microsoft Networks enabled
A computer being scanned remotely	Any Windows operating system, XP, or later IIS 4.0, 5.0, 6.0, 7.0. 8.0, 8.5, and 10.0 (required for IIS product and administrative vulnerability checks) SQL Server 7.0, 2000, 2005, 2008, 2008 R2, 2012, 2014, or SQL Server Data Engine (MSDE) 1.0, 2000, or Windows Internal Database (required for SQL product and administrative vulnerability checks) Office 2016, 2013, 2010, 2007, 2003, 2000, or XP (required for Office product and administrative vulnerability checks) Server and Remote Registry services and File and Print Sharing enabled

Table 8-3   Minimum system requirements for MBSA

Like the original HFNetChk tool, you can run MBSA from the command line, which enables you to use scripts. Figure 8-2 shows the output of running mbsacli.exe on a Windows 10 system.

```
Administrator: Command Prompt                                    —    □    ×
C:\Program Files\Microsoft Baseline Security Analyzer 2>mbsacli.exe /target 127.0.0.1
Microsoft Baseline Security Analyzer
Version 2.3 (2.3.2211.0)
(C) Copyright 2002-2013 Microsoft Corporation. All rights reserved.

Scanning...
1 of 1 computer scans complete.

Scan Complete.

Security assessment: Severe Risk
Computer name: WORKGROUP\SALESREP
IP address: 127.0.0.1
Security report name: WORKGROUP - SALESREP (3-6-2016 1-30 PM)
Scan date: 3/6/2016 1:30 PM
Scanned with MBSA version: 2.3.2211.0
Catalog synchronization date: 2016-02-09T03:57:12Z
Security update catalog: Microsoft Update (offline)


  Security Updates Scan Results

     Issue:  Developer Tools, Runtimes, and Redistributables Security Updates
     Score:  Check passed
     Result: No security updates are missing.

        Current Update Compliance

                | MS11-025 | Installed | Security Update for Microsoft Visual C++ 2008 Serv
ice Pack 1 Redistributable Package (KB2538243) | Important |

     Issue:  SQL Server Security Updates
     Score:  Check passed
     Result: No security updates are missing.

        Current Update Compliance

                | MS06-061 | Installed | MSXML 6.0 RTM Security Update  (925673) | Critical
```

Figure 8-2   Scanning with the `mbsacli.exe /target` command

Source: © 2016 Microsoft

Activity 8-2: Using MBSA to Scan the Local Computer (Optional)

Time Required: 30 minutes

Objective: Use MBSA to scan the local computer for weak or missing passwords.

Description: In this activity, you scan your computer with MBSA to discover vulnerabilities, including weak or missing passwords. At the end of the activity, submit a summary of your findings to your instructor, along with brief recommendations for correcting the problems you found.

1. Start MBSA, if necessary and click the **Scan a Computer** link.

2. Click the **dropdown button** next to **Computer name** and select your computer's name. Accept the scan default settings and click **Start Scan**.

3. When the scan is finished, the report window displays the results (see Figure 8-3). What problems did MBSA find? Did it find any password vulnerabilities or other vulnerabilities? Are any results unexpected?

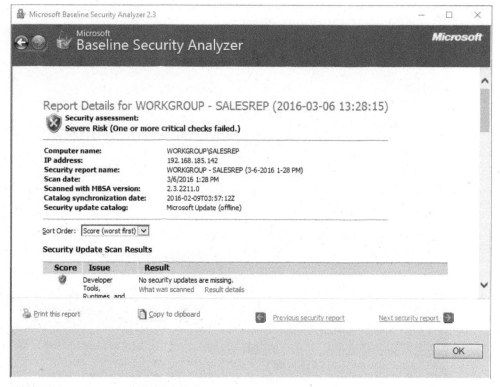

Figure 8-3   Viewing the MBSA report

Source: © 2016 Microsoft

4. Write a brief summary of vulnerability problems that MBSA found. If time permits, discuss your results with your classmates and instructor. Close the MBSA window, and log off Windows for the next activity.

Best Practices for Hardening Windows Systems

As a penetration tester, your job is to find vulnerabilities and report them as defined in your contract. Your responsibility ends there. However, a security tester must not only find vulnerabilities; he or she must be familiar with methods of correcting them. Typically, managers want solutions included with reports of potential problems, particularly for technologies they might not fully understand.

Although the only way to make a system truly secure is to unplug it and lock it away in a vault, this approach defies the purpose of a network. Because you can't lock network computers away to keep them secure, the best option is to be vigilant. A security breach is only one undiscovered vulnerability away, but with careful management, most systems can be secured adequately and still meet users' needs. There are some general things you can do to make and keep a network secure, discussed in the following sections.

Patching Systems

The best way to keep systems secure, operating at peak performance, and using the newest features is to *keep systems under your care up to date*. As noted, many attacks have taken advantage of a known vulnerability that has a patch available. There are several methods for obtaining service packs, hotfixes, and patches. If you have only a few computers to maintain (10 or fewer), accessing Windows Update manually from each computer works fine, but this method is still time consuming. Depending on the Windows version, you can configure Automatic Updates on each machine. This option is usually better because it helps ensure that machines are always up to date without the administrator or user's intervention. The downside is that some patches can cause problems, so testing a patch before applying it to a production system is preferable, particularly in large networks.

For a large network, applying updates manually isn't feasible. Configuring Automatic Updates is an option if you have physical access to all computers, but downloading patches to each machine can slow network performance. There are a couple of options for patch management. From 1994 to 2005, Microsoft's **Systems Management Server (SMS)** was the standard for managing Windows security patches on multiple computers in a network. This service assessed machines in a defined domain and could be configured to manage patch deployment. (Although this service had many other capabilities, for the purposes of this chapter, you simply need to know that it can be used for patch management.)

In 2005, **Windows Software Update Services (WSUS)** became available. WSUS is a client/server technology designed to manage patching and updating system software from the network. Instead of downloading updates to each computer, WSUS downloads patches and publishes them internally to servers and desktop systems. Unlike Automatic Updates, which downloads and installs updates automatically, the administrator has control over which updates are deployed. This feature is a major advantage, considering that some updates can cause problems with certain network and application configurations and should be tested before being deployed.

In 2007, Windows **System Center Configuration Manager (SCCM)** became the new standard. SCCM includes a suite of tools to help administrators deploy and manage servers alongside updated patch-management functionality. SCCM even allows for administrators to control mobile devices running Android, iOS, and Windows Mobile OS.

Third-party patch-management solutions are also available from vendors such as BigFix, Tanium, and BladeLogic. Whatever patch-management tools you use, remember that keeping systems up to date is one of the most critical steps in keeping systems secure. As a security tester, often you'll find that patches aren't current on the system you're testing. An effective patch-management scheme might seem like common sense, but administrators often get so busy with other complicated issues that they forget the simple solutions. You must recommend effective patch management to your clients and be able to explain why it's crucial to system security.

Antivirus Solutions

Whether you're working with an enterprise network consisting of thousands of servers and tens of thousands of clients or a small business network of 15 systems and one server, an antivirus solution is essential. For small networks, desktop antivirus tools with automatic updating might be enough, but in a large network, a corporate-level solution is needed. Several excellent products are available, and selecting the right one requires some research. What's important to remember about an antivirus tool is that it must be planned, installed, and configured correctly to ensure the best protection. An antivirus tool is almost useless if it isn't updated regularly. Ideally, an antivirus tool should automatically download and install updates daily. If your examination of a system reveals that no antivirus tool is running, you should recommend installing one immediately. You must also stress keeping it up to date for the best protection.

Enable Logging and Review Logs Regularly

Logging is a crucial function for monitoring system security. It must be configured carefully to record only useful statistics, because overly verbose logging can easily overwhelm analysts. Review logs regularly for signs of intrusion or other problems on the network. It's always important to build prevention and detection by considering what attackers might do if they compromised your network. If you were an attacker and broke into a network you weren't familiar with, you would probably run some Windows administrative commands to understand more about the network. Commands like ipconfig /all, netstat -r, net view, gpresult, especially when grouped together, could be seen as suspicious, given the proper context. If you suddenly see a non-technical user making a bunch of administrative requests, it might be time to investigate further. Scanning through thousands of log entries is time consuming, and missing important entries is likely. A log-monitoring tool is best for this task. Several are available, depending on network needs and budget. Some of these tools even include customizable automation that can give you an edge on an attacker by automating response (e.g., disable a remote systems network adapter) when known malicious activities are occurring.

Disable Unused Services and Filtering Ports

Disabling unneeded services and deleting unnecessary applications or scripts make sense because they give intruders a potential point of entry into a network. For example, if you have a Windows Server 2016 system acting as a file server, you certainly don't need DNS services running on it; doing so leaves port 53 TCP/UDP open and vulnerable to attack. The idea is simple: Open *only* what needs to be open, and close everything else—also known as reducing the attack surface. (The **attack surface** is the amount of code a computer system exposes to unauthenticated outsiders.) With fewer services exposed, there's less chance of an attacker being able to find an unpatched vulnerability.

In addition, filtering out unnecessary ports can protect systems from attack. Some ports frequently subject to attack include the following:

- FTP (20 and 21 TCP)
- TFTP (69 UDP)
- Telnet (23 TCP)
- DNS (53 TCP/UDP)
- NTP (123 UDP)
- NetBIOS (135 TCP/UDP, 137 and 138 UDP, 139 TCP)

- SMB (445 TCP/UDP)
- Remote Desktop Protocol (3389 TCP)
- SNMP (161 and 162 TCP/UDP)
- Windows RPC programs (1025 to 1039 TCP/UDP)

The best way to protect a network from SMB attacks is to make sure perimeter routers and firewalls filter out ports 137 to 139 and 445. Blocking ports 139 and 445 has the added benefit of protecting against external null session attacks. Windows Server 2003 doesn't disable SMB on port 445 by default. In fact, if the computer is a domain controller, you need to provide access to SMB. The server's job is to make sure the person attempting to log on to the network is indeed authorized to access network resources. Because you usually want to share resources on a server, closing port 445 could create other problems, such as users not being able to access shared folders and printers.

An attacker can gain entry through many other ports. It isn't possible to close all avenues of attack and still offer the functionality users need, but with careful planning, an administrator can make sure there are fewer ways in. For a complete list of ports and services, consult IANA's Assigned Port Number page at *www.iana.org/assignments/port-numbers*.

 Use caution when disabling services and blocking ports. Make sure that no required services depending on a port or other service are disabled.

Other Security Best Practices

In addition to keeping software up to date, running antivirus tools, and disabling services, you can take the following steps to help minimize the risks to a Windows network:

- Minimize the number of users with administrative rights.
- Implement software to prevent sensitive data from leaving the network.
- Use network segmentation to make it more difficult for an attacker to move from computer to computer.
- Restrict the number of applications that are allowed to execute on a computer connected to the network.
- Delete unused scripts and sample applications.
- Delete default hidden shares and unnecessary shares.
- Use a different unique naming scheme and passwords for public interfaces.
- Ensure passwords' length and complexity are sufficient.
- Be careful of default permissions, configurations, and passwords.
- Use packet-filtering technologies, such as host-based software firewalls, enterprise-class hardware firewalls, and intrusion detection and prevention systems, that are suited to the environment.
- Use open-source or commercial tools to assess system security.

- Use a file-integrity checker to monitor unauthorized file system modifications and send alerts of these changes.

- Disable the Guest account.

- Disable the local administrator account.

- Make sure there are no accounts with blank passwords. A good password policy is crucial.

- Use Windows group policies to enforce security configurations on large networks efficiently and consistently.

- Develop a comprehensive security awareness program for users to reinforce your organization's security policy.

- Keep up with emerging threats. Check with Microsoft, SANS, US-CERT (*www.us-cert .gov*), and other security organizations for the newest developments.

The security field is changing rapidly, and security professionals must keep up with new developments, threats, and tools. Securing Windows systems can be challenging, but a number of tools can be used to pinpoint problems.

Linux OS Vulnerabilities

Like any OS, Linux can be made more secure if users are aware of its vulnerabilities and keep current on new releases and fixes. It's assumed you have some experience working with a *nix OS, so basics of the Linux OS and file system aren't covered in this chapter. Many Linux versions are available, with differences ranging from slight to major. For example, Red Hat and Fedora Linux use the yum command to update and manage RPM (Red Hat Package Manager) packages, and Ubuntu and Debian (and the Linux version included with the Kali Linux DVD) use the apt-get command to update and manage DEB (Debian) packages. Whatever Linux version you use, it's important to understand the basics, such as run control and service configuration, directory structure, file system, basic shell commands and scripting, and package management. (If you're unfamiliar with these *nix basics, spending some time reviewing them is highly recommended. One of the quickest ways security testers can make a poor impression on clients is to show a lack of knowledge about the systems they're testing.)

Guide to Operating Systems, Fourth Edition (Michael Palmer, Course Technology, 2012, ISBN 1111306362) is highly recommended for more information on Linux as well as Windows and Macintosh OSs. A thorough understanding of OSs is essential for security testers.

A typical Linux distribution has thousands of packages developed by many contributors around the world. With such diverse sources of code, it's inevitable that flaws will happen and sometimes be discovered only after they have been incorporated in the final product. Too many network administrators believe Windows is easier to attack and view *nix OSs as inherently more secure. Security professionals must understand that making these assumptions can be dangerous because vulnerabilities exist for all OSs. When conducting a security test on systems running Linux, you should follow the same rules you would for any OS.

Samba

Users expect to be able to share resources over a network, regardless of the OS used, and companies have discovered that users no longer tolerate proprietary systems that can't co-exist in a network. To address the issue of interoperability, a group of programmers created **Samba** (*www.samba.org*) in 1992 as an open-source implementation of CIFS. With Samba, *nix servers can share resources with Windows clients, and Windows clients can access a *nix resource without realizing that the resource is on a *nix computer. Samba has been ported to non-*nix systems, too, including OpenVMS, NetWare, and AmigaOS. At the time of this writing, security professionals should have a basic knowledge of SMB and Samba because many companies have a mixed environment of Windows and *nix systems.

For a Windows computer to be able to access a *nix resource, CIFS must be enabled on both systems. On networks that require *nix computers to access Windows resources, Samba is often used. It's not a hacking tool; this product was designed to enable *nix computers to "trick" Windows services into believing that *nix resources are Windows resources. A *nix client can connect to a Windows shared printer and vice versa when Samba is configured on the *nix computer. Most new versions of Linux include Samba as an optional package, so you don't need to download, install, and compile it.

Tools for Identifying Linux Vulnerabilities

Visiting the CVE Web site is a good first step in discovering possible avenues attackers might take to break into a Linux system. Table 8-4 lists a small portion of the CVEs and CANs found when searching on the keyword "Linux." To give you an idea of the multitude of Linux vulnerabilities, more than 500 entries were found. Many of these vulnerabilities can no longer be exploited on systems that have been updated.

CVE/CAN	Description
CVE-2015-0235	A buffer overflow in the Linux kernel's glibc module allows remote attackers to execute code on the victim system by using a specially crafted gethostbyname request sent over the network.
CVE-2009-1389	A buffer overflow in a Linux kernel NIC driver allows remote attackers to crash the system by sending a specially crafted large packet.
CVE-2015-3331	Prior to version 3.19.4, the Linux kernel did not properly allocate memory before receiving user-supplied encrypted data. An attacker could make a specially crafted crypto API call and execute code on the victim system.

Table 8-4   Linux vulnerabilities found at CVE

You can use CVE information when testing Linux computers for known vulnerabilities. Security testers should review the CVE and CAN information carefully to ensure that a system doesn't have any vulnerabilities listed on the CVE Web site and has been updated.

In Chapter 6, you learned how tools such as OpenVAS (a.k.a. Greenbone Security Assistant) can be used to enumerate multiple OSs. A security tester, using enumeration tools, can do the following:

- Identify a computer on the network by using port scanning and zone transfers.
- Identify the OS the computer is using by conducting port scanning and enumeration.
- Identify via enumeration any logon accounts and passwords configured on the computer.
- Learn the names of shared folders by using enumeration.
- Identify services running on the computer.

The following example shows OpenVAS enumerating and finding vulnerabilities on a Linux computer. Figure 8-4 shows the OpenVAS report after a Linux computer with the IP address 192.168.185.131 has been scanned. The figure indicates that OpenVAS discovered a Red Hat Enterprise Linux 5.7 system.

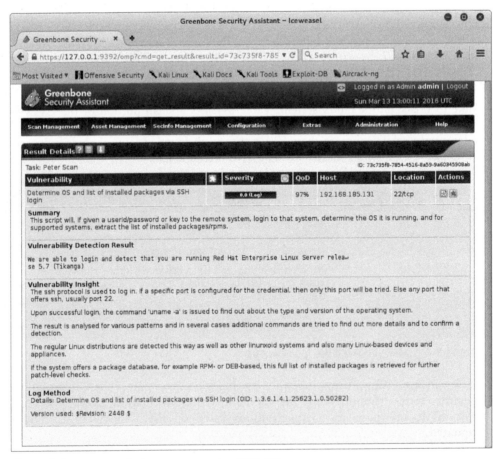

Figure 8-4 OpenVAS finds a system running RHEL 5.7

Source: GNU General Public License (GNU GPL)

In Figure 8-5, note that OpenVAS discovered 118 high-risk vulnerabilities, 106 medium-risk vulnerabilities, and 13 low-risk vulnerabilities. You can tell this machine hasn't been patched in a while.

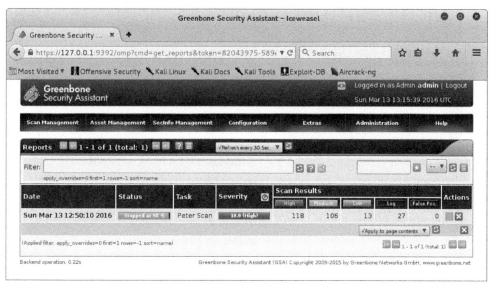

Figure 8-5 Viewing an OpenVAS scan report on a Linux computer

Source: GNU General Public License (GNU GPL)

You can view individual vulnerabilities by using the result page under the scan management tab, as shown in Figure 8-6.

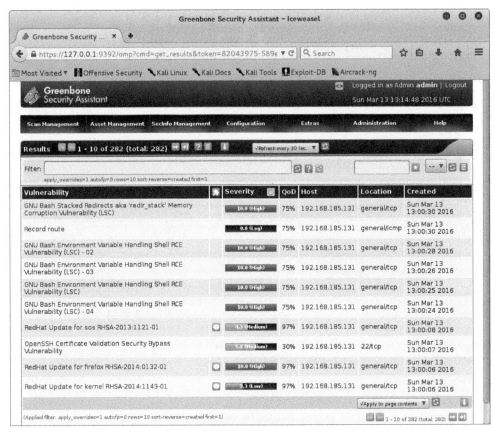

Figure 8-6   Viewing OpenVAS results on a Linux computer

Source: GNU General Public License (GNU GPL)

Figure 8-7 shows details of a vulnerability result for "CPE Inventory." OpenVAS has enumerated a list of active software on the system and their versions—not immediately damaging information, but certainly information that attackers can use. You can see how this information might be troubling, given your experience researching vulnerabilities earlier in this book.

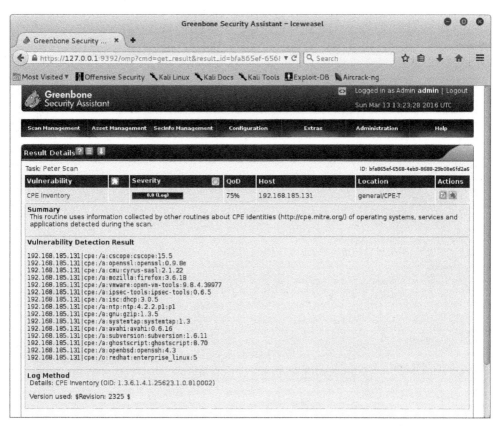

Figure 8-7   Viewing installed software and versions

Source: GNU General Public License (GNU GPL)

With 118 high-risk vulnerabilities, there's enough information in the results displayed in Figure 8-7 to take up an entire chapter, but we're using it to indicate how OpenVAS can be used for security testing. Figure 8-8 shows that OpenVAS discovered a critical "GNU Bash Environment Variable Handling Shell RCE Vulnerability (LSC) - 04" vulnerability. This is the technical name for a vulnerability you may have heard of: the Bash Bug, or Shellshock vulnerability. Released in late 2014, this was a very serious bug that affected many Linux machines and could be exploited over the Internet. Attackers would send specially crafted commands to a Linux machine, and if the conditions were right, could execute whatever code they wanted to.

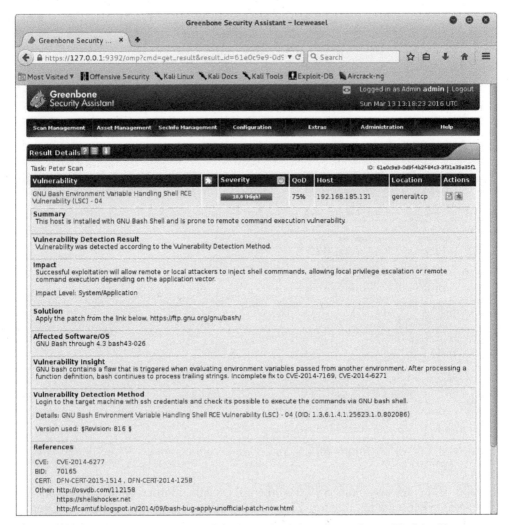

Figure 8-8   OpenVAS revealing a security hole resulting from the Bash Bug (Shellshock)

Source: GNU General Public License (GNU GPL)

Many of the vulnerabilities OpenVAS has discovered allow running remote code, which means attackers could gain complete access to the system. If you research the Internet for the Bash Bug vulnerability, you'll find that exploit code for this vulnerability has been published. If this system is an Internet-facing server in the comptroller's office of a Fortune 1000 company, for example, this vulnerability represents a serious risk.

Activity 8-3: Installing and Using OpenVAS to Discover Vulnerabilities on a Linux Computer

Time Required: 45 minutes

Objective: Install and use OpenVAS to discover vulnerabilities on a Linux computer.

Description: OpenVAS is a helpful tool for enumerating an OS. Not only does it warn testers of possible vulnerabilities, but it also makes recommendations to help correct any problems that are discovered. In this activity, you configure OpenVAS to scan your partner's Linux computer and discover any vulnerabilities an attacker might use to gain access. For this exercise, you'll need a computer that has at least 4 GB of RAM.

1. Boot into the Kali Linux DVD.

2. Open a Terminal shell and determine your computer's IP address by typing **ifconfig** and pressing **Enter**. Write down the IP address, and give it to your partner. Next, start the ssh daemon (sshd) by typing **/etc/init.d/ssh start** and pressing **Enter**. This command allows OpenVAS on your partner's computer to log in and check for vulnerabilities.

3. Type **apt-get install openvas** and press **y** when prompted. Wait until this process completes. This downloads and installs the OpenVAS package.

4. Type **openvas-setup**. This will start the OpenVAS setup process and will take a few minutes to complete. Watch out for the line **User created with password: <long-random string>**. That long random string is the password for the admin account. If you don't see this line and/or need to reset the admin password, use the following command: **openvasmd --user=admin --new-password=<your new password>**.

5. Now we make sure that the OpenVAS services are running using the command **openvas-start**.

6. Once OpenVAS is installed and started, you can access it by opening your Web browser and browsing to *https://127.0.0.1:9392*. Use **admin** for the username and the long random string you observed in Step 3 for the password. Step 3 also has instructions for resetting this password. Once you authenticate, you'll see a window similar to what is shown in Figure 8-9.

8

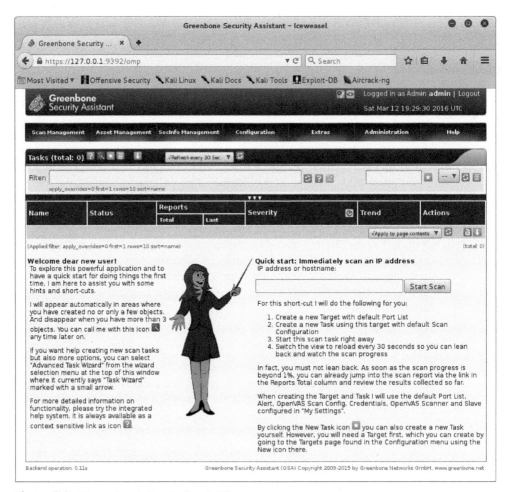

Figure 8-9   The main window in OpenVAS

Source: GNU General Public License (GNU GPL)

7. For this next step, we will need to create a directory using the mkdir command. We need to do this because of compatability issues between Kali and OpenVAS. Run the following command: **mkdir /var/lib/openvas/gnupg/**.

8. Hold your mouse over the **Configuration** tab and select **Credentials** from the drop-down list. Select the light blue icon with the white star to **add a new credential**. Allow your partner to enter his/her system's root credential in the **New Credential** form, similar to Figure 8-10. Once you press **submit**, OpenVAS will need a little bit of time (a few minutes) to process this request.

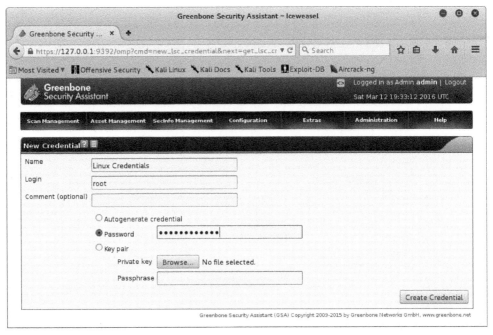

Figure 8-10   Adding a new credential to OpenVAS

Source: GNU General Public License (GNU GPL)

9. Hold your mouse over the **Configuration** tab and select **Targets** from the drop-down list. Select the light blue icon with the white star to **add a new target**. Fill out the New **Target** form with your partner's system information. Name your task *partner* **computer** (replacing *partner* with your partner's name). Make sure to select the SSH credential you set up, similar to Figure 8-11.

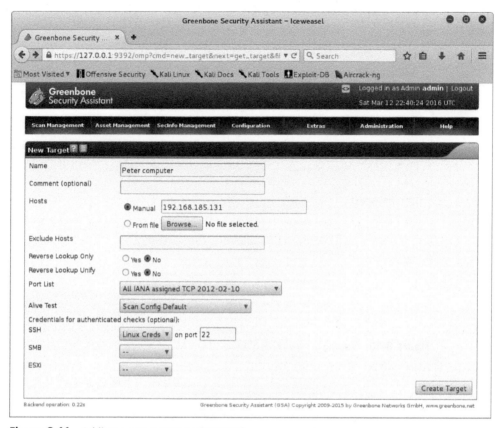

Figure 8-11 Adding a new target to OpenVAS

Source: GNU General Public License (GNU GPL)

10. Hold your mouse over the **Scan Management** tab and select **Tasks** from the drop-down menu. Next to the "Tasks (total : 0)" text, select the light blue icon with the white star to **add a new scan task**. Name your task *partners* **scan** (replacing *partners* with your partner's name). Select your partner's computer in the drop-down list named Scan Targets. Then click **Create Task**. Your end results should look similar to what is shown in Figure 8-12.

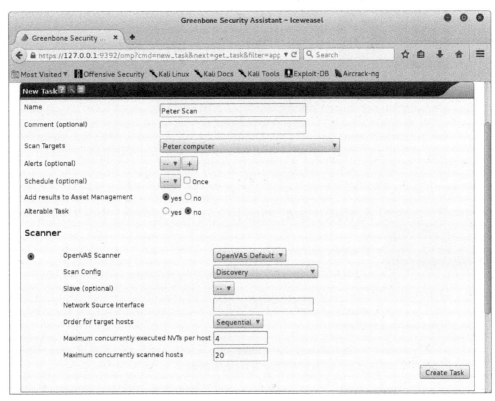

Figure 8-12 Entering a new task in OpenVAS

Source: GNU General Public License (GNU GPL)

11. Now that everything is set up, launch the scan by pressing the green **play** button. Wait for your scan to complete. You might not find many vulnerabilities if your partner's system is up to date.

12. When our scan is complete, we can view the results by clicking the **1** next to **Reports**. To dig in deeper, click on the date and time of the scan.

13. Using the information OpenVAS discovered, write down what you think is the most critical vulnerability on your partner's system and why, and include the CVE reference ID. What recommendation does OpenVAS make to fix this vulnerability?

14. To exit OpenVAS, close the window. When prompted to save the report, click **No**, and then click **Quit** in the OpenVAS Setup dialog box. Leave Linux running for the next activity.

Some software packages on the Kali Linux DVD aren't the most recent versions. Even after just a few months of not having patches installed, a Linux system can become a bonanza of vulnerabilities for an attacker. A security tester would probably recommend upgrading the version before spending time looking for vulnerabilities. You can use the `apt-get update && apt-get upgrade` command to update your Kali Linux system with the most current patches.

After attackers discover a vulnerability, they can go to a Web site describing exploits that take advantage of the vulnerability. In Activity 8-4, you visit another Web site with information on exploits as well as many articles and tools for security testers.

Activity 8-4: Discovering Exploits for Linux Systems

Time Required: 20 minutes

Objective: Research the Internet to discover Linux exploits.

Description: In this activity, you visit a Web site listing exploits you can use to attack different OSs. As a security tester, you should be aware of the resources available to both security testers and attackers.

1. If necessary, boot your computer into Linux with the Kali Linux DVD. Start a Web browser and go to **www.securityfocus.com**.

2. On the Security Focus home page, click **Search all vulnerabilities** and choose **Wireshark** from the Vendor drop-down list. Click **Submit**.

3. Review some of the documents in the search results. Click the **discussion, exploit,** and **solution** tabs in each document to find more information. In which versions of Wireshark are vulnerabilities reported? Find at least one vulnerability for which an exploit or proof of concept (code used to demonstrate the vulnerability) has been published and included for download from the Security Focus Web site.

4. To determine the version of Wireshark running on your computer, open a Terminal shell, and then type **wireshark –v** and press **Enter**.

5. What version of Wireshark is running on your system?

6. Would the exploit you found in Step 3 work on your system?

7. Close the Wireshark Network Analyzer window and the Terminal shell, but leave your Web browser open for the next activity.

Checking for Trojan Programs One method of attacking networks remotely is installing Trojan programs that record keystrokes and other processes without users' knowledge. Trojan programs can be installed after users click an attachment to an e-mail, or users might download a file from the Internet thinking it's a patch or a security fix for the OS they're running. Because the Web server logs the IP address of all visitors, when users download a file from the Internet, attackers then know the IP address of the person who downloaded the Trojan. When a Trojan is installed on a computer, it can carry out many actions. Sometimes, it advertises enumerated victim information to a specific port, so the attacker needs to monitor or connect to that port to gather the information. Other times, a Trojan can be programmed to automatically connect back to an attacker machine. Most Trojan programs perform one or more of the following functions:

- Allow remote administration of the attacked system
- Create a hidden file server on the attacked computer so that files can be loaded and downloaded without the user's knowledge
- Steal passwords and enumerate installed software from the attacked system and send them to the attacker
- Log all keystrokes a user enters and e-mail the results to the attacker or store them in a hidden file the attacker can access remotely
- Encrypt all of the user's files and hold them ransom
- Destroy all of the data on a victim system

Linux Trojan programs are sometimes disguised as legitimate programs, such as `df` or `tar`, but contain program code that can wipe out file systems on a Linux computer or allow for remote administration. Trojan programs are more difficult to detect today because programmers develop them to make legitimate calls on outbound ports that an IDS or a firewall wouldn't normally detect. Because the generated traffic looks just like normal network traffic, it's difficult to detect. For example, a Trojan program called Dyre makes HTTPS `POST` requests over port 443. There's certainly nothing strange about these requests occurring on a network. The Web server could then be configured to issue commands that are carried out on a Linux computer. The HTTPS traffic appears to be normal network traffic, but the commands sent from the Web server could contain other commands requesting that the attacked computer download or copy sensitive files to a remote Web server. Some recent Trojan programs are controlled by encoded, or even encrypted, commands that attackers post on social networking Web sites. To someone monitoring network traffic coming from these infected systems, it might look like a normal user browsing through Facebook or Twitter, for example.

Protecting Linux computers against Trojan programs that IT professionals have already identified is easier. For example, the Linux.Backdoor.Kaiten Trojan program logs on to an Internet Relay Chat (IRC) site automatically and waits for commands from the attacker (controller). Linux antivirus software from McAfee, Sophos, and Symantec can detect this backdoor Trojan.

Even more dangerous are rootkits containing Trojan binary programs ready to be installed by an intruder who has gained root access to a system. Attackers can then hide the tools they use to perform further attacks on the system and have access to backdoor programs. A common Linux rootkit is Linux Rootkit 5 (LRK5), but malware coders create other rootkits almost daily. When a rootkit is installed, legitimate commands are replaced with Trojan programs. For example, if the LRK5 rootkit is installed on a Linux computer, entering the Trojaned `killall` command allows the attacker's processes to continue running, even though the Linux administrator thinks all processes were killed. The `ls` command doesn't show files the attacker uses, and the `netstat` command doesn't show suspicious network connections the attacker makes. So everything looks normal to Linux administrators because they're using commands that have been Trojaned.

Activity 8-5: Using Tools to Find Linux Rootkits

Time Required: 15 minutes

Objective: Learn how to find Linux rootkits on the Internet and use a rootkit-checking program.

Description: Attackers can locate rootkits for many Linux platforms easily. In this activity, you visit the *www.packetstormsecurity.org* Web site, which has thousands of tools and exploits that attackers or security professionals can use. You also run a rootkit detection program included with Kali Linux to find rootkits running on your system.

1. If necessary, boot your computer into Linux with the Kali Linux DVD, and start a Web browser. Go to **www.packetstormsecurity.org**.

2. On the home page, click **Search** in the navigation bar, type **LRK5** in the text box that's displayed, and press **Enter**. At the bottom of the page, you'll see a few results for this search.

3. Look through the list for Linux Rootkit 5. The description shows some Linux commands that are Trojaned when using this rootkit. List five of these commands.

4. Open a Terminal shell, and then type **chkrootkit** and press **Enter** to check for rootkits on your system. Do you recognize any of the Linux commands you wrote down in Step 3?

5. Log off the Kali Linux session but leave your computer running for the case projects at the end of the chapter.

As a security tester, you should check Linux systems periodically for installed rootkits.

More Countermeasures Against Linux Attacks

You've learned about some defenses against Linux vulnerabilities, and in this section, you learn about additional countermeasures for protecting a Linux system, especially from remote attacks. The most critical tasks are training users, keeping up on kernel releases and security updates, and configuring systems to improve security. Having a handle on these tasks is an essential start to protecting any network.

User Awareness Training Making it difficult for social engineers to get information from employees is the best place to start protecting Linux systems from remote attacks. Tell users that no information should be given to outsiders, no matter how harmless the information might seem. Inform them that if attackers know what OS the company is running, they can use that information to conduct network attacks. Make users aware that many exploits can be downloaded from Web sites, and emphasize that knowing which OS is running makes it easier for attackers to select an exploit.

Teach users to be suspicious of people asking questions about the systems they're using and to verify that they're talking to someone claiming to be from the IT Department. Asking for a phone number to call back is a good way to ensure that the person does work for the same company. A 30-minute training session on security procedures can alert users to how easily outsiders can compromise systems and learn proprietary information.

Keeping Current Software vendors are in a never-ending battle to address vulnerabilities that attackers discover. As soon as a bug or vulnerability is discovered and posted on the Internet, OS vendors usually notify customers of upgrades or patches. Installing these fixes promptly is essential to protect your system.

Most Linux distributions now have warning methods for informing users when they're running outdated versions. These warnings in the latest versions of Fedora and Ubuntu Linux are hard to ignore. Figure 8-13 shows the warning that's displayed when a user logs on to a Ubuntu 15 Linux system that isn't current.

Figure 8-13   The Ubuntu 15 security updates warning

Source: GNU General Public License (GNU GPL)

Secure Configuration Many methods and tools can be used to configure a Linux system to help prevent intrusions. Vulnerability scanners not only detect missing patches, but also help identify when a system is configured poorly. You should use built-in Linux tools, too. Security Enhanced Linux (SELinux), a National Security Agency (NSA) project, is now built into many of the main Linux distributions. SELinux contains several features and modules that use **Mandatory Access Control (MAC)**, an OS security mechanism that enforces access rules based on privileges for interactions between processes, files, and users. If an intrusion happens on a system running SELinux, it's less likely the intruder will be able to take complete control of the system. Classes from enterprise Linux vendors cover use of this tool, and you can find more information at *www.nsa.gov/research/selinux* or by searching for SELinux on any Linux distribution Web site.

One of the best ways to measure and report objectively on how an OS is secured is to use the free benchmark tools provided by the Center for Internet Security (CIS, *www .benchmarks.cisecurity.org*). These benchmarks are available for many versions of *nix and Windows. When you take the time to work through securing a Linux OS by following recommendations in the CIS benchmark tool, your knowledge of Linux security, and Linux in general, will improve.

Finally, a commercial tool worth mentioning is Security Blanket (*https://op.trustedcs.com*) from ForcePoint (formerly Trusted Computer Solutions). You install this program on Red

Hat, CentOS, or Solaris *nix systems to tighten the system's security configuration by using templates. If your client is required to follow certain security policies, Security Blanket can secure systems quickly and save *nix system administrators from hours of manual configuration work. Security Blanket can be described as the *nix equivalent of using Windows group policies.

Chapter Summary

- Default installations of Windows OSs can contain serious vulnerabilities that attackers exploit. The CVE Web site is a good place to start when checking for Windows vulnerabilities.

- Vulnerabilities in Windows file systems include lack of ACL support in FAT and risk of malicious ADSs in NTFS.

- Other Windows vulnerabilities involve RPC, an interprocess communication mechanism that allows a program running on one host to run code on a remote host; Net-BIOS, which is still used for backward compatibility; and SMB, which is also still used for backward compatibility and contains a vulnerability that enables attackers to intercept SMB traffic and collect usernames and password hashes.

- In Windows, null sessions and default installations can leave passwords blank and resources unprotected, causing major problems.

- Older versions of Microsoft SQL Server have a critical SQL vulnerability called a null SA password that enables remote users to gain System Administrator (SA) access through the SA account on the server.

- Buffer overflow attacks can allow attackers to run arbitrary code.

- Users represent a major security vulnerability, so creating a comprehensive password policy and having user awareness training programs are essential.

- Many tools are available for discovering vulnerabilities in Windows systems, such as MBSA. Learning to use more than one tool is essential.

- Steps you can recommend to secure systems include keeping systems updated with the most current patches and updates, running antivirus tools, enabling logging and reviewing logs regularly, disabling unused or unneeded services, and filtering out unnecessary ports.

- Vulnerabilities of the Linux OS can be discovered with security tools, such as Open-VAS, and at the CVE Web site.

- To address the issue of interoperability, a group of programmers created Samba as an open-source implementation of CIFS.

- Tools such as chkrootkit can detect rootkits installed on Linux systems.

- Built-in Linux tools, such as SELinux, are available for configuring systems securely. In addition, free benchmark tools are available from the Center for Internet Security, and commercial tools with templates can be used to tighten security configurations quickly and easily.

Key Terms

attack surface

Common Internet File System (CIFS)

domain controller

Mandatory Access Control (MAC)

NetBIOS Extended User Interface (NetBEUI)

Remote Procedure Call (RPC)

Samba

Server Message Block (SMB)

System Center Configuration Manager

Systems Management Server (SMS)

Windows Software Update Services

Review Questions

1. MBSA performs which of the following security checks? (Choose all that apply.)
   a. Security update checks
   b. IIS checks
   c. System time checks
   d. Computer logon checks

2. In Windows Server 2016, the administrator must enable IIS manually to use it. True or False?

3. Windows OSs are vulnerable to the Conficker worm because of which of the following?
   a. Arbitrary code
   b. SQL buffer overflow
   c. Blank password
   d. RPC vulnerability

4. Which of the following is a well-known SMB hacking tool? (Choose all that apply.)
   a. SMBRelay
   b. SMBsnag
   c. L0phtcrack's SMB Packet Capture utility
   d. NTPass

5. Which ports should be filtered out to protect a network from SMB attacks?
   a. 134 to 138 and 445
   b. 135, 139, and 443
   c. 137 to 139 and 445
   d. 53 TCP/UDP and 445 UDP

6. For a Windows computer to be able to access a *nix resource, CIFS must be enabled on at least one of the systems. True or False?

7. Applications written in which programming language are especially vulnerable to buffer overflow attacks? (Choose all that apply.)

   a. C

   b. Perl

   c. C++

   d. Java

8. Which of the following programs includes several buffer overflow exploit plug-ins?

   a. Buffercrack

   b. MBSA

   c. Nmap

   d. Metasploit

9. Which of the following is the most efficient way to determine which OS a company is using?

   a. Run Nmap or other port-scanning programs.

   b. Use the Whois database.

   c. Install a sniffer on the company's network segment.

   d. Call the company and ask.

10. List three measures for protecting systems on any network.

11. Employees should be able to install programs on their company computers as long as the programs aren't copyrighted. True or False?

12. Which of the following is an OS security mechanism that enforces access rules based on privileges for interactions between processes, files, and users?

   a. MBSA

   b. Mandatory Access Control

   c. Server Message Block

   d. Systems Management Server

13. A good password policy should include which of the following? (Choose all that apply.)

   a. Specifies a minimum password length

   b. Mandates password complexity

   c. States that passwords never expire

   d. Recommends writing down passwords to prevent forgetting them

14. Linux antivirus software can't detect backdoor Trojans. True or False?

15. Which program can detect rootkits on *nix systems?

    a. chkrootkit

    b. rktdetect

    c. SELinux

    d. Ionx

16. Which organization offers free benchmark tools for Windows and Linux?

    a. PacketStorm Security

    b. CVE

    c. Center for Internet Security

    d. Trusted Security Solutions

Case Projects

CASE PROJECTS

Case Project 8-1: Securing an Older Linux OS

After conducting footprinting and using social-engineering techniques on the Alexander Rocco network, you have determined that the company is running several applications on Linux computers. You also discover that the payroll system runs on several Red Hat Enterprise Linux 5.8 (RHEL 5.8) servers. You need to ensure that this version will be supported with patches from the vendor until the new payroll system is installed in 2017. Based on this information, write a brief report stating whether the systems can be secured until they're replaced in 2017, and include recommendations for securing these systems.

Case Project 8-2: Detecting Unauthorized Applications

In conducting a review of the OSs running on the Alexander Rocco network, you detect a program that appears to be unauthorized. No one in the department knows how this program got on the Linux computer. The department manager thinks the program was installed before his start date three years ago. When you review the program's source code, you discover that it contains a buffer overflow vulnerability. Based on this information, write a report to the IT manager stating what course of action should be taken and listing recommendations for management.

Case Project 8-3: Validating Password Strength for Alexander Rocco Corporation

After discovering that most computers and servers at Alexander Rocco run many different versions of Windows, your supervisor has asked you to write a report on the issue of password vulnerabilities. Write a one-page memo to your supervisor describing the password-cracking areas you will test. Your memo should be based on the information you find in Section 11, "Password Cracking," of the OSSTMM.

## chapter 9

Embedded Operating Systems: The Hidden Threat

After reading this chapter and completing the exercises, you will be able to:

- Explain what embedded operating systems are and where they're used
- Describe Windows IoT (Internet of Things) and other embedded operating systems
- Identify vulnerabilities of embedded operating systems and best practices for protecting them

Embedded systems include their own operating system, called an "embedded operating system," which is the focus of this chapter. Many people use a global positioning system (GPS) device or navigation system to find a bank so that they can withdraw cash from an ATM and don't realize that both the GPS device and ATM may be embedded systems that use an embedded Operating System (OS). Security professionals should understand that any vulnerability in a desktop or server OS might exist for its embedded counterpart. For example, many embedded OSs contain a Web server that's potentially vulnerable to attack, as you will learn in Chapter 10. If this Web server software is required for the device to operate correctly, you might have a problem. In fact, the problem can be worse on an embedded system because of hardware limitations and software compatibility. Software developers often omit many security checks on embedded systems, such as input validation, so that they can "fit" the code on the chip. In a 2014 blog post titled "Security Risks of Embedded Systems," Bruce Schneier points out that chip makers minimize engineering effort to maximize their profit margins. Also, the manufacturers' names aren't on their finished products, so they have little incentive to spend resources securing their chips. You can read more about Bruce Schneier's security concerns with embedded systems on his blog at: *https://www.schneier.com/blog/archives/2014/01/security_risks_9.html.*

When conducting security tests for a company, don't ignore embedded systems. You shouldn't ignore devices simply because they're small, perform simple tasks, or haven't been exploited in the past. As a security tester, part of your job will be identifying potential security problems, and to do this, you need to think outside the box. With embedded OS vulnerabilities, you might have to start thinking inside the "box," too!

Introduction to Embedded Operating Systems

At its most basic, an **embedded system** is any computer system that isn't a general-purpose PC or server. In addition to GPS devices and some ATMs, embedded systems are found in a wide array of electronic consumer and industrial items: toys, kitchen appliances, printers, industrial control systems, spacecraft, and scientific equipment. An **embedded operating system (OS)** can be a small program developed specifically for use with embedded systems, or it can be a stripped-down version of an OS commonly used on general-purpose computers. Embedded OSs are usually designed to be small and efficient, so they don't have some of the functions that general-purpose OSs do, particularly if the specialized applications they run don't use these features. One type of specialized embedded OS is a **real-time operating system (RTOS)**, typically used in devices such as programmable thermostats, appliance controls, and even spacecraft. If you're piloting an F-35 fighter jet, you'll certainly appreciate that the embedded RTOS in your aircraft is designed with an algorithm aimed at multitasking and responding predictably. RTOSs are also found in high-end kitchen ovens, heart pacemakers, and just about every new car.

Security Bytes

As you become acquainted with devices that use embedded OSs, you need to think the way attackers do. What system could you attack that could affect hundreds of systems? Thousands of systems? Something as simple as an attack on a company's heating, ventilation, and air-conditioning (HVAC) system—or even a thermostat, for that matter—could have a serious negative impact on the network infrastructure.

With just a cursory survey of a typical corporate building, you can find many embedded systems, including: firewalls, switches, routers, Web-filtering appliances, network attached storage (NAS) devices, networked power switches, printers, scanners, copy machines, video projectors, uninterruptible power supply (UPS) consoles, Voice over IP (VoIP) phones and voicemail systems, thermostats, HVAC systems, fire suppression systems, closed-circuit TV systems, elevator management systems, video teleconferencing workstations and consoles, and intercom systems. How many embedded systems can you identify in the building you're in right now?

Security Bytes

The place: Las Vegas. The event: the 2009 Black Hat Convention. The audience waited patiently for the three speakers standing on the makeshift stage to begin their presentation. Two attorneys entered the huge conference room, and the speakers announced they were ready to begin. The topic of the presentation? Hacking the San Francisco parking meter system—or better phrased as "Proof of Concept: Parking Meter Vulnerability." The attorneys were there to make sure the speakers didn't say anything that could be incriminating. After all, teaching people how to hack a parking meter is illegal. The presenters were able to keep the discussion legal by presenting it as sharing information with security professionals. After the one-hour lecture, which included many photos depicting what the presenters were able to accomplish, the audience had a better understanding of how an embedded OS could be hacked easily. The good news is that the presenters were the good guys. They were upset that the city of San Francisco didn't think hiring security professionals to conduct a vulnerability study of the $35 million parking meter system was worthwhile. This system was hacked in less than a week by three people who spent less than $1000 on equipment.

Many dismiss the topic of embedded device security to focus on more popular security issues. Most of the media emphasis is on threats that people can understand and relate to, such as the latest network worm, the most recent Windows attack, or the hack of Hillary Clinton's e-mail. However, embedded systems are in all networks and perform essential functions, such as routing network traffic and blocking suspicious packets. Many believe that because devices use an embedded OS, such as the San Francisco parking meters, no one would bother to attack them or take the time and effort to understand how they work. The three San Francisco hackers purchased several parking meters on eBay to do just that—understand how the devices work. They took them apart and looked for any security features and for ways to access the internal hardware from the outside, such as an external USB or serial port. They also tried to determine whether someone could jam a card or gum, for example, into the device to disable it and investigated what type of smart card could be inserted, if any.

Recently, security researchers were able to reverse-engineer the software on a popular firewall's chipset; software residing on a chip is commonly referred to as **firmware**. The researchers were then able to insert modified software to control the firewall's behavior. Hackers who do this could modify a firewall so that they can copy network traffic passing through an interface and give an external IP address full access through the firewall. They can also configure the firewall so that these intrusions could be made without being detected or generating a single log entry. As the value and quantity of targets with embedded systems increase, attackers will start shifting their focus to embedded systems.

Activity 9-1: Researching an Attack on a Jeep Cherokee

Time Required: 20 minutes

Objective: Learn more about potential attacks on embedded systems.

Description: In 2013, Charlie Miler and Chris Valasek demonstrated they could control the steering wheel and the brakes of a vehicle they were plugged into. In 2015, they proved that, from the comfort of their home, they could hack into a Jeep Cherokee that was driving on the highway. This remote attack turned a few heads in the industry and, luckily, was responsibly reported by Charlie and Chris before any real damage could be done.

1. In Windows, start your Web browser and go to **www.google.com.**

2. In the search text box, type **Jeep Hack 2015** and press **Enter.**

3. Select the entry from *http://wired.com* and read the article. When you're finished, use the back arrow to return to the search results page.

4. Scroll through the search results and spend time reading a couple other articles about the attack.

5. What attack vector did the hackers use? Do you think the Jeep designers could have done something to prevent the attack?

6. Do you think the articles you read gave information others could use to hack cars in the future? Explain your answer.

7. What could Charlie and Chris have done if they were malicious?

8. When you're finished, leave the Web browser open for the next activity.

As you learned in this activity, the work of only two people could have wreaked havoc on highways nationwide. Your job as a security tester is to try to prevent attacks like this one.

Windows and Other Embedded Operating Systems

Recycling common code and reusing technologies are sound software engineering practices. After all, why should you pay a developer to write the same code repeatedly if you can just reuse it? Unfortunately, these practices introduce common points of failure in many products. Many viruses, worms, Trojans, and other attack vectors take advantage of shared code, which increases the impact a single vulnerability can have. In Chapter 8, you learned about vulnerabilities in Windows and Linux. Any vulnerability in these OSs might also exist in the embedded version. For example, the embedded versions of Windows 7 and Windows 8 contain the same software and, with few exceptions, operate the same way. Windows XP had a very popular embedded release, which many products continue to use even after extended support expired in January of 2016.

Windows CE was a trimmed-down version of the Windows desktop OS and shouldn't be confused with Windows Embedded 8 or Windows 10 IoT. Some Windows CE source code is available to the public, and much of the rest of it is available to hardware vendors, partners, and developers, based on their licensing level. Windows CE is rare in 2016, but still worth knowing about. Windows Mobile, an old OS based on Windows CE, was designed for use in products such as Personal Data Assistants (PDAs) and smartphones. Now, those devices run a slightly modified version of Windows 8 or Windows 10.

Unlike Windows CE, Windows 10 IoT provides the full Windows API and can perform many of the same tasks that the desktop version can, although Windows 10 IoT does not have a desktop interface. It's designed for use on commodity devices like Raspberry Pi, a small, affordable computer. In addition to commodity devices, Window 10 IoT can underlie any of the systems mentioned above (i.e., GPS, ATM, and Printers). Windows 10 IoT was designed to make things easy for developers.

As you learned in Chapter 8, many tools, such as MBSA, are available for discovering vulnerabilities in Windows systems. You can run some on an embedded OS, and others can be used remotely from the network to discover vulnerabilities in a Windows embedded OS.

Other Proprietary Embedded OSs

VxWorks is a widely used embedded real-time OS developed by Wind River Systems. It's used in many different environments and applications and is designed to run efficiently on minimal hardware. In the next activity, you research the variety of systems powered by VxWorks and other embedded OSs. Figure 9-1 shows creating an embedded OS image with VxWorks Workbench, a development toolkit, running on the desktop version of Fedora Linux.

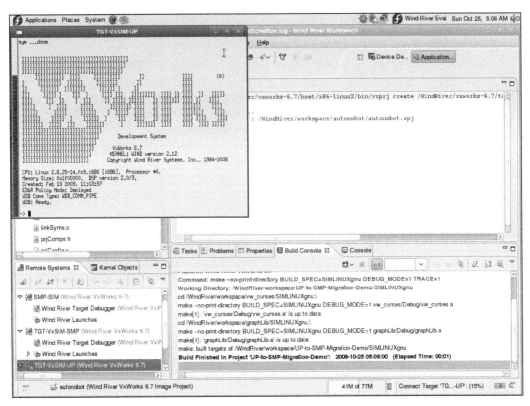

Figure 9-1 Creating an embedded OS image in VxWorks Workbench

To give you an idea of the variety of systems using VxWorks, here's a partial list:

- Clementine spacecraft
- Deep Impact space probe
- James Webb Space Telescope (in development)
- Mars exploration rovers Spirit and Opportunity
- Mars Phoenix Lander
- Mars Reconnaissance Orbiter
- Radvision 3G communication equipment
- Stardust spacecraft
- SAUVIM (a submersible spacecraft designed for deep-ocean operations)

Green Hill Software also produces a variety of embedded OSs. It designed an embedded OS for the F-35 Joint Strike Fighter as well as an embedded OS certified to run multiple levels of classification (such as unclassified, secret, and top secret) on the same CPU without leakage between levels. This type of OS is called **multiple independent levels of security/ safety (MILS)**. The US military uses MILS OSs in high-security environments, and other organizations, such as those controlling nuclear power or municipal sewage plants, use them when separating privileges and functions is crucial. Green Hill also designs embedded OS code used in printers, routers, switches, barcode scanners, and radios. The aforementioned OSs use a microkernel, which sacrifices flexibility for simplicity and fewer hardware resources.

QNX, from QNX Software Systems, is a commercial RTOS used in Cisco's ultrahigh-availability routers and in Logitech universal remotes. Another proprietary embedded OS is Real-Time Executive for Multiprocessor Systems (RTEMS), an open-source embedded OS used in space systems because it supports processors designed specifically to operate in space. It's currently running on the Mars Reconnaissance Orbiter along with VxWorks. NASA has improved this spacecraft's survivability by using several small embedded OSs tailored for specific functions instead of a huge monolithic kernel OS that controls every function. However, using multiple embedded OSs also increases the attack surface. Figure 9-2 illustrates the differences in size and resource requirements between monolithic kernel and microkernel OSs.

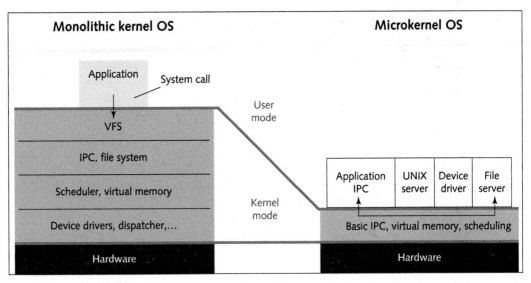

Figure 9-2   Monolithic kernel versus microkernel OSs

*Nix Embedded OSs

Embedded Linux is an example of a monolithic OS used in a multitude of industrial, medical, and consumer items. Embedded versions of Linux and other *nix OSs can be tailored for devices with limited memory or hard drive capacity, such as mobile phones. An advantage of a monolithic kernel is that it can support the widest variety of hardware and allows adding features by using dynamic kernel modules. Other examples of commercial products with *nix embedded OSs are Cisco switches and routers, TomTom and Garmin GPS devices, PDAs, media players, and medical instruments. Even the iPhone has a *nix embedded OS at its core.

In addition to VxWorks, Wind River produces an open-source Linux OS for embedded systems and an OS microkernel extension called Real Time Linux (RTLinux). RTLinux turns "regular" Linux into an RTOS that's suitable for embedded applications requiring a guaranteed response in a mathematically predictable manner. RTLinux is no longer available for download, but patches are being maintained for some builds.

If you want to play around with an RTOS, you can get a copy of FreeRTOS from Sourceforge (*https://sourceforge.net/projects/freertos/files/FreeRTOS/V8.2.3/*).

Another embedded Linux OS that you can download for use at home is dd-wrt (*www.dd -wrt.com/*). Initially designed for use on the Linksys WRT54G wireless, this OS can be run on most small office or home routers. Figure 9-3 shows its bandwidth-monitoring feature.

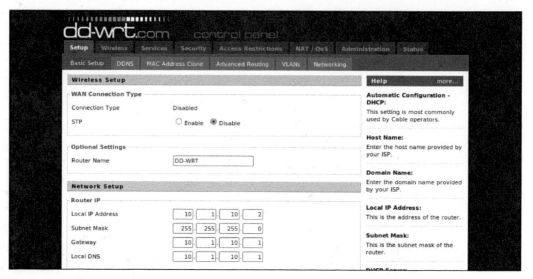

Figure 9-3 The control panel for dd-wrt

Home router embedded systems, such as the Linksys WRT54G, were the target of a large-scale botnet worm attack. Called psyb0t (or the Network Bluepill), this worm spread by exploiting outdated or poorly configured router OSs that contained easy-to-guess passwords. After psyb0t had infected tens of thousands of systems, attackers used it to launch distributed denial-of-service (DDoS) or vulnerability exploitation attacks. If you have a wireless router at home, do you know whether it's protected against threats such as psyb0t?

As you have seen, embedded OSs are everywhere on earth—and beyond, in some cases. As a security tester, you need to know about vulnerabilities in these systems. In the next activity, you research some products using embedded OSs and learn more about their vulnerabilities.

Activity 9-2: Researching Products with Embedded OSs

Time Required: 40 minutes

Objective: Search vulnerability databases to find products using vulnerable embedded OSs.

Description: Until now, most security professionals had little knowledge of the many products that use embedded OSs. In this activity, you search the National Vulnerability Database (NVD) for products using embedded OSs.

1. In Windows, start your Web browser, if necessary, and go to **http://nvd.nist.gov**.

2. Click the **Vulnerability Search Engine** link. Type **vxworks** in the Keyword search text box and press **Enter**.

3. Scroll through the list, and spend some time reading about vulnerabilities of devices using VxWorks OSs.

4. Continue your research by searching for more terms related to embedded OSs, such as **Windows 10 Mobile, embedded Linux, QNX, Netscreen, Lexmark, Jetdirect, Android, Canon printers, Linksys, VOIP, dd-wrt, iPhone, Netgear, Foundry, Cisco, and Nortel.** Write down some examples you find of devices with embedded OSs and describe the vulnerabilities briefly. Spend no more than 20 minutes.

5. How many embedded devices and vulnerabilities were you able you find in 20 minutes? Are any of these vulnerable devices likely to be found in a large company or government agency? How about at home?

6. Leave your Web browser open for the next activity.

Vulnerabilities of Embedded OSs

Some security professionals can remember when computer attacks typically caused damage equivalent to graffiti on a building. Offensive, yes, but not damaging enough to concern most security professionals. However, the impact of attacks has become more serious, and embedded OSs are no exception. In Activity 9-2, you found that many embedded OSs have vulnerabilities. Web sites such as *www.exploit-db.com* and *www.packetstormsecurity.org* have information on what hackers are doing with these vulnerabilities.

9

Many hackers today want more than just notoriety, however; they're criminals looking for ways to steal money. The easiest way to profit from hacking is to attack devices where cash is stored and dispensed by a computer: ATMs. The most common ATM attacks involve using card skimmers or actually stealing the machines. A security researcher, Barnaby Jack of Juniper Networks, announced a vulnerability in a line of popular ATMs that made both local and remote attacks possible. Just before the much anticipated public demonstration of "jackpotting" an ATM in 2009, Juniper Networks chose not to reveal the exploit until the ATM vendor had a chance to protect its devices. In the same year, a major ATM manufacturer, Diebold, announced that hackers had installed malware on more than a dozen ATMs running Windows XP Embedded. An insider, such as an authorized technician, was needed to install the malicious code, and then an accomplice inserted a specially designed control card that allowed complete control of the ATM, including unlimited cash dispensing and printing account numbers and PINs. Considering that an ATM can store hundreds of thousands of dollars, the embedded OS in an ATM is an attractive target to hackers.

Security Bytes

As a security tester, you need to remember that sometimes the biggest security threat to an organization is its employees. System **NOTE** administrators, network managers, and technicians often have unfettered, and unmonitored, access to a company's most critical IT components. They're aware of any gaps in existing security processes and know how to cover up illegal activities. Following the "least privileges principle" can help reduce the insider threat, however. This principle specifies giving personnel only the access they need to perform their job duties and revoking access as soon as they no longer need it.

Activity 9-3: Researching ATM Vulnerabilities

Time Required: 20 minutes

Objective: Examine current ATM vulnerabilities.

Description: As a security tester, you must be aware of attacks that can occur on systems other than the usual workstations and servers. If a bank contracts you to conduct a security test and you neglect to research possible attacks on ATMs, you might find yourself in an embarrassing situation if a major attack happens that results in the bank losing millions of dollars. After reading several articles on ATMs, you should have a better awareness of the methods attackers are using to steal money from banks—without needing masks and guns.

1. Start your Web browser, if necessary, and go to your favorite search engine. Type **Hacking ATM Machines with just a text** in the search text box, and press **Enter**.

2. A **The Hacker News** article discusses how attackers can use malware and smartphones to make ATMs dispense cash. What OS is in use? What suggestion did the security company offer to reduce these risks?

3. Continue your search for articles on ATM hacking and vulnerabilities. Based on your research, what OSs do most ATMs use?

4. Leave your Web browser open for the next activity.

Embedded OSs Are Everywhere

On the eve of the past millennium, experts warned of an imminent global catastrophe: Billions of embedded systems with the Y2K (for "Year 2000") software flaw would suddenly stop or fail when the clock struck midnight. These embedded systems were located everywhere, including critical infrastructure controls for power, communications, transportation, and more, so enormous amounts of time and money were spent fixing them to prevent potential disaster. Today, there are many more embedded devices to be concerned about than in 2000. These embedded devices don't have the Y2K software flaw, but they're under attack from hackers and terrorists who want to further their financial or political causes. This new threat is why addressing the security of embedded systems early in the design phase—not treating it as an afterthought—is essential.

Embedded OSs Are Networked

For reasons of efficiency and economy, connecting embedded systems to a network has advantages. Being able to manage systems and share services while keeping the amount of human resources and expertise to a minimum helps companies reduce costs. Gaining efficiency and reducing costs have a price, however: Any device added to a network infrastructure increases the potential for security problems. Security testers should address questions such as the following for every machine or device on a network:

- What Peripheral Component Interconnect (PCI) devices are present?
- Where were they manufactured? Is the supply chain trustworthy?

- Which devices have embedded OSs stored in rewriteable (nonvolatile) memory? Rewriteable memory can be flashed (that is, erased and rewritten quickly).

- Which embedded OS is currently loaded on each device?

- Can you make sure the embedded OS hasn't been corrupted or subverted with malicious code? This check is called validating the embedded OS's integrity.

Embedded OSs Are Difficult to Patch

In Chapter 8, you learned about the importance of keeping systems patched and antivirus software up to date. With general-purpose desktop OSs, it's normal to wait for a vulnerability to be identified, download and install the patch when it's available, and restart the system, if necessary. This approach doesn't work for many embedded OSs, however, because they must continue operating regardless of the threat, particularly in critical systems, such as power distribution, air traffic control, and medical life support.

Patching on general-purpose computers is usually simple, but patching embedded OSs can be a problem. For example, many skilled system administrators know how to patch a Web server for Linux, Windows, or Solaris UNIX OSs running on standard Sun or x86 PC hardware, but they might have no clue how to patch a Web server running on a tiny chip (called a "16-bit micro-controller") inside a plastic box the size of a deck of cards. Another problem is that buffer overflow attacks might be successful on embedded OSs because few updates are released to correct vulnerabilities. Typically, manufacturers prefer that you upgrade the system rather than the embedded OS, so they might not release updates when vulnerabilities are discovered. Updating the embedded OS on some systems is difficult enough that your clients probably won't do it. Be prepared to explain the best course of action to your clients.

Remember that both general-purpose and embedded OSs use drivers to interface with hardware devices. In both types of OSs, drivers are vulnerable to exploitation and occasionally need to be updated or patched. A while back, a vulnerability in drivers for the Intel wireless chipset made it possible to compromise wireless devices remotely. The vulnerability isn't surprising. What is surprising is that few system administrators updated these drivers because they never showed up in the list of "critical" OS patches in Windows Update.

One reason that some vendors of embedded OSs are using open-source software more is that the cost of developing and patching an OS is shared by the entire open-source community, not just a handful of overworked programmers in a back office. To date, the total cost in programmer hours for developing and patching the Linux kernel is estimated at tens of billions of dollars. Having that much programming expertise available is hard for any company developing embedded systems to turn down. On the other hand, the monolithic Linux kernel was designed to offer the most flexibility and support for sophisticated features; for that reason, it's very large and has many code portions that might need to be patched as vulnerabilities are discovered. For sensitive embedded systems that need only a fraction of the features in the Linux kernel, the risk of having potential vulnerabilities might outweigh the benefits. In this situation, a proprietary kernel might be more suitable.

As a security tester, one day you might identify minor vulnerabilities in embedded OSs that are extremely expensive to fix. However, the amount of time and expertise an attacker would need to exploit this minor vulnerability is extremely high, too. For these types of vulnerabilities, you must weigh the cost of fixing the vulnerability against the importance of the information the embedded system controls. You might recommend not fixing the vulnerability because it's secure enough for the minor risk involved.

Security Bytes

Heart rate monitors and MRI machines are examples of systems that run embedded Windows OSs. Often these systems can't be patched because they're certified at a specific revision level, or the manufacturer never provided a patch method. This problem was apparent when the Conficker worm infected numerous medical systems around the world. Even in embedded systems that weren't connected directly to the Internet, versions of Conficker spread through removable media. A simple data transfer with USB drives, for example, might be risky.

Embedded OSs Are in Networking Devices

Networking devices, such as routers and switches, usually have software and hardware designed for the tasks of transmitting information across networks. Originally, general-purpose computers were used to perform routing and switching, but high-speed networks now use specialized hardware and embedded OSs. In the past, Cisco mainly used proprietary code in its embedded systems. By using more open-source code, however, Cisco can release new product features more quickly. Cisco uses Linux kernels in its latest VoIP Call Manager appliances and Adaptive Security Appliance (ASA) firewall. Other embedded OSs for networking devices are modified *nix OSs. For example, Juniper's and Extreme Networks' OSs are based on UNIX.

You might wonder why anyone would bother hacking routers or other networking devices, as they don't contain corporate secrets and don't have lots of storage space or processing capacity that could be stolen. The short answer is that when attackers compromise a host, that's all they might get: a single host. When they compromise a router, they might be able to control every host on the network. From the router, attackers can map the entire network, modify packets to and from hosts, redirect traffic to and from other hosts or networks, attack other networks that are accessible from the compromised router, and make free phone calls with VoIP, if it's configured. In short, controlling a router can give attackers complete access to network resources.

To compromise an entire network through a router, attackers follow the usual methods of footprinting, scanning, and enumerating the target. Embedded OSs in routers are often susceptible to many of the same attacks that plague general-purpose OSs, ranging from simple password guessing to sophisticated buffer overflow attacks. A common vulnerability of routers and other network devices with built-in Web management interfaces is the authentication bypass vulnerability. Attackers can take control of a network device or gather sensitive information from it by accessing the device with a specially crafted URL that bypasses the normal authentication mechanism. You might have found examples of authentication bypass vulnerabilities in Activity 9-2. After bypassing authentication, attackers can launch other network attacks by using the access they gained through compromising the router.

can detect rootkits and prevent them from being installed. However, the problem becomes more difficult if the OS has already been compromised. Installing these tools on an infected system doesn't normally trigger alerts because rootkits can monitor the OS for anti-rootkit tools and neutralize them. Rootkits that pose the biggest threat to any OS (embedded or general-purpose) are those that infect a device's firmware. They're more dangerous because they tend to be extremely small, are loaded in low-level nonvolatile storage that anti-rootkit tools can't access readily, and can persist even after the hard drive has been reformatted. Defenses against low-level rootkits include using Trusted Platform Module (TPM), a cryptographic firmware boot-check processor installed on many new computer systems. TPM ensures that the OS hasn't been subverted or corrupted, such as with a firmware rootkit. It's now the ISO standard ISO/IEC 11889. For more information on this standard, visit *www .iso.org*.

A computer might have several megabytes of flash ROM on the motherboard and controller cards, such as the Ethernet controller. Firmware rootkits are hard to detect because the code for firmware often isn't checked for possible corruption. Insider hacking is harder to detect with malicious code hidden in a system's flash memory. Disgruntled employees, for example, could install a BIOS-based rootkit in company computers' flash memory before they leave a company. They could then use this BIOS rootkit, which would survive having the OS reinstalled, to gain access to the corporate network later.

Security Bytes

For demonstration purposes, Microsoft and University of Michigan researchers developed a BIOS-level rootkit, called SubVirt, for desktop computers that can survive hard disk replacement and OS reinstallation. It modifies the boot sequence and loads itself before the OS so that it can operate outside the OS and remain hidden from many rootkit-detection tools. By exploiting hardware virtualization technology from CPU manufacturers, SubVirt can load the original OS as a virtual machine and then intercept the OS's calls to hardware.

What if the system you're using is compromised before it's even purchased? Criminals in Europe have tampered with credit card machines while they're still in the supply chain. The compromised devices continue to function like normal credit card readers with one notable exception: They copy customers' credit card information and transmit it to criminals via a cell phone network. The only way to get rid of these types of infections is to flash (rewrite) the BIOS with a known clean copy, wipe the hard drive, and reload the OS from clean installation media. These tasks can be hugely expensive in both time and money, but at least a method for removing the malware is available.

A popular laptop theft-recovery service, LoJack for Laptops, has some design-level vulnerabilities that rootkits can exploit. Researchers from Core Security Technologies reconfigured LoJack with a custom BIOS rootkit that takes advantage of LoJack's vulnerabilities. Because the infection resides in the computer's BIOS, it persists even after the OS is reinstalled or the hard drive is replaced. Of more concern to security professionals is that the LoJack BIOS agent is stored in a part of the BIOS that isn't overwritten when you flash it. The LoJack BIOS agent periodically "calls home" to a central monitoring authority for instructions in case a laptop is reported stolen. The call-home mechanism allows the monitoring authority to instruct the LoJack BIOS agent to wipe all information as a security measure or to track

9

the stolen system's location. Because so many laptops have this agent installed, and it can't be removed, it's an attractive target to attackers.

Now that you have a better understanding of embedded OS vulnerabilities, continue reading to learn how you can improve their security.

Best Practices for Protecting Embedded OSs

You've learned that your job as a security tester is to discover and document vulnerabilities and recommend ways to fix them. Now that you know embedded OSs have vulnerabilities similar to those in general-purpose OSs as well as additional security challenges, what can you do?

- Identify all embedded systems in an organization.
- Prioritize the systems or functions that depend on these embedded systems.
- Follow the least privileges principle for access to embedded systems.
- Use data transport encryption, when possible, for embedded system communication.
- Configure embedded systems as securely as possible and follow manufacturers' recommendations.
- When possible, use cryptographic measures, such as TPM, for booting embedded systems, especially when a loss of data or a modification in the system's behavior is a major risk.
- Install patches and updates, when available, to address vulnerabilities. Make sure doing so is possible on the embedded system you're working with, however; some embedded systems can't have any downtime for installing updates and patches.
- Reduce the potential of vulnerabilities by restricting network access to only the IP addresses that need to communicate with embedded systems, and reduce the attack surface of embedded systems by disabling or blocking unneeded services.
- Upgrade or replace embedded systems that can't be fixed or pose an unacceptable risk.

Chapter Summary

- An embedded system is any computer system that isn't a general-purpose server or PC. An embedded OS and its hardware are the main components of an embedded system.
- An RTOS is a specialized embedded OS designed with algorithms aimed at multitasking and responding predictably; it is used in devices such as programmable thermostats, appliance controls, planes, and spacecraft.
- Most corporate networks and buildings have numerous embedded systems, such as routers and switches, firewalls, copiers, printers, faxes, digital phones, HVAC systems, intercoms, and fire-suppression systems.
- Microsoft offers several different embedded OSs. Windows 10 IoT, the most modern of these offerings, is similar to older versions of Windows Embedded Standard.

Windows CE was an embedded OS designed for mobile devices, and Windows Embedded Standard was an example of a Windows desktop OS modified for use in embedded systems.

- Microkernel embedded OSs, such as QNX, GreenHills, and VxWorks, trade flexibility for more security and simplicity and are often used when security and safety are crucial.

- *Nix-based embedded OSs are often used for devices in which flexibility and a wide range of feature and hardware support is needed, such as GPSs, PDAs, and iPhones.

- Embedded OSs are more common now than during the most recent worldwide panic caused by the Y2K vulnerability. The fact that they're everywhere emphasizes the importance of incorporating security into the design phase of an embedded OS.

- Embedded OSs are usually networked to increase efficiency. However, they're difficult to patch, which can increase the cost of securing them. Vulnerabilities in embedded OSs are often the same as in general-purpose OSs. Exploiting embedded systems, such as ATMs, can be quite profitable for criminals.

- Embedded systems are in network devices and peripherals on nearly every network, and compared with general-purpose computing systems, their vulnerabilities are often overlooked.

- SCADA systems are used for critical infrastructure systems, such as power generation and distribution, air traffic and rail control, dams and public works, and heavy industry. Damage to these embedded systems could cause catastrophic consequences.

- Smartphones are examples of an ever-evolving embedded system that can be exploited to steal sensitive corporate and personal information.

- Smartphones can be infected with malicious Trojan software and exploited just like your Windows and Linux systems.

- Firmware rootkits pose the biggest threat to an embedded OS. Cryptographic boot protection, such as that provided by TPM, can help defend against firmware rootkits.

- Following best practices, such as identifying all embedded systems, patching when possible, following the least privileges principle, and restricting access, is important to ensure the security of embedded systems.

Key Terms

embedded operating system (OS)	multifunction devices (MFDs)	real-time operating system (RTOS)
embedded system	multiple independent levels of security/safety (MILS)	supervisory control and data acquisition (SCADA) systems
firmware		

Review Questions

1. An embedded OS must be developed specifically for use with embedded systems. True or False?

2. Why are embedded OSs more likely to have unpatched security vulnerabilities than general-purpose OSs do? (Choose all that apply.)

   a. Many security checks are omitted during development to reduce the code size.

   b. Devices with embedded OSs connect to the Internet more frequently.

   c. Manufacturers prefer that you upgrade the system rather than the embedded OS.

   d. Devices with embedded OSs typically can't have any downtime for installing patches.

3. Which of the following describes an RTOS?

   a. An embedded OS capable of multitasking and responding predictably

   b. An embedded OS intended for real-time data manipulation

   c. An embedded OS intended for packet analysis

   d. An embedded OS intended for devices that run multiple OSs

4. Which of the following doesn't use an embedded OS?

   a. An ATM

   b. A workstation running Windows Vista Business

   c. An NAS device running Windows Server 2008 R2

   d. A slot machine

5. Why are rootkits that infect a device's firmware considered the biggest threat to any OS (embedded or general-purpose)?

6. Which of the following is an advantage of Windows CE over other Windows embedded OSs?

   a. It's designed for more advanced devices with complex hardware requirements.

   b. It has many of the same security features as Windows XP.

   c. It provides the full Windows API.

   d. Its source code is available to the public.

7. VxWorks is which of the following?

   a. A Windows embedded OS

   b. A proprietary embedded OS

   c. A Linux embedded OS

   d. A Windows security validation tool

8. Which of the following is a major challenge of securing embedded OSs?

   a. Training users

   b. Configuration

   c. Patching

   d. Backup and recovery

9. The lack of a familiar interface, such as CD/DVD-ROM drives, contributes to the difficulty of updating embedded OSs. True or False?

10. Embedded OSs on routers are susceptible to which of the following? (Choose all that apply.)

    a. Authentication bypass attacks

    b. Buffer overflow attacks

    c. Password-guessing attacks

    d. RTOS clock corruption

11. Multifunction devices (MFDs) are rarely:

    a. Targets of network attacks

    b. Installed on Windows networks

    c. Installed on large networks

    d. Scanned for vulnerabilities

12. SCADA systems are used for which of the following?

    a. Monitoring embedded OSs

    b. Monitoring ATM access codes

    c. Monitoring equipment in large-scale industries

    d. Protecting embedded OSs from remote attacks

13. Cell phone vulnerabilities make it possible for attackers to do which of the following? (Choose all that apply.)

    a. Use your phone as a microphone to eavesdrop on meetings or private conversations.

    b. Install a BIOS-based rootkit.

    c. Clone your phone to make illegal long-distance phone calls.

    d. Listen to your phone conversations.

14. If the time and money required to compromise an embedded system exceeds the value of the system's information, a security tester might recommend not fixing the vulnerability. True or False?

15. Most printers now have only TCP/IP enabled and don't allow default administrator passwords, so they're inherently more secure. True or False?

Case Projects

Case Project 9-1: Protecting Embedded OSs on the Alexander Rocco Network

After performing enumeration tests, you discover that the network consists of 5 systems running Windows 10 IoT, 2 systems running Windows Server 2008 R2 for Embedded Systems, 23 systems running Jetdirect, and 5 network appliances running embedded Linux.

Based on this information, write a one-page memo to Bob Jones, the IT manager, outlining some suggestions on possible weaknesses or vulnerabilities in these systems. The memo should include recommendations to reduce the risk of network attacks and cite specific CVE entries (check *www.cve.mitre.org*).

Case Project 9-2: Identifying Vulnerable Systems That Can't Be Patched

You discover that some devices on the Alexander Rocco network can't be patched against a buffer overflow attack because of FDA certification requirements. What recommendations can you make to reduce the risk these systems pose?

Case Project 9-3: Identifying Vulnerabilities in Mobile Phones

More than three billion mobile phones are in use worldwide, and more people now reach the Internet with mobile phones than they do with desktop computers. Even if your phone can't browse the Web, it probably has some limited Web capability and is at least part of a huge cell phone network. Have you ever thought about someone hacking your phone? Research your phone model on the Internet to determine what OS it uses and any existing or potential vulnerabilities. For example, could your phone be used as a covert listening device or used to send text message spam or perform a DoS attack? Be creative, but use real information that you find in your research. Write a one- to two-page report on your findings.

## chapter 10

Hacking Web Servers

After reading this chapter and completing the exercises, you will be able to:

- Describe Web applications
- Explain Web application vulnerabilities
- Describe the tools used to attack Web servers

The Internet has revolutionized commerce and communications. Web applications and Web services are widely used, and many Web development platforms are available, such as Microsoft Active Server Pages (ASP) and Java Server Pages (JSP).

Normally, a Web application is supported by a Web server that runs on a general-purpose or embedded OS. Each component (application, server, and OS) has its own set of vulnerabilities, but when these components are combined, there's an increased risk of a Web application compromise affecting a network's overall security. Skilled hackers can often exploit a minor vulnerability in one function, such as a Web mail application, and use it as a stepping stone to launch additional attacks against the OS. With the growth in available platforms and e-commerce Web sites, it's no wonder that security vulnerabilities abound.

Chapter 8 covered OS vulnerabilities; this chapter gives you an overview of Web applications, explains the vulnerabilities of many Web components, and describes the tools used to hack Web servers.

Understanding Web Applications

As you learned in Chapter 7, writing a program without bugs is really difficult. The bigger the program, the more bugs or defects are possible, and some defects create security vulnerabilities. The more people who have access to a program, the bigger the risk of security vulnerabilities. The following sections describe Web application components and platforms for developing Web applications.

Web Application Components

HTML is still the foundation of most Web applications and is commonly used for creating static Web pages. HTML5 is the latest release in the HTML family. **Static Web pages** display the same information regardless of the time of day or the user who accesses the page. **Dynamic Web pages** can vary the information that's displayed, depending on variables such as current time and date, username, and purchasing history (information collected with cookies or Web bugs, discussed in Chapter 4). For Web pages to be dynamic, their code must consist of more than just the basic tags discussed in Chapter 7. These pages need special components for displaying information that changes depending on user input or information from a back-end server. To do this, a variety of techniques can be used for dynamic Web pages, including the <form> element, AJAX, Common Gateway Interface (CGI), Active Server Pages (ASP), PHP, ColdFusion, JavaScript, and database connector strings, such as Open Database Connector (ODBC). These components are covered in the following sections.

Web Forms The <form> element is used in an HTML document to allow customers to submit information to the Web server. You have probably filled out a form when purchasing a product online or registering for an e-mail newsletter, for example. Some forms can be quite long and ask for a lot of information, and some have only a couple of input fields, such as username and password. A Web server processes information from a form by using a Web application. The following HTML code shows the syntax for a simple form, and Figure 10-1 shows the Web page created with this code.

```
<html>
<body>
<form>
Enter your username:
<input type="text" name="username">
<br>
Enter your password:
<input name="password" type="password">
</form></body></html>
```

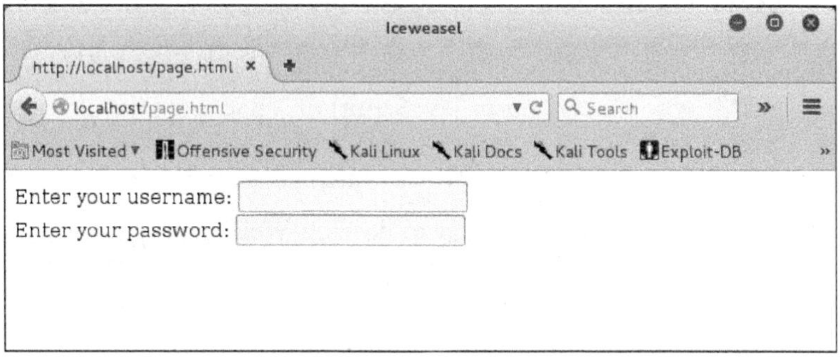

Figure 10-1   An HTML Web page with a form

Common Gateway Interface Another standard that handles moving data from a Web server to a Web browser is **Common Gateway Interface (CGI)**, which enables Web designers to create dynamic HTML Web applications. Many dynamic Web pages are created with CGI and scripting languages. CGI is the interface that determines how a Web server passes data to a Web browser. It relies on Perl or another scripting or programming language to create dynamic Web pages, which is quite different from Active Server Pages (covered in the next section). CGI's main role is passing data between a Web server and Web browser. In fact, the term "gateway" describes this movement of data between the Web server and Web browser.

CGI programs can be written in many programming and scripting languages, such as C/C++, Perl, UNIX shells, Visual Basic, and FORTRAN. Programming languages such as C and C++ require compiling the program before running it. If CGI is implemented with a scripting language, compiling isn't necessary. The following CGI program displays "Hello Security Testers!" in the user's browser. This hello.pl program is written in Perl and would be placed in the cgi-bin directory on the Web server:

```
#!/usr/bin/perl
print "Content-type: text/html\n\n";
print "Hello Security Testers!";
```

To check whether the CGI program works, save the program to the cgi-bin directory of your Web server, and then enter the URL in your Web browser, such as *http://www.myweb.com/cgi-bin/hello.pl.*

Third Party Frameworks and Libraries Spring, JSF, AngularJS, Yeoman, Sass, and Vaadin are just a few of the hundreds of frameworks designed to make programming easier. Frameworks are typically called on for a specific purpose. For example, the Spring Framework's strength is connecting components, and the Sass framework helps you style your Web site to enhance user experience. The use of libraries saves developer time and means less documentation is required for complex routines of custom code. As third-party libraries grow in popularity, keeping them current and secure becomes more and more important.

Active Server Pages Active Server Pages (ASP) is another technology that developers can use to display HTML documents to users on the fly. That is, when a user requests a Web page, one is created at that time. ASP isn't a programming language. It's a technology that enables developers to create dynamic, interactive Web pages and uses scripting languages, such as JScript (Microsoft's version of JavaScript) or VBScript. Like all Internet technologies, ASP has evolved and has been largely replaced by ASP.NET. However, for the purposes of this chapter, ASP and ASP.NET are used interchangeably.

Not all Web servers support ASP, so if you want to develop Web pages with ASP, the server you're using must support this technology. Internet Information Services (IIS) 4.0 and later support ASP, and IIS 5.0 and later support ASP.NET. It's important to understand that the Web server, not the Web browser, must support ASP. In Activities 10-1 and 10-2, you work with IIS to get a better understanding of Web applications.

Activity 10-1: Installing Internet Information Services

Time Required: 30 minutes

Objective: Install IIS on your Windows computer.

Description: To host a Web site, you need to install IIS on your Windows computer. Although IIS is deployed on a server in a production environment, preproduction Web development and testing can be done on workstations. IIS 8 is available in Windows 8.1 (Professional, Ultimate, and Enterprise), and IIS 10 is available in Windows 10. Because IIS isn't installed by default, in this activity you install it and use your Web browser to check that it was installed correctly. This activity assumes you have never installed IIS on the PC you are using and are installing on a Windows 10 PC.

1. Open Control Panel, and then click **Programs**.

2. In the Programs and Features section, click **Turn Windows features on or off** to open the Windows Features dialog box. If the User Account Control (UAC) message box opens, click **Continue**. Click the **Internet Information Services** check box, and then click the plus symbol to expand the IIS options. Click the **World Wide Web Services** check box. Ensure that the **Application Development Features, Common HTTP Features**, and **Security** are checked under **World Wide Web Services**. Click **Web Management Tools** and ensure that **IIS Management Console** and **IIS Scripts and Tools** are selected under **Web Management Tools**. When you are finished, your windows should look like what is shown in Figure 10-2. Don't clear any options that are already selected.

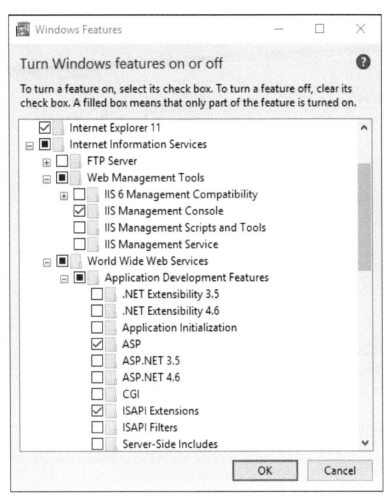

Figure 10-2 Turning Windows features on or off

Source: © 2016 Microsoft

3. Click **OK** to have IIS installed. When you see the "Windows completed the requested changes" message, click **Close**.

4. To check that IIS has been installed, click **Start,** type **inetmgr,** and press **Enter** to open the IIS Manager (see Figure 10-3). Click **Help, About Internet Information Services** from the menu. What version of IIS is installed on your computer?

Figure 10-3 The Internet Information Services (IIS) Manager

Source: © 2016 Microsoft

5. Start a Web browser, type the URL **http://localhost,** and press **Enter** to go to the IIS welcome page. A visitor to your Web site would get an IIS welcome message because you haven't created a default HTML Web page yet. However, clicking the graphic directs you to Microsoft's official IIS Web site, where you can learn more about IIS. When you're finished, close the browser window.

6. Next, you need to create a folder on your Web server to hold any HTML pages you create. When IIS is installed, a new folder called inetpub is created on the C drive. Open File Explorer. Under the C drive (substitute the correct drive letter if your installation is different), click to expand the **inetpub** folder, and then click to select the **wwwroot** folder.

7. Right-click inside the **wwwroot** folder, point to **New,** and click **Folder.** For the folder name, type *YourFirstName* (substituting your first name), and then press **Enter.**

8. Close any open windows, and leave Windows running for the next activity.

To keep attackers from knowing the directory structure you create on an IIS Web server, creating a virtual directory is recommended so that the path a user sees on the Web browser isn't the actual path on the Web server. A **virtual directory** is a pointer to the physical directory. For example, with virtual directories, a user might see *http://www.mycompany.com/jobs/default.asp* instead of *http://www.mycompany.com/security/positions/CEH_Cert/default.asp.*

The simpler structure that a virtual directory offers is often easier for users to memorize and navigate. Using this design strategy is also a good security feature because it helps hide the actual directory structure from attackers.

Activity 10-2: Creating a Virtual Directory

Time Required: 15 minutes

Objective: Learn how to create a virtual directory on an IIS Web server.

Description: After IIS is installed and physical directories are created, a Web administrator should create virtual directories that prevent site visitors from seeing the physical directory structure. In this activity, you create a virtual directory, using the directory you created in Activity 10-1.

1. Click **Start**, type **inetmgr**, and press **Enter**. In the IIS Manager window, click to expand the computer name, **Sites**, and **Default Web Site** (see Figure 10-4).

Figure 10-4 Viewing IIS Web sites

Source: © 2016 Microsoft

2. Right-click the *YourFirstName* folder you created in Activity 10-1 and click **Add Virtual Directory**.

3. In the Alias text box, type your first name. Type (or browse to) the physical path of the folder you created in Activity 10-1 (**C:\inetpub\wwwroot*YourFirstName***), and then click **OK** to create a virtual directory that users can access over the Web.

4. Close all open windows, and leave Windows running for the next activity.

The Web server uses the ASP scripting language to generate HTML pages for the Web browser. How does the Web server know when ASP code is being used? You wrote an

HTML Web page in Chapter 7; now look at a Web page containing ASP statements in Activity 10-3. The best way to learn ASP is to create a Web page with it. To do this, you need three components: a text editor (e.g., Notepad), a Web server (such as an IIS Web server), and a Web browser (such as Internet Explorer, Microsoft Edge, or Firefox).

Activity 10-3: Creating an ASP Web Page

Time Required: 20 minutes

Objective: Use ASP to create dynamic Web pages and be able to recognize ASP Web pages.

Description: ASP Web pages are created on the Web server and enable a developer to create dynamic Web pages. In this activity, you create an ASP Web page and use a Web browser to view the page.

1. To start Notepad with administrative privileges, click **Start**, type **Notepad**, right-click **Notepad**, and click **Run as administrator**. (If necessary, click **Yes** in the UAC message box.) In Notepad, type the following code:

```
<HTML>
<HEAD><TITLE> My First ASP Web Page</TITLE></HEAD>
<BODY>
<H1>Hello, security professionals</H1>
The time is <%=Time %>.
</BODY>
</HTML>
```

2. Save the file as **First.asp** in C:\inetpub\wwwroot*YourFirstName*. Be sure the file is saved with the .asp extension, not the .txt extension. Exit Notepad.

3. To test the First.asp Web page, start your Web browser, type the URL **http://localhost /*YourFirstName*/First.asp**, and press **Enter**. Note that the Web page shows the current time of your location, meaning it's dynamic. That is, it changes each time your Web browser calls for the Web page. The <% and %> tags tell the Web server that ASP is used as the script language.

4. Click **View**, and then click **Source** from the Web browser menu. Does the source code show you the ASP commands you entered?

5. Close the Web browser, and log off Windows for the next activity.

To prevent potential security problems, Microsoft doesn't want users to be able to view an ASP Web page's source code. For example, a Web page containing a connection string that reveals username and password information to users could be used for an attack. Not allowing the source code to be viewed makes ASP more secure than basic HTML Web pages. Connection strings are covered later in "Connecting to Databases."

Apache Web Server As a security tester, you should be aware of another Web server program. Apache Web Server is said to run on more than twice as many Web servers as IIS, so some familiarity with this Web server can be helpful in the security-testing profession. Apache has important advantages over the competition: It works in just about any *nix platform as well as in Windows, and it's free. Installing Apache in Linux is different from installing IIS in Windows, but you don't have to worry about installation because the Apache Web Server daemon (httpd) 2.4 is included on the Kali DVD.

Activity 10-4: Working with Apache Web Server

Time Required: 35 minutes

Objective: Explore basic settings and tasks in Apache Web Server.

Description: Without a doubt, you'll run across Apache Web Server systems when conducting a security test. Because Apache is a sophisticated, modular Web server, mastering its features and options can take considerable time. Apache's layout varies, depending on the OS. For example, Apache in Fedora Linux is different from Apache in Ubuntu Linux. In this activity, you explore basic Apache Web Server commands and learn how to find and modify some configuration options (called "Apache directives"). The goal of this activity is to configure a Web server with a directory that requires authentication.

1. Boot your computer into Linux with the Kali Linux DVD.

2. Open a Terminal shell. At the command prompt, type **apache2ctl start** and press **Enter**. You can safely ignore the "Could not reliably determine the server's fully qualified domain name" error.

3. Start the Iceweasel Web browser. In the address bar, type **localhost** and press **Enter**. The Web site displays instructions on how to manipulate the default apache configuration. Read over this page.

4. Open a Terminal shell. At the command prompt, type **apache2ctl stop** and press **Enter**.

5. Now, we'll view the default apache configuration files. In the Terminal shell, type **cd/etc/apache2** and press **Enter** to change directories. Then type **grep Include apache2.conf** and press **Enter** to see a listing of files and directories where the Apache server searches for additional directives at startup (see Figure 10-5). Note the next to last line, `IncludeOptional sites-enabled/*.conf`. This directory is where Apache checks for Web site configuration files. You can add a Web site by adding its configuration file in this directory without having to change the main configuration file apache2.conf.

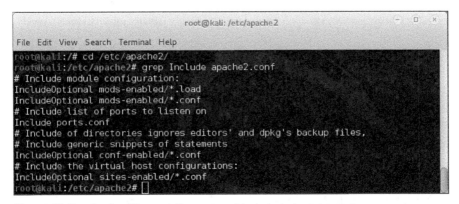

Figure 10-5   Viewing files and directories with an Include statement

Source: GNU GPL

6. Type **cd /etc/apache2/sites-enabled && ls** and press **Enter**.

7. Open the file in the gvim editor by typing **gvim 000-default.conf** and pressing **Enter**.

8. Enter the following lines at the end of the file, below the line `</VirtualHost>`:

```
<Directory /var/www/html/restricted>
        Options Indexes FollowSymLinks
        AllowOverride AuthConfig
        Order allow,deny
        allow from all
</Directory>
```

9. Save your changes and exit the gvim editor by pressing **Esc**, typing **:wq**, and pressing **Enter**.

10. In the Terminal shell, create a new directory by typing **mkdir /var/www/html/restricted** and pressing **Enter**.

11. Type **cd /var/www/html/restricted** to change to the directory you created in Step 12 and press **Enter**. Then type **touch secret.txt** and press **Enter** to create a file in this directory.

12. Next, you create the .htaccess file in the same directory. This file is the local directory configuration file specified in apache2.conf by the AccessFileName directive. If .htaccess exists in any Web site directory, Apache checks it first. In this .htaccess file, you point Apache to the location of AuthUserFile (essentially, a password file). Type **gvim .htaccess** and press **Enter**. Type the following for the file's contents:

```
AuthType Basic
AuthName "Password Required"
AuthUserFile /etc/apache2/.htpasswd
Require user tester
```

13. Exit and save the file by pressing **Esc** and then pressing : (a colon). At the : prompt, type **wq** and press **Enter**. In the Terminal shell, create a password file by typing **htpasswd -c /etc/apache2/.htpasswd tester** and pressing **Enter**. When prompted, enter a password and confirm, and then make note of the password. The .htaccess file you created in Step 12 tells Apache to look in the .htpasswd file for the tester user's password. You can run the command **cat /etc/apache2/.htpasswd** to view the password hash for your new user.

14. Restart Apache by typing **apache2ctl restart** and pressing **Enter**. In Iceweasel, go to **http://localhost/restricted**, and enter the username **tester** and the password you confirmed in Step 13. What file is displayed? If you want to be prompted again for a password, you'll have to close and reopen your browser.

15. See whether others in the class can access your restricted folder by having them enter **http://*yourIPaddress*/restricted** in their browsers (replacing *yourIPaddress* with your IP address). If necessary, type **ifconfig eth0** and press Enter to find your IP address.

16. Why is entering your credentials on a Web site not secured with SSL, such as this site, a problem? What is the fix for this problem?

17. Research Basic Authentication security weaknesses on the Internet. Are there any problems with Basic Authentication?

18. Close the Terminal shell, exit Firefox, and log off Linux for the next activity.

Using Scripting Languages

Web pages can be developed with several scripting languages, such as VBScript and JavaScript. You won't learn how to be a Web developer by reviewing the scripting languages covered in this chapter, but you should be able to recognize when one is being used because many security-testing tools are written with scripting languages. Also, most macro viruses and worms, and all worms that take advantage of cross-site scripting vulnerabilities (discussed later in the chapter), are based on scripting language.

PHP Hypertext Processor Similar to ASP, **PHP Hypertext Processor (PHP)** enables Web developers to create dynamic Web pages. PHP, an open-source server-side scripting language, is embedded in an HTML Web page by using the PHP tags <?php and ?>. Because PHP Web pages run on the server, users can't view the source code in their Web browsers. PHP was originally used mainly on UNIX systems, but it's used more widely now on many platforms, including Macintosh and Windows. The following excerpt is a code example for a static PHP Web page showing the use of PHP tags:

Bolded lines in these code examples show how different scripting languages are indicated.

```
<html>
<head>
<title>My First PHP Program</title>
</head>
<body>
<?php echo "<h1>Hello, Security Testers!</h1>"; ?>
</body>
</html>
```

This page would need to be created on your Web server as a .php file, similar to the ASP Web page you created in Activity 10-3. After you have identified that a Web server is using PHP, you should use the methods you have learned in this book to investigate further for specific vulnerabilities. For example, several versions of PHP running on Linux can be exploited because of a line in the Php.ini file: The line `file_uploads=on` permits file uploads; however, this setting might allow a remote attacker to run arbitrary code with elevated privileges. The best solution is to upgrade to the latest version of PHP, but if that's not possible, change the line to `file_uploads=off`.

You should also be familiar with LAMP (which stands for Linux, Apache, MySQL, and PHP) because it's a collection of open-source software used for many sophisticated, high-traffic Web applications. LAMP is known as a "solution stack" because it stacks several programs into one integrated Web application solution. For more information, do an Internet search on the term "LAMP" combined with the Linux version you're using, such as "Ubuntu" or "Fedora."

ColdFusion ColdFusion is another server-side scripting language for developing dynamic Web pages. Created by Allaire Corporation, it's now owned by Adobe Systems, Inc. ColdFusion integrates Web browser, Web server, and database technologies. It uses proprietary tags written in ColdFusion Markup Language (CFML), and Web applications written in CFML can contain other client-side technologies, such as HTML and JavaScript. The following code is an example of HTML code with a CFML tag that redirects the user to a Web page. All CFML tags begin with the letters CF. For example, the column tag is <CFCOL>.

```
<html>
<head>
<title>Using CFML</title>
</head>
<body>
<CFLOCATION URL="www.isecom.org" ADDTOKEN="NO">
</body>
</html>
```

As with the PHP example, security testers should become familiar with vulnerabilities associated with a Web server using ColdFusion. A quick search of the Adobe security page (*http://helpx.adobe.com/security.html*) can narrow your research time, allowing you to focus on the vulnerabilities that affect your situation.

VBScript Visual Basic Script (VBScript) is a scripting language developed by Microsoft. You can insert VBScript in your HTML Web pages to convert static Web pages into dynamic Web pages. The biggest advantage of using a scripting language is that you have the features of powerful programming languages at your disposal. For those who have programming experience, VBScript will be really easy for you to pick up quickly. Take a look at a simple example to help you recognize when VBScript is being used. The following code is entered in an .html file in Notepad, as you did earlier:

```
<html>
<body>
<script type="text/vbscript">
document.write ("<h1>Hello Security Testers!</h1>")
document.write ("Date Activated: " & date())
</script>
</body>
</html>
```

Figure 10-6 shows the Web page generated from the preceding VBScript code.

Figure 10-6 A Web page created with VBScript

Source: © 2016 Microsoft

The Microsoft Security Bulletin Search page (*https://technet.microsoft.com/en-us/security/bul letin*) is an excellent starting point for investigating VBScript vulnerabilities. A search on a specific Security Bulletin produces a wealth of information, including the severity rating and patch information.

To see an example of a VBScript Security Bulletin, visit *https://technet.microsoft.com/en-us /library/security/ms08-022.aspx*.

JavaScript Another popular scripting language for creating dynamic Web pages is JavaScript, which also has the power of a programming language. As with VBScript, you can branch, loop, and test (the BLT you learned in Chapter 7) and create functions and procedures in HTML Web pages. The following code is a simple HTML snippet with JavaScript code added:

```
<html>
<head>
<script type="text/javascript">
function chastise_user()
{
alert("So, you like breaking rules?")
document.getElementById("cmdButton").focus()
}
</script>
</head>
<body>
<h3>"If you are a Security Tester, please do not click the command
button below!"</h3>
<form>
<input type="button" value="Don't Click!" name="cmdButton"
onClick="chastise_user()" />
</form>
</body>
</html>
```

This code is a little more complex than the previous examples, but it shows you how scripting languages can include functions and alerts. Notice that the third line specifies that Java-Script is the language being used. Next, the `chastise_user()` function is defined; this function simply displays an alert message. The `getElementById()` function is a method (a sequence of statements that perform a routine or task) defined by the World Wide Web Consortium (W3C) Document Object Model (DOM). Basically, it returns an object—in this case, a command button you click. The remaining code is fairly self-explanatory. To see how this code works, take a look at the output shown in Figure 10-7.

Figure 10-7   A command button created with JavaScript

Source: © 2016 Microsoft

If the user accepts the security warning and clicks the command button, the alert message box shown in Figure 10-8 is displayed.

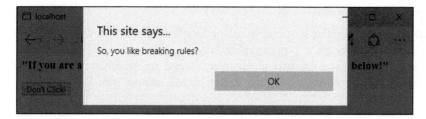

Figure 10-8   An alert message created with JavaScript

Source: © 2016 Microsoft

JavaScript is widely used, and a variety of vulnerabilities have been exploited in older Web browsers. Security testers and administrators should inspect every computer for unpatched or outdated browser versions and keep up with vulnerabilities. For example, Cyber Security Alert TA09-133B, Adobe Reader and Acrobat Vulnerabilities (*https://www.us-cert.gov/ncas /alerts/TA09-133B*) describes a JavaScript vulnerability.

Connecting to Databases

Most Web pages that display company information to users are stored on a database server. Web pages that prompt a user for information, such as name, phone number, address, and so on, store the information users enter in a database. The technology used to connect a Web application to a database server might vary depending on the OS, but the theory is the same. The following sections discuss some technologies used to connect to a database or an external file system from a Web application.

Open Database Connectivity Open Database Connectivity (ODBC) is a standard database access method developed by the SQL Access Group. The ODBC interface allows an application to access data stored in a database management system (DBMS), such as Microsoft SQL, Oracle, or any system that can recognize and issue ODBC commands. Interoperability between back-end DBMSs is a key feature of the ODBC interface, allowing developers to focus on the application without worrying about a specific DBMS. The ODBC interface accomplishes this interoperability by defining the following:

- A standardized representation for data types
- A library of ODBC function calls that allow an application to connect to a DBMS, run SQL statements, and retrieve the results
- A standard method of connecting to and logging on to a DBMS

Object Linking and Embedding Database Object Linking and Embedding Database (OLE DB) is a set of interfaces that enable applications to access data stored in a DBMS. Microsoft designed it to be faster, more efficient, and more stable than its predecessor, ODBC. OLE DB relies on connection strings that allow the application to access data stored on an external device. Depending on the data source you're connecting to, you might use a different provider. For example, connecting to an SQL database requires using SQLOLEDB as the provider instead of Microsoft.ACE.

Table 10-1 shows some OLE DB providers available for developers. When conducting a security test on a Web server, you should verify how the Web server is connecting to a database and, of course, what type of database or resource data is being collected. The following code line is an example of a connection string used to access data in a Microsoft Access database named Personnel:

```
Provider=Microsoft.ACE.OLEDB.12.0;Data Source=C:\Personnel.accdb;
User ID=; Password=;
```

OLE DB provider	Description in connection string
Microsoft Active Directory Service	Provider=ADSDSOOBJECT
Advantage	Provider=Advantage OLE DB Provider
AS/400 (from IBM)	Provider=IBMDA400
AS/400 and VSAM (from Microsoft)	Provider=SNAOLEDB
MS Commerce Server	Provider=Commerce.DSO.1
DB2	Provider=DB2OLEDB
Microsoft Jet	Provider=Microsoft.Jet.OLEDB.4.0
Microsoft.ACE	Provider=Microsoft.ACE.OLEDB.12.0
MS Exchange	Provider=EXOLEDB.DataSource
MySQL	Provider=MySQLProv
Oracle (from Microsoft)	Provider=msdaora
Oracle (from Oracle)	Provider=OraOLEDB.Oracle
MS SQL Server	Provider=SQLOLEDB

Table 10-1   OLE DB providers

ActiveX Data Objects ActiveX Data Objects (ADO) is a programming interface for connecting a Web application to a database. ActiveX defines technologies that allow applications, such as Word or Excel, to interact with the Web. For example, you can place an Excel spreadsheet in a Web page. To access a database from an ASP Web page, you follow these general steps:

1. Create an ADO connection to the database you want to access.
2. Open the database connection you created in Step 1.
3. Create an ADO recordset, which contains rows from the table you're accessing.
4. Open the recordset.
5. Select the data you need from the recordset, based on particular criteria.
6. Close the recordset.
7. Close the database connection.

Next, take a look at how these steps are performed and what the result looks like in an ASP Web page. The following ASP code creates and opens the ADO connection:

```
<%
set conn=Server.CreateObject("ADODB.Connection")
conn.Provider="Microsoft.Jet.OLEDB.4.0"
conn.Open "c:\MyDatabase\employee.mdb"
%>
```

Now you need to create a recordset to contain records from a table in your employee.mdb database:

```
<%
set rs=Server.CreateObject("ADODB.recordset")
rs.Open "Select * FROM Employee", conn
.....
rs.close
conn.close
%>
```

You would probably use a loop to print all the records to the Web page, but that's not important here. You want to understand the technology so that you can recognize vulnerabilities when they exist. Now that you have a good foundation on the components of a Web application, the following section discusses some of these vulnerabilities.

Understanding Web Application Vulnerabilities

Many platforms and programming languages can be used to design a Web site. Each platform has its advantages and disadvantages. Some are free, and others cost quite a bit; some require only basic skills in creating Web applications, and others require an in-depth knowledge of programming. Regardless of the platform, security professionals need to assess the system and examine potential methods for attacking it.

Network security is essential to protect company data and resources from attack. Application Security, often referred to as AppSec, was once overlooked by professionals because it is a very specialized practice. One reason is that many security professionals have experience in networking but little or no experience in programming. In fact, most network security books don't have much programming coverage because the topic can overwhelm students. No matter how efficient a company's firewalls or intrusion detection systems are, most systems allow the content of HTTP traffic. Therefore, an attacker can bypass supposed security boundaries as well as any OS hardening that network administrators have done. Simply stated, Network-layer protection doesn't always prevent Application-layer attacks from occurring. All an attacker needs is an understanding of some basic programming concepts or scripting languages. To add to the mayhem, attackers usually don't need special tools, and detection of a manual attack on a Web application is often difficult. After attackers gain control of a Web server, they can use a number of post-exploitation actions, including:

- Defacing the Web site
- Attempting to destroy the application's database or selling its contents
- Attempting to gain control of user accounts
- Launching secondary attacks from the Web server or infecting site visitors' systems with malware
- Attempting to gain access to other servers that are part of the network infrastructure

Application Vulnerabilities and Countermeasures

Luckily, there's an organization that helps security professionals understand the vulnerabilities in Web applications. Much like ISECOM, **Open Web Application Security Project (OWASP)** is a not-for-profit foundation dedicated to finding and fighting the causes of Web application vulnerabilities. OWASP (*www.owasp.org*) publishes the Ten Most Critical Web Application Security Risks paper, which has been built into the Payment Card Industry (PCI) Data Security Standard (DSS). The PCI DSS is a requirement for all businesses that sell products online. Visiting the OWASP Web site to learn more about Web application vulnerabilities is recommended. As a security tester, you might need to analyze vulnerabilities such as the following ones in the OWASP Top Ten list:

- *A1—Injection vulnerabilities* occur when untrusted data is accepted as input to an application without being properly validated. Any piece of data sent from a Web browser to a server could be manipulated and thus represents a potential point of attack. If an attacker is able to make assumptions about how data might be handled on the server, they can make educated attempts at exploiting the server. There are many types of injection vulnerabilities, including SQL, code, LDAP, and command injection.

- *A2—Authentication flaws and weaknesses* are prevalent when poor session management, weak encryption schemes, and/or weak logic is used to control or protect the authentication process. Developers will often "roll their own" authentication or encryption schemes instead of leveraging existing, vetted libraries. One small oversight by a developer can lead to major weaknesses.

- *A3—Cross-site scripting (XSS)* vulnerabilities, like injection vulnerabilities, result from a server accepting untrusted, unvalidated input. There are two types of XSS vulnerabilities: stored and reflected. Stored, sometimes referred to as "persistent XSS," is especially harmful because it can be delivered to subsequent users of the application. Reflected XSS relies on social engineering to trick a user into visiting a maliciously crafted link or URL. In either case, the attacker's goal is to execute code on a remote user's computer. In order to accomplish this, the attacker injects code into a susceptible parameter of the application. The server sends this code to the victim's browser. The user's browser then runs the injected code, causing some harmful action on the user's computer.

Security Bytes

In 2005, an XSS worm called JS.Spacehero was spread by hijacking browsers visiting the MySpace Web site. The worm's creator uploaded a malicious script to his MySpace profile page, and anyone visiting this page was redirected automatically into sending him a friend request. The worm was then embedded in the hijacked user's profile page. In less than 24 hours, more than a million MySpace profile pages were infected, making the JS.Spacehero worm one of the fastest spreading worms ever. MySpace had to shut down the site to clean up the infection, and the worm's creator earned himself a felony conviction.

- *A4—Insecure direct object reference* is a combination of poorly implemented access control and the programmer's use of guessable names when calling database records. For example, if Ted and Mary register with a Web site and are assigned customer numbers of 301 and 302, the application is likely assigning sequential customer numbers. The next users will likely be assigned 303, 304, and so on. If this sequential customer number is sent from the browser to the server when requesting account information, this is called a direct object reference. In the case of an insecure direct object reference, the application does not verify that users are authorized to view the information they are requesting. Ted, in our example, could edit the customer number parameter passed from the browser to the server from his customer number, 301, to Mary's, 302. If the application is vulnerable, Mary's information will be displayed to Ted.

- *A5—Security misconfigurations* result from poorly configured technologies that a Web application runs on top of. This includes operating system, application server, Web server, services used for maintenance, and so on. Configuration baselines and checklist can help administrators prevent security misconfigurations.

- *A6—Sensitive data exposure* occurs when the proper precautions are not taken to protect application data at rest and in transit. Client-side exposure can include sensitive information that is cached and remnant on the user's hard drive after an application is used. This is especially dangerous if a user checks his or her bank account balance on a Internet cafe's PC and cached information contains sensitive banking details that an attacker can use to conduct fraud. Server-side encryption of data-at-rest should be used to protect sensitive data, such as passwords and other customer information. In order to preserve the secrecy of data-in-transit, encryption must always be forced by the application.

- *A7—Missing function level access control*, described in A4, means an application does not properly verify that users are authorized to view the information they are requesting. Attackers can use a technique called forced browsing to view pages that they should not have access to because the application does not validate access rights.

- *A8—Cross-site request forgery* is sometimes referred to as a session-riding attack because it is conducted against a user who already has an active session with an application. The attacker tricks a user of the application into clicking on a link, which performs an action in the application (think money transfer or password change). The attacker never has access direct to the user's session, but by tricking the user to click a link, the user unknowingly performs an action on the attacker's behalf.

- *A9—Using components with known vulnerabilities* refers to vulnerabilities in third-party libraries, OSs, databases, applications, and Web servers. These components should always be kept up to date to avoid introducing risk to an application.

- *A10—Unvalidated redirects and requests* occur when an application accepts any target URL for the application to redirect to before or after a specified action occurs. Applications should only allow redirects to a whitelist of target URLs.

The OWASP paper on the top 10 vulnerabilities might cover some areas beyond the skills of a beginning security tester, so OWASP offers Broken Web Apps and **WebGoat,** an online utility that helps beginning security testers understand the Web application vulnerabilities covered in this list.

OWASP developed the WebGoat project to help security testers learn how to conduct vulnerability testing on Web applications. Experts from all over the world use WebGoat and offer their input. The OWASP developers want to encourage security students to think about how to launch an attack, so solutions aren't given for all exercises. In the following paragraphs, you walk through an example of using WebGoat to learn about some basic Web application attacks. You can follow along, if you like, or just review the steps and figures.

Assuming you've booted in to Kali Linux, you will need to download the easy-run executable jar version of WebGoat from: *https://s3.amazonaws.com/webgoat-war/webgoat -container-7.0.1-war-exec.jar.* Next, open a terminal window and browse to where you downloaded the easy-run jar. Type **java -jar webgoat-container-7.0.1-war-exec.jar** to run the executable. Now, open a browser and go to *http://localhost:8080/WebGoat.* You should see the WebGoat start page shown in Figure 10-9.

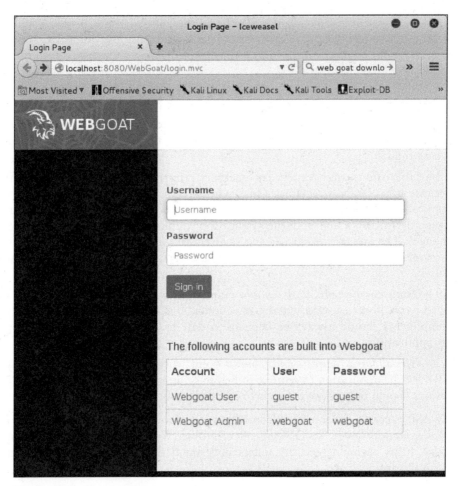

Figure 10-9 The WebGoat start page

Source: GNU GPL

Once you authenticate with the credentials listed on the start page, you are taken to the introduction module "How to Work with WebGoat." Read through the introduction, then click the **General** link from the navigation panel on the left and select **Http Basics**. After you enter a name, the server accepts the HTTP request and reverses the input. For example, entering the name "student" returns the value "tneduts." You can click the **Hints** menu shown in Figure 10-10 to see tips, Java code, and any cookies or parameters used.

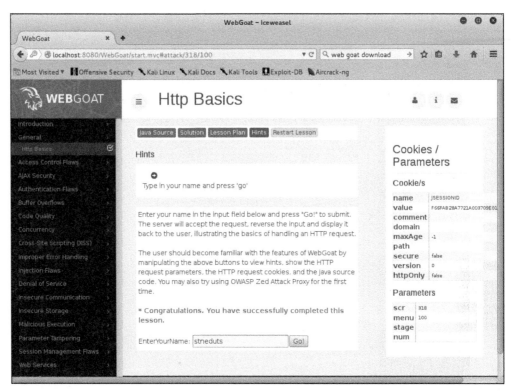

Figure 10-10 The WebGoat Hints menu

Source: GNU GPL

The exercises become more complex after this one, so you probably won't be able to do them quickly. For example, the **Asynchronous JavaScript and XML (AJAX)** security exercise on XML injection involves AJAX code, which is used to create sophisticated dynamic Web applications, such as Facebook and Google Apps. To help you learn about AJAX vulnerabilities, WebGoat has set up a fictitious travel rewards Web site (see Figure 10-11); your goal is to add more reward miles to your account than are allowed. Perhaps you can get enough points to earn the WebGoat Hawaii cruise!

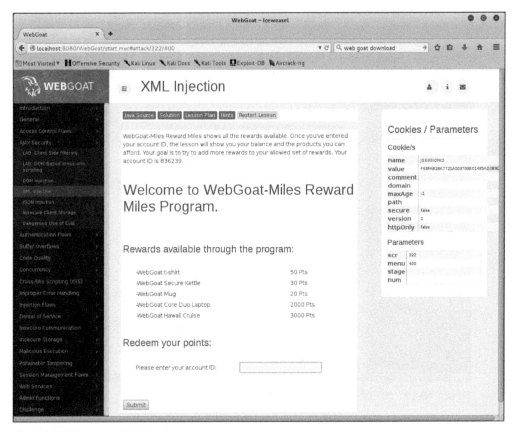

Figure 10-11 The AJAX XML injection exercise

Source: GNU GPL

Other exercises show different aspects of Web security. For example, one requires setting up a client/server configuration so that you can sniff traffic containing credentials to a Web site; another involves launching a DoS attack by creating too many concurrent logons to the database. The last exercise, called the Challenge (see Figure 10-12), takes beginning students to a higher level: breaking an authentication scheme, stealing credit cards from a database, and then defacing a Web site. No solutions are given for this exercise, but knowing how to search the Web can give you additional hints.

The SQL statement is then the following:

```
SELECT * FROM customer
WHERE tblusername = ' OR 1 = 1 - - AND tblpassword = ' '
```

Because 1 = 1 is always true, the query is carried out successfully. Double hyphens (--) are used in SQL to indicate a comment. Are there more tricks to hacking into a database? Take a look at a couple of other things an attacker could have entered when prompted for a username and password:

```
Please enter username: ' OR 1 = 1 - -
Please enter password: ' OR 1 = 1 - -
```

The SQL statement is then as follows:

```
SELECT * FROM customer
WHERE tblusername = ' OR 1 = 1 - - AND tblpassword =' OR 1 = 1 - -
```

Instead of the SQL statement comparing values the user enters with values in the Customer table, it compares a quotation mark to another quotation mark, which of course returns a true condition. Hence, all rows are returned. It's surprising that this vulnerability exists on many systems connected to the Internet. You shouldn't test for this vulnerability by attempting SQL injections on Web sites because this attack is considered intrusive and is subject to criminal prosecution. However, you should test any Web applications when you're performing a security test and are authorized in writing to do so. Basic testing should look for the following:

- Whether you can enter text containing punctuation marks of any kind
- Whether you can enter a single quotation mark followed by any SQL keywords, such as WHERE, SELECT, INSERT, UNION, and so on
- Whether you get any sort of database error when attempting to inject SQL statements (meaning SQL injection is possible)
- Sometimes, a Web application will give a tester no indication that a SQL statement was run. OWASP calls this "Blind SQL injection," and it has its own set of tests that are required for detection. An attacker can inject a waitfor delay '00:00:10' - command to MSSQL. If the SQL statement is successfully processed, it will instruct the server to wait for 10 seconds before responding. If not successful, the server responds without delay. This, and other tricks, can be used to detect Blind SQL injection.

Security Bytes

When students apply for graduate school, waiting for an acceptance letter can be painful, but a hacker offered them a way of getting an answer quickly. Still not identified at the time of this writing, the hacker gained access to internal admissions records for Harvard, Stanford, MIT, and other top business schools by exploiting vulnerabilities discovered in a Web application called ApplyYourself. The hacker then posted hacking hints on *Business Week*'s online forum. To read more, visit *www.thecrimson.com/article/2005/3/3/hacker-tips-off-b-school-applicants-tipped/*. Applicants, regardless of their hacking background, could now find out whether they had been accepted. Harvard Business School identified 119 applicants who hacked the system and stated that it would reject their admissions because of the ethics violation. Some people thought the problem was the lack of security on the ApplyYourself Web server, which allowed an attacker to simply modify the Web server's displayed URL. The applicants who were caught used their logon names and changed only the URL when connected to the Web server. They didn't attempt to hide their tracks or guess passwords. Was what they did unethical? This question might seem difficult to answer, but Harvard had no problem doing just that.

Error Handling A Web application can be configured or written to handle errors in a variety of ways. For example, when an application needs to undergo troubleshooting, developers can enable debugging, which provides rich logging information helpful to diagnose issues. Sometimes, after troubleshooting, debugging mode might be left on, which provides a rich source of information for attackers. Developers should minimize the amount of information shared with attackers when an application encounters an error. Optimally, no information or only a generic message should be displayed to users in these error cases.

Cryptography Testing Cryptography can be an intimidating thing for junior security testers. The important thing to remember is that you don't need to understand integer factorization and discrete logarithm functions to find flaws in the implementation of cryptography. Many problems in cryptography are due to simple things: using bad random number generators; using a known weak method of encryption; an application that doesn't actually enforce the use of secure channels; using a self-signed certificate instead of a purchased certificate. To discover flaws in the actual algorithms, you might need to add a team member who has experience analyzing cryptographic routines for flaws. Often, when developers decide to create their own crytographic schemes instead of using the common crypto frameworks, an experienced tester can find a way to subvert it. Crypto concepts are covered further in Chapter 12.

Business Logic Testing Business logic refers to the flow a user is expected to follow in an application to accomplish a goal. For example, before conducting a wire transfer, a user must first satisfy the requirement of having at least that amount of money in the transferring account. If the user doesn't have adequate funds, the transfer should be halted. Business logic testing involves utilizing creative ways to bypass these types of checks. Can you somehow trick the application into thinking you have $1,000,000 in your account when you only have $100? What implications might this have for the bank that authorizes a wire transaction for $1,000,000 from an account with $100? These types of flaws can expose a company to legal, financial, and reputational issues and should be a point of focus during application testing.

Client-Side Testing Client-side issues arise from code executing on the user's machine, typically within the Web browser. Often, when a developer doesn't want a field to be changed, he or she will use client-side javascript to "grey out" or disable that field. A regular user cannot edit this field, but an attacker or tester can use an intercepting proxy to tamper with it in transit. Client-side controls are insufficient on their own and should be paired with server-side controls that cannot be bypassed. Some other key areas to consider with a client-side test are: Does the application store sensitive information on the client's machine in an insecure manner? Does the application allow for client browser redirection if the server is fed a specially crafted request?

Activity 10-5: Researching SQL Injection Vulnerabilities

Time Required: 30 minutes

Objective: Recognize the many platforms that have SQL injection vulnerabilities.

Description: After determining that a Web application is using a back-end database server to store data, a security tester should attempt to test the Web application for SQL injection vulnerabilities. In this activity, you visit the Common Vulnerabilities and Exposures (CVE) Web site to identify some known vulnerabilities.

1. Start your Web browser, if necessary, and go to **www.cve.mitre.org**.

2. On the CVE home page, click the **Search & Downloads** link on the left.

3. On the **CVE List and CCEMaster Copy** page, type **SQL injection** in the **By Keyword(s)** text box and click **Submit**. How many CVE entries are listed?

4. Scroll through the list of vulnerabilities and candidates, and read the descriptions for each entry on the first page. When you get to the end of the list, click the **Back** button on your browser, type **SQL injection phpbb** in the **By Keyword(s)** text box, and click **Submit**. How many entries are listed?

5. When an attacker discovers a vulnerability, as you did in this activity, the next step is trying to find out which businesses use the software. To find this information, you can use a search engine. For example, many Web sites using the phpBB software add a footnote to home pages stating "Powered by phpBB." Go to your favorite search engine and search **"powered by phpbb."** (including the quotation marks). How many Web sites are listed in the search results? Do you think most sites corrected the vulnerability you discovered?

6. Because hackers use the same process to find vulnerable Web sites to hack, it's likely that some of these Web sites contain malicious code designed to infect *your* system. Visiting these Web sites isn't recommended, unless you're using a Live Linux DVD, such as Kali. What are the security ramifications of listing the type of software you're running on a Web site?

7. Exit the Web browser.

As you learned in this activity, many Web sites use phpBB. After attackers discover a vulnerability, they look for as many targets as possible to attack. As you can see, notifying clients when you discover a vulnerability is crucial—and the faster, the better!

Tools for Web Attackers and Security Testers

After vulnerabilities of a Web application or an OS platform are discovered, security testers or attackers look for the tools that enable them to test or attack the system. For example, if you learn of a vulnerability in CGI, the next step is discovering whether any systems are using CGI. As you saw in the previous section, all platforms and Web application components have vulnerabilities. No matter which platform is used to develop a Web application, there's probably a security hole in it and a tool capable of breaking into the system.

Web Tools

You have already seen that most tools for performing a security test or attacking a network can be found on the Internet and are usually free. The Kali DVD is packed with free tools for hacking Web applications, which you can find in the Kali, Web Application Analysis menu. You can install new tools with a simple `apt-get install` *packagename* command. However, there are always other tools that might be more suitable for a specific task. The following sections cover some popular tools for hacking Web applications. Web sites for finding other Web application testing tools include *https://www.owasp.org/index.php/Appendix_A: _Testing_Tools* and *http://packetstormsecurity.org*. As a security tester, you should visit these sites before a test to keep track of any new tools and to browse through the multitude of available exploits. Exploits posted on the Packet Storm Web site are often added to Metasploit plug-ins.

Firefox and Chrome Built-In Developer Tools Firefox and Chrome each come with a similar set of developer tools that are also useful for an application security tester. These tools allow for an attacker to view parameters in requests, examine cookies, and even tamper with and resend requests. These tools can be accessed through the settings menu in Firefox and Chrome. Figure 10-13 shows the Network tab of Firefox's developer tools in action and the shortcut menu with the "Edit and Resend" feature.

Figure 10-13 Firefox Developer Tools

Source: Mozilla Public License ("MPL") 2016

Burp Suite and Zed Attack Proxy Burp Suite is included in Kali Linux and offers the tester a number of features for testing Web applications and Web services. It allows you to intercept traffic between the Web browser and the server to inspect and manipulate requests before sending to the server. It can also crawl, scan, and brute force applications. In fact, it has many commonalities with Zed Attack Proxy, which we described in Chapter 5. Burp Suite Pro and Zed Attack Proxy can often be used interchangeably. Figure 10-14 shows Burp Suite's intercepting proxy functionality, which allows a security tester to inspect request and response details.

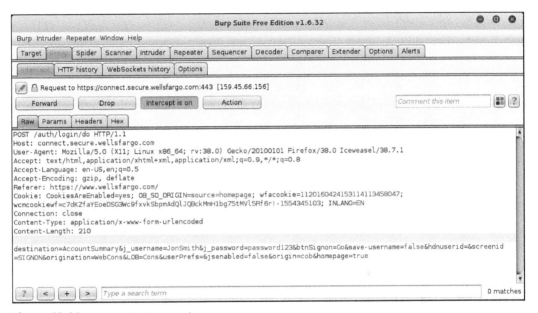

Figure 10-14   Burp Suite intercepting proxy

Wapiti Wapiti is a Web application vulnerability scanner that uses a black box approach, meaning it doesn't inspect code. Instead, it inspects a Web site by searching from the outside for ways to take advantage of XSS, SQL, PHP, JSP, and file-handling vulnerabilities. Although Wapiti can detect common forms that allow uploads or command injection, it uses what's called "fuzzing"—trying to inject data into whatever will accept it. In this way, even new vulnerabilities can be discovered. Other scanners search for only known vulnerability signatures. Wapiti is just one of the many Web application vulnerability tools included on this book's DVD. To start it, use the `wapiti http://`*URL* command (replacing *URL* with the URL of the Web site you're inspecting) in a Terminal shell.

Wfetch If you're tired of all these text-mode programs, Wfetch is a GUI tool that can be downloaded free from Microsoft and is included in the IIS Resource Kit. The 1.4 version works in Windows XP through Windows 7. Microsoft warns users that Wfetch has advanced features that might expose a server to potential security risks, so be careful. Despite these cautions, this helpful tool enables security testers to query a Web server's status and attempt authentication by using any of the methods in the fourth bullet in the following list. Wfetch 1.4 offers these features:

- Multiple HTTP methods, such as GET, HEAD, TRACE, POST, and OPTIONS
- Configuration of hostname and TCP port
- HTTP 1.0 and HTTP 1.1 support
- Anonymous, Basic, NTLM, Kerberos, Digest, and Negotiate authentication types
- Multiple connection types, such as HTTP, HTTPS, PCT 1.0, SSL 2.0, SSL 3.0, TLS 1.1, and TLS 1.2
- Proxy support
- Client-certificate support
- Capability to enter requests manually or have them read from a file
- Onscreen and file-based logging

Figure 10-15 shows the information Wfetch gathers, which would tell an attacker the IIS version the user is running as well as the type of authentication (Anonymous, in this example) the Web server is using.

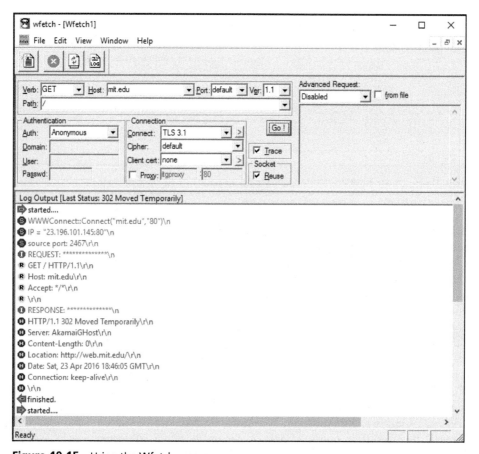

Figure 10-15   Using the Wfetch program

Source: © 2016 Microsoft

Chapter Summary

- Web applications can be developed on many different platforms. HTML Web pages can contain forms, ASP, CGI, and scripting languages, such as VBScript and JavaScript. Note, however, that scripting languages account for more than half of Web server attacks.

- Many static Web pages have been replaced by dynamic Web pages, which are created on the fly when a user calls the page. Dynamic Web pages can be created with a variety of techniques, including CGI, ASP, PHP, ColdFusion, JavaScript.

- Web forms allow developers to create Web pages that visitors can interact with. Care should be taken, however, to ensure that form fields can't be manipulated by attackers.

- Web applications use a variety of technologies to connect to databases, such as ODBC, OLE DB, and ADO. These technologies create a front-end interface, allowing a Web application to connect to a back-end database.

- You can install IIS to test your Web pages in Windows.

- Web application vulnerabilities can have damaging consequences for a company. An attacker might be able to deface the company Web site, destroy a critical database, gain access to user accounts, or even gain access to the admin account or root access to other application servers on the network.

- When conducting security tests on Web applications, determine whether dynamic Web pages were used, whether the Web application connects to a back-end database, whether a separate server is used for authenticating users, and what platform was used to develop the Web application.

- Web applications that interact with databases might be vulnerable to SQL injection exploits. Unicode exploits are possible in older versions of IIS.

- Many tools for testing Web application vulnerabilities (and attacking Web servers) are available, such as Burp Suite and Wapiti. In addition, OWASP offers open-source software to help security professionals learn about Web application vulnerabilities.

Key Terms

Active Server Pages (ASP)

ActiveX Data Objects (ADO)

Asynchronous JavaScript and XML (AJAX)

ColdFusion

Common Gateway Interface (CGI)

dynamic Web pages

Dynamic Application Security Testing (DAST)

Object Linking and Embedding Database (OLE DB)

Open Database Connectivity (ODBC)

Open Web Application Security Project (OWASP)

PHP Hypertext Processor (PHP)

SQL injection (SQLi)

static Web pages

Static Application Security Testing (SAST)

virtual directory

WebGoat

Review Questions

1. The following code is an example of what language?

```
<Body>
<%
Dim strLastname, strFirstname
strLastname = Request.Form("Last")
strFirstname = Request.Form("First")
%>
```

   a. PHP

   b. HTML

   c. ASP

   d. JScript

2. Which of the following can be used to create dynamic Web pages? (Choose all that apply.)

   a. ColdFusion

   b. PHP

   c. ASP

   d. MySQL

3. Which of the following can be used to connect a Web server to a back-end database server? (Choose all that apply.)

   a. ODBC

   b. OLE DB

   c. ADO

   d. HTML

4. What tag is used to indicate ASP code?

5. What is DAST?

   a. Dynamic Application Static Testing

   b. Dynamic Application Server Takeover

   c. Delivery Application Server Testing

   d. Dynamic Application Security Testing

6. What is authorization testing?

   a. Testing to ensure that an application is properly sanitizing input

   b. Testing an application's access control mechanisms to ensure only users who should have access to resources do

   c. Tests focused on client-side code and the execution of scripts in the user's browser

   d. Testing that is specific to source code, otherwise referred to as Static Application Security Testing (SAST)

7. Entering the value OR 1=1 in a Web application that has an "Enter Your PIN" field is most likely an example of which attack?

   a. SQL injection

   b. Code injection

   c. Buffer overflow

   d. Ethernet flaw

8. HTML Web pages containing connection strings are more vulnerable to attack. True or False?

9. The AccessFileName directive in Apache, along with a configuration file (such as .htaccess), can be used to perform which of the following on a Web site?

   a. Run malicious code in the browser.

   b. Protect against XSS worms.

   c. Restrict directory access to those with authorized user credentials.

   d. Scan for CGI vulnerabilities.

10. Which of the following is an open-source technology for creating dynamic HTML Web pages?

    a. ASP

    b. PHP

    c. Java

    d. Oracle

11. CGI is used in Microsoft ASP pages. True or False?

12. Name three Web application vulnerabilities from OWASP's top 10 list.

13. If a Web server isn't protected, an attacker can gain access through remote administration interfaces. True or False?

14. Which of the following is used to connect an ASP Web page to an Oracle database? (Choose all that apply.)

    a. ADO

    b. HTML

    c. CGA

    d. OLE DB

15. List an organization with online resources for learning more about Web application vulnerabilities.

16. What tags identify ColdFusion as the scripting language?

    a. <# #>

    b. <% %>

    c. The letters CF

    d. <! /!>

17. What tags identify PHP as the scripting language?

    a. `<# #>`

    b. `<% %>`

    c. `<? ?>`

    d. `<! /!>`

18. An HTML Web page containing ASP code must be compiled before running. True or False?

19. Which of the following can be used to detect a new application vulnerability on a Web site?

    a. PHP

    b. Nmap

    c. Wapiti

    d. Wfetch

20. IIS is used on more than twice as many Web servers as Apache Web Server. True or False?

Case Projects

CASE PROJECTS

Case Project 10-1: Determining Vulnerabilities of Web Servers

After conducting preliminary security testing on the Alexander Rocco Corporation network, you have identified that the company has seven Web servers. One is a Windows 2003 Server system running IIS 6.0. Curt Cavanaugh, the Webmaster and network administrator, says the Web server is used only by sales personnel as a front-end to update inventory data on an Oracle database server. He says this procedure needs to be done remotely, and it's convenient for sales personnel to use a Web browser when out of the office. Based on this information, write a one-page report on any possible vulnerabilities in the current configuration of the company's Web server. Use the tools and techniques you have learned to search for possible vulnerabilities of IIS 6.0. Your report should include any recommendations that might increase Web security.

Case Project 10-2: Discovering Web Application Attack Tools

After discovering that Alexander Rocco Corporation has multiple Web servers running on different platforms, you wonder whether your security tools can assess Web application vulnerabilities thoroughly. You have only two tools for conducting Web security tests: Wapiti and Wfetch.

Based on this information, write a two-page report on other tools for security testers conducting Web application vulnerability testing. Use the skills you have gained to search the Internet and explore the Kali DVD to find tools for Windows and *nix platforms. The report should state the tool's name, describe the installation method, and include a brief description of what the tool does.

1

## chapter 11

Hacking Wireless Networks

After reading this chapter and completing the exercises, you will be able to:

- Explain wireless technology
- Describe wireless networking standards
- Describe the process of authentication
- Describe wardriving
- Describe wireless hacking and tools used by hackers and security professionals

The term "wireless" is generally used to describe equipment and technologies operating in the radio frequency (RF) spectrum between 3 Hz and 300 GHz. Examples of wireless equipment include cell phones, smartphones, AM/FM radios, wireless networking devices, and radar systems. Most wireless networking equipment operates in a smaller portion of the RF spectrum, between 2.4 GHz and 66 GHz. Wireless technology, especially in the Internet of Things (IoT), continues to grow more and more popular, which has made securing wireless networks from attackers a primary concern.

This chapter gives you an overview of wireless networking technology and standards, explains the process of authentication, describes wardriving, and covers some tools attackers use on wireless networks.

Understanding Wireless Technology

For a wireless network to function, you must have the right hardware and software as well as a technology that sends and receives radio waves. At one time, when seeing the comic strip character Dick Tracy talk to his wristwatch, people wondered whether that would ever be possible. The idea that a phone could work without a wire connected to it astounded them, even though Alfred J. Gross had invented the walkie-talkie in 1938. In fact, the creator of *Dick Tracy* asked for Gross's permission before using a wireless wristwatch in his comics. (To read more about Al Gross, visit *www.retrocom.com.*) In 1973, 35 years after the walkie-talkie, Martin Cooper invented the first cell phone, which weighed in at close to 2 pounds.

Wireless technology is part of your daily life. Here are some wireless devices many people use daily:

- Baby monitors
- Keyless entry systems
- Cell phones
- Smartphones
- Global positioning system (GPS) devices
- Remote controls
- Garage door openers
- Two-way radios
- Bluetooth compatible speakers

Components of a Wireless Network

Any network needs certain components to work: communication devices to transmit and receive signals, protocols, and a medium for transmitting data. On a typical LAN, these components are network interface cards (NICs), TCP/IP, and an Ethernet cable (the wire serving as the connection medium). As complex as wireless networks might seem, they too have only a few basic components:

- **Wireless network interface cards (WNICs)**, which transmit and receive wireless signals, and access points (APs), which are the bridge between wired and wireless networks

- Wireless networking protocols, such as Wi-Fi Protected Access (WPA)
- A portion of the RF spectrum, which replaces wire as the connection medium

The following sections explain how an AP and a WNIC function in a wireless network.

Access Points An **access point (AP)** is a radio transceiver that connects to a network via an Ethernet cable and bridges a **wireless LAN (WLAN)** with a wired network. It's possible to have a wireless network that doesn't connect to a wired network, such as a peer-to-peer network, but this topology isn't covered because security testers are seldom, if ever, contracted to secure a peer-to-peer wireless network. Most companies where you conduct security tests use a WLAN that connects to the company's wired network topology.

An AP is where RF channels are configured. Figure 11-1 shows APs detected on channel 11 by ViStumbler (an AP-scanning program covered in "Understanding Wardriving" later in this chapter). APs are what hackers look for when they drive around with an antenna and a laptop computer scanning for access. Channels are explained in more detail later in "The 802.11 Standard." For now, think of a channel as a range or frequency that data travels over, just like a channel on the radio.

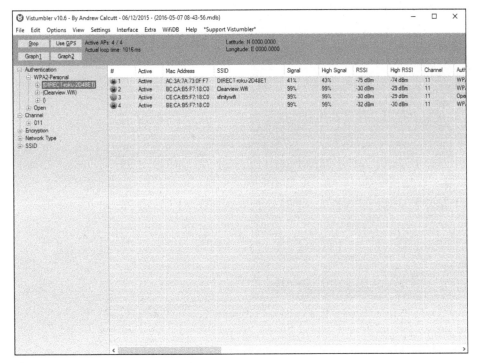

Figure 11-1 AP channels detected

Source: GNU General Public License (GNU GPL)

An AP enables users to connect to a LAN with wireless technology. It can be configured to transmit and receive only within a defined area or square footage, depending on the technology. If you're 20 miles away from an AP, you're probably out of range.

Service Set Identifiers A *service set identifier* (SSID) is the name used to identify a WLAN, much the same way a VLAN ID is used to identify network VLANs. An SSID is configured on the AP as a unique, 1- to 32-character, case-sensitive alphanumeric name. For wireless-enabled computers to access the WLAN the AP connects to, they must be configured with the same SSID as the AP. The SSID name, or "code," is attached to each packet to identify it as belonging to that wireless network. The AP usually beacons (broadcasts) the SSID several times a second so that users who have WNICs can see a display of all WLANs within range of the AP's signal. In Figure 11-2, the Windows 10 wireless connection manager shows SSIDs advertised by APs within range of the wireless computer. Some WNICs come with built-in wireless connection software that looks different from the Windows utility.

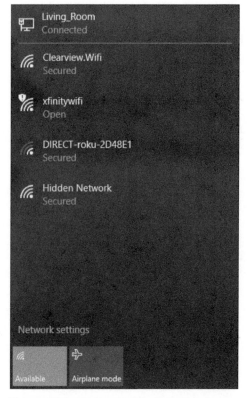

Figure 11-2   SSIDs advertised to a Windows computer

Source: © 2016 Microsoft

Many vendors have SSIDs set to a default value. For example, Cisco APs previously used the default SSID "tsunami." Table 11-1 shows some default SSIDs as of this writing, but this list changes often, sometimes daily. As a security professional, you must research constantly and gather information to keep abreast of changes in this industry. If an AP is configured to not provide its SSID until after authentication, wireless hackers can attempt to guess the SSID by using the information in Table 11-1. Make sure your client isn't using a default SSID.

Sometimes, a default SSID can tell an attacker how old or out of date the target AP is. A more exhaustive list of default SSIDs can be found at WikiDevi.com (*https://goo.gl /1dF9OH*).

Vendor	Default SSIDs
3Com	3Com, comcomcom,101
Apple	Apple Network XXXXXX
Belkin (54G)	Belkin54g, belkin.XXX
Cisco	HOME-XXXX-2.4, HOME-XXXX-5, tsunami
D-Link	dlink, default, dlink-XXXX
Dell	Wireless
Linksys	linksys, linksys-a, linksys-g
Microsoft	MSHOME
Netgear	Wireless, NETGEAR, NETGEARXX
TP-LINK	TP-LINK_XXXX

Table 11-1   Default SSIDs

Activity 11-1: Finding Vulnerabilities with Default SSIDs

Time Required: 30 minutes

Objective: Learn how recognizing a default SSID can open the door to discovering vulnerabilities.

Description: As you learned in Chapter 6, recognizing which OS a customer or client is using is essential before you can detect vulnerabilities in a system or network. This is also true when you're attempting to discover vulnerabilities in an AP. When conducting a security test on a WLAN, you start by looking for SSIDs advertised over the air to determine the type of AP the company is using.

1. If necessary, start your computer in Windows or boot into Linux with the Kali Linux DVD, and start a Web browser. Go to **http://nvd.nist.gov**. Click the **Vulnerability Search Engine** link, type **dlink wireless** in the search text box, and click the **Search** button. Review some recent vulnerabilities with a Common Vulnerability Scoring System (CVSS) severity score of 10.0 (the highest).

2. Click the **CVE** link, and read the vulnerability summary information to learn more about each vulnerability. Is an exploit or attack demonstration available?

3. Is the router's default SSID listed in Table 11-1? Because router models (and URLs) change constantly, you might want to use your search skills to find the default SSID for the router make and model you selected, if it isn't listed in Table 11-1.

4. What solution would you offer to a client using the router you selected in Step 3?

5. Leave your Web browser open for the next activity.

Configuring an Access Point Configuring an AP varies, depending on the embedded OS supplied by the manufacturer. With most APs, users can access the software through a Web browser because the AP has an embedded OS supporting a Web server. The following example shows options for the dd-wrt Linux embedded OS that replaces the embedded OS used on hundreds of routers from Linksys, D-Link, Netgear, Belkin, Microsoft, U.S. Robotics, Dell, Buffalo, and many others. You see how an AP administrator can determine the SSID and channel and configure security (covered later in this chapter in "Understanding Authentication"). This example outlines the steps a security professional takes to access and reconfigure a wireless router running dd-wrt with the IP address 192.168.1.1:

1. After entering the IP address in a Web browser, the user is prompted for a logon name and password. In dd-wrt, the default username is "root," and the default password is "admin." For security reasons, changing these credentials is essential.

2. After a successful logon, you click the **Status** item at the top to display the window shown in Figure 11-3. Notice the router model and CPU model listed under Router Information.

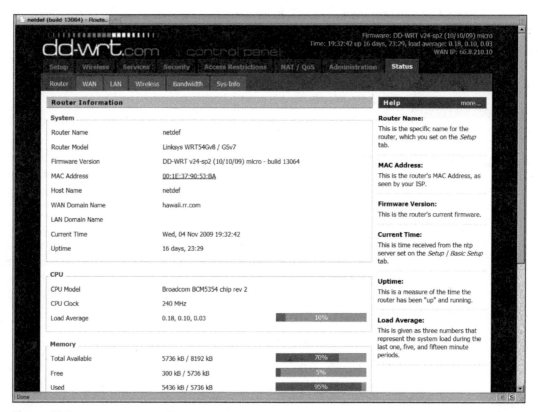

Figure 11-3   Viewing status information in dd-wrt

Source: Copyright © 2016 embeDD GmbH

3. After clicking the **Wireless** tab at the top, you see the window shown in Figure 11-4. The user entered "koko" for the SSID. (*Note:* The default SSID for wireless routers running dd-wrt is "dd-wrt.") The user could have changed the default name to "Cisco" to try to trick attackers into believing the router is a Cisco product; however, picking a name that's not associated with a manufacturer or an OS might be more effective at discouraging attacks. Notice that Channel 6, the default channel for many wireless router OSs, has been selected. To improve security, you might want to disable SSID broadcasts because advertising who you are and whether you're using encryption increases the chance of attack. In dd-wrt, disabling SSID broadcasts is easy: Just click the **Disable** option button.

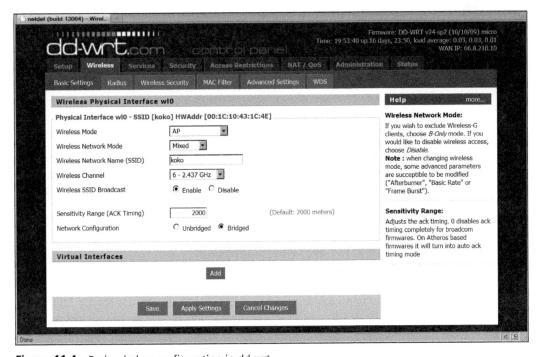

Figure 11-4 Basic wireless configuration in dd-wrt

4. To configure security, you click the **Wireless Security** tab. In Figure 11-5, the user has entered a password (called a "WPA shared key" in dd-wrt) that must be supplied by the wireless computer.

WNIC manufacturers usually supply connection management software that you can use instead of the built-in Windows utility.

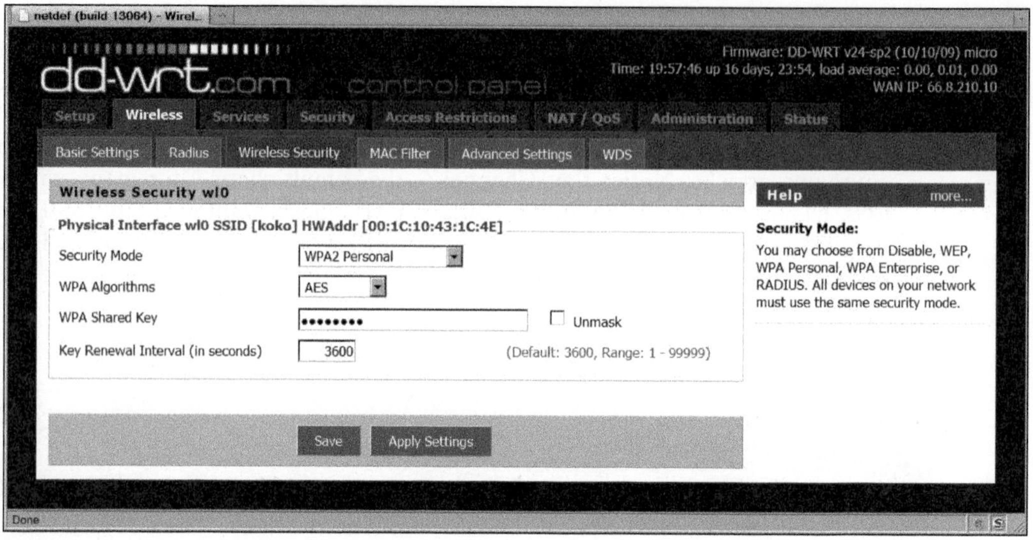

Figure 11-5   Configuring wireless security in dd-wrt

Source: Copyright © 2016 embeDD GmbH

If a company doesn't change its default SSID but decides to disable SSID broadcasts, a determined intruder can use a passive wireless sniffer, such as Kismet (covered later in "Understanding Wardriving"). Kismet can detect SSIDs in WLAN client traffic. If the user didn't assign a WLAN key or change the default administrator password to the AP, you can see how easily an attacker could access the WLAN. As a security tester, you must verify that these vulnerabilities don't exist on a WLAN; if they do, you should recommend that the company close the holes as quickly as possible.

Wireless NICs   For a computer to be able to send information over any medium, it must follow the rules for the medium it's traversing, so the correct software and drivers for the NIC must be installed. For example, data traveling over a copper wire must follow rules for how Ethernet signals are sent over that medium. For wireless technology to work, each node or computer must have a WNIC, which converts the radio waves it receives into digital signals the computer understands.

There are many WNICs on the market, but be careful deciding which one to purchase if you're considering using specific tools for detecting APs and decrypting WEP keys or using antennas that can cover a large distance. For instance, AirCrack NG, a program for cracking WEP encryption on a WLAN, requires using a specific chipset on a WNIC, so only certain brands of WNICs can be used.

Understanding Wireless Network Standards

A standard is a set of rules formulated by an organization. All industries have standards, and a WLAN is no exception. Just as the **Institute of Electrical and Electronics Engineers (IEEE)** has standards specifying maximum cable length in an Ethernet network, there are rules to follow for wireless networks.

Working groups (WGs) of the IEEE are formed to develop new standards. After a WG has reached consensus on a proposal for a standard, the Sponsor Executive Committee must approve the proposal. Finally, after the proposal is recommended by the Standards Review Committee and approved by the IEEE Standards Board, you have a new standard.

IEEE Project 802 was developed to create LAN and WAN standards. (The first meeting was held in February 1980, so the project was given the number 802, with "80" representing the year and "2" representing the month.) WG names are also assigned numbers, such as 11 for the Wireless LAN group, and letters to denote approved projects, such as 802.11a or 802.11b. In this chapter, you learn about the 802 standards pertaining to wireless networks.

The 802.11 Standard

The first wireless technology standard, **802.11**, defined specifications for wireless connectivity as 1 Mbps and 2 Mbps in a LAN. This standard applied to the Physical layer of the OSI model, which deals with wireless connectivity issues of fixed, portable, and moving stations in a local area, and the Media Access Control (MAC) sublayer of the Data Link layer. Often, multiple transmitters are nearby, so radio signals can mix and have the potential to interfere with each other (as signal collision). For this reason, carrier sense multiple access/collision avoidance (CSMA/CA) is used instead of the CSMA/CD method (collision detection, used in Ethernet).

Many definitions of terms are included in the more than 500 pages of the 802.11 standard. One important distinction is that wireless LANs don't have an address associated with a physical location, as wired LANs do. In 802.11, an addressable unit is called a **station (STA)**. A station is defined as a message destination and might not be a fixed location. Another distinction is made between mobile stations and portable stations. A mobile station is one that accesses the LAN while moving; a portable station is one that can move from location to location but is used only while in a fixed location.

The Basic Architecture of 802.11 802.11 uses a **basic service set (BSS)** as its building block. A BSS is the collection of devices (AP and stations or just stations) that make up a WLAN. A **basic service area (BSA)** is the coverage area an AP provides. A WLAN running in what's called **infrastructure mode** always has one or more APs. An independent WLAN without an AP is called an **ad-hoc network**; independent stations connect in a decentralized fashion. As long as a station is within its BSA, it can communicate with other stations in the BSS. You have probably experienced losing cell phone connectivity when you're out of range of your service area. Similarly, you can lose network connectivity if you aren't in the WLAN's coverage area. To connect two BSSs, 802.11 requires a distribution system (DS) as an intermediate layer. Basically, BSS 1 connects to the DS, which in turn connects to BSS 2. However, how does a station called STA 1 in BSS 1 connect to STA 2 in BSS 2? 802.11

defines an AP as a station providing access to the DS. Data moves between a BSS and the DS through the AP. This process sounds complicated, but Figure 11-6 should clear up any confusion.

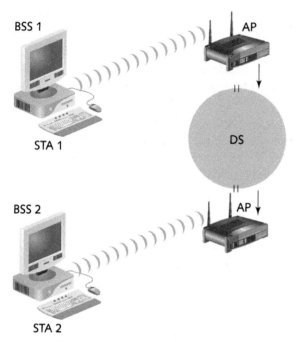

Figure 11-6 Connecting two wireless remote stations

The IEEE specifications also define the operating frequency range of 802.11. In the United States, the range is 2.4 to 2.4835 GHz. Think of the frequency as a superhighway in the sky where data travels, and this superhighway encompasses many highways (frequency bands). Each frequency band contains **channels**, which break up the band into smaller frequency ranges. For example, channel 1 of a frequency band ranging from 2.4 GHz to 2.4835 GHz might use the 2.401 GHz frequency, and channel 2 of this frequency band might use 2.406 GHz. The 802.11 standard defines 11 channels in the 2.4 to 2.462 GHz range. If channels overlap, interference could occur.

Sound travels through the air just as waves move in the ocean, and like ocean waves, a sound wave's length is measured from the peak of one wave to the next. A sound wave's **amplitude** (height) and **frequency** (rate at which a sound wave repeats) determine its volume and pitch. Surfers know they must wait for the next set of waves to occur and get quite accurate in determining frequency (the time it takes a set of waves to repeat). The completion of a repeating pattern of sound waves is called a cycle. For surfers, a cycle can be minutes. Sound waves, however, repeat at a much faster frequency. For example, a tuning fork vibrates at 440 hertz (Hz), or cycles per second. That's 440 waves per second—too fast for a surfer. Different technologies use different frequencies, referred to as bands, to transmit sound. Table 11-2 lists frequency bands. For example, AM radio stations use the medium frequency (MF) band; FM radio stations and search-and-rescue stations use the very high frequency (VHF) band. The distance sound waves need to travel also determines which frequency band to use.

Frequency	Range	Wavelength
Extremely low frequency (ELF)	3–30 Hz	100,000 km–10,000 km
Super low frequency (SLF)	30–300 Hz	10,000 km–1000 km
Voice frequency (VF) or ultra low frequency (ULF)	300 Hz–3 KHz	1000 km–100 km
Very low frequency (VLF)	3–30 KHz	100 km–10 km
Low frequency (LF)	30–300 KHz	10 km–1 km
Medium frequency (MF)	300 KHz–3 MHz	1 km–100 m
High frequency (HF)	3–30 MHz	100 m–10 m
Very high frequency (VHF)	30–300 MHz	10 m–1 m
Ultra high frequency (UHF)	300 MHz–3 GHz	1 m–10 cm
Super high frequency (SHF)	3–30 GHz	10 cm–1 cm
Extremely high frequency (EHF)	30–300 GHz	1 cm–1 mm

Table 11-2   Frequency bands

An Overview of Wireless Technologies

Now that you understand the different frequencies on which radio waves can travel, take a look at the three technologies WLANs use:

- *Infrared*—Infrared light can't be seen by the human eye. **Infrared (IR)** technology is restricted to a single room or line of sight because IR light can't penetrate walls, ceilings, or floors.

- *Narrowband*—**Narrowband** technology uses microwave radio band frequencies to transmit data. The most common uses of this technology are cordless phones and garage door openers.

- *Spread spectrum*—For data to be moved over radio waves, it must be modulated on the carrier signal or channel. **Modulation** defines how data is placed on a carrier signal. For example, **spread spectrum** modulation means data is spread across a large-frequency bandwidth instead of traveling across just one frequency band. In other words, a group of radio frequencies is selected, and the data is "spread" across this group. Spread spectrum, the most widely used WLAN technology, uses the following methods:

  - *Frequency-hopping spread spectrum* (FHSS): Data hops to other frequencies to avoid interference that might occur over a frequency band. This hopping from one frequency to another occurs at split-second intervals and makes it difficult for an intruder or attacker to jam the communication channel.

  - *Direct sequence spread spectrum* (DSSS): DSSS differs from FHSS, in that it spreads data packets simultaneously over multiple frequencies instead of hopping to other frequencies. Sub-bits are added to a packet as it travels across the frequency band and are used for recovery, in much the same way RAID-5 uses parity bits to rebuild a hard disk that crashes. Sub-bits are called "chips," and every bit of the original message is represented by multiple bits, called the **chipping code**.

- *Orthogonal frequency division multiplexing* (OFDM): The bandwidth is divided into a series of frequencies called tones, which allows a higher throughput (data transfer rate) than FHSS and DSSS do.

Additional IEEE 802.11 Projects

The IEEE WG developed some additional 802.11 projects, releasing the 802.11a and 802.11b standards in October 1999. 802.11b quickly became the more widely used standard, probably because its hardware was less expensive. Also referred to as Wi-Fi, 802.11b operates in the 2.4 GHz band and increased the throughput to 11 Mbps from the 1 or 2 Mbps of the original 802.11. It allows a total of 11 separate channels to prevent overlapping signals. However, because of each channel's bandwidth requirements, effectively only three channels (1, 6, and 11) can be combined without overlapping and creating interference. This standard also introduced Wired Equivalent Privacy (WEP), which gave many users a false sense of security that data traversing the WLAN was protected. WEP is covered later in "Understanding Authentication."

802.11a has a different operating frequency range than 802.11 and 802.11b do; it operates in three distinct bands in the 5 GHz range. In addition, throughput was increased to 54 Mbps, much faster than 802.11b.

The 802.11g standard, released in 2003, operates in the 2.4 GHz band, too. However, because it uses a different modulation, it uses the OFDM method, which increases throughput to 54 Mbps.

The 802.11i standard introduced Wi-Fi Protected Access (WPA) in 2004, which is covered in "Understanding Authentication." For now, just know that 802.11i corrected many security vulnerabilities in 802.11b. For security professionals, the 802.11i standard is probably the most important.

The 802.11e standard, released in 2005, had improvements to address the problem of interference. When interference is detected, the signal can jump to another frequency more quickly, improving the quality of service over 802.11b.

The 802.11n standard, finalized in 2009, operates in the same frequency (2.4 or 5 GHz band) and uses the same encoding as 802.11g. However, by using multiple antennas and wider bandwidth channels, throughput has been increased to 600 Mbps in this standard.

The 802.11ac standard, released in 2014, utilizes the 5 GHz band. The 802.11ac standard allows for higher throughput (up to 1 gigabit per second) by multiplying the number of MIMO links and using high-density modulation.

The 802.11ad standard, dubbed "WiGig," allows for transfer rates of up to 7 gigabits per second over the 2.4 GHz, 5 GHz, and 60 GHz bands. In January 2016, TP-Link revealed the first wireless router to support the 802.11ad specification.

Additional IEEE 802 Standards The 802.15 standard addresses networking devices in one person's workspace, which is called a **wireless personal area network (WPAN)**. The maximum distance between devices is usually 10 meters. With the Bluetooth telecommunication specification, a fundamental part of the WPAN standard, you can connect portable devices, such as cell phones and computers, without wires. Bluetooth version 2.0 uses the 2.4 GHz band and can transmit data at speeds up to 12 Mbps. It's not compatible with the 802.11 standards. The most recent Bluetooth version, 4.0, was released in 2010 and has moved to the 802.11 band to support speeds of up to 24 Mbps. In 2005, the IEEE began work on using different technologies for the WPAN standard. ZigBee, a current example, is used for automation systems, such as smart lighting systems, temperature controls, and appliances.

The 802.16 standard covers wireless **metropolitan area networks (MANs)**. This standard defines the Wireless MAN Air Interface for wireless MANs and addresses the limited distance available for 802.11b WLANs. The most widely used implementation of wireless MAN technology is called **Worldwide Interoperability for Microwave Access (WiMAX)**. WiMAX was marketed as a viable alternative to so-called last-mile Internet access, which is normally provided by cable and DSL. There are mobile (802.16e) and fixed (802.16d) versions of WiMAX. A typical real-world speed of WiMAX is about 10 Mbps, quite a bit less than the theoretical 120 Mbps maximum of the 802.16 standard. WiMAX was a failed venture, and efforts ended in 2015. Another MAN standard, 802.20, with a goal similar to mobile WiMAX is called **Mobile Broadband Wireless Access (MBWA)**. It addresses wireless MANs for mobile users sitting in trains, subways, or cars traveling at speeds up to 150 miles per hour. The most common implementation of MBWA, iBurst, is used widely in Asia and Africa.

Table 11-3 summarizes the wireless standards in common use today but doesn't include some wireless standards beyond the scope of this book, such as the licensed 802.11y 3.6 GHz bands, the 4.9 GHz band for U.S. public safety networks, and mobile phone wireless technologies—Evolution Data Optimized (EVDO), Enhanced Data GSM Environment (EDGE), and 3G, 4G/LTE, for example.

Standard	Frequency	Maximum rate	Modulation method
802.11	2.4 GHz	1 or 2 Mbps	FHSS/DSSS
802.11a	5 GHz	54 Mbps	OFDM
802.11b	2.4 GHz	11 Mbps	DSSS
802.11g	2.4 GHz	54 Mbps	OFDM
802.11n	2.4 GHz & 5 GHz	600 Mbps	OFDM
802.11ac	5 GHz	1 Gbps	OFDM
802.11ad	2.4 GHz, 5 GHz, & 60 GHz	7 Gbps	OFDM
802.15	2.4 GHz	2 Mbps	FHSS
802.16 (WiMAX)	10–66 GHz	120 Mbps	OFDM
802.20 (Mobile Wireless Access Working Group)	Below 3.5 GHz	1 Mbps	OFDM
Bluetooth	2.4 GHz	24 Mbps	Gaussian frequency shift keying (GFSK)
HiperLAN/2	5 GHz	54 Mbps	OFDM

Table 11-3 Summary of approved wireless standards

Activity 11-2: Visiting the IEEE 802.11 Web Site

Time Required: 30 minutes

Objective: Learn more about IEEE wireless standards.

Description: You can find a wealth of information at the IEEE Web site, and the standards are available for download. In this activity, you visit the IEEE Web site and research a new and exciting project at IEEE.

1. Start a Web browser, if necessary, and go to **http://www.ieee802.org/11/Reports /tgay_update.htm**.

2. Review project goals of the IEEE 802.11ay specification.

3. What is the theoretical throughput of 802.11ay? Looking at Table 11-3, what is the throughput of commonly used protocols 802.11a, b, g, and n?

4. Visit the Wikipedia entry for 802.11 at **https://en.wikipedia.org/wiki/IEEE_802.11**.

5. Review the **Security** section of the Wikipedia article.

6. Explain why a security professional might suggest disabling Wi-Fi Protected Setup (WPS) on a router. We talk about WPS more in the following section.

7. Exit your Web browser.

Understanding Authentication

The problem of unauthorized users accessing resources on a network is a major concern for security professionals. An organization that introduces wireless technology to the mix increases the potential for security problems. The 802.1X standard, discussed in the following section, addresses the issue of authentication. Some routers, by default, do not require authentication, which could leave a corporate network at risk.

The 802.1X Standard

Because there must be a method to ensure that others with wireless NICs can't access resources on your wireless network, the **802.1X standard** defines the process of authenticating and authorizing users on a network. This standard is especially useful for WLAN security when physical access control is more difficult to enforce than on wired LANs. To understand how authentication takes place on a wireless network, you review some basic concepts in the following sections.

Point-to-Point Protocol Many ISPs use Point-to-Point Protocol (PPP) to connect dial-up or DSL users. PPP handles authentication by requiring a user to enter a valid username and password. PPP verifies that users attempting to use the link are indeed who they say they are.

Extensible Authentication Protocol Extensible Authentication Protocol (EAP), an enhancement to PPP, was designed to allow a company to select its authentication method. For example, a company can use certificates or Kerberos authentication to authenticate a user connecting to an AP. A certificate is a record that authenticates network entities, such as a server or client. It contains X.509 information that identifies the owner, the certification authority (CA), and the owner's public key. (For more information on certificates and keys, see Chapter 12.) You can examine an X.509 certificate by going to *www.paypal.com*. This Web site redirects you to the secure (HTTPS) URL, where you click the padlock icon at the right of the address bar in Internet Explorer 11, and then click View Certificates to see the certificate information shown in Figure 11-7.

Figure 11-7 Viewing information about an X.509 certificate

Source: © 2016 Microsoft

The following EAP methods can be used to improve security on a wireless network:

- *Extensible Authentication Protocol-Transport Layer Security* (EAP-TLS)—This method requires assigning the client and server a digital certificate signed by a CA that both parties trust. This CA can be a commercial company that charges a fee, or a network administrator can configure a server to issue certificates. In this way, both the server and client authenticate mutually. In addition to servers requiring that clients prove they are who they say, clients also want servers to verify their identity.

- *Protected EAP*—**Protected EAP** (PEAP) uses TLS to authenticate the server to the client but not the client to the server. With PEAP, only the server is required to have a digital certificate. (See RFC-2246 for more information on TLS.)

- *Microsoft PEAP*—In Microsoft's implementation of PEAP, a secure channel is created by using TLS as protection against eavesdropping.

802.1X uses the following components to function:

- *Supplicant*—A **supplicant** is a wireless user attempting access to a WLAN.
- *Authenticator*—The AP functions as the entity allowing or denying the supplicant's access.
- *Authentication server*—This server, which might be a Remote Access Dial-In User Service (RADIUS) server, is used as a centralized component that authenticates the user and performs accounting functions. For example, an ISP using RADIUS can verify who logged on to the ISP service and how long the user was connected. Most RADIUS servers are *nix based, but the Microsoft implementation of RADIUS is called Internet Authentication Service (IAS) in Windows Server 2000 and Windows Server 2003 and is called Network Policy Server after Windows Server 2008.

Figure 11-8 shows the process of 802.1X, described in the following steps:

1. An unauthenticated client (supplicant) attempts to connect with the AP functioning as the authenticator.
2. The AP responds by enabling a port that passes only EAP packets from the supplicant to the RADIUS server on the wired network.
3. The AP blocks all other traffic until the RADIUS server authenticates the supplicant.
4. After the RADIUS server has authenticated the supplicant, it gives the supplicant access to network resources via the AP.

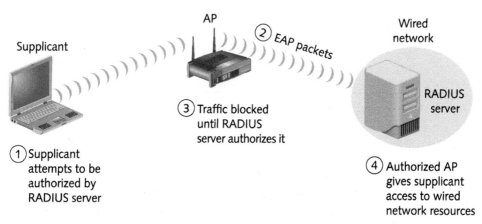

Figure 11-8 A supplicant connecting to an AP and a RADIUS server

Until EAP and 802.1x were used on wireless LANs, a device, not a user, was authenticated on the WLAN. Therefore, if a computer was stolen from a company, the thief was able to connect to resources on the WLAN because the computer could still be authenticated. The following sections describe security features introduced in 802.11b and 802.11i.

Wired Equivalent Privacy Wired Equivalent Privacy (WEP), part of the 802.11b standard, was developed to encrypt data traversing a wireless network. For some time, it gave many security professionals a false sense of security that wireless technology could be just as safe as wired networks. Unfortunately, WEP has been torn to shreds by security professionals, professors from major universities, and hackers who post ways to crack WEP encryption. Some argue that WEP is still better than no security at all, and when it's combined with the security of a virtual private network (VPN), they claim that WEP works well for home users or small businesses. Still, many saw a need for a better way to protect WLANs.

Wi-Fi Protected Access Wi-Fi Protected Access (WPA and WPA2), specified in the 802.11i standard, is the replacement for WEP, which is known to have cryptographic weaknesses. WPA improves encryption by using Temporal Key Integrity Protocol (TKIP). TKIP has four enhancements that address encryption vulnerabilities in WEP:

- *Message Integrity Check* (MIC)—MIC, also called Michael, is a cryptographic message integrity code. Its main purpose is to prevent forgeries, which are packets that attackers create to look like legitimate packets. For example, an MIC uses a secret authentication key, which only the sender and receiver know, and creates a tag (message integrity code) generated from the key and message that's sent to the receiver. The sender sends the message and tag to the receiver, who must enter the key, tag, and message in a program that verifies whether the tag created with the three input fields is equal to the tag the program should have created. You don't need to memorize how this process takes place, but understanding that MIC corrects a known vulnerability in WEP is important.

- *Extended Initialization Vector (IV) with sequencing rules*—This enhancement was developed to prevent replays. In a replay, an attacker records or captures a packet, saves it, and retransmits the message later. To prevent a replay from occurring, a sequence number is applied to the WEP IV field. If a packet is received with an IV equal to or less than the sequence number received earlier, the packet is discarded.

- *Per-packet key mixing*—This enhancement helps defeat weak key attacks that occurred in WEP. MAC addresses are used to create an intermediate key, which prevents the same key from being used by all links.

- *Rekeying mechanism*—This enhancement provides fresh keys that help prevent attacks that relied on reusing old keys. That is, if the same key is used repeatedly, someone running a program to decipher the key could likely do so after collecting a large number of packets. The same key being used repeatedly was a big problem in WEP.

WPA also added an authentication mechanism using 802.1X and EAP, which weren't available in WEP.

Since the release of WPA, weaknesses have been found in TKIP, which called for a more advanced WPA2. WPA2 has replaced WPA in the official Wi-Fi standard. The main difference between WPA and WPA2 is the requirement in WPA2 to use AES encryption instead of TKIP (discussed in Chapter 12).

Wi-Fi Protected Setup (WPS) Wi-Fi Protected Setup (WPS) is a wireless authentication standard created to allow users to easily add devices to a wireless network securely.

WPS makes this process easier by eliminating the need for a user to enter a passphrase. Rather, the user simply presses a button on the router and the WPS-able device pairs with the router. Chances are, if you have a modern router at home, it is capable of WPS.

WPS might sound like a great solution, but a major security flaw was discovered in late 2011. This flaw allows an attacker to gain access to a network remotely without knowing the WPA2 password.

Understanding Wardriving

It's probably no secret that hackers use **wardriving**—driving around with inexpensive hardware and software that enables them to detect access points that haven't been secured. Surprisingly, some APs have no passwords or security measures, so wardriving can be quite rewarding for hackers. As of this writing, wardriving isn't illegal; using the resources of networks discovered with wardriving is, of course, a different story. Wardriving has now been expanded to include warflying, which is done using drones with an antenna and the same software used in wardriving. The testers used Kismet, covered later in this section, which identifies APs that attempt to "cloak" or hide their SSIDs.

How It Works

To conduct wardriving, an attacker or a security tester simply drives around with a laptop computer containing a WNIC, an antenna, and software that scans the area for SSIDs. Not all WNICs are compatible with scanning software, so you might want to look at the software requirements first before purchasing the hardware. Antenna prices vary, depending on their quality and the range they can cover. Some are as small as a cell phone's antenna, and some are as large as a bazooka, which you might have seen in old war films. The larger ones can sometimes return results on networks miles away from the attacker. The smaller ones might require being in close proximity to the AP.

Most scanning software detects the company's SSID, the type of security enabled, and the signal strength, indicating how close the AP is to the attacker. Because attacks against WEP are simple and attacks against WPA are possible, any 802.11 connection not using WPA2 should be considered inadequately secured. The following sections introduce some tools that many wireless hackers and security professionals use.

Security Bytes

An ethical hacker in Houston, previously employed by the county's Technology Department, was accused of breaking into a Texas court's wireless network. While he was conducting scans as part of his job, he noticed a vulnerability in the court's wireless network and was concerned. He demonstrated to a county official and a local reporter how easily he could gain access to the wireless network with just a laptop computer and a WNIC. He was later charged with two counts of unauthorized access of a protected computer system and unauthorized access of a computer system used in justice administration. After a 3-day trial and 15 minutes of jury deliberation, he was acquitted. If he had been found guilty of all charges, he would have faced 10 years in prison and a $500,000 fine.

Vistumbler Vistumbler (*https://www.vistumbler.net/*) is a freeware tool written for Windows that enables you to detect WLANs using 802.11a, 802.11b, 802.11g, 802.11n, and 802.11ac access points. It's easy to install, but not all wireless hardware works with the software, so you must follow the directions carefully and verify that the hardware you have is compatible. Vistumbler was designed to assist security testers in the following:

- Verifying the WLAN configuration

- Detecting other wireless networks that might be interfering with a WLAN

- Detecting unauthorized APs that might have been placed on a WLAN

Vistumbler is also used in wardriving, but remember that in most parts of the world, using someone's network without permission is illegal. This law includes using someone's Internet connection without his or her knowledge or permission.

Another feature of Vistumbler is its capability to interface with a GPS, enabling a security tester or hacker to map out locations of all WLANs the software detects (see Figure 11-9).

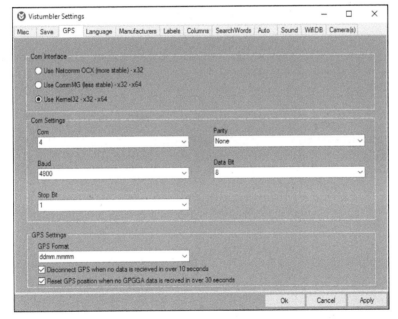

Figure 11-9   Configuring GPS settings in the Vistumbler Settings dialog box

Source: GNU General Public License version 2 (GNU GPL v2)

When the program identifies an AP's signal, it logs the SSID, MAC address of the AP, manufacturer of the AP, channel on which the signal was heard, strength of the signal, and whether encryption is enabled (but not a specific encryption type). Attackers can detect any APs within a 350-foot radius, but with a good antenna, they can locate APs a couple of miles away. For those with mechanical ability, numerous Web sites have instructions on building your own antenna with empty bean cans, potato chip cans, and the like. You can also purchase a decent antenna for about $50.

For directions on building an antenna from a tin can, visit *www.wikihow .com/Make-a-Cantenna.*

Activity 11-3: Discovering APs with Wifite

Time Required: 15 minutes

Objective: See what information a wireless scanner, such as Wifite, can gather.

Description: When testing a network for vulnerabilities, don't neglect checking for vulnerabilities in any WLANs the company has set up. Wifite is a free Wi-Fi scanner, similar to Vistumbler, included on this book's DVD. Wifite also offers attack features you can use to break insecure wireless networks. For this activity, we will examine the scanner functionality of Wifite. You can verify available APs and their SSIDs. In this activity, you run Wifite from the DVD. If your classroom doesn't have wireless NICs or an AP, you can do the activity later where equipment is available, such as your home or office.

1. If necessary, boot into Linux with the Kali Linux DVD.

2. Open a Terminal shell and enter **wifite**, then press **Enter** to start Wifite. If you're in an area with a few APs, your Wifite terminal window might look like Figure 11-10.

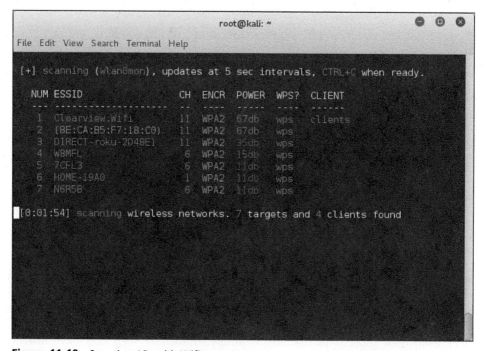

Figure 11-10 Scanning APs with Wifite

Source: GNU General Public License version 2 (GNU GPL v2)

3. If SSIDs start to populate your screen, examine the CH column. This displays the channel information for each AP. As you can see, many systems in this figure use channel 6, which could indicate congestion. If you discovered this information during a security test, you might suggest configuring some APs on different channels to your client.

4. Hit **ctrl-c** twice to exit Wifite. Close any open windows.

Kismet Another common product for conducting wardriving attacks is Kismet (*www .kismetwireless.net*), written by Mike Kershaw. This product is free and runs on Linux, BSD UNIX, Mac OS X, and even Linux PDAs. The software is advertised as being more than just a wireless network detector. Kismet is also a sniffer and an intrusion detection system (IDS, covered in Chapter 13) and can sniff 802.11b, 802.11a, 802.11g, and 802.11n traffic. It offers the following features:

- Wireshark- and Tcpdump-compatible data logging
- Compatible with AirSnort and AirCrack (covered later in "Tools of the Trade")
- Network IP range detection
- Detection of hidden network SSIDs
- Graphical mapping of networks
- Client/server architecture that allows multiple clients to view a single Kismet server at the same time
- Manufacturer and model identification of APs and clients
- Detection of known default AP configurations
- XML output
- Support for more than 25 card types (almost any card that supports monitor mode)

Kismet is a passive scanner, so it can detect even hidden network SSIDs. Kismet can be used to conduct wardriving, but it can also be used to detect rogue APs on a company's network. If you need GPS support, the Kali Linux DVD includes several tools that work with Kismet, such as the GPS daemon (GPSD), GISKismet, and Kisgearth, that can come in handy for accurate AP geopositioning. When Kismet is configured to use GPSD, the output displays coordinates pinpointing the location of the AP being scanned. This coordinate data can then be fed into Google Earth to create maps.

Understanding Wireless Hacking

Hacking a wireless network isn't much different from hacking a wired LAN. Many of the port-scanning and enumeration tools you've learned about can be applied to wireless networks. The following sections describe some additional tools that attackers use, and you can use them to conduct security tests, too.

Tools of the Trade

A wireless hacker usually has a laptop computer, a WNIC, an antenna, sniffers (Tcpdump or Wireshark, for example), tools such as Vistumbler or Kismet, and lots of patience. After using Vistumbler or Kismet to determine the network name, SSID, MAC address of the AP, channel used, signal strength, which type of encryption is enabled, and whether or not WPS is enabled, a security tester is ready to continue testing.

What do attackers or security testers do if WEP or WPA is enabled on the AP? Several tools address this issue. Aircrack-ng, covered in the following sections, is what prompted organizations to replace WEP with the more secure WPA as their authentication method. However, some companies still use 802.11b with WEP enabled, and some even leave their network completely unsecured.

Aircrack-ng As a security professional, your job is to protect a network and make it difficult for attackers to break in. You might like to believe you can completely *prevent* attackers from breaking in, but unfortunately, this goal is impossible. Aircrack-ng (included on the Kali Linux DVD or available free at *www.aircrack-ng.org*) is the tool most hackers use to access WEP-enabled WLANs. Aircrack-ng replaced AirSnort, a product created by wireless security researchers Jeremy Bruestle and Blake Hegerle, who set out to prove that WEP encryption was faulty and easy to crack. AirSnort was the first widely used WEP-cracking program and woke up nonbelievers who thought WEP was enough protection for a WLAN. Aircrack-ng took up where AirSnort (and the slightly older WEPCrack) left off. It has some useful addons, such as a GUI front-end called Fern WIFI Cracker, shown in Figure 11-11 (also included on the Kali Linux DVD).

Figure 11-11   Fern WIFI Cracker interface

Source: 2016 Fern Pro

WiFi Pineapple Wi-Fi hacking enthusiasts Darren Kitchen and Sebastian Kinne created a Swiss-army knife for wireless hacking called the WiFi Pineapple. It can perform scans for wireless access points and can set up fake APs to social-engineer users or confuse attackers using airbase-ng. The WiFi Pineapple has another dangerous feature that allows an attacker to emulate any network that a client requests. To understand this, keep in mind that wireless devices are constantly probing for networks they've previously connected to. A feature in the WiFi Pineapple listens for these probes and responds to them as if it was the AP the client had requested to connect to. After the client revives the response from the WiFi Pineapple, the client connects to the fake network, and any of the client's traffic is at risk of being sniffed. You can read more about it on the WiFi Pinapple's Web site (*https://www.wifipineapple.com/*). The tool's main page is shown in Figure 11-12.

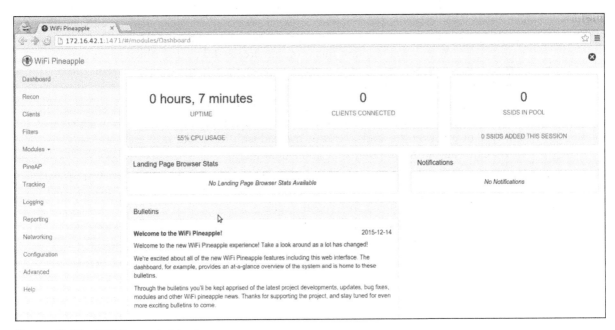

Figure 11-12   WiFi Pineapple interface

The Kali Linux DVD includes a wide range of analysis tools for testing wireless networks.

Countermeasures for Wireless Attacks

Protecting a wireless network is a challenge for security professionals because of the inherent design flaws of wireless technology and because, to some extent, engineers are attempting to place a band-aid over a gaping chest wound. Some countermeasure techniques discussed in this section, such as using certificates on all wireless devices, are time consuming and costly.

If you approach securing a wireless LAN as you would a wired LAN, you'll have a better chance of protecting corporate data and network resources. Would you allow users to have access to network resources simply because they plugged their NICs into the company's switch or hub? Of course not. Then why would you allow users to have access to a wireless LAN simply because they have WNICs and know the company's SSID?

If a company must use wireless technology, your job is to make it as secure as possible. Be sure wireless users are authenticated before being able to access any network resources. Here are some additional guidelines to help secure a wireless network:

- Consider using anti-wardriving software to make it more difficult for attackers to discover your WLAN. In Chapter 13, you learn about honeypots, which are hosts or networks available to the public that entice hackers to attack them instead of a company's real network. IT personnel can study how an attack is made on the honeypot, which can be useful in securing the company's actual network. To make it more difficult for wardrivers to discover your WLAN, you can use airbase-ng, available on the Kali Linux DVD. As its name implies, this program creates fake APs, which keeps wardrivers so busy trying to connect to nonexistent wireless networks that they don't have time to discover your legitimate AP.

- There are measures for preventing radio waves from leaving or entering a building so that wireless technology can be used only by people in the facility. One is using a certain type of paint on the walls, but this method isn't foolproof because some radio waves can leak out if the paint isn't applied correctly.

- Use a router to only allow approved MAC addresses to access your network. Unfortunately, some exploits enable attackers to spoof authorized addresses, but this measure makes exploits more difficult for typical attackers.

- Consider using an authentication server instead of relying on a wireless device to authenticate users. A RADIUS server that can refer all users to a server running Windows Server 2016 with Active Directory can be used to authenticate wireless users attempting to access network resources. This method can also prevent an intruder from sending or receiving HTTP, DHCP, SMTP, or any network packets over the network before being authenticated.

- Consider using EAP, which allows using different protocols that enhance security. For example, EAP enables using certificates for authentication, or wireless vendors can implement password-based authentication by using the EAP standard. EAP offers more options for increasing security.

- Consider placing the AP in the demilitarized zone (DMZ, covered in Chapter 13) and using a firewall in front of the company's internal network that filters out traffic from unauthorized IP addresses.

- WEP with 104-bit encryption is only marginally better than WEP with 40-bit encryption. If possible, replace WEP with WPA2 for better security, and replace hardware that can't be upgraded to support WPA2. WEP encryption can be cracked easily with just the tools on the Kali Linux DVD, and researchers have shown that breaking WPA isn't beyond a determined attacker's abilities.

- Assign static IP addresses to wireless clients instead of using DHCP.

- Disable WPS, which removes the known WPS attacks vectors.

- Change the default SSID and disable SSID broadcasts, if possible. If you can't disable SSID broadcasts, rename the default SSID to make it more difficult for attackers to determine the router's manufacturer. For example, leaving the default SSID of Netgear makes it easy for an attacker to determine what router is being used. Changing its SSID to another manufacturer's default SSID or to one not associated with any vendor might deter an attacker.

These methods aren't foolproof. In fact, by the time you read this book, there could be a way to crack WPA2 and other security methods for protecting wireless LANs. That's what makes the security field fun and dynamic. There are no easy fixes. If there were, these fixes wouldn't last long, unfortunately.

Chapter Summary

- Wireless technology defines how and at what frequency data travels over the radio frequency (RF) spectrum. The term "wireless" generally describes equipment operating in the RF spectrum between 3 Hz and 300 GHz, although most wireless networking equipment operates between 2.4 GHz and 66 GHz.

- The basic components of wireless networks are WNICs, which transmit and receive wireless signals; access points (APs), which are the bridge between wired and wireless networks; wireless networking protocols; and a portion of the RF spectrum that acts as a medium for carrying the signal.

- A service set identifier (SSID) is configured on the AP and used to identify a WLAN. It's a unique, 1- to 32-character, case-sensitive alphanumeric name.

- IEEE's main purpose is to create standards for LANs and WANs. 802.11 is the IEEE standard for wireless networking and includes many additional standards that address security and authentication.

- A BSS is the collection of all devices (APs and stations) that make up a WLAN. A BSA is the wireless coverage area that an AP provides to stations in a WLAN running in infrastructure mode. Although infrastructure mode is the most common in WLANs, independent stations can also establish an ad-hoc decentralized network that doesn't require an AP.

- WLANs use three technologies: infrared, narrowband, and spread spectrum. For data to be moved over radio waves, it must be modulated on the carrier signal or channel. The most common modulation methods for spread spectrum are DSSS and OFDM.

- Bluetooth is the most popular form of WPAN technology (802.15 standard), which usually has a more limited range than a typical WLAN. On the other end of the spectrum is a MAN (802.16 standard), which has a much larger coverage area than a WLAN. LTE is the most common implementation of a wireless MAN.

- WEP, WPA, and WPA2 are wireless encryption standards used to protect WLANS from unauthorized access and eavesdropping. WEP is easy to crack, WPA is harder to crack, and WPA2 is the most secure of these three.

- Authentication is usually used in combination with wireless encryption standards to ensure that access to a WLAN is authorized. 802.1x is an example of WLAN authentication and has three components: the supplicant, a wireless user attempting access to a WLAN; the authenticator, the AP that allows or denies a supplicant's access; and the authentication server, such as a RADIUS server.

- Wardriving and warflying involve driving in a car or flying in a plane with a laptop computer, a WNIC, an antenna, and software that scans for available APs.

- WLANs can be attacked with many of the same tools used for hacking wired LANs. For example, a sniffer such as Wireshark can also be used to scan WLANs for logon and password information. Specialized wireless tools include, such as Vistumbler, which can survey APs as part of a wardriving scan, and Kismet, a sophisticated multipurpose wireless tool that can detect hidden network SSIDs.

- Some methods for protecting a wireless network are disabling SSID broadcasts, renaming default SSIDs, using an authentication server, placing the AP in the DMZ, using EAP, upgrading to WPA2, assigning static IP addresses to wireless clients, and using a router to only allow approved MAC addresses to have access to a network.

Key Terms

802.11

802.1X standard

access point (AP)

ad-hoc network

amplitude

basic service area (BSA)

basic service set (BSS)

channels

chipping code

Extensible Authentication Protocol (EAP)

frequency

infrared (IR)

infrastructure mode

Institute of Electrical and Electronics Engineers (IEEE)

metropolitan area networks (MANs)

Mobile Broadband Wireless Access (MBWA)

modulation

narrowband

Protected EAP (PEAP)

service set identifier (SSID)

spread spectrum

station (STA)

supplicant

wardriving

Wi-Fi Protected Access (WPA and WPA2)

Wi-Fi Protected Setup (WPS)

Wired Equivalent Privacy (WEP)

wireless LAN (WLAN)

wireless network interface cards (WNICs)

wireless personal area network (WPAN)

Worldwide Interoperability for Microwave Access (WiMAX)

Review Questions

1. Which IEEE standard defines authentication and authorization in wireless networks?

   a. 802.11

   b. 802.11a

   c. 802.11b

   d. 802.1X

2. Which EAP method requires installing digital certificates on both the server and client?

   a. EAP-TLS

   b. PEAP

   c. EAP-SSL

   d. EAP-CA

3. Which wireless encryption standard offers the best security?

   a. WPA2

   b. WEP

   c. WPS

   d. WPA

4. Name a tool that can help reduce the risk of a wardriver attacking your WLAN.

5. What protocol was added to 802.11i to address WEP's encryption vulnerability?

   a. MIC

   b. TKIP

   c. TTL

   d. EAP-TLS

6. What IEEE standard defines wireless technology?

   a. 802.3

   b. 802.5

   c. 802.11

   d. All 802 standards

7. What information can be gathered by wardriving? (Choose all that apply.)

   a. SSIDs of wireless networks

   b. Whether encryption is enabled

   c. Whether SSL is enabled

   d. Signal strength

8. Disabling SSID broadcasts must be configured on the computer and the AP. True or False?

9. What TKIP enhancement addressed the WEP vulnerability of forging packets?

   a. Extended Initialization Vector (IV) with sequencing rules

   b. Per-packet key mixing

   c. Rekeying mechanism

   d. Message Integrity Check (MIC)

10. Wi-Fi Protected Access (WPA) was introduced in which IEEE 802 standard?

    a. 802.11a

    b. 802.11b

    c. 802.11i

    d. 802.11

11. Wardriving requires expensive hardware and software. True or False?

12. What is a known weakness of wireless network SSIDs?

    a. They're broadcast in cleartext.

    b. They're difficult to configure.

    c. They use large amounts of bandwidth.

    d. They consume an excessive amount of computer memory.

13. Bluetooth technology is more vulnerable to network attacks than WLANs are. True or False?

14. Which of the following channels is available in 802.11b for attempting to prevent overlapping? (Choose all that apply.)

    a. 1

    b. 5

    c. 6

    d. 11

15. Which authentication mechanisms and standards are currently exploitable?

    a. WEP

    b. WPA

    c. WP2

    d. WPS

16. An access point provides which of the following?

    a. Access to the BSS

    b. Access to the DS

    c. Access to a remote station

    d. Access to a secure node

17. The IEEE 802.11 standard pertains to which layers and sublayers of the OSI model?

18. The operating frequency range of 802.11a is 2.4 GHz. True or False?

19. Which of the following typically functions as the 802.1x authenticator, allowing or denying a supplicant's access to a WLAN?

    a. AP

    b. RADIUS server

    c. CA

    d. Public key issuer

20. List three tools for conducting wireless security testing.

Case Projects

Case Project 11-1: Determining Vulnerabilities of Wireless Networks

After conducting a security test on the Alexander Rocco network, you discover that the company has a wireless router configured to issue IP addresses to connecting stations. Vistumbler indicates that channel 6 is active, the SSID is linksys, and WEP is enabled. Based on this information, write a one-page report listing possible vulnerabilities of the WLAN's current configuration. Your report should include recommendations for improving wireless security.

Case Project 11-2: Maintaining Security on Wireless Systems

Bob Smith, the IT manager at Alexander Rocco, has just purchased a laptop computer. The company has asked you to ensure that privacy and security are maintained on this wireless system. Based on this information, write a one-page report using the information in the OSSTMM, Section E, Wireless Security available at *http://www.isecom.org/mirror/OSSTMM.3.pdf*. Your report should outline guidelines for ensuring the laptop's security.

## chapter 12

Cryptography

After reading this chapter and completing the exercises, you will be able to:

- Summarize the history and principles of cryptography
- Describe symmetric and asymmetric encryption algorithms
- Explain public key infrastructure (PKI)
- Describe possible attacks on cryptosystems
- Compare hashing algorithms and how they ensure data integrity

Protecting data as it traverses the Internet or while it's stored on a computer is one of a network security professional's most important jobs. Companies as well as users don't want others to be able to view confidential documents and files.

In this chapter, you examine the cryptography technologies that security professionals use to protect a company's data. You see how information can be converted into an unreadable format and how only those with the correct key or "decoder" can read the message. You also look at cryptography attacks and some of the tools used to conduct these attacks.

Understanding Cryptography Basics

Cryptography is the process of converting **plaintext**, which is readable text, into **ciphertext**, which is unreadable or encrypted text. Cryptography can be used on data that people or organizations want to keep private or data that should be accessible to only certain users. In other words, cryptography is used to hide information from unauthorized users. Decryption is the process of converting ciphertext back to plaintext (also called cleartext). As a kid, you might have had a decoder ring from a box of cereal that you could use to write a letter to a friend in secret code. If your friend had the same decoder ring, he or she could decode your letter and read it.

History of Cryptography

Cryptography has been around for thousands of years. For example, some Egyptian hieroglyphics on ancient monuments were encrypted. Parts of the Book of Jeremiah were written using a **cipher**, or key, known as Atbash. This simple cipher reversed the alphabet—replacing A with Z, for example—and only the person who knew the mapping could decipher (decrypt) the message. This type of cryptography is called a substitution cipher. Julius Caesar developed a similar **substitution cipher** for encrypting messages by shifting each letter of the alphabet three positions. For example, A was encoded as the letter D. Every culture seems to have used some form of hiding or disguising plaintext. *The Kama Sutra*, written by the Indian scholar Vatsyayana almost 2000 years ago, recommends that men and women learn and practice the art of cryptography, which it defines as "the art of understanding writing in cipher and the writing of works in a peculiar way."

NOTE — You can find an excellent timeline of cryptography in *The Codebreakers: The Comprehensive History of Secret Communication from Ancient Times to the Internet, Revised Edition*, written by David Kahn (Scribner, 1996, ISBN 0684831309).

As long as people attempt to create encryption algorithms to protect data, others will endeavor to break them. The study of breaking encryption algorithms is called **cryptanalysis**. It's taught in universities and by government agencies, but hackers also find the challenge of breaking an encryption algorithm intriguing and continue to force developers of encryption algorithms to push the envelope in finding harder-to-break algorithms. When a new encryption algorithm is developed, cryptanalysis is used to ensure that breaking the code is impossible or would take so much time and so many resources that the attempt would be impractical. In other words, if breaking an encryption algorithm requires the processing power of a $500 million supercomputer and 500 years, the algorithm can be considered secure enough for practical purposes.

When cryptanalysis is feasible with a reasonable amount of computing power, however, an attack on the algorithm is deemed "practical," and the algorithm is considered weak.

The War Machines The most famous encryption device was the Enigma machine, developed by Arthur Scherbius and used by the Germans during World War II. Most books on cryptography discuss this device. How did it work? The operator typed a letter to be encrypted, and the machine displayed the substitution character for the letter. The operator then wrote down this substitution character and turned a rotor or switch. He or she then entered the next letter and again wrote down the substitution character Enigma displayed. When the message was completely encrypted, it was transmitted over the airwaves. Of course, the message could be decrypted only by the Enigma machine at the other end, which knew in what positions to shift the rotors. The code was broken first by a group of Polish cryptographers, and then by the British and Americans. The machine British and American cryptologists used for breaking the code, developed by British mathematician Alan Turing, was called the Bombe.

During World War II, the Japanese developed another notable war machine, called the Purple Machine, that used techniques discovered by Herbert O. Yardley. A team led by William Frederick Friedman, a U.S. Army cryptanalyst known as the Father of U.S. Cryptanalysis, broke the code. The FBI had employed Mr. Friedman and his wife to assist in decrypting radio messages sent by bootleggers and smugglers during the 1930s. These encryption codes proved to be more difficult and complex than those used during wartime.

The main purpose of cryptography is to hide information from others, and there are methods of hiding data that don't use encryption. One is **steganography**, a way of hiding data in plain view in pictures, graphics, or text. For example, a picture of a man standing in front of the White House might have a hidden message embedded that gives a spy information about troop movements. In 1623, Sir Francis Bacon used a form of steganography by hiding bits of information in variations of the typeface used in books.

Activity 12-1: Creating a Substitution Cipher

Time Required: 30 minutes

Objective: Learn how to create a substitution cipher and encrypt a message.

Description: To better understand cryptography, break into groups of four students. Each group should create a short message no longer than five words in plaintext. Your group encrypts the message with a substitution cipher, and then the other groups (the decrypters) try to decode the message. Each group should create one encrypted message and decrypt each message created by the other groups.

1. The encrypting group writes a five-word message on a blank sheet of paper.

2. Create a substitution cipher to encrypt the message. For example, each character can be shifted three characters so that, for example, the letter A becomes the letter D.

3. Write down the ciphertext message you created with your group's cipher.

4. When instructed to do so, hand your ciphertext messages to the other groups to decrypt.

5. When a group decrypts the message, the group leader should shout "Finished!" so that the instructor can see which group completed the task the fastest.

6. After all groups have had a chance to try decrypting messages, discuss the ciphers each group created.

Security Bytes

Did you know that Thomas Jefferson invented a wheel cipher in the 18th century that the Navy redeveloped and used during World War II and named M-138-A? The more things change, the more they remain the same.

Understanding Symmetric and Asymmetric Algorithms

Modern cryptography uses encryption algorithms to encrypt data, banking transactions, online Web transactions, wireless communication (WEP and WPA encryption), and so on. An **encryption algorithm** is a mathematical function or program that works with a key. The algorithm's strength and the key's secrecy determine how secure the encrypted data is. In most cases, the algorithm isn't a secret; it's known to the public. What is secret is the key. A **key** is a sequence of random bits generated from a range of allowable values called a **keyspace**, which is contained in the algorithm. The larger the keyspace, the more keys that can be created. For example, an algorithm with a 256-bit keyspace has 2^{256} possible keys. The more random keys that can be created, the more difficult it is for hackers to guess which key was used to encrypt the data. Of course, using only eight random keys (as shown in Figure 12-1) makes the algorithm too easy to crack and is shown as an example only.

Key length of 3 bits allows creating 2^3 (8) different random keys.

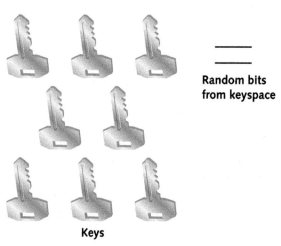

Random bits from keyspace

000 001 010 011 100 101 110 111

Keyspace

The larger the keyspace, the more random keys can be created.

Keys

Figure 12-1   Selecting random keys from a keyspace

Simply put, a **cryptosystem** converts between plaintext and ciphertext. Most attempts to break a cryptosystem are related to guessing the key. No matter how strong the algorithm or how large the keyspace, if the key isn't protected, an attacker can decrypt the message. If users share their keys with someone, all bets are off! Table 12-1 summarizes the three types of algorithms.

Type of algorithm	Description
Symmetric	Uses a single key to encrypt and decrypt data. Both the sender and receiver must agree on the key before data is transmitted. Symmetric algorithms support confidentiality but not authentication and nonrepudiation (covered later in "Asymmetric Algorithms"). However, they're at least 1000 times faster than asymmetric algorithms.
Asymmetric	Uses two keys: one to encrypt data and one to decrypt data. Asymmetric algorithms support authentication and nonrepudiation but are slower than symmetric algorithms. Asymmetric algorithms are also known as public key cryptography.
Hashing	Used for verification. Hashing takes a variable-length input and converts it to a fixed-length output string called a hash value or message digest.

Table 12-1   **Symmetric, asymmetric, and hashing algorithms**

Having a cryptologist's skills isn't necessary for security testers, but understanding basic cryptology terms is helpful. For example, if you see the description "Blowfish is a block cipher with a key size up to 448 bits," you want to know enough to understand what it means. The following sections examine these algorithm types in more detail and explain some basic terms.

Symmetric Algorithms

Cryptosystems using **symmetric algorithms** have one key that encrypts and decrypts data. If a user wants to send a message to a colleague, he or she encrypts the message with the secret key, and the colleague, who must have a copy of the same key, decrypts the message. If the user wants to encrypt a different message and send it to another colleague, a different secret key must be used. If hundreds of colleagues are placed in the equation, keeping track of which secret key to use becomes a big problem. To calculate the number of keys needed to support a symmetric system, you use the formula $n(n - 1)/2$. For example, if five users need to use secret keys to transmit data, you need $5(5 - 1)/2$ keys, or 10 keys.

Another problem with secret keys is how to send one to the colleague decrypting your message. E-mailing it can be dangerous because the message can be intercepted. You can try putting the secret key on a CD-R or USB drive, but either medium can be misplaced or stolen.

Because two users share the same key in symmetric algorithms, there's no way to know which user sent the message. In other words, symmetric algorithms don't support authentication and nonrepudiation (covered in more detail in "Asymmetric Algorithms").

As you can see, there are some problems with symmetric algorithms, but as Table 12-1 states, they're fast. They're perfect mechanisms for encrypting large blocks of data quickly and are difficult to break if a large key size is used. The advantages of symmetric algorithms are as follows:

- Much faster than asymmetric algorithms
- Difficult to break if a large key size is used
- Only one key needed to encrypt and decrypt data

12

Symmetric algorithms have the following disadvantages:

- Require each pair of users to have a unique secret key, making key management a challenge
- Difficult to deliver keys without risk of theft
- Don't provide authentication or nonrepudiation for users

Two types of symmetric algorithms are used currently: stream ciphers and block ciphers. **Stream ciphers** operate on plaintext one bit at a time. Messages are treated as a stream of bits, and the stream cipher performs mathematical functions on each bit, which makes these algorithms great candidates for hardware or chip-level encryption devices. **Block ciphers** operate on blocks of bits. These blocks are used as input to mathematical functions that perform substitution and transposition of the bits. Sometimes, when a block cipher separates input into blocks, it must add padding to fill a given block. This padding leaves the cipher susceptible to attack. Publicized attacks include CRIME, BEAST, and Lucky 7, which are all types of Padding Oracle attacks. You can read more detail about Padding Oracle attacks on The Grymoire Blog (*https://grymoire.word press.com/2014/12/05/cbc-padding-oracle-attacks-simplified-key-concepts-and-pitfalls/*).

In the following sections, you take a look at some of the symmetric algorithms that have become standards in the industry. Regardless of the standard, however, symmetric algorithms rely on one and the same key to encrypt and decrypt data.

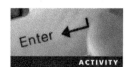

Activity 12-2: Hacking DVD Encryption Methods

Time Required: 20 minutes

Objective: Use the Internet to find information on DVD encryption methods.

Description: In this activity, you use the Internet to research the encryption method used for DVDs.

1. In Windows, start a Web browser, go to any search engine, and type **DeCSS** for the search keyword. How does DeCSS relate to DVD encryption?

2. On the search page, type **Why the DVD Hack was a Cinch** as the search phrase. It should take you to an article at *www.wired.com* by Andy Patrizio. Read the two-page article. What does CSS stand for?

3. Go to several other links related to CSS encryption. Were any lawsuits brought against the DeCSS program? If yes, describe them briefly.

4. Exit your Web browser, and log off Windows for the next activity.

Data Encryption Standard A discussion of symmetric algorithms must include **Data Encryption Standard (DES)**. The National Institute of Standards and Technology (NIST) wanted a means of protecting sensitive but unclassified data, so in the early 1970s, it invited vendors to submit data encryption algorithms. The best algorithm would become the standard encryption method for government agencies and private-sector companies. IBM had already created a 128-bit algorithm called Lucifer. NIST accepted it as the standard encryption algorithm; however, the National Security Agency (NSA) wanted to make some modifications before allowing it to be used. The NSA decided to reduce the key size from 128 bits

dictionary attack

digital signature

encryption algorithm

hashing algorithm

HTTP Strict Transport Security (HSTS)

International Data Encryption Algorithm (IDEA)

key

keyspace

man-in-the-middle attack

mathematical attack

message digest

Message Digest 5 (MD5)

nonrepudiation

OpenPGP

plaintext

Pretty Good Privacy (PGP)

private key

public key

public key cryptography

public key infrastructure (PKI)

rainbow table

RC4

RC5

replay attack

salt

Secure Hash Algorithm 1 (SHA-1)

Secure Multipurpose Internet Mail Extension (S/MIME)

SSL/TLS downgrade attack

steganography

stream cipher

substitution cipher

symmetric algorithm

Triple Data Encryption Standard (3DES)

Review Questions

1. Digital signatures are used to do which of the following?
    a. Verify that a message was received
    b. Ensure that repudiation is provided
    c. Provide authentication and nonrepudiation
    d. Encrypt sensitive messages
2. What is the standard for PKI certificates?
    a. X.500
    b. X.400
    c. X.509
    d. MySQL.409
3. List the three MIT professors who developed the RSA algorithm.
4. A hash value is a fixed-length string used to verify message integrity. True or False?
5. OpenPGP is focused on protecting which of the following?
    a. Web content
    b. E-mail messages
    c. Database systems
    d. IPSec traffic

6. Intruders can perform which kind of attack if they have possession of a company's password hash file?

   a. Dictionary

   b. Scan

   c. Ciphertext

   d. Buffer overflow

7. Intercepting messages destined for another computer and sending back messages while pretending to be the other computer is an example of what type of attack?

   a. Man-in-the-middle

   b. Smurf

   c. Buffer overflow

   d. Mathematical

8. A certification authority (CA) issues private keys to recipients. True or False?

9. Write the equation to calculate how many keys are needed to have 20 people communicate with symmetric keys.

10. Why did the NSA decide to drop support for DES?

   a. The cost was too high.

   b. The encryption algorithm was too slow.

   c. The processing power of computers had increased.

   d. It was too difficult for government agencies to use.

11. Symmetric algorithms can be block ciphers or stream ciphers. True or False?

12. Which of the following describes a chosen-plaintext attack?

   a. The attacker has ciphertext and algorithm.

   b. The attacker has plaintext and algorithm.

   c. The attacker has plaintext, can choose what part of the text gets encrypted, and has access to the ciphertext.

   d. The attacker has plaintext, ciphertext, and the password file.

13. Two different messages producing the same hash value results in which of the following?

   a. Duplicate key

   b. Corrupt key

   c. Collision

   d. Message digest

14. Which of the following is a program for extracting Windows password hash tables?
    a. Nmap
    b. Fgdump
    c. John the Ripper
    d. L0phtcrack

15. Advanced Encryption Standard (AES) replaced DES with which algorithm?
    a. Rijndael
    b. Blowfish
    c. IDEA
    d. Twofish

16. What cryptographic devices were used during World War II? (Choose all that apply.)
    a. Enigma machine
    b. Black Box
    c. Purple Machine
    d. Bombe

17. Asymmetric cryptography systems are which of the following?
    a. Faster than symmetric cryptography systems
    b. Slower than symmetric cryptography systems
    c. The same speed as symmetric cryptography systems
    d. Practical only on systems with multiple processors

18. Diffie-Hellman is used to encrypt e-mail messages. True or False?

19. Hiding data in a photograph is an example of which of the following?
    a. Steganography
    b. Stenography
    c. Ciphertext
    d. Cryptology

20. Which of the following is an asymmetric algorithm?
    a. DES
    b. AES
    c. RSA
    d. Blowfish

Case Projects

Case Project 12-1: Determining Possible Vulnerabilities of Microsoft CA Root Server

In conducting security testing on the Alexander Rocco network, you have found that the company configured one of its Windows Server 2016 computers as an enterprise root CA server. You have also determined that Ronnie Jones, the administrator of the CA server, selected MD5 as the hashing algorithm for creating digital signatures. Based on this information, write a one-page report explaining possible vulnerabilities caused by signing certificates with MD5. The report should cite articles about MD5 weaknesses and include recommendations from Microsoft about using MD5 in its software.

Case Project 12-2: Exploring Moral and Legal Issues

After conducting research for Case Project 12-1, you have gathered a lot of background about the release of information on hashing algorithms. Articles on vulnerabilities of SHA-1, MD4, and MD5 abound. The proliferation of programs for breaking DVD encryption codes and the recent imprisonment of an attacker who broke Japan's encryption method for blocking certain images from pornographic movies have raised many questions on what's moral or legal in releasing information about hashing algorithms. Based on this information, write a one- to two-page report addressing moral and legal issues of releasing software or code for breaking these algorithms. Your paper should also answer these questions:

- Should people who are able to break a hashing algorithm be allowed to post their findings on the Internet?

- Do you think the reporters of the DVD (DeCSS) crack were exercising their First Amendment rights when including the source code for breaking the DVD encryption key in an article? What about displaying the source code on a T-shirt?

- As a security professional, do you think you have to abide by a higher standard when sharing or disseminating source code that breaks hashing algorithms? Explain.

## chapter 13

Network Protection Systems

After reading this chapter and completing the exercises, you will be able to:

- Explain how routers are used as network protection systems
- Describe firewall technology and tools for configuring firewalls and routers
- Describe intrusion detection and prevention systems and Web-filtering technology
- Explain the purpose of honeypots

Hackers have many tools at their disposal to attack a network. You have seen how port scanning and enumeration make it possible for attackers to determine the services running on computers and gain access to network resources. In this chapter, you look at network protection systems that can be used to reduce exposure to these attacks and reduce their occurrence.

Routers, hardware and software firewalls, Web filtering, intrusion detection and prevention systems, and honeypots are covered in this chapter. A network protection system can also include a security incident response team, which is a team of people with the responsibility of protecting a large network.

Understanding Network Protection Systems

To protect a network from attack, security professionals must know how to use network protection systems, such as routers, firewalls, intrusion detection and prevention systems, Web filtering, and honeypots. For the purposes of this book, a **network protection system** is simply any device or system designed to protect a network. The term **Unified Threat Management (UTM)** device is used to describe a single device that combines many network protection functions, such as those performed by routers, firewalls, intrusion detection and prevention systems, VPNs, Web-filtering systems, and malware detection and filtering systems. For instance, modern Cisco routers can perform firewall functions, address translation (Network Address Translation and Port Address Translation), and intrusion prevention in addition to their router function. The term **security appliance** can be used to describe both UTMs and network protection systems. As hardware technology gets more powerful, security appliances can perform the same functions that once required using several dedicated systems. They also reduce administrative effort because multiple network protection functions are managed via a common interface. In this section, you start learning about network protection systems by seeing how routers are used to reduce network attacks.

Understanding Routers

Routers, which operate at the Network layer of the TCP/IP protocol stack, are hardware devices used to send packets to different network segments. Their main purposes are to reduce broadcast traffic passing over a network and choose the best path for moving packets. For example, if Router A in Spain wants to send a packet to Router B in Iowa, the packet can probably take several paths. Routers use routing protocols in this best-path decision-making process that function in the following ways:

- *Link-state routing protocol*—A router using a **link-state routing protocol** sends link-state advertisements to other routers; these advertisements identify the network topology and any changes or paths discovered recently on the network. For example, if a new router or path becomes available for a packet, this information is sent to all other routers participating in the network. This method is efficient because only new information is sent over the network. An example of a link-state routing protocol is Open Shortest Path First (OSPF).

- *Distance-vector routing protocol*—If a router is using a **distance-vector routing proto-col**, it passes its routing table (containing all possible paths it has discovered) to neighboring routers on the network. These neighbor routers then forward the routing table to *their* neighbors. Two examples of distance-vector routing protocols are Routing Internet Protocol version 2 (RIPv2) and Enhanced Interior Gateway Routing Protocol (EIGRP).

- *Path-vector routing protocol*—A **path-vector routing protocol** uses dynamically updated paths or routing tables to transmit packets from one autonomous network to another. It isn't used on LANs because it's used mainly by ISPs and large organizations with multiple Internet connections to other ISPs and organizations. The main path-vector routing protocol is Border Gateway Protocol (BGP), a routing protocol that an ISP uses to transmit packets to their destinations on the Internet

Security Bytes

BGP does have some security vulnerabilities. For example, attackers might hijack IP space belonging to another ISP by injecting a malicious BGP routing advertisement for a network prefix they don't own. This type of attack happened in summer 2008, when the IP space for YouTube.com was hijacked by an ISP in Pakistan, causing YouTube.com to be completely unreachable. For more information about this BGP hijacking event, visit *https://www.ripe.net/publications/news/industry-developments/youtube-hijacking-a-ripe-ncc-ris-case-study*.

For more information on routing protocols, see *CCNA Guide to Cisco Networking Fundamentals, Fourth Edition* (Kelly Cannon, Kelly Caudle, and Anthony V. Chiarella, Course Technology, Cengage Learning, 2009, ISBN 1418837059).

As a security professional, your main concern is confirming that a router filters certain traffic, not designing a router infrastructure and determining the routing protocol an organization uses. The following section explains how a Cisco router is configured to filter traffic.

Understanding Basic Hardware Routers

In this section, Cisco routers are used as an example because they're widely used; millions of Cisco routers are used by companies around the world. Because Cisco has become such a standard among network professionals, vendors offering competitive products often design their configuration interfaces to be similar to Cisco's. So although the information in this section can assist you in performing security tests on companies using Cisco routers in their networks, you won't be completely lost if you see a product from a Cisco competitor, such as Juniper. The principles you learn in this chapter can be applied to other types of routers. In Activity 13-1, you visit the Cisco Web site and review some Cisco products. If you've never seen a router or worked with the interfaces discussed in this section, the product photographs on this site can give you an idea of what you'll be working with as a security professional. As you learned in Chapter 9, a Cisco router is an embedded system that uses Cisco Internetwork Operating System (IOS) to function.

Activity 13-1: Visiting the Cisco Web Site

Time Required: 30 minutes

Objective: Learn more about Cisco routing products.

Description: Cisco routing products will be an important part of your job as a security professional because many companies use them. In this activity, you visit the company's Web site and review the type of vulnerability information Cisco makes available to its customers. This information can be helpful if you're performing a security test on a network using Cisco routers.

1. Start a Web browser, and go to **www.cisco.com**. On the Cisco home page, point to **Products & Services** in the top menu, and click **Routers**.

2. At the time of this writing, Cisco groups its routers into three categories. Explore the types of products available. In which category does the main router at your school fall? You might need to ask your instructor which type of router your school uses. If it isn't a Cisco product, who is the vendor?

3. Go to **https://tools.cisco.com/security/center/**. In the Search Security text box, type **ios** and click **Go**. Examine some recent vulnerabilities in Cisco IOS.

4. Go to **http://nvd.nist.gov**, click the **Vulnerability Search Engine** link, type **Cisco ios** in the Keyword search box, and then press **Enter**. At the time of this writing, the CVE Vulnerability Database was much faster than the Cisco security search site, so for the remainder of this activity, you use this site.

5. Examine the search results. How many records were returned?

6. Choose a specific vulnerability with a Common Vulnerability Scoring System (CVSS) severity score of at least 7, and click the link beginning with **CVE-** to read the summary information. What does the flaw allow an attacker to do? For software flaws, the NVD Web site supplies links to the vendor's Web site to find a patch or workaround. Click the link to the Cisco Web site and read the information. What does Cisco recommend?

7. Exit your Web browser and log off Windows for the next activity.

As you can see from your reading, vulnerabilities exist in Cisco IOS as they do in any OS, so security professionals must consider the type of router used when conducting a security test

Security Bytes

At a Black Hat computer security conference in 2005, a 24-year-old researcher named Michael Lynn was instructed by Cisco not to give a presentation on vulnerabilities he found in Cisco's Internet routers. Mr. Lynn claimed the vulnerabilities would allow hackers to take over corporate and government networks. Cisco argued that releasing his findings to the general public was illegal and that Mr. Lynn found the vulnerabilities by reverse-engineering Cisco's product, also illegal in the United States. Most technology companies don't want vulnerabilities in their products to be released to the public until they have the chance to correct the problem themselves or they can control what information is given to the public. The issue of disclosure will be here for quite some time and will most certainly affect security testers.

Cisco Router Components To help you understand how routers are used as network protection systems, this section describes the components of a Cisco router. Just as a system administrator must understand commands for configuring a server, Cisco router administrators must know commands for configuring a Cisco router. Many components of a Cisco router are similar to those of a computer, so the following components should seem familiar:

- *Random access memory (RAM)*—This component holds the router's running configuration, routing tables, and buffers. If you turn off the router, the contents stored in RAM are erased. Any changes you make to a router's configuration, such as changing the prompt displayed, are stored in RAM and aren't permanent unless you save the configuration.

- *Nonvolatile RAM (NVRAM)*—This component holds the router's configuration file, but the information isn't lost if the router is turned off.

- *Flash memory*—This component holds the IOS the router is using. It's rewriteable memory, so you can upgrade the IOS if Cisco releases a new version or the current IOS version becomes corrupted.

- *Read-only memory (ROM)*—This component contains a minimal version of Cisco IOS that's used to boot the router if flash memory gets corrupted. You can boot the router and then correct any problems with the IOS, possibly installing a new, uncorrupted version.

- *Interfaces*—These components are the hardware connectivity points to the router and the components you're most concerned with. An Ethernet port, for example, is an interface that connects to a LAN and can be configured to restrict traffic from a specific IP address, subnet, or network.

As a security professional, you should know some basic Cisco commands to view information in these components. For example, to see what information is stored in RAM, a Cisco administrator uses this command (with bolded text indicating the actual command):

RouterB# **show running-config**

Here's an example of the abbreviated output of this command for a production router:

Building configuration…

Current configuration : 4422 bytes

! version 12.4

service timestamps debug datetime msec localtime

service timestamps log datetime msec localtime

no service password-encryption

!

hostname R3825_2

!

```
boot-start-marker
boot-end-marker
!
card type t100
logging buffered 51200 debugging
!
no aaa new-model
!
resource policy
!
clock timezone Hawaii -10
network-clock-participate wic 0
network-clock-select 1 T1 0/0/0
ip subnet-zero
ip cef
!
interface GigabitEthernet0/0
description $ETH-LAN$$ETH-SW-LAUNCH$$INTF-INFO-GE 0/0$
ip address 192.168.10.3 255.255.255.0
duplex auto
speed auto
media-type rj45
negotiation auto
h323-gateway voip interface
h323-gateway voip bind srcaddr 192.168.10.3
!
interface Serial0/0/0:23
no ip address
isdn switch-type primary-ni
isdn incoming-voice voice
isdn bind-l3 ccm-manager
```

Demilitarized Zone A demilitarized zone (DMZ) is a small network containing resources that a company wants to make available to Internet users; this setup helps maintain security on the company's internal network. A DMZ sits between the Internet and the internal network and is sometimes referred to as a "perimeter network." Figure 13-2 shows how outside users can access the e-mail and Web servers in the DMZ, but the internal network is protected from these outside Internet users.

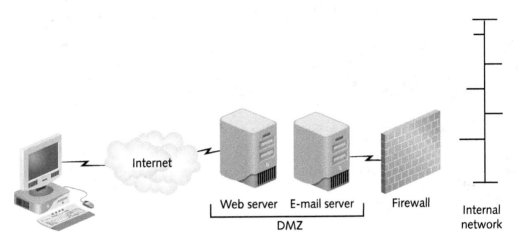

Figure 13-2 A DMZ protecting an internal network

Note that Internet users can access the DMZ without going through the firewall. A better security strategy is placing an additional firewall in the network setup (see Figure 13-3).

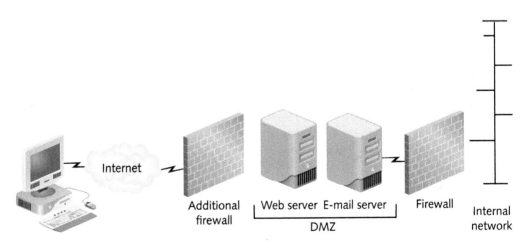

Figure 13-3 An additional firewall used to protect the DMZ

For users to access the internal network from the Internet, they need to pass through two firewalls. This setup is probably the most common design for an enterprise firewall topology.

Understanding the Cisco Adaptive Security Appliance Firewall

A good way to learn how a firewall operates is to look at the configuration of one of the most widely used firewalls: the Cisco Adaptive Security Appliance (ASA) firewall. Cisco ASA has replaced the Cisco PIX firewall and added advanced modular features, such as intrusion detection and prevention and more sophisticated application layer inspection. In the following sections, you view some configuration commands for an ASA firewall to get an idea of what security professionals need to know. We will walk through configuring an ASA to create rules to segment network servers from terminals that only allow traffic on a few ports.

 Cisco has classes and books on configuring ASA, so the information in this section is just the tip of the iceberg.

Configuring the ASA Firewall After logging on to an ASA firewall via SSH, you see a logon prompt that's similar to the prompt for logging on to a Cisco router:

```
If you are not authorized to be in this XYZ Hawaii network device, log out
immediately!

Username: admin

Password: ********
```

In this example, the administrator created a banner warning that anyone attempting to connect must be authorized before continuing. This banner might seem like a waste of time, but it serves a legal purpose. If the banner had said "Welcome, please log on," intruders might not be prosecuted if they hack into your network. The U.S. legal system has already dropped charges against hackers who entered sites with the word "Welcome" in banners.

After you log on with the correct password, the firewall displays the following information:

```
Type help or '?' for a list of available commands.

ciscoasa>
```

The prompt is the same one you saw when logging on to a Cisco router—the router name followed by a > symbol—so you know you're in user mode. To enter privileged mode, you enter the same `enable` (en, in this example) command used for a Cisco router and are then prompted to enter a password:

```
ciscoasa> en

Password: ********
```

After entering the correct password, you're placed in privileged mode, indicated by the # prompt. Entering the ? character reveals more commands available in privileged mode. Next, to enter configuration mode in ASA, you use the same command as on a Cisco router: `configure terminal` or `configure t`.

Next, look at how the firewall uses access lists to filter traffic. The following access list named PERMITTED_TRAFFIC shows the specific VPN connections to several wiring closets:

```
ciscoasa(config)# show run access-list

access-list PERMITTED_TRAFFIC remark VPN-CONC1 TO TERMINAL CLOSET1B

access-list PERMITTED_TRAFFIC extended permit ip host 10.13.61.98

host 10.13.61.18

access-list PERMITTED_TRAFFIC remark VPN-CONC2 TO TERMINAL CLOSET1B

access-list PERMITTED_TRAFFIC extended permit ip host 10.13.61.99

host 10.13.61.19

access-list PERMITTED_TRAFFIC remark VPN-CONC3 TO TERMINAL CLOSET1B

access-list PERMITTED_TRAFFIC extended permit ip host 10.13.61.100

host 10.13.61.20

access-list NONE extended deny ip any any log

access-list CAP-ACL extended permit ip any any
```

Next, look at the object group listing in the ASA configuration. An object group is a way to organize hosts, networks, services, protocols, or ICMP types into groups so that a firewall rule can be applied to all objects at once, instead of one at a time. In this example, several hosts are members of the VIRTUAL_TERMINALS object group:

```
ciscoasa# show run object-group

object-group network VIRTUAL_TERMINALS

network-object host 10.11.11.67

network-object host 10.11.11.68

network-object host 10.11.11.69
```

In the following example, notice the object group for networks. It's called AD_SERVERS, a name the firewall administrator chose to represent Active Directory servers. Currently, there's only one host in the group, but the firewall administrator might expand it when more Active Directory servers are added. Next is the object group for services, which is organized as AD_TCP and AD_UDP. In Chapter 8, you learned which ports must be open on a firewall for domain controller Active Directory services to function, so the ports listed in this example should look familiar.

```
object-group network AD_SERVERS

network-object host 10.0.0.25

object-group service AD_TCP tcp

port-object eq domain
```

```
port-object eq 88

port-object eq 135

port-object eq ldap

port-object eq 445

port-object eq 1026

object-group service AD_UDP udp

port-object eq domain

port-object eq 88

port-object eq ntp

port-object eq 389
```

Finally, the application services that should be allowed through the firewall are organized in the APP_SERVICES object group. Notice that Web (WWW, HTTPS), FTP (FTP, FTP-data), e-mail (POP3, SMTP), and file sharing (port 445) are allowed:

```
object-group service APP_SERVICES tcp

port-object eq ftp-data

port-object eq ftp

port-object eq smtp

port-object eq www

port-object eq pop3

port-object eq https

port-object eq 445
```

Using Configuration and Risk Analysis Tools for Firewalls and Routers

As you learned in Chapter 8, patching systems is only one part of protecting them from compromise. You must also configure them securely. Fortunately, plenty of resources are available for this task. One of the best Web sites for finding configuration benchmarks and configuration assessment tools for Cisco routers and firewalls is the Center for Internet Security (CIS, *benchmarks.cisecurity.org*). A benchmark is an industry consensus of best configuration practices on the hows (using step-by-step guidance) and whys (explaining the reasons for taking these steps) of securing a Cisco router or firewall. For Cisco devices, use the CIS Cisco IOS Benchmark; the most recent version is currently 4.0. Reviewing all the configuration steps in these benchmarks can take quite a bit of time. For this reason, CIS offers a useful tool called Configuration Assessment Tool (CAT) that's faster and easier to use. CAT versions are available for both *nix and Windows systems. If you have time and access to a lab with a Cisco router or firewall, download the CAT tool and run it on your Windows or Kali Linux system.

A commercial tool worth mentioning is RedSeal (*redseal.co*), a unique network risk analysis and mapping tool. Like the CIS RAT tool, RedSeal can identify configuration vulnerabilities in routers or firewalls, but it also generates professional-looking reports that can be customized with your company logo. In addition to analyzing configuration files from routers and firewalls, RedSeal can analyze IPSs as well as OS vulnerability scans of a network to produce a detailed analysis and mapping. Figure 13-4 shows the network risk map that's generated when you enter Cisco router and firewall configuration files and Nessus scans in RedSeal. It analyzes the configurations of all devices on the network to identify what access is allowed. In considering the architecture to use for network protection, access is determined by combining the rules and ACLs in each device along a network path. The thicker lines in Figure 13-4 represent every subnet that can access a network's data center. To see details of an allowed path, simply click the corresponding line.

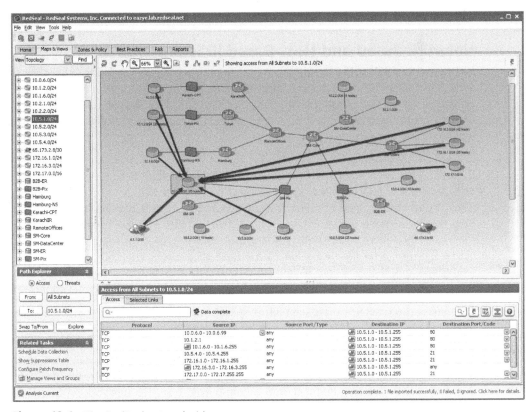

Figure 13-4   The RedSeal network risk map

RedSeal is unique in that it shows a graphical representation of vulnerabilities discovered in the context of the network on which they're found. A RedSeal report and map can be especially useful in conveying information to senior management; the graphical format is easier to understand than pages of wordy reports. (Remember the old adage: A picture is worth a thousand words.) For representing a network's security status, RedSeal is a handy tool.

Understanding Intrusion Detection and Prevention Systems

Intrusion detection systems (IDSs) monitor network devices so that security administrators can identify attacks in progress and stop them. For example, for users to be able to access a Web server, a firewall must allow port 80 to be open. Unfortunately, opening this port can also allow a hacker to attack the Web server. An IDS examines the traffic traversing the connection to port 80 and compares it with known exploits, similar to virus software using a signature file to identify viruses. If an attacker attempts to exploit a known vulnerability in the Web server, the IDS sends an alert of the attack so that the Web server administrator can take action. **Intrusion prevention systems (IPSs)** are similar to IDSs, but they take the additional step of performing some sort of action to prevent the intrusion, instead of just alerting administrators of the attack. The following section describes two types of intrusion detection and prevention systems: network-based and host-based.

Network-Based and Host-Based IDSs and IPSs

Network-based IDSs/IPSs monitor activity on network segments. Essentially, they sniff traffic as it flows over the network and alert a security administrator when something suspicious occurs. Some of these systems can also block traffic. **Host-based IDSs/IPSs** are most often used to protect a critical network server or database server, although they can also run on workstations. The IDS or IPS software is installed on the system you're attempting to protect, just like installing antivirus software on your desktop system.

IDSs can also be categorized by how they react when they detect suspicious behavior. Systems that don't take any action to stop or prevent an activity are called **passive systems**. They do, of course, send an alert and log the activity, much like a security guard at a shopping mall witnessing an armed robbery. **Active systems** also log events and send alerts, but they can also interoperate with routers and firewalls to stop an attack. For example, an active IDS can send an access list to a router that closes an interface to prevent attackers from damaging the network. Some active IDSs send spoofed reset packets that fool the TCP/IP stacks of both the victim and attacker into tearing down the malicious connection.

Of course, the time from the start of an attack to the time it compromises a system can be mere milliseconds, too fast for a human to take action. For this reason, vendors have started focusing their marketing efforts on IPSs. There's a difference between an active IDS and a true IPS. A true network-based IPS is installed inline to the network infrastructure, meaning traffic has to pass through the IPS before going into or out of the network. An active IDS just sniffs traffic and can be turned off or unplugged from the network without affecting network connectivity. Because an IPS is inline, generally it's more capable of stopping malicious traffic than an active IDS is, especially against UDP-based attacks. Many current IDSs include IPS features and often have optional modules, such as malware detection and Web filtering. In addition, host-based IPSs are available; they operate at the OS (or kernel) level and intercept traffic that's not allowed by the host policy. Because host-based IPSs share resources with the OS they run on, they can slow down performance if the hardware isn't adequate.

(1)

- (A) a fine under this title or imprisonment for not more than ten years, or both, in the case of an offense under subsection (a)(1) of this section which does not occur after a conviction for another offense under this section, or an attempt to commit an offense punishable under this subparagraph; and

- (B) a fine under this title or imprisonment for not more than twenty years, or both, in the case of an offense under subsection (a)(1) of this section which occurs after a conviction for another offense under this section, or an attempt to commit an offense punishable under this subparagraph;

(2)

- (A) except as provided in subparagraph (B), a fine under this title or imprisonment for not more than one year, or both, in the case of an offense under subsection (a)(2), (a)(3), or (a)(6) of this section which does not occur after a conviction for another offense under this section, or an attempt to commit an offense punishable under this subparagraph;

- (B) a fine under this title or imprisonment for not more than 5 years, or both, in the case of an offense under subsection (a)(2), or an attempt to commit an offense punishable under this subparagraph, if—

  - (i) the offense was committed for purposes of commercial advantage or private financial gain;

  - (ii) the offense was committed in furtherance of any criminal or tortious act in violation of the Constitution or laws of the United States or of any State; or

  - (iii) the value of the information obtained exceeds $5,000; and

- (C) a fine under this title or imprisonment for not more than ten years, or both, in the case of an offense under subsection (a)(2), (a)(3) or (a)(6) of this section which occurs after a conviction for another offense under this section, or an attempt to commit an offense punishable under this subparagraph;

(3)

- (A) a fine under this title or imprisonment for not more than five years, or both, in the case of an offense under subsection (a)(4) or (a)(7) of this section which does not occur after a conviction for another offense under this section, or an attempt to commit an offense punishable under this subparagraph; and

- (B) a fine under this title or imprisonment for not more than ten years, or both, in the case of an offense under subsection (a)(4), or (a)(7) of this section which occurs after a conviction for another offense under this section, or an attempt to commit an offense punishable under this subparagraph;

(4)

- (A) except as provided in subparagraphs (E) and (F), a fine under this title, imprisonment for not more than 5 years, or both, in the case of—

  - (i) an offense under subsection (a)(5)(B), which does not occur after a conviction for another offense under this section, if the offense caused (or, in the case of an attempted offense, would, if completed, have caused)—

- (I) loss to 1 or more persons during any 1-year period (and, for purposes of an investigation, prosecution, or other proceeding brought by the United States only, loss resulting from a related course of conduct affecting 1 or more other protected computers) aggregating at least $5,000 in value;

- (II) the modification or impairment, or potential modification or impairment, of the medical examination, diagnosis, treatment, or care of 1 or more individuals;

- (III) physical injury to any person;

- (IV) a threat to public health or safety;

- (V) damage affecting a computer used by or for an entity of the United States Government in furtherance of the administration of justice, national defense, or national security; or

- (VI) damage affecting 10 or more protected computers during any 1-year period; or

- (ii) an attempt to commit an offense punishable under this subparagraph;

- (B) except as provided in subparagraphs (E) and (F), a fine under this title, imprisonment for not more than 10 years, or both, in the case of—

  - (i) an offense under subsection (a)(5)(A), which does not occur after a conviction for another offense under this section, if the offense caused (or, in the case of an attempted offense, would, if completed, have caused) a harm provided in subclauses (I) through (VI) of subparagraph (A)(i); or

  - (ii) an attempt to commit an offense punishable under this subparagraph;

- (C) except as provided in subparagraphs (E) and (F), a fine under this title, imprisonment for not more than 20 years, or both, in the case of—

  - (i) an offense or an attempt to commit an offense under subparagraphs (A) or (B) of subsection (a)(5) that occurs after a conviction for another offense under this section; or

  - (ii) an attempt to commit an offense punishable under this subparagraph;

- (D) a fine under this title, imprisonment for not more than 10 years, or both, in the case of—

  - (i) an offense or an attempt to commit an offense under subsection (a)(5)(C) that occurs after a conviction for another offense under this section; or

  - (ii) an attempt to commit an offense punishable under this subparagraph;

- (E) if the offender attempts to cause or knowingly or recklessly causes serious bodily injury from conduct in violation of subsection (a)(5)(A), a fine under this title, imprisonment for not more than 20 years, or both;

- (F) if the offender attempts to cause or knowingly or recklessly causes death from conduct in violation of subsection (a)(5)(A), a fine under this title, imprisonment for any term of years or for life, or both; or

- (G) a fine under this title, imprisonment for not more than 1 year, or both, for—

- (i) any other offense under subsection (a)(5); or

- (ii) an attempt to commit an offense punishable under this subparagraph.

(d)

- (1) The United States Secret Service shall, in addition to any other agency having such authority, have the authority to investigate offenses under this section.

- (2) The Federal Bureau of Investigation shall have primary authority to investigate offenses under subsection (a)(1) for any cases involving espionage, foreign counter-intelligence, information protected against unauthorized disclosure for reasons of national defense or foreign relations, or Restricted Data (as that term is defined in section 11y of the Atomic Energy Act of 1954 (42 U.S.C. 2014 (y)), except for offenses affecting the duties of the United States Secret Service pursuant to section 3056 (a) of this title.

- (3) Such authority shall be exercised in accordance with an agreement which shall be entered into by the Secretary of the Treasury and the Attorney General.

(e) As used in this section—

- (1) the term "computer" means an electronic, magnetic, optical, electrochemical, or other high speed data processing device performing logical, arithmetic, or storage functions, and includes any data storage facility or communications facility directly related to or operating in conjunction with such device, but such term does not include an automated typewriter or typesetter, a portable hand held calculator, or other similar device;

- (2) the term "protected computer" means a computer—

  - (A) exclusively for the use of a financial institution or the United States Govern-ment, or, in the case of a computer not exclusively for such use, used by or for a financial institution or the United States Government and the conduct constituting the offense affects that use by or for the financial institution or the Government; or

  - (B) which is used in or affecting interstate or foreign commerce or communica-tion, including a computer located outside the United States that is used in a manner that affects interstate or foreign commerce or communication of the United States;

- (3) the term "State" includes the District of Columbia, the Commonwealth of Puerto Rico, and any other commonwealth, possession or territory of the United States;

- (4) the term "financial institution" means—

  - (A) an institution, with deposits insured by the Federal Deposit Insurance Corporation;

  - (B) the Federal Reserve or a member of the Federal Reserve including any Federal Reserve Bank;

  - (C) a credit union with accounts insured by the National Credit Union Administration;

  - (D) a member of the Federal home loan bank system and any home loan bank;

- (E) any institution of the Farm Credit System under the Farm Credit Act of 1971;
- (F) a broker-dealer registered with the Securities and Exchange Commission pursuant to section 15 of the Securities Exchange Act of 1934;
- (G) the Securities Investor Protection Corporation;
- (H) a branch or agency of a foreign bank (as such terms are defined in paragraphs (1) and (3) of section 1(b) of the International Banking Act of 1978); and
- (I) an organization operating under section 25 or section 25(a) of the Federal Reserve Act;
- (5) the term "financial record" means information derived from any record held by a financial institution pertaining to a customer's relationship with the financial institution;
- (6) the term "exceeds authorized access" means to access a computer with authorization and to use such access to obtain or alter information in the computer that the accesser is not entitled so to obtain or alter;
- (7) the term "department of the United States" means the legislative or judicial branch of the Government or one of the executive departments enumerated in section 101 of title 5;
- (8) the term "damage" means any impairment to the integrity or availability of data, a program, a system, or information;
- (9) the term "government entity" includes the Government of the United States, any State or political subdivision of the United States, any foreign country, and any state, province, municipality, or other political subdivision of a foreign country;
- (10) the term "conviction" shall include a conviction under the law of any State for a crime punishable by imprisonment for more than 1 year, an element of which is unauthorized access, or exceeding authorized access, to a computer;
- (11) the term "loss" means any reasonable cost to any victim, including the cost of responding to an offense, conducting a damage assessment, and restoring the data, program, system, or information to its condition prior to the offense, and any revenue lost, cost incurred, or other consequential damages incurred because of interruption of service; and
- (12) the term "person" means any individual, firm, corporation, educational institution, financial institution, governmental entity, or legal or other entity.

(f) This section does not prohibit any lawfully authorized investigative, protective, or intelligence activity of a law enforcement agency of the United States, a State, or a political subdivision of a State, or of an intelligence agency of the United States.

(g) Any person who suffers damage or loss by reason of a violation of this section may maintain a civil action against the violator to obtain compensatory damages and injunctive relief or other equitable relief. A civil action for a violation of this section may be brought only if the conduct involves 1 of the factors set forth in subclauses (I), (II), (III), (IV), or (V) of subsection (c)(4)(A)(i). Damages for a violation involving only conduct described in subsection (c)(4)(A)(i)(I) are limited to economic damages. No action may be brought under this subsection unless such action is begun within 2 years of the date of the act complained of or the date of the discovery of the damage. No action may be brought under this subsection for the negligent design or manufacture of computer hardware, computer software, or firmware.

(h) The Attorney General and the Secretary of the Treasury shall report to the Congress annually, during the first 3 years following the date of the enactment of this subsection, concerning investigations and prosecutions under subsection (a)(5).

(i)

- (1) The court, in imposing sentence on any person convicted of a violation of this section, or convicted of conspiracy to violate this section, shall order, in addition to any other sentence imposed and irrespective of any provision of State law, that such person forfeit to the United States—

  - (A) such person's interest in any personal property that was used or intended to be used to commit or to facilitate the commission of such violation; and

  - (B) any property, real or personal, constituting or derived from, any proceeds that such person obtained, directly or indirectly, as a result of such violation.

- (2) The criminal forfeiture of property under this subsection, any seizure and disposition thereof, and any judicial proceeding in relation thereto, shall be governed by the provisions of section 413 of the Comprehensive Drug Abuse Prevention and Control Act of 1970 (21 U.S.C. 853), except subsection (d) of that section.

(j) For purposes of subsection (i), the following shall be subject to forfeiture to the United States and no property right shall exist in them:

- (1) Any personal property used or intended to be used to commit or to facilitate the commission of any violation of this section, or a conspiracy to violate this section.

- (2) Any property, real or personal, which constitutes or is derived from proceeds traceable to any violation of this section, or a conspiracy to violate this section.

Resources

Books

Chapter 1

Ruhl, Janet. *The Computer Consultants Guide*. Wiley, 1997. ISBN 0471176494.

Meyer, Peter. *Getting Started in Computer Security*. Wiley, 1999. ISBN 0471348139.

Paioff, Mitch. *Getting Started as an Independent Computer Consultant*. Consulting Training Institute, 2008. ISBN 978-0-98192-970-5.

Weiss, Alan. *The Consulting Bible: Everything You Need to Know to Create and Expand a Seven-Figure Consulting Practice*. Wiley, 2011. ISBN 978-0-470-92808-0.

Chapter 8

Palmer, Michael. *Guide to Operating Systems, Enhanced Edition*. Course Technology, Cengage Learning, 2007. ISBN 1418837199.

Chapter 12

Kahn, David. *The Code Breakers: The Comprehensive History of Secret Communication from Ancient Times to the Internet, Revised Edition*. Scribner, 1996, ISBN 0684831309.

Schneier, Bruce. *Applied Crytopgraphy: Protocols, Algorithms, and Source Code in C, Second Edition*. Wiley, 1996. ISBN 0471117099.

Chapter 13

Cannon, Kelly, Kelly Caudle, and Anthony V. Chiarella. CCNA *Guide to Cisco Networking Fundamentals, Fourth Edition*. Course Technology, Cengage Learning, 2009. ISBN 1418837059.

Web Sites
Chapter 1
Professional Certifications, Security Jobs, and Applicable Laws

www.comptia.org

www.eccouncil.org

www.giac.org

www.isc2.org

www.isecom.org

www.kali.org

www.monster.com/jobs/search

www.ncsl.org/research/telecommunications-and-information-technology.aspx

www.offensive-security.com

www.sans.org

toool.us/laws.html

www.youtube.com/watch?v=vXr-2hwTk58 (The Internet's Own Boy: The Story of Aaron Swartz)

Chapter 2
Protocols

www.cisco.com/security_services/ciag/documents/v6-v4-threats.pdf

www.iana.org

www.ietf.org

www.rapidtables.com/convert/number/ascii-to-hex.htm (ASCII to Hex Converter)

Chapter 3
Identifying Malware

www.spywareguide.com

Searching for Known Vulnerabilities and Exposures

www.cve.mitre.org

www.exploit-db.com

www.kb.cert.org/vuls

www.lysator.liu.se/mit-guide/MITLockGuide.pdf

www.osvdb.org

www.packetstormsecurity.com

www.securityfocus.com

www.symantec.com

technet.microsoft.com/en-us/security/bulletins.aspx

www.us-cert.gov

Macro Viruses
www.virusbulletin.com/virusbulletin/2014/07/vba-not-dead

Chapter 4

Footprinting
www.arin.net
bitbucket.org/LaNMaSteR53/recon-ng
centralops.net/co/domaindossier.aspx
www.elevenpaths.com/labstools/foca/index.html
github.com/zaproxy
gnuwin32.sourceforge.net
groups.google.com
www.isc.org/downloads/bind/
www.knowprivacy.org
www.namedroppers.com
nmap.org/ncat
www.nscan.org
www.owasp.org/index.php/OWASP_Zed_Attack_Proxy_Project
www.parosproxy.org
www.paterva.com/web4/index.php/maltego
www.rafasoft.com
www.securityfocus.com/tools/139
www.severus.org/sacha/metis
toolbar.netcraft.com/site_report
www.whitepages.com
www.whois.net

Chapter 5

Port Scanning and Service Mapping
www.cve.mitre.org
www.fping.com
www.hping.org
www.nessus.org
nmap.org/nsedoc/categories/default.html
www.unicornscan.org
www.us-cert.gov

Chapter 6
Enumeration

www.kali.org/penetration-testing/openvas-vulnerability-scanning/

www.l0phtcrack.com/download.html

www.nessus.org

www.systemtools.com

Chapter 7
Programming

www.activestate.com/activeperl

history.perl.org/PerlTimeline.html

www.metasploit.com

perldoc.perl.org/Net/Ping.html

www.plenz.com/reverseshell

search.cpan.org/~jdb/Win32-0.52/Win32.pm

www.w3c.org

Chapter 8
Desktop and Server OSs

www.cisecurity.org/benchmarks.html

www.cve.mitre.org

github.com/SELinuxProject

www.iana.org/assignments/port-numbers

www.ionx.co.uk

logrhythm.com/index.html

www.microsoft.com/en-us/download/details.aspx?id=7558

www.microsoft.com/technet/security/Bulletin/MS09-044.mspx

technet.microsoft.com/en-us/security/cc297183.aspx

www.nsa.gov/what-we-do/research/selinux/

www.ntsecurity.nu/toolbox/lns/

www.packetstormsecurity.com

www.samba.org

www.securityfocus.com

support.microsoft.com/en-us/kb/325864

technet.microsoft.com/en-us/sysinternals/bb897440.aspx

www.tripwire.com

https://op.trustedcs.com

www.us-cert.gov

Chapter 9
Embedded OSs

www.cve.mitre.org

www.dd-wrt.com

exploit-db.com

hackaday.com

www.iso.org

nvd.nist.gov

www.packetstormsecurity.org

www.rtlinuxfree.com

www.schneier.com/blog/archives/2014/01/security_risks_9.html

www.wired.com/2015/07/hackers-remotely-kill-jeep-highway/

Chapter 10
Web Server Security

www.cve.mitre.org

helpx.adobe.com/security.html

technet.microsoft.com/en-us/security/bulletin

technet.microsoft.com/library/security/ms08-022

www.owasp.org

www.owasp.org/index.php/Web_Application_Penetration_Testing

www.owasp.org/index.php/Appendix_A:_Testing_Tools

www.packetstormsecurity.org

poweryogi.blogspot.com/2005/03/hbsapplyyourself-admit-status-snafu.html

s3.amazonaws.com/webgoat-war/webgoat-container-7.0.1-war-exec.jar

www.us-cert.gov/ncas/alerts/TA09-133B

Chapter 11
Wireless Networking

www.aircrack-ng.org

en.wikipedia.org/wiki/IEEE_802.11

goo.gl/1dF9OH

www.ieee802.org/11/Reports/tgay_update.htm

www.isecom.org/mirror/OSSTMM.3.pdf

www.kismetwireless.net

nvd.nist.gov

www.retrocom.com

www.vistumbler.net

www.wifipineapple.com

www.wikihow.com/Make-a-Cantenna

Chapter 12
Cryptography

csrc.nist.gov

www.mandylionlabs.com/documents/BFTCalc.xls

www.nsa.gov/ia/programs/suiteb_cryptography

www.phreedom.org

www.rsa.com

www.symantec.com/products/information-protection/encryption

veracrypt.codeplex.com

Chapter 13
Network Protection Systems

benchmarks.cisecurity.org

www.bluecoat.com

www.ca.com

canary.tools

www.cert.org

www.enterasys.com

glastopf.org

www.honeyd.org

www.honeynet.org

www.ibm.com

www.isc.sans.org/weblogs

www.keyfocus.net/kfsensor

labrea.sourceforge.net

www.mcafee.com

www.micheloosterhof.com/cowrie

opencanary.org

nvd.nist.gov

www.redseal.co

www.ripe.net/publications/news/industry-developments/youtube-hijacking-a-ripe-ncc-ris-case-study

www.securityfocus.com/infocus/1659

www.snort.org

www.sourcefire.com

www.specter.com or www.spectorcne.com

www.symantec.com

tools.cisco.com/security/center

valhalahoneypot.sourceforge.net

www.websense.com

Glossary

802.11 A set of IEEE standards that define protocols for implementing wireless local area networks (WLANs).

802.1X standard An IEEE standard that defines the process of authenticating and authorizing users on a network before they're allowed to connect.

access point (AP) A radio transceiver that connects to a network via an Ethernet cable and bridges a wireless network with a wired network.

ACK A TCP flag that acknowledges a TCP packet with SYN-ACK flags set.

Active Server Pages (ASP) A scripting language for creating dynamic Web pages.

active systems An IDS or IPS that logs events, sends out alerts, and can interoperate with routers and firewalls.

ActiveX Data Objects (ADO) A programming interface for connecting a Web application to a database.

ad-hoc network A wireless network that doesn't rely on an AP for connectivity; instead, independent stations connect to each other in a decentralized fashion.

Advanced Encryption Standard (AES) A symmetric block cipher standard from NIST that replaced DES. *See also* Data Encryption Standard (DES).

adware Software that can be installed without a user's knowledge; its main purpose is to determine users' purchasing habits.

algorithm A set of directions used to solve a problem.

amplitude The height of a sound wave; determines a sound's volume.

anomaly-based IDS A type of IDS that sends alerts on network traffic varying from a set baseline.

application-aware firewall A firewall that inspects network traffic at a higher level in the OSI model than a traditional stateful packet inspection firewall does.

assembly language A programming language that uses a combination of hexadecimal numbers and expressions to program instructions that are easier to understand than machine-language instructions.

asymmetric algorithm Encryption methodology that uses two keys that are mathematically related; also referred to as public key cryptography.

Asynchronous JavaScript and XML (AJAX) A Web development technique used for interactive Web sites, such as Facebook and Google Apps; this development technique makes it possible to create the kind of sophisticated interface usually found on desktop programs.

attack Any attempt by an unauthorized person to access, damage, or use resources of a network or computer system.

attack surface The amount of code a computer system exposes to unauthenticated outsiders.

authentication The process of verifying that the sender or receiver (or both) is who he or she claims to be; this function is available in asymmetric algorithms but not symmetric algorithms.

backdoor A program that an attacker can use to gain access to a computer at a later date. *See also* rootkit.

basic service area (BSA) The coverage area an access point provides in a wireless network.

basic service set (BSS) The collection of connected devices in a wireless network.

birthday attacks Attacks used to find the same hash value for two different inputs and reveal mathematical weaknesses in a hashing algorithm.

black box model A model for penetration testing in which management doesn't divulge to IT security personnel that testing will be conducted or give the testing team a description of the network topology. In other words, testers are on their own.

block cipher A symmetric algorithm that encrypts data in blocks of bits. These blocks are used as input to mathematical functions that perform substitution and transposition of the bits.

Blowfish A block cipher that operates on 64-bit blocks of plaintext, but its key length can be as large as 448 bits.

botnet A group of multiple computers, usually thousands, that behave like robots to conduct an attack on a network. The computers are called zombies because their users aren't aware their systems are being controlled by one person. *See also* zombies.

branching A method that takes you from one area of a program (a function) to another area.

brute-force attack An attack in which the attacker uses software that attempts every possible combination of characters to guess passwords and keys.

buffer overflow attack An exploit written by a programmer that finds a vulnerability in poorly written code that doesn't check for a predefined amount of memory space use, and then inserts executable code that fills up the buffer (an area of memory) for the purpose of elevating the attacker's permissions.

bug A programming error that causes unpredictable results in a program.

certificate A digital document that verifies that a server or party is who it claims to be. Each certificate has a unique serial number and must follow the X.509 standard.

certification authority (CA) A third party, such as Symantec, that vouches for a company's authenticity and issues a certificate binding a public key to a recipient's private key.

Certified Ethical Hacker A certification designated by the EC-Council.

Certified Information Systems Security Professional (CISSP) Non-vendor-specific certification issued by the International Information Systems Security Certification Consortium, Inc. (ISC²).

channels Specific frequency ranges within a frequency band in which data is transmitted.

chipping code Multiple sub-bits representing the original message that can be used for recovery of a corrupted packet traveling across a frequency band.

cipher A method of converting plaintext into ciphertext.

ciphertext Plaintext (readable text) that has been encrypted.

class In object-oriented programming, the structure that holds pieces of data and functions.

closed ports Ports that aren't listening or responding to a packet.

ColdFusion A server-side scripting language for creating dynamic Web pages; supports a wide variety of databases and uses a proprietary markup language known as CFML.

Common Gateway Interface (CGI) An interface that passes data between a Web server and a Web browser.

Common Internet File System (CIFS) A remote file system protocol that enables computers to share network resources over the Internet.

competitive intelligence A means of gathering information about a business or an industry by using observation, accessing public information, speaking with employees, and so on.

compiler A program that converts source code into executable or binary code.

computer security The security of stand-alone computers that aren't part of a network infrastructure.

connectionless With a connectionless protocol, no session connection is required before data is transmitted. UDP and IP are examples of connectionless protocols.

connection-oriented protocol A protocol for transferring data over a network that requires a session connection before data is sent. In TCP/IP, this step is accomplished by sending a SYN packet.

conversion specifier Tells the compiler how to convert the value indicated in a function.

cookie A text file containing a message sent from a Web server to a user's Web browser to be used later when the user revisits the Web site.

crackers Hackers who break into systems with the intent of doing harm or destroying data.

cryptanalysis A field of study devoted to breaking encryption algorithms.

cryptosystem Software or hardware that converts between plaintext and ciphertext.

data at rest Any data not moving through a network or being used by the OS; usually refers to data on storage media.

Data Encryption Algorithm (DEA) The encryption algorithm used in the DES standard; a symmetric algorithm that uses 56 bits for encryption. *See also* Data Encryption Standard (DES).

Data Encryption Standard (DES) A NIST standard for protecting sensitive but unclassified data; it was later replaced because the increased processing power of computers made it possible to break DES encryption.

demilitarized zone (DMZ) A small network containing resources that sits between the Internet and the internal network, sometimes referred to as a "perimeter network." It's used when a company wants to make resources available to Internet users yet keep the company's internal network secure.

denial-of-service (DoS) attack An attack made to deny legitimate users the ability to access network resources.

dictionary attack An attack in which the attacker runs a password-cracking program that uses a dictionary of known words or passwords as an input file against the attacked system's password file.

digital signature A method of signing messages by using asymmetric encryption that ensures authentication and non-repudiation. *See also* authentication and nonrepudiation.

distance-vector routing protocol A routing protocol that passes the routing table (containing all possible paths) to all routers on the network. If a router learns one new path, it sends the entire routing table again, which isn't as efficient as a link-state routing protocol.

distributed denial-of-service (DDoS) attack An attack made on a host from multiple servers or computers to deny legitimate users from accessing network resources.

do loop A loop that performs an action and then tests to see whether the action should continue to occur.

domain controller A Windows server that stores user account information, authenticates domain logons, maintains the master database, and enforces security policies for a Windows domain.

drive-by downloads A type of attack in which Web site visitors download and install malicious code or software without their knowledge.

dumpster diving Gathering information by examining the trash that people discard.

SQL injection A type of exploit that takes advantage of poorly written applications. An attacker can issue SQL statements by using a Web browser to retrieve data, change server settings, or possibly gain control of the server.

SSL/TLS downgrade attack An attack that occurs when an attacker who intercepts the initial traffic between a Web server and a Web browser forces a vulnerable server to insecurely renegotiate the encryption being used down to a weaker cipher.

state table A file created by a stateful packet filter that contains information on network connections. *See also* stateful packet filters.

stateful packet filters Filters on routers that record session-specific information in a file about network connections, including the ports a client uses.

stateless packet filters Filters on routers that handle each packet separately, so they aren't resistant to spoofing or DoS attacks.

Static Application Security Testing (SAST) Analysis of an applications source code for vulnerabilities.

static Web pages Web pages that display the same information whenever they're accessed.

station (STA) An addressable unit in a wireless network. A station is defined as a message destination and might not be a fixed location.

steganography A method of hiding secret data in image, text, or other files alongside non-secret data.

stream cipher A symmetric algorithm that operates on plaintext one bit at a time.

substitution cipher A cipher that maps each letter of the alphabet to a different letter. Parts of the Book of Jeremiah were written by using a substitution cipher called Atbash.

supervisory control and data acquisition (SCADA) systems Systems used for equipment monitoring and automation in large-scale industries and critical infrastructure systems, such as power plants and air traffic control towers; these systems contain components running embedded OSs.

supplicant A wireless user attempting access to a WLAN.

symmetric algorithm An encryption algorithm that uses only one key to encrypt and decrypt data. The recipient of a message encrypted with a key must have a copy of the same key to decrypt the message.

SYN A TCP flag that signifies the beginning of a session.

SYN-ACK A reply to a SYN packet sent by a host.

SysAdmin, Audit, Network, Security (SANS) Institute Founded in 1989, this organization conducts training worldwide and offers multiple certifications through GIAC in many aspects of computer security and forensics.

System Center Configuration Manager (SCCM) A Microsoft software product for server configuration, server deployment, software management, and patch management.

Systems Management Server (SMS) This service includes detailed hardware inventory, software inventory and metering, software distribution and installation, and remote troubleshooting tools.

TCP flag The six flags in a TCP header are switches that can be set to on or off to indicate the status of a port or service.

testing A process conducted on a variable that returns a value of true or false.

three-way handshake The method the Transport layer uses to create a connection-oriented session.

Transmission Control Protocol/Internet Protocol (TCP/IP) The main protocol used to connect computers over the Internet.

Triple Data Encryption Standard (3DES) A standard developed to address the vulnerabilities of DES; it improved security, but encrypting and decrypting data take longer.

Trojan program A program that disguises itself as a legitimate program or application but has a hidden payload that might send information from the attacked computer to the creator or to a recipient located anywhere in the world.

Unified Threat Management (UTM) A single device that combines many network protection functions, such as those performed by routers, firewalls, intrusion detection and prevention systems, VPNs, Web-filtering systems, and malware detection and filtering systems.

User Datagram Protocol (UDP) A fast, unreliable Transport layer protocol that's connectionless.

user mode The default method on a Cisco router, used to perform basic troubleshooting tests and list information stored on the router. In this mode, no changes can be made to the router's configuration.

virtual directory A pointer to a physical directory on a Web server.

virus A program that attaches itself to a host program or file.

virus signature file A file maintained by antivirus software that contains signatures of known viruses; antivirus software checks this file to determine whether a program or file on your computer is infected.

vulnerability A weakness or flaw in a computer that allows for an attacker to disclose, alter, or destroy systems or data.

vulnerability assessment A test performed by security professionals to enumerate an many vulnerabilities as possible.

wardriving The act of driving around an area with a laptop computer that has a WNIC, scanning software, and an antenna to discover available SSIDs in the area.

Web bug A small graphics file referenced in an <IMG> tag, used to collect information about the user. This file is created by a third-party company specializing in data collection.

WebGoat A Web-based application designed to teach security professionals about Web application vulnerabilities.

while loop A loop that repeats an action a certain number of times while a condition is true or false.

white box model A model for penetration testing in which testers can speak with company staff and are given a full description of the network topology and technology.

whitelisting Restricting the execution of all programs not on an approved list.

Wi-Fi Protected Access (WPA and WPA2) An 802.11i standard that addresses WEP security vulnerabilities in 802.11b; improves encryption by using Temporal Key Integrity Protocol (TKIP). *See also* Wired Equivalent Privacy (WEP).

Wi-Fi Protected Setup (WPS) A wireless authentication standard that allows users to easily add devices to a wireless network securely.

Windows Software Update Services (WSUS) A free add-in component that simplifies the process of keeping Windows computers current with the latest critical updates, patches, and service packs. WSUS installs a Web-based application that runs on a Windows server.

Wired Equivalent Privacy (WEP) An 802.11b standard developed to encrypt data traversing a wireless network.

wireless LAN (WLAN) A network that relies on wireless technology (radio waves) to operate.

wireless network interface cards (WNICs) Controller cards that send and receive network traffic via radio waves and are required on both APs and wireless-enabled computers to establish a WLAN connection.

wireless personal area network (WPAN) A wireless network specified by the 802.15 standard; usually means Bluetooth technology is used, although newer technologies are being developed. It's for one user only and covers an area of about 10 meters.

Worldwide Interoperability for Microwave Access (WiMAX) The most common implementation of the 802.16 MAN standard. *See also* metropolitan area networks (MANs).

worm A program that replicates and propagates without needing a host.

zombies Computers controlled by a hacker to conduct criminal activity without their owners' knowledge; usually part of a botnet. *See also* botnet.

zone transfer A method of transferring records from a DNS server to use in analysis of a network.

Index